Praise for *Copperheads: The Rise and Fall of Lincoln's Opponents in the North*

"Jennifer Weber has written a wonderful and timely book that explores the nature and value of wartime dissent. *Copperheads* describes a genuine, thoughtful opposition to war and the concentration of governmental power. In a well-crafted study, she explains how individuals could perceive a war to create civil rights by destroying slavery as a war that trampled civil liberties in the process."—Joseph Glatthaar, author of *Forged in Battle: The Civil War Alliance of Black Soldiers and White Officers*

"This excellent study of the most conservative element of the Democratic Party during the Civil War offers a powerful reminder that the North, even as it sought to put down the Confederate rebellion, suffered from deep political divisions. It fruitfully argues that Copperheads more than once threatened the Union war effort before ending the conflict as a group despised only slightly less in the North than the vanquished rebels. Weber's study supersedes older works and is now the obvious place to begin any study of the Copperhead movement."—Gary W. Gallagher, author of *The Confederate War*

"Jennifer Weber's *Copperheads* dispels outworn myths in her compelling narrative of Abraham Lincoln's all too real opponents in the North. Her fresh research has established a new baseline for all future interpretations of an often overlooked movement."—Ronald C. White Jr., author of *Lincoln's Greatest Speech: The Second Inaugural* and *The Eloquent President: A Portrait of Lincoln Through His Words*

"Historians of the Civil War era will raise a joyful hymn to Jennifer Weber for this fine study of Copperhead dissenters. Combining deep research, assured judgment, shrewd insights, and energetic writing, *Copperheads* challenges the prevailing orthodoxy, showing how anti-war northerners constituted a very real threat to the Union administration's effective conduct of the war. It is a compelling case, engagingly and persuasively made."—Richard Carwardine, author of *Lincoln: A Life of Purpose and Power*

"Perhaps the greatest contribution that this book will make is to encourage historians to reevaluate their comfortable notion that dissenters were marginal and that the 'peace wing' of the Democratic Party not a real threat. Weber has rendered magnificent service to Civil War historians by reminding us of that fact."—Adam I. P. Smith, *American Historical Review*

Copperheads

THE RISE AND FALL
OF LINCOLN'S OPPONENTS IN THE NORTH

Jennifer L. Weber

OXFORD
UNIVERSITY PRESS

OXFORD

UNIVERSITY PRESS

Oxford University Press, Inc., publishes works that
further Oxford University's objective of excellence
in research, scholarship, and education.

Oxford   New York
Auckland   Cape Town   Dar es Salaam   Hong Kong   Karachi
Kuala Lumpur   Madrid   Melbourne   Mexico City   Nairobi
New Delhi   Shanghai   Taipei   Toronto

With offices in
Argentina   Austria   Brazil   Chile   Czech Republic   France   Greece
Guatemala   Hungary   Italy   Japan   Poland   Portugal   Singapore
South Korea   Switzerland   Thailand   Turkey   Ukraine   Vietnam

Copyright © 2006 by Jennifer L. Weber

First published by Oxford University Press, Inc., 2006
198 Madison Avenue, New York, NY 10016

www.oup.com

First issued as an Oxford University Press paperback, 2008

Oxford is a registered trademark of Oxford University Press

Library of Congress Cataloging-in-Publication Data
Weber, Jennifer L., 1962–
Copperheads : the rise and fall of Lincoln's opponents in
the North / Jennifer L. Weber.
p. cm.
Includes bibliographical references and index.
ISBN 978-0-19-534124-9
1. Lincoln, Abraham, 1809–1865—Adversaries.
2. Democratic Party (U.S.)—History—19th century.
3. Copperhead movement.
4. Dissenters—United States—History—19th century.
5. United States—History—Civil War, 1861–1865—Protest movements.
6. United States—Politics and government—1861–1865.
I. Title
E458.8 .W43 2006
973.7/12 22—dc22
2006010827

Printed in the United States of America
on acid-free paper

For Mom and Dad

Contents

Foreword

James M. McPherson

IN JANUARY 1863 PRESIDENT ABRAHAM LINCOLN said that he feared "the fire in the rear" even more than the Union's military chances against Confederate armies as a threat to the survival of the United States as one nation, indivisible. The fire in the rear was kindled by the antiwar wing of the Democratic Party. Branded as "Copperheads" as early as 1861 by Ohio Republicans, the Peace Democrats were stuck with that label through the entire war and beyond. Some of them turned the Copperhead image from a negative to a positive one by wearing a lapel pin made from the Goddess of Liberty on the copper penny to symbolize their defiance of efforts to suppress their antiwar rhetoric. Northern military defeats in the winter of 1862–63 and at other times in the Civil War gave a boost to the Copperhead argument that the Union could never be restored by the war, especially now that Lincoln had turned it into an unconstitutional war against slavery. Under the slogan "The Union as it was, the Constitution as it is," the Peace Democrats relentlessly attacked every one of the Lincoln administration's war policies.

A speech in the House of Representatives by Congressman Clement Vallandigham in January 1863 laid out the themes that provoked Lincoln's concern about "the fire in the rear." What had this wicked war accomplished? asked Vallandigham. "Let the dead at Fredericksburg and Vicksburg answer." The South could never be conquered; the only trophies of the war were "defeat, debt, taxation, sepulchres . . . the suspension of *habeas corpus*, the violation . . . of freedom of the press and of speech . . . which have made this country one of the worst despotisms on earth for the past twenty months." What was the solution? "Stop fighting. Make an armistice. . . . Withdraw your army from the

seceded States" and start negotiations for peaceful reunion. Vallandigham had no use for the "fanaticism and hypocrisy" of the abolitionist
argument that an armistice would preserve slavery. "I see more of bar-
barism and sin, a thousand times, in the continuance of this war . . .
and the enslavement of the white race by debt and taxes and arbitrary
power" than in African American slavery. "In considering the terms of
settlement we [should] look only to the welfare, peace, and safety of
the white race, without reference to the effect that settlement may have
on the African."

Rhetoric like this got Vallandigham arrested and convicted of treason by a military court. Lincoln commuted his prison sentence to banishment to the Confederacy, from which Vallandigham made his way
to Canada, where he ran for governor of Ohio—and lost. Vallandigham
and his fellow Copperhead politicians figure prominently in Jennifer
Weber's splendid new study of the Peace Democrats. She makes clear,
however, that Copperheadism was a grassroots movement that pitted
neighbor against neighbor in many communities, and sometimes even
members of the same family against each other. Her vivid narration of
this localized civil war within the national Civil War is one of the most
significant contributions of this important book on antiwar dissent in
the North. But it is far from the only fresh insight on the Copperheads
that readers will find in the following pages. In a challenge to the reign-
ing interpretation, she shows that they represented a genuine and dangerous threat to the Lincoln administration's ability to carry on the war.
In the 1864 presidential election they wrote the Democratic platform,
which in effect demanded peace at any price, even the price of defeat
and disunion. Weber shows the naïveté of the Copperheads' insistence that an armistice and negotiations would bring Confederate states
back into the Union. Southern leaders repeatedly and unambiguously
proclaimed that recognition of Confederate independence was a precondition for negotiations.

In times of defeat and discouragement, the Peace Democrats made a
great deal of headway among Northern Democrats with their argument that the war could never be won and indeed was not worth winning. But they made no headway with Northern soldiers. Not only did
soldiers vote against Copperhead candidates by far larger margins than
civilian voters, but they also helped persuade family members and
friends back home to vote for candidates who supported the Lincoln
administration's determination—and their own—to fight this war
through to unconditional victory. Weber's fascinating analysis of the
soldiers' political role adds a key dimension to our understanding of
the mobilization of the Northern population for the war effort.

Until now the foremost historian of the Copperheads was the late Frank L. Klement, whose several books advanced the central thesis that the Copperhead "fire in the rear" was mostly "a fairy tale," a "figment of Republican imagination" compounded of "lies, conjecture, and political malignancy." Republicans did exaggerate the Copperhead menace for political advantage, to be sure, and their accusations of treason were mostly false. But the danger to the Northern war effort posed by Copperhead political activities was far more than a figment of Republican imagination. Weber disentangles the myths and realities of antiwar dissent in vigorous, lucid prose grounded in exhaustive research. In the large and growing literature on the Civil War, only a few books stand out above the crowd. *Copperheads* is one of those few.

Acknowledgments

I READ OFTEN of the loneliness of researching and writing, of the solitary nature of those pursuits. That has not been my experience with this book. At every step of the way, I have had a battery of smart people with whom to exchange ideas. I met countless wonderful people on my research travels. Once words started to spit from my computer, many people were gracious enough to read drafts—in a couple of cases, multiple drafts. My thinking and my writing have only become sharper for the input I have received, and I count myself lucky to have made several new friends along the way.

I visited a number of archives for this project, and the archivists at each site were knowledgeable, courteous, and hospitable. They also put up with my speed reading and requests for multiple carts each day with unfailing good humor. I cannot thank the staffs at the following archives enough: The Illinois State Historical Library (now the Lincoln Library), State Historical Society of Iowa (Des Moines and Iowa City branches), Ohio Historical Society, Wisconsin Historical Society, Minnesota Historical Society, Indiana Historical Society, Indiana State Library, Indiana State Archives, William L. Clements Library, Lilly Library, Huntington Library, New York State Archives, New-York Historical Society, New York State Library Manuscripts and Special Collections, Connecticut State Library, Connecticut State Archives, Connecticut Historical Society, Massachusetts Historical Society, Firestone Library at Princeton University, Library of Congress, and the National Archives and Records Administration.

As I made my way through these various places, several people were particularly generous with their time, allowing me to bounce my still-forming ideas off them. They are: Illinois State Historian Tom Schwartz, who was the first person I talked with about writing on the Copper-heads and who has continued to be remarkably generous toward me; Stephen Towne of the Indiana University–Purdue University India-napolis library's special collections department, who prompted me to think about things that had not occurred to me; and Michael Musick of the National Archives and Records Administration, who is a wonder-ful source for anything having to do with the Civil War.

I have also been the beneficiary of other generous people and insti-tutions. My wonderful and funny cousin Jay Ellis and his family have opened their home to me more times than I can count now. In the early stages of this book, I received much-welcome financial support from the Illinois State Historical Library, the Gilder-Lehrman Institute, the Iowa State Historical Society, and the Minnesota Historical Society. John Adler and HarpWeek were more than generous in allowing me full access to the still-beta version of "Abraham Lincoln and the Civil War," where I found nearly all the images used in this book. I look forward to the day when anyone can have access to John's marvelous collection. At the University of Kansas, the staff at the Word Processing Center has been a godsend.

Princeton University is a special place. Both the university and the history department were incredibly generous in their financial sup-port of this project. That, perhaps, I could repay; the intellectual gener-osity I received from so many members of the department and the university I cannot. In particular, I would like to thank John Murrin and Sean Wilentz, members of my dissertation committee who con-stantly pushed me to dig deeper, ask more questions, and challenge my assumptions. Eric Foner asked relevant and penetrating questions that have made this a much better book.

My graduate school friends were wonderfully supportive and pro-vided many welcome diversions. Liz Lunbeck and Angela Creager and their families made my graduate school experience so much richer than it otherwise would have been by taking me into their homes and their families. Liz, Angela, and Gary Gerstle have offered me much sound professional guidance, too. Lisa Bailey and her husband, James Cunningham, go down as some of the best people ever to hang out with. I also thank them for teaching me the basics of World Cup soccer, hockey, and cricket. Tania Munz can always make me laugh. She and Lisa both were good enough to read early chapters of this book, de-spite the fact that it was not in their fields.

My California friends have been with me in spirit if not in body all these years. Kris Sanders is the sister I never had. Joe and Sharon Cutcliffe and their children have made me an adjunct member of their family, for which I will always be grateful. Kathleen Deeringer is my academic alter ego. Pat Linehan, many years ago, opened up my world when she introduced me to the life of the mind. Richard Kassebaum read the manuscript at a key moment and provided not just good feedback, but also continuing moral support. Kathy Morrison brought her keen eye to the book to give it a final vetting before it was printed.

Two more recent friends have been incredibly giving of their time and support. Richard Carwadine and William Miller read through the manuscript, chapter by chapter, and offered sharp insights and excellent suggestions. I am deeply indebted to both of them, especially since both men were deeply involved in their own projects. I count myself lucky to have them as friends and advisers. I also would like to thank the Junior League—the junior faculty in the University of Kansas history department—for reading and offering advice on a particularly troublesome chapter.

Without a doubt, my greatest intellectual debt is to Jim McPherson, who has read more drafts of this than he probably would care to think about. To call him an influence is an understatement. He has been unstintingly generous with his time and input. He has given me many remarkable opportunities, and I cannot begin to repay him. He is the model teacher, adviser, and mentor. It is a privilege to know him, and to call him my friend.

I would also like to thank my editor at Oxford, Peter Ginna, and the rest of the staff who did such a marvelous job on this book.

All my readers have saved me from embarrassing errors, missteps, and typos. Should anything have slipped past my early readers, it is in spite of their efforts, not because of them. My mistakes are all my own.

Finally, I would like to thank my parents, who have been unceasingly supportive. They may not always understand my decisions, but they always stand behind me. With that kind of net, I can never fall too far. It is to them that I dedicate this book.

COPPERHEADS

Introduction

IN LATE AUGUST 1864 the conservative, antiwar wing of the Democratic Party was at the height of its influence. The Peace Democrats, also known as Copperheads, were so powerful that their strength nearly matched that of the War Democrats, who supported Abraham Lincoln's war policies. The growing authority of the Copperheads within the Democratic Party was most apparent at the national convention, which was held that year at the end of the month in Chicago. The peace men gained control of the committee responsible for writing the party platform, and the final document, which laid out the Democrats' philosophy for the coming presidential contest, amounted to a Copperhead manifesto. The conservatives' clout was also evident in the makeup of the ticket. A War Democrat, General George B. McClellan, occupied the top spot, but his running mate was an Ohio congressman who was one of the country's most outspoken—and notorious—antiwar men.

By the time of the election two months later, the Copperheads were entirely disgraced. Most Northerners considered them to be traitors to the Union cause, and many who had sympathized with the Peace Democrats struggled to distance themselves from their previous political associations. The party itself, whose values the hard-liners claimed to represent in their purest form, was hardly in better shape. It was so tainted by the exploits of the Peace Democrats that only two Democrats occupied the Executive Mansion between 1868 and 1932, by which time most of the Civil War generation had died.[1]

This book, which focuses on the war years, has four central findings. First, it shows that antiwar sentiment was not the peripheral issue that many Civil War histories have made it out to be. Lincoln was confronted with widespread disaffection at home, hostility so profound by the summer of 1864 that he appeared certain to lose his reelection effort. The Peace Democrats, whose influence waxed and waned in counterpoint to the Union armies' successes and failures, were nearly powerful enough that fateful summer to take over their party. Second, the Civil War has often been called a brothers' war, but this book demonstrates that in the North it was a neighbors' war as well. Disagreements over how the war was being prosecuted—indeed, whether the war should even have been waged—divided towns and counties throughout the Union. Violence burst out with surprising frequency in many parts of the North, urban and rural, East and West. Third, the peace wing's opposition to the administration damaged the army's ability to prosecute the conflict efficiently. Dissidents' resistance to conscription and their encouragement of less ideologically minded Americans to dodge the draft or desert the army forced the military to divide its attention and at times send troops home to keep order there. Finally, the book tracks the politicization of Union soldiers. Their fury at the antiwar faction helped bring most of the army behind the Emancipation Proclamation within a year of Lincoln's first announcing it, and turned many soldiers into lifelong Republicans. The troops' unqualified support of Lincoln helped maintain his political viability even when he appeared doomed, and their victories at a crucial moment sealed Lincoln's reelection, which in turn guaranteed a reunited nation and freedom for African Americans. Lincoln has sometimes been credited with holding the Union together single-handedly, but he could not have done so without the moral and military support of the soldiers.[2]

Dissent had another by-product, which historian Eric L. McKitrick pointed out years ago and which this book confirms. The activities of the Peace Democrats drove Republican governors to embrace the Lincoln administration to a degree they otherwise might not have. In dealing with this resistance, they turned repeatedly to the federal government for help, even if that meant surrendering state powers and becoming more dependent on a centralized infrastructure in the process. By comparison, the lack of organized political parties in the Confederacy kept President Jefferson Davis from exercising the kind of political discipline over local officials that parties allow.[3]

Who were the Copperheads, and how did they fall so quickly from grace, taking the entire party down with them? Broadly speaking, Copperheads were antiwar Democrats. They went by a number of names. They most often called themselves conservatives. They were that, given their commitment to the narrowest possible interpretation of the Constitution. Republicans started calling them Copperheads in the summer of 1861, when an anonymous letter-writer to the *Cincinnati Commercial* suggested this would be an apt term for Ohio's Peace Democrats, whose motto the writer thought should be drawn from Genesis 3:14: "Upon thy belly shalt thou go, and dust shalt thou eat all the day of thy life."[4] Copperheads are poisonous snakes, but after the term came into widespread use in 1862, conservatives tried to turn it to their own advantage. "Copperhead" was also a contemporary term for the penny, and the penny at that time had Lady Liberty—the perfect symbol for people deeply concerned about incursions on their rights—on one side of it. Some Peace Democrats adopted the term as their own and sported Lady Liberty pins made from pennies to signify their loyalties. Dissenters in the lower Midwest were also known as "Butternuts" because of their Southern roots (butternut being the color of their homespun clothes and therefore a term sometimes used to describe impoverished Confederate soldiers). This was another term they used for themselves, but Republicans used it, too. "Peace Democrats" is a more neutral term that historians have chosen. Except for Butternut, which is geographically constrained, I use all these terms interchangeably.

Whatever people chose to call them, or they chose to call themselves, they were consistent, and constant, in their demand for an immediate

A Copperhead Meeting.

Republican publications were fond of depicting antiwar Democrats in the most grotesque terms, and this cartoon is no exception. A slave driver doles out toad soup to the Copperheads while King Cotton looks on in the background. (*Nick-Nax*/Courtesy of HarpWeek LLC)

peace settlement. At times they were willing to trade victory for peace. One persistent problem for conservatives was their refusal or reluctance to offer a realistic and comprehensive plan for peace. It remains unclear to this day how they expected the nation to return to the *status quo ante bellum*. Once seceded, the Confederates insisted that all they wanted was their independence. Lincoln came to realize this fact by 1862, but the peace wing never acknowledged Confederate wishes, even though Northerners regularly read excerpts from the Southern press in their own newspapers, and not even after Southern editors directly confronted the North's foremost Copperhead, Clement Laird Vallandigham, with their demands for independence. To the extent the Peace Democrats had a plan, it was to resurrect the Crittenden Compromise, which included a constitutional amendment to protect slavery in the South forever. The Senate narrowly defeated the measure in January 1861, three months before the war broke out, but conservatives stopped calling for it only after Lincoln stomped the Democrats in November 1864.

Besides the desire for peace, the common denominator for all conservatives was their concern about personal liberties. Peace men were strict constructionists about the Constitution; they saw no interpretive wiggle room in the document. It said what it said, and what was not there could not be read into it by courts or presidents. They considered themselves the heirs of Andrew Jackson and Thomas Jefferson, who believed in limited governmental powers. Jackson was particularly popular for his conservative approach to the Constitution, which mirrored theirs. Like Jefferson and Jackson, the Copperheads drank deeply from an old ideology, republicanism, that warned against tyranny, executive usurpation, and big government.[5] (Ironically, Lincoln's Republican Party had sought to capitalize on those same fears in the 1850s by portraying a Slave Power in league with Democratic presidents and Northern sympathizers. Of course, the Copperheads were targeting a different constituency than the Republicans.) The rhetoric of the most prominent Copperheads was quite similar to the language that the Patriots used against George III during the American Revolution. Their fears about the threats of government power, combined with their understanding of the Constitution, made them extremely wary of, and often alarmed by, the way Lincoln wielded power during the war— indeed, in some cases, by the very fact of the war itself.

The conservatives' fears had real foundation. Lincoln and his representatives were making incursions on civil liberties. In the first two years of the war, Lincoln suspended habeas corpus and even declared martial law in some areas. Officials sometimes padlocked the doors of

Abduction of the Yankee Goddess of Liberty.

This cartoon, of the devil kidnapping Lady Liberty, appeared in a Southern humor magazine, but it expressed the precise thoughts of Copperheads in the North. (*Southern Punch*/Courtesy of HarpWeek LLC)

newspapers whose views they did not like or refused to let the mail carry suspect circulars. Opposition newspaper editors could be hauled off and jailed, sometimes for several months, without charge. Military tribunals tried some dissidents, even though the civilian court system was functioning. The draft, when it was introduced in March 1863, had the potential to deprive every military-age man of his freedom. Moreover, it brought with it a huge new bureaucracy that had greater reach and authority than any agency Americans had ever known. Lincoln was also instituting a number of measures for which there was no precedent in federal history, including income taxes and a national currency made of paper.

And then, of course, there was emancipation. Even in a time when a racist view of the world was the norm, the attitude of these Democrats toward African Americans was startlingly virulent. Peace Democrats universally supported slavery, believing it to be the best situation for a degraded race. Their most charitable view of abolitionists was as zealots whom one should regard warily. Many conservatives blamed the abolitionists for starting the war. Southerners, by this account, were the innocent victims. The Emancipation Proclamation confirmed the Copperheads' worst fears and suspicions about Republican aims. They thought the president was acting beyond his constitutional purview in issuing the proclamation, and they raved about what freemen would do to Northern workers, not to mention their wives and daughters. Their combination of fundamentalist constitutional interpretation and deeply held racism was like dry tinder and a fat log. When Lincoln turned the war from one whose only goal was saving the Union to one that also sought to free the slaves, he struck the match.

One important note about who the Copperheads were not: Their ranks did not include religious objectors to war, such as many Quakers and Mennonites, who preferred to sit out the Civil War on the grounds that war was wrong—not just this war, but any war. The Copperheads' ideology did not encompass pacifism.

Peace Democrats never recognized the magnitude of the emergency confronting the nation. They criticized Lincoln harshly and relentlessly. Blinkered by ideology, they remained insistent on a strict constructionist reading of the Constitution. Their interpretation would have barred Lincoln from employing most of the flexible and creative initiatives that helped the Union to win the war. Rather than offering realistic alternative solutions for the problems the war posed, Copperheads were obstructionists, doing little more than laying into Lincoln and his policies. "The Constitution as it is, the Union as it was" became their rallying cry. But as the violence of the war increased and the death toll mounted, their commitment to a simpler past and to a rigid interpretation of the Constitution took on a bizarre, even reckless quality. Their refusal to deal with the complexity of the war and of governance nearly consigns their ideas to the realm of fantasy.

For their many faults, though, most Copperheads were not traitors. Though some made no bones about their Southern sympathies, most were genuinely committed to the well-being of the nation. Their efforts may have been misguided and at times damaging, and they may have been blind to or ignorant of the consequences of their actions, but

ABE LINCOLN'S LAST CARD; OR, ROUGE-ET-NOIR.

The British publication *Punch* was routinely critical of Lincoln, and it was typically blunt in depicting emancipation as a potentially explosive decision. Note the slave's face sketched into the satanic-looking Lincoln's ace of spades. (*Punch*/Courtesy of HarpWeek LLC)

the vast majority were loyal to the Union. They were sincere in their belief that the Lincoln administration and the Republican Congress were overstepping their constitutional bounds. They did not want the Confederacy to win or the Union to split. They just wanted the nation to return to the *status quo ante bellum.*

Copperheadism developed in three distinct phases. The first came with secession. While some Copperheads actively supported the Confederate cause, that was very much a minority view. Many who opposed the war from its outset did not support the rebels per se but thought secession was legal because the Constitution did not expressly forbid it. (The Constitution was stone silent on the question of what it meant for states to have ratified it. Only the Civil War clarified the question of whether states that had voluntarily entered the Union could voluntarily leave it.) When the war started and Lincoln began, in their view, bending the Constitution to his own needs, they grew increasingly distressed about threats to liberty, especially Lincoln's decision to suspend habeas corpus. Conservative Democrats who actively opposed the war at this point made up the inner core of the Copperhead movement and deeply influenced the terms with which it would express itself as the war continued.

The second phase began with the preliminary Emancipation Proclamation in September 1862 and extended into the following spring, when the Union adopted a draft. In this phase, Democrats who had been sitting, sometimes uncomfortably, on the prowar side joined the opposition because they had become increasingly alarmed over the actions of the Lincoln administration. Deeply racist Democrats who had supported the war when its only purpose was maintaining the Union jumped to the opposition when the confrontation became an effort to free the slaves. The idea was too repugnant to them. Others, already worried by growing government power, drew the line at the draft, which was the most coercive measure Lincoln had adopted to that point. The Copperheads who joined the movement in the first two years of the war melded with the first group to create an even larger core of true believers. They insisted they were patriots acting out of concern for the nation, the only true defenders of republican government in a time of upheaval. Although some were content to let the Southern states go—the constitutional issue again—most insisted that they wanted to reunite the country. This was a vague, hand-waving promise, though. They never offered a coherent alternative to Lincoln's plan—war—nor did they ever acknowledge the Confederates' own resolve to gain independence.

Inklings of the third phase of development predated the second. In the summer of 1862, the federal armies were losing. Dispirited Northerners who had supported the war a year earlier began to question why they were fighting at all. The impulse to quit ebbed and flowed among Northerners like an ocean tide for the next two years but reached its height in the summer of 1864. Confronted by Union armies that seemed to have stalled on all fronts and by casualties that stagger the imagination—sixty thousand in six weeks from Grant's army alone—thousands of Northerners were clamoring for peace. The Copperheads, with their antiwar stance and harsh criticisms of the president, offered an appealing alternative to Lincoln's stubborn determination to stay the course. The people who linked arms with the Copperheads at this point did not necessarily share their ideological vision; they just wanted the war to end. So when the Union army and navy enjoyed a dramatic reversal of fortune late in the summer and into the fall, the war-weary quickly abandoned their antiwar position and returned to the president's fold with all the fervor of the newly converted.

The strength of the Peace Democrats generally ran in inverse relation to the successes (or failures) of the armies. When the war was going well for the Union forces, Copperheads were relatively weak. But when the Northern armies were losing, civilian morale dropped. Americans began to ask pointed questions about the government and the president. Another, more objective way of considering public confidence is in the price of gold. Generally speaking, the price rises when people feel uneasy about the future and are looking for a safe investment. During the Civil War this was true, although the price was skewed at times by efforts to corner the gold market and by an inflation rate that raised the consumer price index by 79 percent over the course of the war. (The chart is not corrected for inflation.)[6]

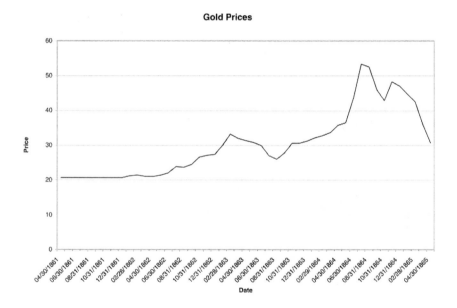

Gold Prices

Clearly, the Copperheads' fate, like that of Abraham Lincoln himself, was inextricably tied to that of the Union armies. Lincoln realized this, at least in regard to his own career. "I claim not to have controlled events, but confess plainly that events have controlled me," he told the editor of the Frankfort, Kentucky, *Commonwealth* in April 1864. The Copperheads, however, lacked Lincoln's understanding of the times. Locked into their own worldview, certain of their rectitude, they failed to appreciate that they did not control their own destiny. They never knew what hit them.[7]

It is partly because of the magnitude of the Copperheads' loss that most Americans do not know about them. If the Democratic candidate, George B. McClellan, had beaten Abraham Lincoln in the 1864 election, the Copperheads would surely have had a strong voice in his administration and therefore a higher profile on the historical stage. As it was, McClellan, the Democrats, and especially the Copperheads were humiliated. Contemporaries commented on Peace Democrats in their neighborhoods all but vanishing; they certainly stopped talking about politics. Neither they nor their family members donated much in the way of letters and diaries to archives. This kind of material from the leading Copperheads is particularly hard to find. Most of what they have to say can be found only in the public record, not among private writings.

Historians also have something to do with the shallow footprint the Peace Democrats left. Only three major books have been written about the Copperheads, and the last of those came out in 1960.[8] All three focused on the peace movement in the Midwest, and all dealt with the question of whether the Copperheads were trying to overthrow government at either the state or federal level. It was the wrong question to ask. Rather than concentrating on conspiracy theories, it is more productive—and illuminating—to concentrate on how widespread dissent was and whether it made a difference in mainstream politics. In any case, the most influential of those three books has been the last of them, Frank L. Klement's *The Copperheads in the Middle West*. In it, Klement contended that the Copperheads were mostly a fiction. As far as a political threat, he argued, they were mostly the product of fevered Republican imaginations. That has set the image of the Peace Democrats for nearly two generations: that they were a fringe group at best. My research finds to the contrary: that the peace movement was broad, and so influential by August 1864 that it very nearly took over the Democratic Party.

An important caveat at this point: It is impossible to quantify the strength of the Copperheads. Public opinion polls did not exist in the nineteenth century. The closest thing would be elections, which of course are the ultimate opinion polls. That leaves me to base my conclusions partly on election results, if there are any, and partly on impressions drawn from reading hundreds of documents from the period. When I talk about the relative strength or weakness of the Peace Democrats, then, I define those terms in two ways. First, how widely accepted did the conservatives' ideas seem to be? Second, how influential were they within their own party?

Carl von Clausewitz, the nineteenth-century German war theoretician, wrote that in order for a nation to wage war successfully, the "paradoxical trinity"—the people, the army, and the politicians—had to be working in concert. "The passions that are to be kindled in war must already be inherent in the people; the scope which the play of courage and talent will enjoy in the realm of probability and chance depends on the particular character of the commander and the army; but the political aims are the business of government alone," he wrote. In other words, civilians must back the war, and they need to maintain the will—the morale—to continue it. This is particularly true in a country such as the United States, which traditionally has not had a large standing army, preferring instead to draw troops when needed from the civilian populace. This creates a close relationship between the civilian and military worlds and an environment in which the morale on one side can easily affect the morale of the other. Civilian support, especially in a democratic republic such as the United States, is also crucial for giving politicians a reason to keep pressing the war and for maintaining high morale among the troops. The politicians have to articulate the strategy, or the grand objectives, of the war to military leaders and to the people at large to bolster and maintain the will to wage war. Finally, the military leaders need to execute the directives effectively, which in turn bolsters confidence in military leaders and politicians. If any leg of this tripod buckles, the war effort may founder entirely.[9]

Historians have rarely considered these three branches together when writing about wartime. They have tended to focus on one facet: the military, the home front, or the political. This is particularly true of the Civil War. Hundreds of books have described the military sweep of the war, the drama of a single battle, the experiences of a particular regiment or an individual soldier. Scores more have focused on politics, especially Northern politics. Still others have looked at what was happening at home, although this piece of the war remains the least studied and the ripest for further scholarship.

Applying Clausewitz's paradoxical trinity in relation to dissent in the North yields a much deeper understanding of the complexities that war presented to the Union: We learn more about the pressures that the public brought to bear on Lincoln and his administration with each turn of military fortunes. We gain greater insights into the expectations that civilians had of the army and navy and the demands that soldiers and sailors had of the people they left at home. Finally, this approach shows us that the war spilled over into a great many Northern communities. Copperheads, it turns out, were not part of a fringe movement but a broad faction that divided many neighborhoods and threatened to undermine Lincoln's war effort. Indeed, one of the major surprises of this project is how strongly people in many parts of the

country felt about Lincoln's policies, whether in support or opposition.[10] Where neighbors had once agreed to disagree over politics, their
feelings about the war proved so divisive that people on both sides of
the question feared that others in their community were about to hurt
or kill them or their family, burn their homes or barns, or destroy their
crops and livestock. These fears proved to be justified in many communities, particularly those in the lower Midwest. Anger over the war
threatened to have larger consequences, too. At times dissent was so
bitter that observers were sure that the Northwest, as they called what
we now think of as the Midwest, would secede from the Union if the
South were successful in its efforts to break away. (Except for the clearer
"lower Midwest," I generally do not use the more modern term, "Midwest." Instead, I refer to the northern tier between the Appalachians
and the Rockies as the "West" or "Northwest," which were the contemporary terms for the region.) Lincoln was well aware of what was
happening across the country and was concerned about its implications. Faced with a war to his front, he called this "the fire in the rear."
Without an understanding of that fire in the rear, our knowledge of the
war at the front is incomplete. This book tells that story.[11]

1

In the Shadows

IT WAS STILL DARK THE MORNING of April 12, 1861, when Confederate shells started to burst over Fort Sumter. The assault was the culmination of a three-and-a-half-month standoff between the federal government and the Confederates, who regarded the Union presence in the mouth of Charleston Harbor to be an affront to them and their recently declared independence. President Abraham Lincoln, who had inherited the situation from his predecessor James Buchanan, was determined not to give up the island fortress. Neither would he be the first to open fire on Americans, seceded though they might be. But by April the newly inaugurated president had to make a decision. The men at Fort Sumter were running short on food and supplies. Having informed the rebels of his plan, Lincoln ordered ships bearing supplies to sail to Charleston. This humanitarian mission, as Lincoln called it, sparked the bloodiest war in American history. The rebels opened fire before the supply ships ever arrived. The 4:30 A.M. attack was a spectacle that drew Charlestonians out of their beds and up to their rooftops or to the Battery to watch. After holding off the Southerners for thirty-three hours, the commander of the garrison, Major Robert Anderson, surrendered. The Civil War, which claimed at least 620,000 lives, began with a battle in which neither side lost a single man.[1]

News of the attack on Sumter spread quickly through the North and was greeted with a combination of excitement and grief. Most Northerners—Republicans and Democrats alike—quickly closed ranks behind the president. But not all of them. In pockets throughout the country, especially in the lower Midwest and urban areas, there were Democrats who opposed the war even amid the war fever that gripped most of the nation. Dissidents came from various backgrounds and arrived at the antiwar movement with assorted motives, but they coalesced around republican ideology. They had a very conservative understanding of the Constitution and were deeply suspicious of any attempts—real or perceived—by Lincoln to expand his powers or those of the government.

While people in many Northern communities were aware of serious objections to the war, and a handful of Democratic congressmen made their own questions plain on the House floor, one would hardly know from reading the national press that there was anything but wholehearted support for Lincoln's efforts. It is partly for that reason that historians have overlooked the presence of an antiwar movement from the very moment the cannons started to boom at Sumter. There is another reason that this conservative movement has not broken into the historiography of the early war, and that is that many people who had doubts about the war kept their uncertainties quiet, waiting to see what would happen. The people who opposed the war from its outset were committed conservatives, and they would form the core of the antiwar movement. They would be joined over the next year and a half by many of those quietly sitting on the fence in April 1861. In the meantime, dissent hardly penetrated the national consciousness.

Before Sumter, Northerners were divided on how to deal with secession. Many Democrats, especially those in the conservative wing, strongly supported the Crittenden Plan. Proposed by Senator John J. Crittenden of Kentucky in December 1860, this involved a series of constitutional amendments protecting slavery along with plans to strengthen and enforce fugitive slave laws. Lincoln opposed the idea, and the measure narrowly failed in the Senate just a few days before he was sworn into office. Legally dead, the plan lived on for years in conservative minds. The day before Fort Sumter, the *Crisis* in Columbus, Ohio, called for the resurrection of the Crittenden Plan. The best way to achieve peace, it said, was through "manly and prudent discussion . . . in accordance with popular government and *constitutional guarantees*" on all sides. The editors fretted about protecting the rights of the minority, i.e., the South, and insisted that abolitionists, not Southerners, were to blame for the current state of affairs. It carried a clipping from the *Cincinnati Commercial* that same day. This piece argued that if the North would only "thross off the shackles and stigma of negro equality," put men in power who supported the Crittenden compromise, and broker honestly with the seceded states while guaranteeing them their "constitutional rights," then "all our calamities would disappear in a twelvemonth, and our national harmony be re-established on a firmer and more lasting foundation than ever." These utopian fantasies would reappear regularly over the next four years.[2]

They would lose most of their audience the next day. After the firing on Sumter, the mood of the North was electric. "The news spread like wildfire, and but one sentiment seemed to pervade every mind—where would the strife, now so terribly commenced, end," reported the *New York Herald*, whose offices were thronged with crowds trying to learn the news. Most Northerners quickly rallied behind the president. In New York, thousands of people jammed into Union Square in a show of support for the nation. "Wave upon wave of human beings, thousands, and thousands, upon tens of thousands, poured through the streets, for hours together, actuated by a sentiment, neither of joy, nor of triumph; but of inflexible determination that, whatever the cost may be, the Union shall be preserved," the *Herald* said.[3]

Rage militaire swept over the young men of the Union, who responded in such enormous numbers to Lincoln's modest demand for seventy-five thousand volunteers that many were turned away. "The country was on martial fire," a New Jersey railroad manager said. Watching young men go to war, a Connecticut bank cashier slipped into a reverie: "Oh! what a stirring sight! Soldiers born under the shaddow of Bunker Hill! Men with the dust of Lexington in their bones! You can see the throbbings of their hearts in their stern and flashing eyes and the heroism of their purpose and their unalterable devotion *shines* in their faces." He could not look at the new soldiers without weeping.[4]

People in the North, as in the South, were confident of quick and decisive victory. Both sides anticipated a ninety-day war. A Rhode Island man dismissed the idea that the rebels were more "natural" military men. He told his brother that the men and material available to the North, along with the new feeling of martial spirit, would allow Lincoln's boys to "wipe out that palmetto, pelican, rattlesnake region entirely. . . . The South *may* be courageous but I doubt it, they can *gas* and *hag* first rate; they can lie and steal to perfection, but I really do believe that they cannot fight—'Barking dogs never bite.'"[5]

With the war now upon the country, support for the administration was nonpartisan as Americans rallied around the Union. In Kalamazoo, Michigan, the Democratic and Republican poles were taken down, spliced, and reerected as a symbol of unity. The message that political differences were to be set aside was most potent coming from Senator Stephen A. Douglas, Lincoln's longtime political rival in Illinois. He now stood squarely behind the president. "There can be but two parties, the party of patriots and the party of traitors. We [Democrats] belong to the former." Douglas, the North's leading Democrat, was unrelenting in his belief that anyone who did not back the president and his war policies was a turncoat. But not all Democrats agreed with

him. With his blunt statement, the lines between War and Peace Democrats were drawn. Douglas was among the first public figures to paint
those not supportive of the war effort as traitors, and his comment
would echo through the next four years. Most Democrats, including
Douglas, agreed, though, that the war should have one aim: to reunite
the country. Altering Southern institutions, especially slavery, was not
among their objectives.[6]

The early peace wing of the party did not endorse the war at all.
Many conservatives regarded the secession of Southern states as wholly
legal. The Constitution, after all, said nothing at all about the terms of
ratification: whether signing the document meant being in the Union
forever. It was completely silent on the issue of secession. The idea of
getting out from under the thumb of an overbearing government one
regarded as oppressive was so attractive that the Copperhead mayor
of New York, Fernando Wood, took advantage of secession fever in
January 1861 to suggest that his city part ways with New York State,
which was too closely allied with abolitionist interests for his comfort.
While Wood did not outright suggest that the city would become its
own country or ally itself with the Confederacy, he did suggest that its
financial interests lay in maintaining "a continuance of uninterrupted
intercourse with every section. . . . It behooves every distinct community, as well as every individual, to take care of themselves."[7]

But the stunning news out of Charleston Harbor and the patriotic
frenzy it sparked set the tone for the first year of the conflict. The overwhelming support in the North for Lincoln and the war effectively
neutralized the opposition. Newspapers that already had spoken fe-
verishly against Lincoln or would do so later were surprisingly muted
in their response to Sumter. The *Dubuque Herald,* which would become
one of Lincoln's fiercest critics, carried a highly diplomatic editorial on
April 14 acknowledging sincere differences of opinion between the
North and the South and reminding both sides that their pursuits of
abstract rights could end up hurting citizens on each side. If the Union
and the Confederacy could not agree to reunite under some sort of
constitutional agreement, they should agree to separate, editor Dennis
A. Mahoney wrote. His moderation would last a single day before he
would return to attacking Lincoln. Sharp sentiments were evident elsewhere, too. The *Indianapolis Sentinel* announced the attack on Fort
Sumter by proclaiming that "the abolition war of Seward, Lincoln and
Company" was under way: "The Abolition and disunion administration have attempted the coercion of the Confederate States. Such are
the first fruits of Republicanism—the end no one can foresee."[8]

The agree-to-disagree tone Mahoney and many other Democratic editors adopted may have characterized the public dissent of many of the elites—politicians and editors, especially—in the first year of the war, but such polite language was not the norm among rank-and-file Copperheads. From the moment fighting broke out, it was obvious that many people in the North opposed the war and the administration's efforts to put down the rebellion. Dissidents disputed the president's policies loudly, immediately, and sometimes violently, and they terrorized many of their Unionist neighbors with threats of what they planned to do on behalf of the Confederacy or in defense of the Constitution. While they generally had little national attention, they were well known in areas where they were active. They represented the first phase, and the hard core, of the Copperhead movement. Unfortunately, it is impossible to know how many people were part of the opposition, or what percentage of the country they represented, at this point in the war or later. Because this was long before polling began, we are left to view public opinion through a gauzy lens, with newspapers, letters, and election results to guide us.

GENERALLY SPEAKING, men who were from the South or whose parents had emigrated from the South were more likely to have reservations about the war than their neighbors who were born in Northern states. While statistics about parents' state of origin are impossible to find, census-takers did record state of birth in 1860. It quickly becomes apparent that many of the areas where flare-ups over the war occurred had significant numbers of Southern-born "Butternuts": the southern tier of Indiana, Illinois, and Ohio, and areas along the rivers or southern border of Iowa. In Indiana and Illinois, which became the center of gravity for antiwar activity, between 10 and 12 percent of the population in 1860 was born in a Southern state. Eight percent of Iowa's population was from the South, and Ohio was home to nearly 135,000 native-born Southerners, who composed nearly 6 percent of the state's population. California and Oregon both had large Southern-born populations, and both of those states had areas of strong dissent, most notably Los Angeles. They were so far from the center of action, though, that they did not attract much attention nationally. Kansas, another state with a large number of people born in the South, had fought its own bloody civil war in the mid-1850s. There were various reasons for this migration. Some families moved from the South in search of better land or economic opportunities. Others may have left, as Lincoln's own father did, because of property title disputes or, another factor in the Lincolns' case, because they were uncomfortable with slavery.[9]

Like people with Southern roots, German and Irish immigrants—especially Catholics—were less inclined to support the war than native-born Northerners. Many of these newcomers did not regard the Civil War as their fight. Besides, Catholics and immigrants had long been targets for Whigs and the nativist Know-Nothings, who had tried either to reform them or drive them out of the country. When those parties collapsed in the first part of the 1850s, many of their members found a new home in the Republican Party. The hostility that Catholics in particular felt toward Republicans meant that states with large Catholic immigrant populations had a higher probability of experiencing antiwar activities, especially in the cities where many immigrants had settled. So it was no surprise that New York State, where the Irish composed 13 percent of the total population, Massachusetts, whose Irish immigrants accounted for 15 percent of the population, and Wisconsin, where Germans made up 16 percent of the residents, all found violent antiwar protesters within their borders during the war. [10]

There was a third element in dissidence: strict constitutional constructionism. This ideology, which drew on a particularly fundamentalist strain of Jeffersonian-Jacksonian democracy, was the great unifying theme of all Peace Democrats. Regardless of social or economic background, opponents of the war tapped the deep roots of republican ideology, which had as its foundation suspicions of centralized government and concentrated power (or tyrannical rule), standing armies, and, most of all, threats to liberty. Republican thinking went back as far as Machiavelli, but blossomed in seventeenth- and eighteenth-century England with Court-Country political debates. It gained a strong following in the American colonies after the Stamp Act passed in 1765 and thereafter became a philosophy on which to base a revolution. In the early years of the republic, its followers gravitated to its leading advocate in the new nation, Thomas Jefferson.[11] Alarmed about the actions and ideas of John Adams and Alexander Hamilton, he and James Madison believed the powers of the president and the federal judiciary should be circumscribed. The government's ability to raise money and spend it should be limited, and the federal government should remain small and relatively powerless. Most authority should rest with state and local governments, which are closer to the voters. Jefferson became the country's first strict constructionist (although he violated some of his own notions about federal authority when he agreed to the Louisiana Purchase). Jefferson's faction ultimately won the debate after the War of 1812, when the Federalist Party died.[12]

Jefferson may also be the first—he is certainly the most prominent—secessionist. In 1798 he ghostwrote the Kentucky Resolves, which said that states could invalidate federal law if they thought the law was unconstitutional and could secede from the Union if they could not otherwise resolve their differences with the federal government. (The Virginia Resolves, which carried a similar message, were much less strident as written by James Madison.) This was a dangerous position, and although Jefferson's language did not find a broad and receptive audience in his own time, his threat bore fruit in December 1860, when South Carolina left the United States and other Southern states soon followed.

Conservatism lay dormant for about a decade after the War of 1812 ended but reemerged forcefully with Andrew Jackson, the other leading light for the Copperheads. Responding to the early years of the market revolution, with its dependent laborers, capitalist bosses, and money-lending bankers, he and his followers hearkened back to fundamentalist Jeffersonian ideals of simplicity and small government— the "spirit of '98" (an allusion to the Virginia and Kentucky Resolves). Jackson dismantled the National Bank, demanded purity in government, fought with the Supreme Court over who had the last word in arguments between state and federal governments, and opposed federal involvement in monopolies. Like Jefferson, Jackson proved to be no absolutist. While he did not favor anything that would lead to a strong centralized government, he demonstrated during the Nullification Crisis of 1832—when he denounced South Carolina's efforts to nullify federal tariffs, its claims of state supremacy over federal law, and its talk of secession—that he nevertheless believed in the preeminence of the federal government on key matters.[13]

Jackson's ideas about small government both reflected and shaped the actual size and powers of the federal government. The bond between Americans and their government was strongest on the local and state levels, where voters could expect regular contact with their elected officials and visible evidence of some sort of administration. This connection was most obvious in newer parts of the North, where many of the men casting ballots either had helped establish local government, held some sort of office, or served on a jury. The federal government in the antebellum era, by contrast, was geographically distant and relatively powerless, its most observable function being the delivery of mail. Jackson's defense of the Union notwithstanding, secession remained an open question. It rose yet again in the 1850s, fueled by the addition of more than half a million square miles of territory ceded to the United States by Mexico. Whether that land would be free or slave helped drive the nation into the abyss of civil war.[14]

Republicanism was the philosophical underpinning that conservatives agreed on, regardless of whether they were Southern born or

foreign born, Protestant or Catholic. Ideas stemming from this ideology totally informed their understanding of politics and government
in both their possibilities and their potential for harm. Falling back
again and again on the Constitution, hearkening back to the examples
of Jefferson and Jackson, they steadfastly defended their liberties against
what they regarded as a steady incursion by the tyrant Abraham Lincoln and his Republican minions.

The election of 1860 did not foreshadow the divisions to come in the
wartime North. To the contrary, the election suggested a North united
behind the Republicans or the pro-Union Douglas Democrats (with
some limited support for John Bell's Union-extolling Constitutional
Union Party). The Southern Democratic candidates in that election, John
C. Breckinridge and Joseph Lane, posted anemic numbers in the North.
One might expect that, because he was from the border state of Kentucky, Breckinridge's performance in the Northern states might shed
light on where resistance would be a problem in the North. The theory
does not hold. In the states of the wartime Union, Breckinridge put in
a strong showing in only four: his home state, although he lost it to
Bell; its fellow border state of Maryland, where he took six counties
but again lost the state; California, where he performed well in the
Central Valley, the foothills, and a handful of coastal counties but still
came in third after Lincoln and Douglas; and Oregon, where only Lincoln outpolled him. His support barely registered in the border states
of Missouri and Delaware. In the areas of the country (outside the border states) where antiwar sentiment was most virulent during the war—
most notably the lower Midwest—Breckinridge had little discernible
following. In Indiana, he drew only 4.3 percent of the total vote, placing no better than third in any county in the state. In Illinois, his best showing was in Union County, in the southern tip of the state, where he placed
second. In Dubuque County, Iowa, the home county of Dennis Mahoney,
one of the most notorious Copperhead editors in the North, Breckinridge
received a mere 1 percent of the vote. He logged similar numbers in the
counties bordering the Ohio River in the Buckeye State. On the other hand,
he took second place in three of Connecticut's eight counties and two
Maine counties. The election of 1860, then, offered no inkling to the
dissent that would emerge only months later; nor did it provide a clue
as to where the hotbeds of opposition would be.

Outright Southern sympathizers were relatively rare in the North,
although there were some. They believed the Southern states had every
right—a responsibility even, given the abolitionist talk in the North—
to secede. "I am cauld a Disunionest a Secesenest a trator & god allmitey

knows what else for no other reason then for vindicating the ondely Set of princiables that can posable accomplis a compremise & a union— of all the States," wrote a Virginia-born Oregonian who swore he would have fought for the Confederacy if he had not had a family. "*Equle rights to all the states* without that we can not posibely exspect a union of all the states." Other Northerners offered their services to Jefferson Davis's government. Thomas Yeatman of New Haven, Connecticut, promised the Confederate president he would raise and equip two companies of one hundred men each for service to the South. Although Republicans tried to paint all antiwar Democrats as secessionists, that describes only a fanatical minority. Most dissidents shared the feelings of a Connecticut man who wrote that the South was justified in thinking its rights were imperiled. "Without some further guarantees, they are sure to be overborne by the progressive antislavery feeling of the North," he said.[15]

Southern sympathizers were a distinct minority, though. For more Peace Democrats, the idea that dominated their thinking was strict constructionism. From the war's outset, most of the objections that dissidents registered were cloaked in constitutional terms. Antiwar Democrats insisted repeatedly that they supported the North but thought the rebels should be persuaded to return to the Union at a negotiating table, not at gunpoint. If the North could not bring the South back into the Union through peace talks, some Democrats believed, it was better for the country to grant the Confederacy its independence. As one New Yorker wrote, the "sane portion of our people" were those who "do not esteem cutting the throats of one's countrymen as proof of patriotism or rely upon the bombardment of a city as the best way of cultivating union and fraternal love with its inhabitants."[16]

In the frenzied days after Fort Sumter, the distinctions between loyal dissent and treason were lost on most Northerners. Actually, many Northerners would *never* see the difference. Anyone who was not firmly behind Lincoln was suspect—even former presidents. After receiving an anonymous letter at the end of 1861, Secretary of State William H. Seward wrote Franklin Pierce to tell him that he had been accused of being a member of a secret society whose object was to overthrow the government. "Any explanations upon the subject, which you may offer, would be acceptable," Seward wrote. Allegations of treachery led to extraordinary proclamations of loyalty. In Chicago, the publisher of the *Daily Chicago Times*, Cyrus McCormick, responded to threats that the paper would be sacked with a front-page letter to readers. Though he had been born and raised in the South, he assured them, "I am a citizen of Illinois and of the United States, and as such shall bear true allegiance to the Government. . . . I am and ever shall be on the side of my country in war—without considering whether my country is right or wrong." Inside, on the editorial page, the editors insisted that they did not support secession, apologizing for an infelicitously worded earlier editorial that had suggested otherwise.[17]

Besides place of birth, religion, and political ideology, one last issue deeply split the Peace Democrats from the Republicans: emancipation. Conservative Democrats had suspected from the earliest days of the Republican Party that abolitionists controlled it and that the party's main objective was to free the slaves. "The Congregational clergymen of New England in my opinion—are the worst disunionists in the land," wrote William Jarvis, a Connecticut executive and father-in-law of gun manufacturer Samuel Colt. If Jarvis were dictator for a week, he said, he would "banish the whole tribe on pain of death, and ship them to self righteous England—to 'agitate' for her institutions—and as a fitting token of gratitude for the presents she made us of Puritanism and slavery." Peace Democrats were sure that the abolitionists "running" the Republican Party actively pursued war to achieve their goals. The day after Fort Sumter, the *Dubuque Herald* accused the administration of goading Southerners into war:

> Nothing will satisfy the fanatics of the North but a provocation to civil war, in which they may accomplish their darling object—that which they have toiled for many years: the incitement of slaves to insurrection against their masters, and ... the consequent emancipation of those slaves, the abolition of slavery, and the ruin and subjugation of the South to the political thraldom of Northern fanaticism.

Even War Democrats were wary of a hidden agenda to get rid of slavery. One, John Campbell of Philadelphia, suspected that a scheming Britain was behind the abolitionist movement "to do us all the mischief she is able." Nevertheless, he thought the administration "must not be crippled in its efforts to suppress rebellion and punish traitors."[18]

Suspicions about the Republicans' real aims ran so deep among some Democrats that Lincoln met with scoffs when he insisted that he had no intention of touching slavery where it already existed. Dissidents' skepticism did not ease as the Civil War rolled through its first year. Feelings against the abolitionists ran so high in Cincinnati that in early 1862 a crowd pelted Wendell Phillips with eggs when he tried to deliver a speech there. The police did nothing to stop the mob. When Horace Greeley of the *New York Tribune* wrote that this war was one of ideas—specifically freedom versus slavery—James Gordon Bennett of the *New York Herald* shot back, "If this is a war of ideas then let the abolitionists fight for their ideas, and let all others stand back." People who did not believe in freeing the slaves should not have to fight for it if that was really what the Civil War was about, he said. Although Bennett was not a Peace Democrat, at least not consistently, his thoughts on this matter were widely shared in the Copperhead community.[19]

Copperheads were notable for the depth and virulence of their racism. Like many Southerners, they regarded African Americans as inferior beings who were best off in bondage. Copperhead rhetoric throughout the war was filled with allusions to racial mixing that were designed to play on whites' deepest fears. Well before emancipation was on Lincoln's front burner, the Copperhead elite stirred up their followers by saying that freed slaves would come north and take the jobs of hardworking white men. *"Free the blacks and enslave* the whites; that seems to be the policy of the Lincoln dynasty. If freemen are pleased with this, they may get enough of it," former Connecticut governor Thomas Seymour wrote. Not surprisingly, this kind of rhetoric reinforced and inflamed existing bigotry.[20]

With anxieties running high, neighbors were quick to turn on each other. Before the war, they might have agreed to overlook political differences, but that moment was over. With civil war the stakes were too high for tolerance, much less compromise. Neighbors who had lived next to each other for years quickly came to regard each other with suspicion, fear, and loathing. Especially in parts of the country where Southern ties were common, people on each side of the political fence regarded those on the other as a threat to their property, safety, and even their lives.

Heightened levels of fear and suspicion resulted in an avalanche of mail to Republican governors. Unionists reported on the activities of their neighbors: Men in their communities were making public statements against the government. They advocated assassination of the president. They openly supported the Confederate government, or said Jefferson Davis was a better president than Lincoln. The Butternuts, which quickly became synonymous with antiwar Democrats, were meeting secretly in the woods or brazenly in the local schoolhouse. Some men were talking about arming themselves and joining the Confederate army. Typical was this letter from an anonymous writer in southern Illinois, a part of the state commonly known as Egypt. Like many other frightened correspondents, he urged Governor Richard Yates to pay attention to the rebels there. "Some of them Say they are going to help Jeff Davis & others Say they are going to hang cut throtes & shoott every Republican

in egypt   they Say it will be sport . . . killing the Republicans as they are
scatiring." Two men in Union County, Illinois, had similar fears. Claiming theirs was the "most intensely Pro-Slavery county in the State," they
reported that the lives and property of all twenty Republican families in
their neighborhood were in peril. Many of the most influential Democrats in the area were rebel sympathizers "and would gladly seek their
vengeance on such Republicans in their reach as have assisted to establish [the federal government]. Many of them swear they will drive out
every negro and 'Black Republican' from the county." In Newburgh,
Indiana, loyalists could not publicly offer any opinions for fear that
secessionists in that town and from across the river in Kentucky might
kill them. Reports that armed organizations were forming came even
out of New England, the cradle of abolitionism. Many of the letters asked
for immediate aid in the form of soldiers or arms, but the governors,
already overwhelmed by having to outfit regiments for the front, were
rarely able to send either.[21]

As if they did not have enough panic to contend with already, governors also had to deal with allegations that political or military appointees, or candidates for those posts, were disloyal. Letters to this effect
were prevalent in the first half of the war, when governors had the power
to appoint regimental officers. Reports of an appointee's disloyalty often came from men the governor knew and men whose information he
could trust, generally Republicans. But they were nearly as likely to come
from complete strangers, often men whose tenuous grasp of the literary
arts adds poignancy to their earnest letters. While some of the men whose
loyalties came into question were removed or asked to resign from the
posts, action on most of these allegations is unclear.

Governors also received alarmed letters about men who were putting together militia companies for local defense. Who was in the militia was of particular concern because local militias had access to
state-issued arms or the regional armory. Many letters to governors
warned that traitors were assembling militia companies under false
pretenses in order to gain access to armaments. An even darker and
more prevalent fear was that such men would turn their muskets and
rifles against either the local population or the local or state government. In some areas, Democrats readily admitted to putting together
their own units. In Talon County, Indiana, for instance, they were doing so "in order to Keep things in a safe condition," Jacob C. Adams
told a political ally. This comment not only confirms that Democrats
were forming companies but also suggests that, like the Unionists, they
were worried about their personal safety.[22]

One of the most frightening prospects, and one that showed up regularly in these letters, was that a number of local men had formed units of the Knights of the Golden Circle, a paramilitary organization modeled after the secret fraternal orders that were so popular in the antebellum United States. George Bickley, a Virginia-born doctor, formed the KGC in 1859 or 1860 in Cincinnati with the goal of overthrowing the Mexican government and colonizing Mexico. Now that the Civil War had broken out, the KGC was determined to serve as a "rallying army for secessionists," according to one historian who has studied the organization. This "army" was especially active in the lower Midwest, again because of the area's historic Southern influences. An Illinois businessman returning from a trip to Randolph and Jackson counties described events that were typical of those taking place throughout the region. Men were taking the oath of the KGC and the organization was growing fast, he said. Estimates varied as to the size of the group—100 by one account, 250 by another—and the ringleader was supposed to be recruiting more men from Union County, he reported. "The union men are talking of scattering them But so many have volunteered in that region that I doubt the ability of the union men to cope with them,—especially as the mass of them is unknown," he said. As a result, local Unionists felt remarkably vulnerable. With so many loyal men gone to war, that sense of defenselessness pervaded many parts of the Northwest.[23]

Frank Klement, who devoted his career to studying the Copperheads, argued that clandestine organizations such as the KGC were the products of overheated imaginations and Republican propaganda. Klement completely discounted their significance and dismissed their potential to create havoc.[24] Some of these letters were no doubt the result of overactive minds. Other letters almost surely were an attempt to even a score with an old political foe—a nineteenth-century analog to McCarthyism. But the vast majority were legitimate reports that historians cannot dismiss. First, these kinds of letters exist from too many different parts of the country and too many disparate sources. Second, too many different people wrote letters expressing their concerns. The sheer volume of mail from so many people to so many readers—powerful or not—suggests that something important was happening. Third, not all of the mail expressing fear about neighbors' activities went to government officials. Much of it was private letters sent between friends and family members. There would be no reason for people to fabricate Copperheads for that kind of audience. Finally, it is clear that not every writer had strong political predilections. What is obvious from the sources is that many people in the North believed the Copperheads posed a threat in their neighborhoods, and both they and government officials acted according to that belief. What it is impossible to know given the existing sources is how serious the threat of Butternut violence was. Still, one cannot help but come to an abrupt stop when encountering an ominous note such as this, written in July 1861 by a man who thought Jefferson Davis was a far better man than Lincoln: "Times will not be better until this foolish Republican war policy is by *practical demonstrations* proved to be *ruinous and suicidal*."[25]

In some parts of the country, allegations of disloyalty led to banishment by friends or colleagues. The most dramatic illustration of this was the U.S. Senate's ejection in February 1862 of Jesse D. Bright of Indiana. In March 1861 the senator had written a letter to Jefferson Davis introducing a friend from Texas who had "an improvement in firearms" to show Davis. His colleagues charged Bright, a Democrat who had once owned slaves and defended slavery in his official capacity, with treason and booted him from the Senate. He was the only Northern member of Congress to suffer this ignominy during the war, but he was not the only high-profile politician to suffer public humiliation. In Hartford, the Connecticut State Senate voted to remove the portraits of former governors Isaac Toucey and Thomas Seymour from the chamber because they opposed the war. Many prominent citizens refused even to acknowledge Toucey, who also had served under Buchanan as secretary of the navy, when he passed them on the street. Such treatment did not sit well with some of the men who were spurned as traitors. When a railroad president refused to grant discounted tickets to a meeting in Terre Haute, Indiana, because he believed one of the speakers was disloyal, a group of Democrats signed a petition denying that the speaker or they were turncoats. They accused the railroad executive of having been swayed by local Republicans "whose partyism rises far above their patriotism—whose principal vocation for the last four months has been to

Former Connecticut governor Thomas Seymour was an outspoken opponent of the war from its inception. He so upset legislators in his home state that they had his portrait removed from the state capitol. (*The Old Guard*/Courtesy of HarpWeek LLC)

misrepresent and slander all persons who have refused to endorse the ultra war policy and unconstitutional acts of the present administration." Regardless of how indignant Copperheads became or how strenuously they defended their loyalty, reports of treachery continued to stream across the desks of Republican officials.[26]

Union men were not the only ones worried about their safety. Men who disagreed with the administration also feared that they could become targets of violence. When Iowa Democrats tapped Charles Mason—a West Point graduate, a prominent patent attorney, and the first chief justice of Iowa's Supreme Court—as their gubernatorial nominee in the summer of 1861, Mason worried about being mobbed by "republican scoundrels." He need not have worried. The party reconsidered the wisdom of naming an antiwar candidate and asked Mason to step aside two weeks after nominating him. In Indiana, a Democrat wrote that he suspected "the craven hearted wretches" in his neighborhood would either hang or assassinate him, based on what he had read in the Republican press. He boasted that Republicans had too little courage to do anything else to him. Many men in Indiana were less sanguine, though. They took precautions against the perceived threat of their Unionist neighbors by banding together in mutual protection societies. In Terre Haute, one such society included former Democratic congressman John G. Davis and his successor, Daniel W. Voorhees, among its members. This group organized assembly points and a system of signals to use if violence broke out.[27]

WHILE NORTHERNERS WERE COMING TO TERMS with the idea that their neighbors might mean them harm, yet another issue was simmering in the Old Northwest: Western secession. This could mean joining the Confederacy or breaking off and forming a third nation from the old Union. A strong Western identity—one predicated in many ways on hostility toward the East—had existed for years. Clement L. Vallandigham, a conservative congressman from Ohio who became the most notorious Copperhead in the nation, articulated the feelings of many, though certainly not most, Westerners in 1859 when he said he was "as good a fire-eater as the hottest salamander [Southern secessionist] in this House." Like many others from the Old Northwest, Vallandigham refused to identify himself with either the North or the South. He was a "Western sectionalist," he said, who would maintain that feeling "to the day of my death."[28]

Sectional talk like that did not subside with the outbreak of a sectional war. To the contrary, it took on a new urgency. For some people in the West, the stakes in the Civil War were all the higher because of its status as a precedent. The West's most ardent sectionalists believed that if the Southerners succeeded in their bid for independence, the Northwest could be the next to break off from the hated Yankees of the Northeast. Discussions of Western secession were especially rampant in the Midwest's southern tier, where so many Butternuts had settled in the antebellum era. Southern Illinois, whose tip reaches farther south than much of Kentucky or Virginia, threatened early in the war to secede not only from the state but from the Union as well. Democratic congressman James Addison Cravens of Indiana privately wrote that if the North and South could not settle on a compromise, and if Indiana could not join the Confederacy (his own preference as a native Virginian), then he would like to see the southern portions of Indiana and Illinois secede, form a new state called Jackson, and have that join the Confederacy.[29]

Western hostility toward Yankees before the war was rooted in economics and politics. Westerners believed that the monied interests in New York and Boston had chiseled them repeatedly in the prewar years and had the support of Congress in doing so. Indeed, Easterners appeared to have a lock on Congress, especially after Southerners left to form the Confederacy. New Englanders, who tended to serve longer in Washington than Western politicians, had the advantage of seniority and therefore dominated many of the committees. Besides serving together for years, the Yankees often shared family ties and educational backgrounds that drew them closer together and created a certain elitism. They routinely blocked Westerners from joining their circle.[30]

Hard feelings against the East only increased when the war began and scores of "unsound banks closed across the Northwest, putting the pinch on farmers. These banks had secured their circulating notes with bonds from border and slave states—bonds whose value tanked after secession. Only 15 percent of Illinois's antebellum banks survived 1861; nearly half of Wisconsin's went belly-up. Farmers, many of whom had held stock in the now-defunct banks, saw their financial standing erode further when the Mississippi River closed commercially at the beginning of the war. Many Western farmers and businessmen who had always sold their goods to towns and cities along the Big Muddy regarded New Orleans as their principal port. The loss of the Mississippi River trade was a blow to the Northwest that, for the moment at least, resulted in lower prices for its products, higher prices for finished goods from the East, and a depressed economy all around. Hog prices dropped by more than half, and farmers could not get even ten cents for a bushel of corn. Freight rates doubled, meanwhile, as railroads struggled to cope with increased demand for their services now that the Mississippi was closed. Compounding the misery in 1861 was the fact that the price of finished goods and staples such as coffee and sugar rose quickly, partly because of war-induced shortages and partly because of the Morrill Tariff Act that Congress had passed in February of that year. Western Democrats, conservatives especially, were deeply resentful that their part of the country was paying the price for a law written to protect the interests of Eastern mill owners.[31]

Producers and merchants need not have worried in the long run. During the 1850s the Northwestern economy had begun to wean itself from river-based trading and turn instead to the rails. Railroad mileage in the West had increased nearly ninefold during that decade, linking the Northern interior decisively to the ports of the East. Many people in the West did not realize it in the early months of the war, but their economic well-being was already tied to the Eastern seaboard, and the Civil War only cemented that bond. Thanks to the combination of bumper crops and high demand for their grain, farmers ultimately fared well during the war.[32]

Economic hardship was not confined to the West, of course. All across the North, prices started to rise shortly after Fort Sumter. Inflation in the Union averaged 13 percent annually over the course of the war. Shortages also became apparent, especially of cotton goods and household staples. The only part of the economy that seemed to be doing well in 1861 was the nascent military-industrial sector, which provided arms, uniforms, shoes, tents, food, and other provisions to the army, the navy, and their soldiers and sailors. These goods often were so poorly made that they fell apart or spoiled quickly. "Shoddy" products and contractors drew the wrath of conservative Democrats, who accused the government of corruption in granting contracts to profiteers at the expense of the boys in blue. People in the East did not experience these hardships to the same degree those in the West did, though, and Westerners were aware of that. Insulated from the suffering of the Northwest, James Gordon Bennett, the editor of the *New York Herald*, could write confidently that the war might impinge on prosperity and would certainly cause much sorrow, but party differences would never divide Northerners. Besides, he continued, men who were out of work could find jobs in the military, and the infusion of money from the federal government would kick-start manufactures. "Public interests and feelings give way before the public welfare," he said.[33]

Although bread-and-butter issues appealed to people at home, economic grievances never became a central theme for the Peace Democrats. That was because Lincoln's actions quickly moved them onto another topic, one that became the cornerstone for every argument

THE FAIR THING.

Northern Lady *who* "*sympathizes*" *with the Rebels to Grocer's Boy.* "Why, gracious!
Hans.   Your Master has charged me *awful prices!* Three Dollars per pound for Tea—
Soap a Dollar per Bar—Butter Two Dollars per Pound—"
Hans. "Yes, Ma'am.   The Boss says as you like to *talk* Secesh, perhaps you would'nt
mind *paying* Secesh prices."

Conservative women were not immune from criticism. *Harper's Weekly* mocked
Copperhead women who complained about rising prices in the North by saying
that perhaps they should experience the kind of inflation that their beloved
rebels did. (*Harper's Weekly*/Courtesy of HarpWeek LLC)

conservatives made during the rest of the war: the constitutionality of
his policies. These concerns started shortly after the attack on Fort
Sumter, first with Lincoln's proclaiming war without Congress making any sort of declaration, and then with his calling for seventy-five
thousand troops without the blessing of Congress. Lincoln also started
spending money to fight the war—again without the approval of Congress, which supposedly controlled the nation's purse strings. For a
group of men already fearful of abuse of power and deeply suspicious

of the president's agenda, Lincoln's actions were alarming. Vallandigham, the Ohio congressman, accused the administration of "highhanded usurpations of power" and of conspiring to overthrow the government in its present form and replace it with a strong, centralized government. Just six weeks into the war, he called for Lincoln's impeachment. In the *Dubuque Herald*, Dennis Mahoney wrote that Lincoln treated the Constitution as "so much blank paper" that he could ignore if he thought popular sentiment was with him. This disregard for the Constitution was a "menacing and dangerous" foreshadowing of what was to come, Mahoney warned.[34]

What galled conservative Democrats even more than Lincoln's failure to consult Congress was his decision to suspend habeas corpus in parts of the country. This first came to pass in April 1861 in Maryland, a state with a significant pro-Confederate population, especially in its eastern half. On April 19 a secessionist mob in Baltimore attacked Massachusetts troops on their way to Washington, D.C. Claiming that other Northern soldiers might retaliate for the mob action, local officials—many of them Southern sympathizers—burned the main railroad bridges out of town, thereby cutting off the nation's capital from the rest of the Union. Lincoln suspended habeas corpus from Washington, D.C., to Philadelphia the same day the Maryland legislature declared the war unconstitutional. Federal troops occupied Baltimore, and dissenting editors and citizens supportive of the Confederacy were clapped in jail. When Chief Justice Roger Taney, a Marylander himself, ruled in *ex parte Merryman* that the president could not suspend habeas corpus and that the military could not arrest civilians for violating federal law, Lincoln ignored him.[35]

Hard-core conservatives were apoplectic. Representative George H. Pendleton of Ohio predicted the country was headed down a perilous path. "If [Lincoln] may suspend one of these constitutional provisions, he may suspend two, or he may suspend all ... ," he said. "And thus, according to this new theory,

When Chief Justice Roger Taney ruled that Lincoln could not suspend habeas corpus, Lincoln ignored him. The full Supreme Court never heard the case.
(*Frank Leslie's Illustrated Newspaper*/Courtesy of HarpWeek LLC)

the President may supersede entirely the Constitution and the laws"
and perhaps even displace the entire system of government. Pendleton
spoke for many peace men when he said that the only way to preserve
the government was to protect and cherish the Constitution and insisted that the entire document remained in effect even in wartime.
"You cannot make a nation jealous of its rights by teaching it that, in
times of great public danger, the citizen has no rights," he argued. Then
he invoked some of the most fundamental values of the Victorian age:
"You cannot increase its manhood or its constancy, or make it sensitive
to dishonor, by teaching that in times of danger it must rely not on its
own virtue and courage, but on the power and good will of its rulers."
The masculine angle of his argument would disappear, but the rights
talk would become central to all Copperhead arguments during the war.[36]

The administration's actions at this moment may not have been as
dire as they first appear. Historian James G. Randall, who closely examined Lincoln and the constitutional issues he confronted, wrote that
the president suspended habeas corpus only with great reluctance and
while the Congress was in recess. Military authorities were instructed
to use this power only as a last resort and in fact showed a good deal of
restraint, according to Randall. In addition, the men the federal government reeled in "were there for good reason." Mark Neely seconds
this argument. Lincoln was motivated not by politics but by a desire to
keep Washington connected to the rest of the country, according to
Neely, whose study of civil liberties during the war is the most thorough of its kind.[37]

The constitutional implications of his measures were not lost on Lincoln, who, after all, was a lawyer. The president acknowledged the
potential legal problems when Congress finally convened on July 4,
1861. Lincoln maintained he had little choice but to bend the law in
response to the crisis. He defended his actions by asking, "Must a government, of necessity, be too strong for the liberties of its own people,
or too weak to maintain its own existence?" He had no time to call
Congress into session when the fighting broke out, he said. In fact, he
had no choice under such circumstances "but to call out the war power
of the Government; and so to resist force, employed for its destruction,
by force, for its preservation." As for suspending habeas corpus and
declaring martial law, Lincoln pointed out that under Article I, Section
9 of the Constitution, habeas corpus could be suspended legally in the
event of a rebellion. The constitutional question was which branch had
the power to suspend habeas corpus, and on that issue the wording, in
passive voice, was ambiguous: "The privilege of the writ of habeas
corpus shall not be suspended, unless when in cases of rebellion or

invasion the public safety may require it." Lincoln urged Congress therefore to consider the big picture. "Are all the laws, but one, to go unexecuted, and the government itself go to pieces, lest that one be violated?" he asked. "Even in such a case, would not the [president's] official oath be broken, if the government should be overthrown, when it was believed that disregarding the single law, would tend to preserve it?"[38]

Many conservatives who still supported Lincoln shifted uneasily over his early actions but stayed with him. The *Crisis* pointed out that the country was moving toward "a pure military despotism" and called on Americans to preserve their institutions (including slavery). "In preserving them we preserve our liberties also. . . . We are hourly in danger at such times as these, of slipping thoughtlessly out of our constitutional moorings, and then all is lost." Other conservatives shrugged off Lincoln's decisions. The *Chicago Times*, now under the proprietorship of Wilbur Storey and destined to become a staunch opposition newspaper, called the suspension of habeas corpus "a grievous calamity" but said Lincoln had to do something, and this action was within his constitutional powers.[39]

The most hardened conservatives, on the other hand, were unmoved by the president's appeal. Vallandigham dismissed Lincoln's message to Congress as a "labored and lawyerly vindication" of a policy "which has precipitated us into a terrible and bloody revolution." He announced to his colleagues, "I am for *peace*, speedy, immediate, honorable PEACE, with all its blessings." His lengthy speech, in which he disputed nearly everything the president had done so far, fell mostly on deaf ears. The Republicans and War Democrats who filled the Congress backed the president. Like most Americans on both sides of the Mason-Dixon line, they believed the war would be over quickly. Under pressure to go along with the administration, hard-core Peace Democrats stewed quietly. But Lincoln, with his crucial early decisions of the war, had given them the first arrows in what would become a well-stocked quiver.[40]

THE FIRST REAL TEST of the nation's morale came July 21, when the blue and the gray armies clashed at Manassas Junction, Virginia. Both armies were inexperienced but, still in the grip of war fever, itching for a fight. Before the clash a lust for battle seemed to pervade much of the North. "Anything is pardonable now but inaction," the *Indianapolis Journal* said. "The Country clamors for energy, decision and determination." The headline "Forward to Richmond" appeared in a *New York Tribune* editorial June 26, and "On to Richmond" remained standing on the editorial page for a week. Some historians believe this prompted the

Union attack at Manassas, also known as Bull Run. When it became apparent that the fighting would actually break out there, picnic-toting civilians from Washington streamed into the Virginia countryside to watch. The battle was not the glorious sight that *Tribune* editor Horace Greeley and so many other Yankees had anticipated. It was an embarrassing and bloody defeat that sent Union soldiers and civilian observers flying down the roads toward Washington. With nearly 4,900 casualties, three-fifths of them Union, First Bull Run was the bloodiest fight the nation had seen to that time.[41]

Northern newspapers labeled Manassas a "disastrous defeat," but the battle had little effect on the national morale, at least as far as the foot soldiers and civilians were concerned. The La Crosse, Wisconsin, *Democrat*, which would later oppose Lincoln virulently, wrote that it would continue to support Lincoln even though it did not find him up to the job. "The time for argument is past. We have submitted the question to the arbitrament of the sword. No matter whether that was the wisest thing we could have done or not. It has been done. We must abide by its decision," the paper commented. Not all papers were so understanding. The *Niles Republican* in Michigan blamed Horace Greeley's "On to Richmond" headline for instigating the battle in the first place. The loss was because of abolitionist congressmen who created a panic in their flight from the field, the paper said.[42]

Some communities saw tensions break out into the open as a result of the battle in Virginia. The Republican and Democratic editors of Niles's two newspapers got into a fistfight on Main Street over the Republican editor's accusing his Democrat counterpart of treason, despite the man's repeated assurances of loyalty. In Dixon, Illinois, when a shopkeeper mentioned to a conservative Democrat his sorrow over events in Virginia, the Copperhead "expressed his pleasure and declared it served them right." The two men came to blows, but the Copperhead quickly retracted his comment and apologized. While Bull Run may have had little effect on the military zeal of many Northerners, it made a deep impression on the field-grade officers of the Army of the Potomac, the Union's principal army in the East. The battle undermined the confidence of that army's high commanders, leaving them to spend the next two years uncertain of their abilities and convinced that Southern warriors were better than their own men.[43]

After Manassas, the Army of the Potomac went silent for months.[44] The battle had taken place before either the Yankees or the rebels were completely outfitted or trained, and both armies used this time to transform themselves into fighting units. In the months between July and February, only one noteworthy battle occurred: Ball's Bluff, on October 21, which the Confederates won. Otherwise, most military actions were nothing more than skirmishes, and civilian morale remained high until late in the year. Yes, men were dying in battle and even more from disease, but the numbers remained relatively small.

Front-line soldiers did not share in the crisis of confidence that some of their field officers did. These men were volunteers, proud to be serving, and they would become the core of the Union army. Their letters were upbeat and reassuring to their friends, families, and sweethearts at home. As the Civil War unfolded, this correspondence played an important role in determining public attitudes. This was a war that mobilized whole communities. Men from the same area joined up in companies, especially in the two years before the draft. Recruitment practices made companies, sometimes even whole regiments, an extension of a community. One way that communities remained firm was through the mail. Friends and family at home would write about their health, local politics, and neighborhood gossip, and they occasionally would slip the local newspaper or a clipping into the mail. In return, the soldiers would report on the men in their unit—not always in a complimentary fashion—their activities, and their opinions about the political scene. When men wrote home with news of seeing the president or of their opinions of a commander, the people at home paid attention. Because they were close to these men at the front, civilians were more apt to be influenced by what they read when it was written by a loved one than by an anonymous reporter or a newspaper editor. This flow of information and opinion would play an important part in shaping opinions about the president's policies and dissent behind the lines as the war wore on.[45]

Unlike the military situation in the fall of 1861, the political front was anything but calm. To begin with, the threat of Western secession still cast a shadow over the North. Southern Illinois had threatened all spring to join the Confederacy. The intervention of the area's congressman, John Logan, a Democrat who earlier in the year had been accused of being a traitor, finally squelched the serious secession talk in southern Illinois, although many men in the lower Midwest continued to hold out hopes for an independent Western nation until 1864. Prominent Copperheads occasionally brought up the matter in their speeches, and though they claimed to fear the day when the country broke apart yet again, their statements sounded to the East's elites like little more than thinly veiled threats. In New York City, a law professor did the Western politicians one better. William B. Wedgewood published a tract in which he proposed dividing the country into "two, three, or four Republics," then holding a convention by which these republics would band together into a "Democratic Empire," as he called it. The idea, along with a long and complicated constitution the professor drafted, went nowhere.[46]

While Westerners ruminated on secession, Lincoln had to deal with treason, or allegations thereof, on the East Coast. In New York, local authorities barred four newspapers in August from using the mails because of their incendiary rhetoric: the *Journal of Commerce*, the *Daily News*, the *Day Book*, and the *Freeman's Journal*. The Post Office Department forced the owner of the *Journal of Commerce* to sell the paper before it would resume delivery. Benjamin Wood, owner of the *Daily News* and brother of New York City mayor Fernando Wood, tried to get around the ban by having his paper sent via private express and then hiring newsboys to deliver it. But Wood stopped resisting when U.S. marshals seized all the copies of the paper and arrested a delivery boy in Connecticut. In early September, the administration had nineteen members of the Maryland legislature arrested in the belief that it was about to vote on an act of secession. Who ordered this—Secretary of State William H. Seward, Secretary of War Simon B. Cameron, General George B. McClellan, or Lincoln himself—is not clear. In Washington, Congress passed a conspiracies law "to discourage the plotting of rebellious activities." The punishment was death.[47] Once again, though, the conservatives' reply was fairly passive. "These acts seem to spring from the despotism of the Old World, and naturally excite deep concerns," Horatio Seymour told a crowd gathered in Utica, New York. He urged moderation. Democrats should maintain their confidence in Lincoln "until events prove that confidence is undeserved. We must assume that there are imperative reasons for these unusual measures, which in due time will be given to the American people." The administration would be held to account when the crisis of the moment was over, he assured the gathering.[48]

As the fall rolled along, the nation's financial troubles mounted. The cost of feeding, clothing, and equipping the army and navy in its first months ran to about $2 million a day. Concerns about how to finance such an expensive war grew as government coffers emptied. Republican congressman John B. Alley of Massachusetts, a businessman before going into politics, said the government would have to issue $150 million in paper money, levy a tax to raise $150 million, and produce a national currency. In fact, Congress had adopted a national income tax in the summer of 1861, placing a 3 percent levy on income of more than eight hundred dollars a year, but nervous politicians decided that the tax would not be due until June 30, 1862. This was too far in the future to solve the cash crunch the nation was facing by the end of

1861, and bankers in New York refused to accept treasury notes until they were sure the government could repay the loan. By January 1862, loyal Northerners found themselves in the remarkable position of pleading with their representatives to raise taxes to protect the nation's credit. A new tax bill passed in March levied a 3 percent tax on domestic manufactures, created a two-tier income tax, authorized a federal bureaucracy to collect those taxes (rather than the states, which had collected them in the past), and taxed commodities and services.[49]

Paper money was an option, but the idea was too novel for lawmakers, and Congress balked. So did members of the administration. Treasury Secretary Salmon P. Chase regarded paper money as "unconstitutional, immoral, and destructive," one historian writes. But Chase's feelings on the subject had no impact on Lincoln's final policy. The administration told Congress in January 1862 that it could not hope to pay its bills and continue the war by relying on specie alone. The only way banks could accept paper currency without going bust, though, was for the government to make it legal tender. So at the end of February, Congress authorized a $150 million issue of the new currency with little more than token constitutional objections on the part of conservative Democrats.[50]

Even with paper currency in circulation, several members of Congress insisted that greenbacks (the new, green dollar bills) were not enough to keep the government afloat. They pressed for taxes and a federal currency backed by government bonds. The nation was "upon the eve of bankruptcy," Representative Alley insisted, and vendors were "knocking at the doors of the Treasury for payment of their honest dues until hundreds are already ruined, and unless something is speedily done you may soon count them by the thousands." Congress agreed and passed yet another internal revenue act on April 8. The only no votes came from fifteen Copperheads in the House, who were deeply suspicious of paper currency and of the constitutionality of the revenue measures. Once again, the reaction among conservative Democrats was minimal, and what arguments they made were predicated on the Constitution. As with greenbacks, though, the income tax would reappear in their rhetoric in the coming months.[51]

Democrats were at a severe disadvantage on Capitol Hill. They were the opposition party in a time of war and, at the moment, a time of high support for the war effort. They were also in the minority. When the South pulled out of the Union, a significant number of Democratic congressmen and senators left with it. The House, for instance, lost fifty-five members to secession, most of them Democrats. The party got no compensatory boost from the 1860 election: Only eight of the

Union's twenty-two states, including the border states, sent Democrats to the House of Representatives that year. Three-quarters of the Democrats in the House in 1861 were freshmen, and seven others were only in their second term. The eleven Senate Democrats were similarly hobbled by inexperience. Five were in their first term. The year 1862 would decimate the six Senate veterans: John R. Thompson of New Jersey died, Jesse Bright was expelled, and Andrew Johnson of Tennessee returned home with an appointment as military governor. Copperheads—a distinct minority within their own party, not to mention in Congress—had no choice but to speak up when they could and hope for happier times politically.[52]

While the debates over how to finance the war were taking place, a pall settled over the nation. Northerners wanted a fight. They wanted *the* fight they thought would end the war. George B. McClellan had spent all fall and part of the winter outfitting and training his troops, but there was no sign that his army or those in the West had imminent plans to move. Civilian morale was slipping. Republican congressman John Gurley of Ohio wrung his hands on the House floor in January 1862. The men were ready to fight, but they lacked a commander who had the "will and the requisite enterprise and genius" to win the war, he said. Gurley worried that "the ghost of Bull Run" was still "hovering about and haunting the minds of our commanding generals." In Illinois "people are becoming impatient and disposed to blame somebody very greatly," a woman there reported. Lincoln shared the nation's despondency. On January 10 he asked Quartermaster General Montgomery Meigs: "General, what shall I do? The people are impatient; Chase has no money and he tells me he can raise no more; the General of the Army [McClellan] has typhoid fever. The bottom is out of the tub. What shall I do?"[53]

Like the people at home, soldiers were impatient for battle. Unlike the civilians, though, they were coolly confident. "This regiment would relish a fight now extremely well," a Vermont private wrote home. "When that event takes place you may be assured the Vermont Second will do their share to wipe out the stigma upon our arms, which they have coveted the privilege of doing ever since the Bull Run disaster."[54]

Peace Democrats fretted that the military situation could force the government to turn to African Americans for help. This concern stemmed from their conviction that the war, from its inception, was really about emancipation. Already, Major General John C. Frémont had unilaterally freed all slaves belonging to Confederates or Confederate sympathizers in Missouri, only to have his order countermanded by Lincoln, who feared that Frémont's measure would drive the border states from the Union. The *Chicago Times,* gravitating toward conservatism, insisted that only when white men could not save the Union should they call on the services of blacks. The idea of arming the slaves "is disgraceful to the civilization of the age, and disgraceful to ourselves. The slaves are practically barbarians. Their instincts are those of savages." It was not clear to the editors that the slaves would fight on the side of the Union. In the kind of dramatic and sweeping statement that would become a hallmark of the Copperheads, the editors wrote that if white men could not save their own government, it was better to let it go.[55]

At least one antiwar Democrat saw an opening amid the civilian unrest and sought to take advantage of it. Fernando Wood, a onetime shipping merchant and former congressman who had long been prominent in Democratic politics, was now the mayor of New York City and running for reelection. In a blistering speech, he said Republicans would pursue the war as long as slavery existed, Southern blood was still available to be shed, and "they themselves are removed from the scene of danger. They will get Irishmen and Germans to fill up the regiments and go forth to defend the country under the idea that they themselves remain at home to divide the plunder that is to be distributed." New York City Republicans were furious. The local U.S. marshal was so offended that he requested permission from Secretary of State Seward to arrest the mayor. A prominent Republican also implored Seward to arrest Wood, but their entreaties were in vain. The Copperhead elite, meanwhile, retreated into the safety of silence.[56]

Worries about the army's inactivity came to an end in February, when General Ulysses S. Grant shoved off from Cairo, Illinois, and embarked on a string of victories that thrilled the nation. Working in tandem with the navy, Grant first attacked and overwhelmed the Confederate garrison at Fort Henry on the Tennessee River, clearing that waterway for the Union all the way to Florence, Alabama. Then Grant and his men marched twelve miles overland to the Cumberland River, where he took Fort Donelson on terms of unconditional surrender, earning himself the nickname of "Unconditional Surrender" Grant. In early March, General Samuel R. Curtis and his Yankee troops in Arkansas turned back the rebels at Pea Ridge, giving the Union control over Missouri and northern Arkansas. And on April 7 the bluecoats under General John Pope captured Island No. 10 in the Mississippi River.

Northern morale soared, but worries about the political situation nagged at conservative Democrats at home. Neither the fact that all political prisoners willing to take the oath of allegiance were released in February nor that the issue of political prisoners was shifted from the State Department to the War Department eased their suspicions about the Republicans' real objective. "The North seems to be growing more rabid on the abolition question—by the North I mean the party in power—they will soon throw off the mask and advocate abolition & extermination of the white race in the rebel states," a Connecticut man told former governor Seymour. This was an unusually blunt admission of a deep fear that all Copperheads had. Another was expressed by a Hoosier who believed that the American people had been following a "blasphemous course" for some time and were no longer able to govern themselves. He concluded that the nation's low point had come at the Republican convention in 1860, "wherein it is set forth that the minority [i.e., Democrats] possess no rights but such as the majority may accord to them. This of course is equivalent to denying that our rights come from God or that there is such a thing as unalienable rights. The real rebellion going on in this Country is a rebellion against God, and for which we are now being afflicted."[57]

While Copperhead anxieties grew, Grant's army confronted the rebels at Shiloh. This gave Americans, North and South, their first real inkling of the kind of bloodletting the Civil War would become. The fight opened April 6, 1862, on a plateau beside the Tennessee River. The Yankees were camped near Pittsburg Landing when Albert Sidney Johnston slammed into William Tecumseh Sherman's camp near a church called Shiloh. The rebels pushed the federals back to the river before the bluecoats regrouped and, with the arrival of Major General Don Carlos Buell's army, drove the Confederates off the field and back to Corinth, Mississippi. The Union took 13,000 casualties, the Confederacy 10,700. Shiloh was the bloodiest battle in the history of the Western Hemisphere to that point, but by the end of the Civil War, it would rank only seventh among the conflict's deadliest fights. Northerners were shocked by the carnage but relieved at the outcome.[58]

Still more successes came. At the end of April, Admiral David G. Farragut steamed up the Mississippi past the forts guarding New Orleans, evaded the Confederate navy, and captured the city. Farragut's fleet continued moving upriver, capturing Baton Rouge and clearing the Mississippi for Union traffic from the mighty river's mouth all the way to Vicksburg. Federal forces were slow to follow up on either this victory or the one at Shiloh. General Henry Halleck arrived on the field and took command of the army from Grant after the battle in Tennessee. Three weeks after that fight, Halleck set out for Corinth, Mississippi, at the rate of one mile a day and entrenching each night. By the time he finally reached Corinth on May 30, ready for battle, he discovered that the rebels had pulled out of the city, never having intended to defend it. Halleck broke up his command, sending Grant to Memphis, Don Carlos Buell toward Chattanooga, and John Pope in yet another direction. The navy, too, enjoyed victory. On June 6, it defeated the Confederate river fleet at Memphis, and the city quickly surrendered. Farragut, meanwhile, discovered that the only way to capture Vicksburg was with a significant number of ground troops. Yet he had a land force of only fifteen hundred men. The rebels, on the other hand, had thirty thousand troops in and around what they called the "Gibraltar of the West." Although he was able to run past the city on June 28, Farragut had no hope of taking it. When Confederates threatened to retake Baton Rouge in early August, he headed back down the river. Vicksburg would remain impregnable for months to come.[59]

CASTLE LINCOLN—NO SURRENDER!   FORT DAVIS—IN RUINS.

People in the North were optimistic in the spring of 1862 that the war would be over soon. Here Castle Lincoln (note the profiles) is intact, while Fort Davis has been battered. The appointment of Robert E. Lee to command what became the Army of Northern Virginia turned around Confederate fortunes. (*Frank Leslie's Illustrated Newspaper*/Courtesy of HarpWeek LLC)

In this environment, more moderate elements of the conservative wing continued to support the war effort. The *Pilot*, a Boston newspaper geared toward Irish immigrants, boasted that the war was nearly over and blamed the hated British for instigating the whole affair. "Conquest did not take us to the South! True patriotism did." In La Crosse, Wisconsin, the *Democrat* also remained steadfast behind Lincoln, supporting the financial measures he advocated and insisting that he was operating within constitutional bounds. The president was, the paper said, "a man of nerve." Both newspapers, like many conservative voices, would change their tune in a few months. For the moment, though, everything looked marvelous for the Union. The armies were winning, and the recession in the West was easing, making the outlook there more upbeat than it had been in months.[60]

The North's renewed optimism proved to be short-lived. The real mettle of the Union was about to be tested. Editors and politicians who already opposed the war but had stayed quiet would begin to catch up to the vociferous rabble-rousers who had organized and frightened their neighbors. People who so far had supported the war despite their conservative leanings would join the dissidents' ranks. As a thick fog of disillusion settled over the nation, the Peace Democrats would move out of the wings and onto the main stage of American politics.

2

The Gathering Storm

SUCCESS DID NOT LAST for the Union armies, and with failure came demoralization. For the first time, Northerners were confronted in the late spring and summer of 1862 with the notion that this could be a long, bloody war. Military losses blunted the patriotic fervor that had characterized 1861, and the government had an increasingly difficult time meeting its need for soldiers. Officials turned to a proto-conscription, which also gave them a bureaucracy with which to pursue opponents of the war more effectively. Arrests rose dramatically as a result, giving the Peace Democrats their first truly substantive issue to exploit. More were soon to come. Around the same time that the draft was established, Lincoln was crafting his Emancipation Proclamation as a way to strike at slavery, the soft belly of the Confederacy. As far as the Copperheads were concerned, this act confirmed everything they had been saying since the beginning of the conflict about emancipation being the true objective of the Republicans in this war. The failures of armies in the summer of 1862 gave Copperheads a new strength, but it was the Emancipation Proclamation that gave them their voice.

While the blue-clad armies of the West were rolling up one victory after another in the late winter and spring of 1862, Union forces in the East experienced little but trouble. Much of the difficulty lay with the commanders, especially George B. McClellan. The former railroad executive brought considerable organizational abilities to his command, which proved to be a blessing for the bedraggled Army of the Potomac in the fall of 1861. But McClellan was still so preoccupied with preparing his men the following spring that he seemed reluctant to fight. McClellan also, it turned out, had a habit of overestimating the enemy's strength and then balked at engaging him. The general repeatedly sent

urgent telegrams to Washington insisting that he had to have reinforcements before he could attack. When he had enough men, he said he
did not have enough guns or horses. This pattern had become so obvious by early March that Lincoln and Secretary of War Edwin M. Stanton
worried that McClellan had some ulterior motive for dragging his feet.
So did suspicious Republican editors and congressmen, who hinted
that maybe McClellan wanted to ensure that slavery remained intact,
or maybe he did not want to crush the South as it deserved. Republican doubts about McClellan's commitment to win the war were so
strong that in March Lincoln removed him as general in chief. But strip-
ping Little Mac—one of several nicknames the press gave him—of his
title did nothing to alleviate his sense of caution, which by then had
permeated the officer corps of the Army of the Potomac.[1]

To be fair, the Army of the Potomac faced a much more talented
enemy than did the far more successful federal armies of the West. The
first hints of the creativity, belligerence, and ability of the Confederate
command in the East that had emerged at Bull Run became fully apparent in late March 1862, when Confederate general Thomas J. Jackson, who had earned the sobriquet "Stonewall" at Manassas the
previous summer, attacked a division nearly twice as big as his own
near Winchester, Virginia. The Confederates lost that encounter, but it
had important consequences. Lincoln was unsettled enough to believe
Washington was in danger, a condition he would often be worried about
that year. In early April, the president ordered Irvin McDowell's corps
to remain near Fredericksburg to protect the federal capital instead of
allowing him to join McClellan, who had moved his forces to the tip of
the Richmond Peninsula with the intention of attacking the Confederate capital from below. McClellan's response to the president's orders
was to complain that the administration did not want a Democrat like
himself to succeed.[2]

McClellan's suspicions, combined with his arrogance and petulance,
poisoned his feelings about Lincoln and had hampered their relationship long before Lincoln began to have his own doubts about the general. For his part, Lincoln grew impatient over the winter and then
disgusted with Little Mac's tendency to dawdle. The peninsula campaign did nothing to alleviate the president's concerns. Rather than
confront the rebels at Yorktown, McClellan dug in. Lincoln, who was
always keenly attuned to public sentiment, feared that morale in the
North was flagging because of McClellan's lack of action. "The country will not fail to note—is now noting—that the present hesitation to
move upon an intrenched enemy, is but the story of Manassas repeated," he wrote the general on April 9. "I beg to assure you that I

have never written you, or spoken to you, in greater kindness of feeling than now, nor with a fuller purpose to sustain you, so far as in my most anxious judgment, I consistently can. *But you must act.*" McClellan ignored the plea. His siege on the peninsula lasted until early May, when the rebels abruptly abandoned their works and backed toward Richmond.[3]

McClellan pursued the Confederates, following the Chickahominy River, and breaking up his forces so they straddled the river. Unfortunately for the Young Napoleon, as the general was also known, the river flooded and his troops began to run short of rations. Meantime, Confederate general Joseph E. Johnston decided to attack McClellan's troops on the south side of the Chickahominy. The rain wound up hampering the rebels as much as it did the Yankees. Disorganized and stuck in the mud at times, the graycoats could not coordinate their attack, giving federal general Edwin Sumner enough time to cross the river on a dilapidated bridge and reinforce the Union lines at a critical moment in the fight. Technically, the May 31 battle—called Fair Pines or Seven Oaks—was a draw, but the Yankees wounded General Joseph E. Johnston badly enough that Jefferson Davis had to relieve him of his command and find a replacement.[4]

This looked like good news at first for the Union. Davis named as Johnston's successor Robert E. Lee, the commander of all the Confederate forces in Virginia. Lee had not been taken seriously in his previous Confederate commands, and some of the rebel press had taken to calling him "Granny Lee." The federals quickly found out he was all business, though. He rapidly renamed the Confederate force under him the Army of Northern Virginia and then got to work sizing up his enemy. It did not take him long to figure out that McClellan was loath to fight. The sight of corpses at Seven Pines had unstrung McClellan, who became increasingly reluctant to put his command at risk. After repeatedly promising Lincoln that he would take action, McClellan finally moved June 25 with a hesitant reconnaissance in force. The next day Lee demonstrated the nerve and the aggressive instinct that made him a great general. He took the offensive, and that began the fighting of the Seven Days Battles. The two armies looped northeast, then east, then southeast of Richmond, fighting all the way and finally disengaging after Malvern Hill. About ten thousand Union men were dead or wounded, and the *Chicago Tribune* deemed the weeklong clash a "stunning disaster" for the Union. It and other Republican newspapers started to call for McClellan's ouster while the Democratic press blamed Stanton for the army's failures, saying he did not send McClellan the men he needed. Confederate confidence soared while Northern partisans bickered.

Morale among the blue troops remained relatively upbeat despite the loss because the soldiers believed—mistakenly—that they had been outnumbered, that the politicians had refused to reinforce them, thereby dooming them, and that McClellan had done all he could to keep the casualty levels down.[5]

Even with their high morale, some soldiers could hardly believe the conditions in which they now lived. Having spent much of the first year of the war in camp, the men now had to get used to marching, sleeping, and fighting in every kind of weather and to consuming mostly salt pork, hardtack, and coffee while they were on the move. The life that soldiers led "would kill wild beasts," Massachusetts volunteer Charles Harvey Brewster wrote. Farmers in his hometown "would call it cruelty to animals to keep their hogs in as bad a place as we have to live and sleep."[6]

Public sentiment was not as sanguine as the army's, largely because of Jackson's escapades. Lee may have been the commanding general in Virginia, but Jackson was the man who most captured Northern attention. While McClellan was lackadaisically engaged on the peninsula in May, Jackson was tying up Union general Nathaniel P. Banks with his deftly executed activities in the Shenandoah Valley. Jackson was moving his small army up, down, and across the valley, striking at Front Royal and hammering the federals at Winchester. The rebel troops marched from one place to another so quickly that they became known as "Jackson's foot cavalry." By the time Jackson withdrew from the valley on June 9, his seventeen thousand men had marched 350 miles, fought and won four battles against three armies that, combined, were twice as big as Jackson's, and inflicted twice as many casualties as they took. It was a humiliating loss for the Army of the Potomac and a shock to the Northern public, which the press had repeatedly assured that the end of the war was near.[7]

Northern morale shrank a little more with each of Jackson's moves through the valley and each of McClellan's failures. Unfortunately for the administration, the Western armies—which by now appeared to be bogged down anyway—had only a limited effect on public opinion. The Army of the Potomac, on the other hand, came under close scrutiny: Its men came mostly from the East, where the major newspapers were; it operated in the East and was therefore more easily covered by the press; and it was the army charged with protecting the capital. Between the army's poor performance and the coverage it received, public confidence in it steadily eroded. Even those working inside the Executive Mansion had their doubts about the army's abilities. "McClellan's extreme caution, or tardiness, or something, is utterly exhaustive of all hope and patience, and leaves one in that feverish apprehension that say something *may* go wrong, something most likely *will* go wrong," said John G. Nicolay, one of Lincoln's personal secretaries. "Risks of battle are proverbially uncertain; but I am beginning to feel that the apprehension of defeat is worse than defeat itself is." Lincoln himself was deeply frustrated. He told a friend he was "satisfied McClellan would not fight." By early summer, some of Lincoln's most ardent supporters were sure the end was near for the Union cause. The situation did not improve as the summer wore on. Thousands of men died of their wounds and of diseases they contracted in the army's often disheveled and unsanitary camps. To McClellan's chagrin, Lincoln on July 11 brought Henry Halleck, known as "Old Brains," to Washington from the West to coordinate all the nation's armies. Still, there was no improvement in the Union's military fortunes.[8]

Depression seeped into the public consciousness, and war weariness followed. With defeat after defeat on the battlefield, Copperheads, who were so quiet during the first year of the war, started to criticize the administration more openly. "I abhor the whole scheme of Southern invasion with all its horrible consequences of rapine and plunder. Heaven will frown on such a cause as this; it cannot and will not come to good," a former governor of Connecticut wrote. In Philadelphia, the country's former minister to China, William Bradford Reed, published a pamphlet urging the North to recognize the Confederacy's independence. "If it be a choice between the subjugation of the Southern States and their tenure as military provinces and peaceable recognition, I am for recognition," he wrote. Other Democrats talked about the war becoming a "Trojan horse of tyranny." As he had so often before, Dennis Mahoney blamed abolitionism, because of its "fanaticism and destructiveness," for bringing on the war.[9]

Although public outcry against Lincoln and the war remained fairly limited and posed no serious challenge to the government, it was clearly beginning to percolate further into the culture. Women, who were not allowed to vote and many of whom had been political agnostics, grew more vocal about the matters of the day. "It is a pity that the abolition female saints and the Charleston female patriots could not meet in fair fight and mutually annihilate each other," wrote Maria Lydig Daly, the wife of a pro-war Irish-Democrat judge in New York. For some women, politics was not an abstract matter but something that landed right in the center of their sphere, the family. Feelings were running so high in some Northern families about whether the war should be fought that they were coming apart. "I feel as though I were ritt off from my family by these troubles," wrote one Democratic woman who was the only

Unionist left among her kin. "None of them love me as they once did, but I cannot go against my conviction of what is rights. But I am *no abolitionist.*"[10]

Whole communities in the North, not just families, were riven over the issue of war. Governors, especially in the West, continued to receive reports from men telling the authorities that their neighbors were not loyal to the Union. In New Middleton, Illinois, a resident wrote Governor Richard Yates to inform him that he had heard a local man say Lincoln and all his cabinet should be in the hands of Beauregard's army "so that they could deal justice to them." The writer asked what should be done with sympathizers. Yates responded that the man in question "ought to have been hung ten minutes after he said it—and should he say it again, ought to be hung in five minutes after he has said it."[11]

This was not the kind of response that Lincoln, an unusually tolerant man, would have endorsed. But the losses in the East were eating away at the goodwill of the public and many politicians alike. In Connecticut, a letter signed simply "A Deaf Mute" landed on Governor William A. Buckingham's desk in late June. The author wrote that he had supported Lincoln earlier in the war, but he was so disgusted with how things were going that he was thinking of going south and joining forces with Davis. *"I tell you that you, Lincoln, Seward & the others would not like to have your head & their heads wooled like the negroes!"* he wrote. He blamed the abolitionists for the war and its increasing levels of violence. "The Southerners are made worse than the savages *by the abolitionists!"* If Lincoln had just ordered Sumter surrendered, the South would have rejoined the Union within three years. *"Now. Withdraw your proclamation. Renounce Lincoln! Disband your army which is in your splendid state immediately. Hoist Jefferson Davis' flag. Shout for Jefferson Davis."*[12]

Policy decisions, especially those dealing with racial matters, had some effect on the Copperheads' popularity, but their impact was limited. For the most part, the influence of the antiwar wing of the Democratic Party rose and fell in inverse relation to the armies' failures and successes. Now, in the summer of 1862, the Copperheads were enjoying the benefit of that correlation. They would only gain strength as the year continued.

In the late spring of 1862, conservative Democrats posed the biggest political threat in Lincoln's home state of Illinois, where a convention met to draft a new state constitution. The effort was a blatant power grab, and the chair of the convention made no excuses for wanting a partisan document. If it passed, a group of semi-secessionist Democrats would govern the state for the next decade. Their proposed constitution would strip the governor of his military powers and cut his four-year term in half. It gerrymandered congressional and legislative district lines to the strong favor of the Democrats and barred African Americans from settling in the state. Republicans mobilized their followers and defeated all the elements of the proposed constitution except for that keeping out blacks. Illinois Republicans now in Washington were much relieved at the Democrats' setback, though they seemed to take little notice of the black ban. "Thank God that Destiny at least, if not man's wisdom seems to be on the side of the Union and the cause of Liberty," wrote Lincoln's secretary John Nicolay. Henry Barber told his brother that the outcome of the constitutional vote was a triumph of *"pure Principle* over 'the machinations of the Devil.'—for in truth the Pro Slavery Secession Humbug could not have sprung from any other source." By defeating the proposed constitution, Illinois residents had struck a harder blow against the *"main Element"* of the rebellion than the Union armies had, Barber said. This proved the likes of Congressmen Clement Vallandigham and Daniel Voorhees (another prominent extremist Copperhead) wrong. "The fools! Did they suppose that God would permit them and their unprincipled associates, with blue lights and false beacons in their hands, to ride into power over the dead bodies of ten thousand free and Patriotic Illinoisans?" Barber took additional comfort from his belief—a mistaken one, it turned out—that the election had done in the conservatives. "While they have been howling about 'Negro equality' in and out of Congress, their political graves have been quietly dug, and last Tuesday the People buried them so deep, that I religiously hope no Political Resurrection will ever find them."[13]

The fact that the Unionists carried the day in Illinois was a positive sign that the public continued to support the administration's war policies. But the news for the administration was not all good. The proposed Illinois constitution was a harbinger of growing dissent in the North and the increasing political power of the Peace Democrats. It was also a signal that the Copperheads, many of whom had either remained silent or had confined their activities to the local sphere, could be more outspoken and active in the political arena with less fear of repercussion. More evidence to that effect was coming out of the heartland every day. In Iowa, Governor Samuel J. Kirkwood received a number of reports of secret societies forming in several counties. The Knights of the Golden Circle attracted particular attention and caused a high level of anxiety in many parts of the West. They were "plotting the destruction of our beloved government . . . ," a frightened Iowan wrote. "They sometimes threaten the extermination of abolitionists—sometimes the republicans—sometimes they say this administration must be put down." Although these kinds of letters caused a good deal of excitement in many governors' offices, rational responses generally prevailed. Kirkwood's secretary, for instance, replied to one complaint about Copperheads in Cedar Rapids and Albion by saying that men talking politics was not an offense on which the governor could act.[14]

The scare the Republicans had from the proposed Illinois constitution was not the only indication that support for their war program was slipping. A far more serious problem was developing: Not enough volunteers were enlisting to meet the needs of the army. In late June, Lincoln quietly lined up a number of governors to request a call for 150,000 more men. When the governors complied, Lincoln had Stanton ask him to call for 300,000 more troops. This behind-the-scenes maneuvering tipped the relation of the state and federal governments regarding recruits. The new enlistees still marched under their states' flags, but they were part of a nationalized army in a way that recruits earlier in the war had not been. A lively new song to encourage men to join up, "We Are Coming, Father Abraham, 300,000 More," became one of the most popular tunes in the country. Local newspapers encouraged young men to enlist. Sometimes the press would ask women to help too. "Young ladies, can you not induce some of your gentlemen acquaintances to enlist? TRY IT!" a small-town Massachusetts paper implored.[15]

Enlistment levels remained disappointing nonetheless—a sure sign of sagging support for the war. A fog of disaffection had settled over the North. Democrats were sputtering about the way the army treated their boys in spite of the fact that, in the early years of the war especially, a significant number of the top brass were Democrats.[16] "Every Democratic general is persecuted, and the Republicans do their best to get them out of the way," Maria Lydig Daly said. The Irish, who would make up a significant part of the resistance movement, had a set of their own complaints. "The Irish believe the abolitionists hate both Irish and Catholic and want to kill them off. The abolitionists always, the Irish say, put them in front of the battle," wrote Daly. Her criticism was mild compared to some others. "Any man who would enlist as a volunteer in the United States Army was a G-d d——d fool, besides being a G-d d——d black abolition son of a bitch," a DeKalb County, Illinois, man said, according to witness testimony. This man, who came under the scrutiny of the government, advised one young recruit to run his head into a tree and beat his own brains out rather than serve, and believed that while the Republicans had gotten the country into war they expected the Democrats to fight them out of it.[17]

Increased hostility toward the administration did nothing to change the fact that the army needed men, and lots of them. Congress responded in July 1862 by passing the Militia Act, which allowed Lincoln to call up local militias for nine months of service. It was a "disguised conscription law," a sign that Congress still was not quite ready to institute compulsory service, but it was nevertheless the government's first step toward a true national draft. The Militia Act anticipated a conscription bill by requiring that all men between eighteen and forty-five years old enroll for the draft. It also allowed blacks into the Union army, stipulating that African American soldiers were to be paid ten dollars a month, three dollars less than their white counterparts. Stanton quickly followed up on the Militia Act, later known as the "militia draft," by ordering a call-up of three hundred thousand militiamen. Surprisingly, the leaders of the Peace Democrats raised few objections to the law or to Stanton's demand for what became known as "nine-month men." Much of the Copperhead press—to the extent that one existed at this point—even endorsed the measure. The silence from the most extreme conservatives was mostly a product of timing. Congressmen who would be the logical opponents of the bill, including Vallandigham, had anticipated the end of the session and had gone home to start campaigning for reelection in the fall when the bill came up for a vote.[18]

For the time being, the Militia Act allowed the government to capitalize on local pride and a sense of honor that was well honed in the mid-nineteenth century. Resorting to a draft was an exercise that towns and counties tried to avoid assiduously because of the shame it brought on the community. In this war where home front and battlefield were linked as in no other American conflict, no city, town, or county wanted to be known as one that was not patriotic enough to send its fair share of men to the nation's service. Intense community pressure was therefore brought to bear on men of military age. At the same time, many communities, businesses, and even wealthy men were willing to add a carrot to the stick by putting up money to offer bounties to recruits. Personal pride also spurred young men to join, since being drafted was even more dishonorable to a man than holding a draft was to a community.[19]

Although many of the nation's most prominent Copperheads supported the draft, they did not necessarily represent a majority.[20] Some conservatives disdained not just the draft but anyone who would comply with it. In Connecticut, former governor Thomas H. Seymour wrote in disgust that few men would dare resist "submission to the yoke. The American people are the easiest enslaved of any people in the world. There is nothing of the Roman about them. The only class that show any signs of remaining manhood are the farmers. Something of their native Independence still remains." That, too, would be lost if the war lasted another year, though, and then despotism would be complete, Seymour thought. His loathing extended to the Democrats who were "helping Lincoln carry on a war which is wicked and infamous beyond that of any previous war since the time of the Goths! I wash my hands of it, and defying the powers of darkness calmly await the worst that can befall us."[21]

One problem with the draft was that it seemed to contradict the aims of the war. As William Platt of Newtown, Connecticut, wrote, the war was *"essentially* a trial of power between two systems of labor *free* &c."* A compulsory draft struck him as "a violation of the whole spirit of our institutions and repulsive in the highest degree to the Northern mind." Reaction against the draft led some to make grisly comments. One Connecticut man reportedly was so angry that he told the people of his town he hoped that all the men who went to fight "will leave their Bones to Bleach on the soil" of the South. A New York man wrote about a Republican aunt who said she would chop off a relative's legs if she thought he was serious about joining the army. "Here is the patriotism of the negro Sympathizers," he observed dryly.[22]

While the Militia Act stimulated a number of volunteers to join, it also produced draft dodgers. A major in Burlington, New York, arrested five young men on a single day in August as they tried to flee to Canada. They were just a sampling of numbers of draft-age men from across the country who were passing through his command district and trying to cross the border. Montreal was reported to be brimming with deserters from the Union army who abused the Lincoln government in even worse terms than the rebels did. Europe was said to be another popular destination, though not so easily reached. In Flushing, New York, firefighting companies were flooded with new recruits, not out of a newly inspired sense of public service but because firemen were exempt from the draft. Men across the North visited their doctors seeking certificates of medical disability. "Opticians are run down by those who have suddenly discovered they are near-sighted. Cabinet makers are anticipating a rich harvest from crutches and tin men for ear trumpets," a Long Island newspaper reported. It is impossible to know how many men fled to Canada or the far West to evade the government's reach, but contemporary reports suggest the number was significant. The numbers suggest that draft dodgers and deserters were not limited to Copperheads, either.[23]

In an effort to deal with shirking, the War Department on August 8 issued a new set of rules for military-age men. Those eligible for the military could not leave the country or even their hometowns if they were departing to avoid the draft enrollment. (This rule had the obvious shortcoming of assuming that men would not lie about where they were going or the reason for their travels.) Anyone who tried to evade enrollment could be sentenced to as much as nine months' service in the army. Furthermore, the War Department suspended habeas corpus in any cases of "disloyal practices," meaning those where people discouraged enlistments. This opened the floodgate on arrests.[24]

One of the unintended consequences of the Militia Act was that it significantly broadened the government's ability to enforce the law and to crack down on dissenters. To carry out the law's demand that eligible men be enrolled for a draft, Stanton ordered governors to appoint a commissioner and an enrolling officer in each county in the North. He also instructed the governors to appoint a state provost marshal to arrest deserters. This gave state governments, and the federal government by extension, a reach into local communities they had never before had. Now the federal government had a network of agents that reached into every nook and cranny of the country. These men could report on antiwar activities and, with the state provost marshals, crack down more effectively on transgressors.[25]

Arrests skyrocketed as a result, especially as more men began to speak out against the draft and to discourage others—at least in the eyes of government officials—from joining the army.[26] From August 1862 to almost the end of the war, state and federal files are filled with reports from government agents about the activities of individuals and organizations deemed secret societies. Almost forty men were arrested in Illinois alone; many of them were prominent Democrats and administration critics. In Iowa, most of the men arrested were newspaper editors, including the state's most prominent Copperhead, Dennis A. Mahoney of the *Dubuque Herald*. This was not the first time newsmen had been arrested, and as in earlier cases, few Northerners other than Peace Democrats objected to the detentions.[27]

Although many officials quickly responded to reports in a measured way, that was not always the case. Decisions about dissidents were entirely dependent on the man or men enforcing the laws. Some officials chose to ignore expressions of support for Jefferson Davis and other threatening chatter, believing that men who made such comments were just exercising their right to free speech. Other agents were quick to make arrests and examples of such rabble-rousers. From Washington, the judge advocate in charge of political arrests, Major Levi C. Turner, ordered the federal marshal in Canandaigua, New York, to catch whoever had cut down a flagpole bearing the American flag in that town. Turner said the act was disloyal, and he intended to send the perpetrator to the Old Capitol Prison in Washington before having a military commission try him. In another case, this one in Wilkes-Barre, Pennsylvania, Turner told local officials to do their "utmost" to keep suspects in custody. "Pay no attention to the Habeas Corpus," he said.[28]

A typical arrest was like this one in southern Illinois. A federal marshal rounded up ten men, including two judges, two doctors, and a minister, whom he suspected to be leaders of the Knights of the Golden Circle, then considered the largest and most threatening of the secret societies. Most of the suspects were charged with making statements that would discourage enlistments. One of the judges, William J. Allen of Williamson County, had given a speech in which he said that "the acts of the Administration was unconstitutional, that he condemned their acts, and thought that the peace party of the old Democratic party was the only one that would restore peace to the country," according to one witness. Another man who admitted that he joined the KGC in October 1861 said another of the arrestees told him that the purpose of the organization was "to get all Democrats to join the South and to unite the North with the South." Each KGC member had to promise to arm himself and join in any rebellion against the government, and if any members were arrested, the others were to help prevent the arrest, this witness said. A third suspect, the Reverend Alexander C. Nelson, was quoted as saying that if he had to take sides he would go with Jefferson Davis. Nelson spoke "very violently" against the government, a witness testified, and said that "if the choice was given to him to live with the abolition and Lincoln party—or the Demons of Hell he would prefer to associate with the Demons of Hell."[29]

Politics was only one source of conflict in this case, though. The other was slavery. Samuel H. Bundy allegedly said that "the object of the administration was to kill off the people of the South and liberate the slaves." The administration wanted to deprive the South of its rights, he said, citing as evidence the arming of blacks "to cut the throats of the Women & Children in the South." Dr. John M. Clementson, who like Bundy was from Williamson County, said that the war's "true object was to liberate the niggers," according to witnesses who said they had heard both men speak at a barbecue. Nelson, the minister, said the war was brought on to elevate the black race and degrade the white.[30]

Zealous enforcement of the law inevitably led to questions about the legitimacy of the arrests. Peace Democrats held public rallies at which they read Jefferson's writings, the Declaration of Independence, and the Bill of Rights. They blasted the centralization of the government and the "tyranny" of Lincoln. While historian Mark Neely, who examined civil liberties under Lincoln, argues convincingly that most of the men arrested during the course of the war rightly came under suspicion, records show that the government sometimes made mistakes in whom it chose to detain. In September 1862, for example, the commander of Camp Douglas, a prison in Chicago, wrote to Turner saying that one of his wards probably was innocent of the accusations against him. Nineteen men had sworn in August that Jacob W. Brown, an attorney from Earlville, Illinois, was disloyal and a rebel sympathizer—statements that led to Brown's arrest. Shortly thereafter another man came forward to say that he had never heard Brown say anything to discourage enlistments or damage the government. To the contrary, according to this witness and many other friends, Brown had helped raise a company for the army. Although the Earlville postmaster said that many of the men who were seeking Brown's release were people of "very doubtful character," the colonel in charge of Camp Douglas said he knew three of them and thought them credible.[31] In Wisconsin, the Door County sheriff and the governor wrote Turner a letter saying they thought a man named Lyman Bradley was innocent and recommending that the federal government release him. Bradley thought his accuser, an enlistment officer, had him arrested after Bradley said the officer could not legally arrest men who were drunk when they signed up. Bradley's arrest was a political smear, another of his supporters claimed.[32]

While it is impossible to get to the bottom of these episodes given the limited evidence and the passage of time, the stories raise the likelihood that some detainees were the victims of either a witch hunt or political skullduggery. Turner acknowledged that "in its efforts to crush this accursed Rebellion" the government "may in its manifold and exhausting labors unintentionally do wrong to individuals, and afflict the innocent." That included not only jailing people but also confiscating the property of those convicted of materially aiding the enemy. Turner insisted, however, that he and other officials worked "incessantly" to make sure the government did the just and proper thing, and he justified any mistakes it might make by observing that "the life of the nation is in jeopardy." The imprisonment of men, he said, "is not a cause for complaining."[33]

On the other hand, it is clear that there was serious discussion in some quarters about taking action against the government. A July convention of mainstream and conservative Democrats in Indianapolis passed pointed resolutions supporting the Union (and especially Indiana) troops while also leveling a withering criticism of the administration. At the same time, though, it denounced "as unwise and unpatriotic, all organizations, secret or open, having for their object the nullification of, or resistance to, the laws of the State or of the United States" and urged the disaffected to seek vengeance at the ballot box.[34]

Paradoxically, arrest became something of a badge of honor for some dissidents. When Dana Sheward, the editor of the Fairfield, Iowa, *Constitution and Union*, was arrested and imprisoned, his wife wrote: "Oh, I tell you that your arrest is the greatest honor that they could confer upon you. I feel proud of the day you were arrested and your friends think the same." Other detainees positioned themselves as martyrs to the cause of liberty and found some support in the political arena. William J. Allen of Illinois and Dennis Mahoney, the Dubuque editor, were nominated as congressional candidates while they were in prison, and at least two other detainees were nominated for legislative seats. One of the latter, Dr. Edson B. Olds, was elected in Ohio.[35]

Although opposition to the draft was not organized, the advent of a conscription law proved to be an important turning point for the Peace Democrats. Until the summer of 1862, they had been railing mostly about complicated financial instruments (such as bonds and paper currency) that many Northerners either did not understand or care about, or about a loss of civil liberties that seemed to affect only outright secessionists or men within their own ranks. A draft, with its obligation to enroll every man of a certain age, was different. It reached into hundreds of thousands of homes in a way that nothing else had in the history of the nation. Moreover, with the draft came a system of enforcement, via federal marshals, district attorneys, and most especially provost marshals, that brought the power of the federal government into every congressional district and virtually every community of any size in the nation.[36] Before the war, the post office had been almost the only point of contact with the federal government. Now the government had tentacles that reached farther and more powerfully into people's lives than anything Americans had previously experienced. Elite conservatives had mostly failed to see the opportunity that the draft could give them on the ground. It proved to be a huge boost for the Copperhead cause. It, and its bureaucratic mechanisms, finally gave them an issue that resonated broadly, and their ranks grew accordingly.

With the new and intensely personal stake that the draft foisted on civilian men, politics increasingly became a subject that could sour trust and ruin even long-term relationships. Former Connecticut governor Thomas Seymour lost an old friend, for instance, after writing what the man considered a "subversive" letter to the *Hartford Times*. "I am sorry to recognise in you the degenerate son of a Patriotic ancestry, I must consider you not much less then a *Traitor* to your Cuntry best interest," the man said in breaking off the relationship.[37]

By late summer, the blues seemed to have reached every corner of the country but the White House, where John Nicolay could hardly believe what he was hearing and reading. "I am utterly amazed to find so little real faith and courage under difficulties among public leaders and men of intelligence. The average public mind is becoming alarmingly sensational," he wrote a friend back in Illinois. One piece of bad news "is enough to throw them all into the horrors of despair. I am getting thoroughly disgusted with average human nature."[38]

Meanwhile, racial tensions were building in various sections of the Union. Part of the increasing hostility of whites toward blacks was simply an expression of the racism that had long been a fact of American life. In some areas, resentment was building that whites were underwriting a war that increasingly appeared to be for the benefit of the enslaved, thus making "the white race slaves for the black: which is in direct antagonism with the decrees of providence and order of nature," an anonymous pamphleteer wrote in Indiana. In other parts of the North, the resentment was not just racial but economic as well. The rising number of freedmen presented more competition for jobs. In Toledo, Ohio, white stevedores went on strike July 8. They complained about low pay and that blacks were paid at the same rate—fifteen cents an hour—as whites. African Americans had long been present on the docks of the city, and despite white concerns about blacks flooding into the area, blacks were in fact leaving in fairly significant numbers. The African American population of Toledo dropped by nearly half between March 1, 1861, and March 1, 1863, according to Lucas County auditors who conducted a special census. Still, working-class whites in the city were convinced they were losing ground economically to a steadily growing black community. The white workers began their action by assaulting the blacks with stones and brickbats. But after a black man stabbed one of the whites in self-defense, the crowd exploded. Unable to catch the man with the knife, the mob went to the homes of African Americans, doing what damage they could. A few men were arrested and convicted for disorderly assembly. They were fined fifty dollars apiece and got thirty days' hard labor.[39]

A week later and two hundred miles to the south, Irish workers rioted after being replaced by contrabands in Cincinnati. As in Toledo, the Irishmen beat up black men and targeted homes, this time setting fire to houses. Blacks responded by burning buildings in the Irish part of town. On August 4 in New York City, a mob of as many as three thousand whites—many of them drunk—burst into a tobacco factory shouting, "Down with the nagurs!" Police arrived on the scene and settled the matter by clubbing the black workers who had barricaded themselves onto the second floor. In the following weeks, roving gangs of Irishmen assaulted individual blacks in New York and Brooklyn. It

is impossible to know how many of the people involved in these episodes considered themselves antiwar Democrats, but the disturbances
underscore the resentment many whites felt toward blacks, especially
when they thought the African Americans threatened their livelihoods.[40]

In other quarters, racial fears were breaking down. Driven in part
by soldiers' letters describing the condition of slaves in the South, public
sentiment was building toward turning the conflict into a war of emancipation. Congress in April had abolished slavery in the District of
Columbia and paid owners an average of three hundred dollars per
slave. It also abolished slavery in the territories with no compensa-
tion.[41] Lincoln, who had an uncanny sense for public opinion and an
ability to stay just ahead of it, had come to believe that the war should
end slavery. Working on a plan for gradual emancipation, he opened
negotiations with border-state representatives on how to free the slaves
in those states. He met with the state emissaries twice in the spring
and early summer, and communicated a third time via letter, trying to
work out a deal for compensated emancipation. Lincoln had long supported the colonization movement, and under the president's plan freed
blacks would be sent to other parts of the New World. But Lincoln's
discussions with the border-state men came to nothing. They spurned
each proposal he offered, and talks broke off in July.[42]

Frustrated with the lack of cooperation from the border-state men,
Lincoln decided in mid-July to draft an emancipation proclamation.
Slaves had been fleeing to Union lines since the beginning of the war
(the army recognized them as contraband of war), and it was becoming apparent that those who stayed behind only helped bolster the
Confederate war effort. At about the same time Lincoln first thought
about drafting his proclamation, Congress decided to punish rebels by
striking at their most cherished institution, slavery. It passed the Second Confiscation Act, which said that slaves whose owners supported
the Confederacy were legitimate war seizures and that escaped slaves
who belonged to rebels would not be returned to their masters. Captured or runaway slaves would be "forever free" under the law. The
act also gave Lincoln the authority to employ black contrabands however he thought best and to colonize freedmen overseas. This came at
a critical moment because it gave Lincoln additional legal cover for the
preliminary Emancipation Proclamation. By freeing the slaves who
lived in areas occupied by the federal army—those he could reach—
Lincoln said he would be striking "at the heart of the rebellion." Navy
Secretary Gideon Welles recalled: "He had given the subject much
thought, and had about come to the conclusion that it was a military
necessity, absolutely essential to the preservation of the Union. We must

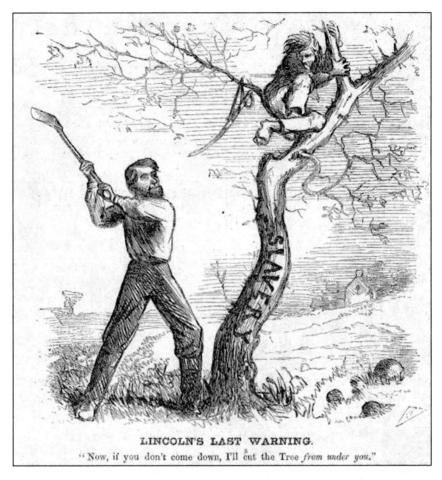

LINCOLN'S LAST WARNING.
"Now, if you don't come down, I'll cut the Tree *from under you.*"

Some commentators saw slavery as the very foundation of the Confederacy. They agreed with Lincoln that by attacking the peculiar institution, the Union would be undercutting the rebel war effort. (*Harper's Weekly*/Courtesy of HarpWeek LLC)

free the slaves or be ourselves subdued." But on the advice of Secretary of State Seward, Lincoln waited for the moment when he could issue the preliminary Emancipation Proclamation from a position of strength rather than having it appear to be a last-ditch attempt to keep the Union war effort alive. Lincoln agreed with his adviser and locked the document in his desk drawer in anticipation of a Union victory.[43]

Although the proclamation remained a secret known only to Lincoln and his cabinet, a belief was spreading through the North that the president intended to make this a war not only to save the Union but also to free the slaves. While this shift was generally regarded favorably, it outraged conservative Democrats who had suspected all along that this was the Republicans' real agenda in fighting the war. Deeply racist and often fearing that blacks would replace them as laborers, Copperheads argued passionately that the president would overstep his constitutional bounds if he liberated the slaves. The prospect of emancipation led many Peace Democrats to start planning what they would do if the slaves were in fact freed. In Clark County, Iowa, five men were arrested on suspicion of discouraging enlistments after they allegedly said that the president and Congress had perjured themselves when they said the war was not to abolish slavery. One of the suspects, James Nailer, also said that if a body that had the power to redress grievances failed to do so, the community "had a perfect right to take up arms in vindication of what they concieved their rights whether they were in the right or wrong," according to a deposition in the case. "He also represented our government on the one hand as a devil and the Secessionist on the other hand as being an other devil and the two in conflict and that his party had a right to put them both down." Another suspect, John Galliher, said that because this was an abolitionist war, the abolitionists could go ahead and fight it. But the war effort was useless against Southerners, who "had whipped us every time," according to a witness's statement.[44]

The army was divided on the subject of emancipation. Some soldiers muttered bitterly to their families about the aims of their efforts. "I came out here to fight for the Constitution & laws of our land, and for *nothing* else, and if it is turned into some other purpose—then those that do it may do the fighting for all me," Sergeant George Upton of Derry, New Hampshire, wrote his wife. "In case of an abolition war— *every* abolishonist should be *compelled* to come out here, and when here to be in the *front rank*—then we would see how long their love for the Darkies would continue." Others, however, welcomed the chance to free the slaves. "I think the fight is freedom or slavery," a member of the 39th Massachusetts said. "I thank God I have the priverlidge of doing what I can to proclaim freedom to all men, white or black."[45]

Regardless of their position on emancipation, soldiers had to keep fighting, and the summer of 1862 was not good to the armies of the North. The Confederates stymied Union efforts to take Chattanooga, an important railroad hub. Worse yet was the Yankees' second battle at Manassas, site of the war's first significant confrontation. Second Bull Run, which took place at the end of August, was an even greater disaster for the men in blue than the first meeting: 16,000 casualties for the North to the South's 9,200. Although Lincoln thought McClellan had willfully withheld assistance from John Pope, the commander on the field, McClellan was nevertheless put back in charge of the Army of the Potomac because of his organizational and defensive abilities.[46]

Union confidence, already flagging at the end of the spring, reached a new low. "This citizen does not despair of the republic," New Yorker George Templeton Strong wrote in his diary. "Most of his friends do. . . . The nation is rapidly sinking just now, as it has been sinking rapidly for two months or more." Maria Lydig Daly bitterly blamed the Southern Democrats for leaving the Union because they had not liked the outcome of the 1860 presidential election: "Had the Southerners waited four years, this bloodshed would have been spared and they would again have been in the ascendant with the whole Democratic party." But if Daly was in the majority in blaming the rebels for starting the war, it was a silent majority.[47]

The most vocal Northerners were those who criticized the administration, not those who defended it. William Augustus Willoughby of New Haven, Connecticut, observed that "soome persons . . . seem to gather satisfaction from our seeming defeat. Whatever satisfaction they take they have got to take now for the time is not far away in which all thier hope will be swept away like a fog before the Sun." Such people should "enlist with the seseshs [secessionists] and they may prove their courage and loyalty at the same time," he added. For the most part, though, soldiers were silent on the subject of Copperheads well into the fall of 1862, an indication that while the strength of the antiwar movement was growing, it was not yet the force that it would be by the following spring.[48]

Lee's victory at Second Bull Run gave him an opening to launch an assault into Maryland, the farthest north the rebels had yet ventured. Leading Confederates believed that Maryland belonged with their country; in fact, the Confederate Congress had announced in December 1861 that its liberation was an explicit war aim. Lee himself seems to have believed as late as early September, as he was preparing to move into Maryland, that it needed help in "throwing off the oppression" to which it had been subjected. But Lee was disabused of this notion shortly after entering the state. The residents of western Maryland, where Lee marched in, were Unionists; the bulk of the Confederacy's supporters were on the other side of the state. So when Lee issued a proclamation to the citizens of Maryland, it was not to announce their liberation but to assure them that they were free to join the Confederacy if and when they chose. In the meantime, he said, his army would "protect all of every opinion."[49]

Lee's objectives were political as well as military. Lee wanted to push France and Britain to recognize Southern autonomy and to tip the North's upcoming elections in the Confederacy's favor. Ever since Jackson had wreaked havoc on the Union army in the Shenandoah Valley, newspapers in Britain and France had been calling for their nations to intervene and end the war. By the middle of July, Napoleon III signaled that the time had come for the two nations to recognize the Confederate States of America, and a Southern-sympathizing member of Parliament had moved for Britain to work with France in brokering a peace agreement. Viscount Palmerston, the prime minister, quashed the motion, saying it was premature but hinting that another victory or two for the South might improve the timing. Lee, who was keenly attuned to politics, was certainly aware of the situation abroad. In a September 8 letter to Jefferson Davis, the general proposed that Davis ask the United States to recognize Confederate independence. This would not be a suit for peace, he said, but would demonstrate to the world that the Confederacy wanted its independence and nothing more. Lee assumed Lincoln would reject the offer, thus proving—by Lee's calculation—that the Republicans pursued a war policy for selfish reasons. That was where the off-year elections factored in: "The proposal of peace would enable the people of the United States to determine at their coming elections whether they will support those who favor a prolongation of the war, or those who wish to bring it to a termination."[50]

Lee's scheme soon went awry. Thanks to a corporal who found a lost set of Lee's campaign plans wrapped around three cigars, McClellan knew his intentions. After his usual lollygagging, McClellan moved and met the Confederates near the town of Sharpsburg, on Antietam Creek. The ensuing fight, as James M. McPherson has described it, was a story of "desperate defense by the Confederates and missed opportunities by the Federals." The September 17 battle was a nightmarish event that remains the bloodiest day ever in American history. Almost 4,100 men died in a matter of hours, and another 2,500 would die later of the wounds they received that day. Another 15,500 wounded men would survive. The dead from this battle alone exceeded the number of combat deaths in the entire Revolutionary War. Some men wrote home with appalling stories of the battle. "There was an awful slaughter," a Vermont sharpshooter wrote home. "The Rebs lay thick on the ground had not been buryed. . . . they were an awful sight hundreds of them piled together." Others said that "words are inadequate to describe the scene" and declined to say anything more. Visitors to the battlefield shortly after the fight described mounds of rotting horse carcasses and the bodies of dead soldiers covering the ground. Bloody Lane, a sunken road where some of the heaviest fighting took place, seemed like "the Valley of Death," a New York officer wrote. "To the feeling man this war is truly a tragedy but to the thinking man it must appear a *madness*," a New Hampshire surgeon wrote. "I pray

God may stop such infernal work—though perhaps he has sent it upon us for our sins. Great indeed must have been our sins if such is our punishment."[51]

Antietam marked the first time Americans at home saw the graphic reality of war. Mathew Brady sent a pair of photographers to the battlefield two days after the fight. A month later, Brady hung an exhibit in his New York studio showing the carnage along Bloody Lane, along Hagerstown Pike, and in other sectors of the battlefield. Civilians had never seen anything like this, and those who looked at the images were appalled at the pictures of shattered bodies and bloated corpses. "Mr. Brady has done something to bring home to us the terrible reality and earnestness of war. If he has not brought bodies and laid them in our dooryards and along the streets, he has done something very like it," the *New York Times* wrote.[52]

For all the bloodshed, the battle at Sharpsburg was a draw. Still, it was close enough to a victory to allow Lincoln to claim it as one and issue his preliminary Emancipation Proclamation. The fact that slaves were among the crucial underpinnings of the Confederate military structure had become increasingly clear over the previous year. While white men were away, the slaves continued to raise the food that fed troops and civilians alike, perform support functions such as cooking and digging for the rebel army, and work in Southern factories. Their importance to the Confederate war effort allowed Lincoln to invoke his powers as commander in chief and free the slaves in areas under rebellion. By classifying his action as military necessity, Lincoln could defend the constitutionality of his action from the inevitable criticism.[53]

Besides the military and humanitarian advantages of freeing the slaves, the Emancipation Proclamation had one other benefit as far as Lincoln was concerned: It would keep the European powers from recognizing Confederate independence. Richard Cobden, an English textile manufacturer, former member of Parliament, and diplomat without portfolio, wrote to Massachusetts senator Charles Sumner that the preliminary proclamation was a turning point in the British view of the war. Beforehand, the ruling classes were more interested in keeping the cotton trade with the South alive, and the remaining Britons were indifferent, Cobden wrote, but the proclamation reinvigorated the antislavery movement in Britain, "and it has been gathering strength ever since."[54]

The attacks on the Emancipation Proclamation came quickly. For conservative Democrats who were already wary of the administration's actions, the proclamation was infuriating. A Circleville, Ohio, newspaper went so far as to urge that abolitionists be hanged "till the flesh rot off their bones and the winds of Heaven whistle Yankee Doodle through their loathsome skelitonz . . . It is a pity that there is not a more tormenting hell than that kept by Beelzebub for such abolition fiends." Horatio Seymour, running for governor of New York, denounced the proclamation as "a proposal for the butchery of women and children, for scenes of lust and rapine, and of arson and murder, which would invoke the interference of civilized Europe." Henry A. Reeves, the editor of the *Republican Watchman* in Greenport, Long Island, was more measured in his response, but his reasoning was typical of many Copperhead newspapers: "In the name of freedom for Negroes, [the proclamation] imperils the liberty of white men; to test an utopian theory of equality of races which Nature, History and Experience alike condemn as monstrous, it overturns the Constitution and Civil Laws and sets up Military Usurpation in their stead." In Springfield, Illinois, the Democratic paper blared, "Home of Lincoln Condemns the Proclamation."[55]

After months of accusing the Republicans of being the pawns of the hated abolitionists, Copperheads shouted their "I told you so's" from every corner. "I have told you that this war is carried on for the Negro.

DOCTOR LINCOLN'S NEW ELIXIR OF LIFE—FOR THE SOUTHERN STATES.

Emancipation was deeply divisive in the North when Lincoln first issued his proclamation. Some people thought it would help the Confederate war effort far more than the Union. (*New-York Illustrated News*/Courtesy of HarpWeek LLC)

There is the proclamation of the President of the United States," David Allen told a crowd in Columbiana, Ohio, on September 27. "Now fellow Democrats I ask you if you are going to be forced into a war against your Britheren of the Southern States for the Negro. I answer No!" "The war is now literally an abolition war," wrote William Jarvis of Connecticut. "It will unite the whole South, and protract the war indefinitely. I did not think Lincoln could be such an obstinate old fool." Jarvis and other Peace Democrats were outraged that young white men were dying for the despised black man, but they also saw the preliminary Emancipation Proclamation as an opportunity to gain some political traction. H. B. Whiting of Connecticut, for instance, thought the measure would remove the scales from the eyes of "those stupid thick-headed persons who persisted in thinking that the President was a conservative man and that the war was for the restoration of the Union under the Constitution."[56]

War Democrats were hardly enamored of the proclamation either, but they were in an awkward position. Democrats historically had enjoyed broad support in the South. Since secession, the party had not eased up on its racist positions, and it particularly had no sympathy for the plight of slaves. On the other hand, Lincoln was using emancipation as a war measure, and War Democrats generally supported the president's war policies. Actively opposing emancipation could demoralize the army and prompt some generals to mutiny. As T. J. Barnett asked Samuel L. M. Barlow, the question came down to this: "Shall we sustain the President, or is a revolution necessary?" For the time being, War Democrats opted for the former, but this question would nag at them for the duration of the conflict and ultimately split the party.[57]

Lincoln further riled the opposition just two days after he issued the preliminary proclamation by suspending habeas corpus all across the North. Lincoln's announcement also authorized military tribunals for "all Rebels and Insurgents" and anyone helping them, anyone who discouraged volunteer enlistments or resisted the militia draft, or anyone engaging in disloyal practices or of providing aid and comfort to the enemy. The reason for this proclamation of suspension, according to Neely, was to enforce the Militia Act that Congress had approved in July. The War Department feared that men would try to evade the draft, and so the declaration ordered that drafted men could not leave the country. Anyone who tried would be taken to the nearest post and mustered into the army immediately. In a brief note at the end of the directive, Stanton wrote that habeas corpus would not apply to detainees or to anyone else arrested for "disloyal practices." Concern over this was not limited just to Lincoln's opponents. One Chicago lawyer thought that the suspension of habeas corpus could result in civil war in the free states.[58]

The timing of the preliminary Emancipation Proclamation and the suspension of habeas corpus were hardly fortuitous for the Republicans, for both measures arrived at the end of a long and dismal summer for the Union armies. The first of the off-year elections was to be held in October and the rest in November, and the two edicts served to alienate many Democrats who had previously supported the administration. While the decision on habeas corpus was deeply troubling to them, the preliminary proclamation was simply too much. They did not believe Lincoln was operating within his constitutional limits, and many defected to the Copperhead camp. Matthew Bulkley of Weston, Connecticut, was typical of the newly galvanized Peace Democrats:

> If we have any desire to maintain, and preserve our government, and free institutions, the heritage of our ancestors, we must follow their example. Sacrifice every thing, but honor & principle & unite as brothers, and give this corrupt, imbecile & as I believe *God abhorred*, administration to understand that they can no longer usurp power and trample upon the sacred rights guaranteed to us by our constitutions and laws. Is there none of the spirit of 1776 left? None of that determined will & energy that would, sooner brook the very devil, than submit to usurpation & tyranny?

Bulkley was incredulous that other people could not perceive the danger he had identified. He himself was ready to "sacrifice the last drop of blood in my veins for the constitution and union of my fathers."[59]

Thus the Copperheads entered the second phase of their growth. The people who joined the ranks over the coming months had for more than a year given Lincoln the benefit of the doubt, but when the end came for them and they jumped to the antiwar ranks, they were as fervent and as vitriolic as the people who had been there from the beginning. More motivated than ever, the increasingly powerful Copperheads rallied their forces. "We must denounce the two proclamations lately made by Mr. Lincoln, or consent to be white slaves for life," Thomas H. Seymour wrote. Six hundred thousand men had been fighting under false pretenses and now were being used "for the infamous purpose of promoting a servile insurrection [in the] South!" Military despotism was complete, he thought, and if opponents of these policies did not react and react strongly, "the knell of our liberties will have been sounded." A Democratic campaign pamphlet in Connecticut denounced the "heresy of secession" but immediately went on to list a series of grievances against the Lincoln administration. "Believing that our silence will be criminal, and may be construed into consent, in deep reverence for our Constitution, which has been ruthlessly violated, we do hereby enter our most solemn protest against these usurpations of power," the writer concluded. In New York, the Democrats' gubernatorial candidate, Horatio Seymour, took the measure of the situation and devised a catchy campaign slogan: "Restore the Union as it was, and maintain the Constitution as it is." This was quickly shortened to "The Union as it was, and the Constitution as it is," which became the rallying cry of conservative Democrats for the rest of the war.[60]

Not all Democrats had faith that their own party would act as an effective counterbalance to the Lincoln juggernaut. In Cincinnati, W. W. Dawson wrote a friend about his frustration not only with Lincoln but with his own party as well. Lincoln may have freed some blacks with the Emancipation Proclamation, Dawson wrote, but he enslaved the whites with his decree against habeas corpus. And what did the Democratic Party do? It "has not one word to say in condemnation!" People wanted to vote against the "outrages of Lincoln," but the Democrats would not give them a chance. "Heart sick" and "well nigh hopeless," Dawson could see nothing in the future "but a Series of Revolutions, the horrors of which I dare not contemplate. . . . What hope then is left for us? None!"[61]

Opinions in the army were divided over the proclamation and the suspension of habeas corpus, although emancipation drew a great deal more attention in the military. Union general Fitz-John Porter, a devoted Democrat and equally committed critic of the administration, said that the Emancipation Proclamation prompted "disgust, discontent, and expressions of disloyalty" among the soldiers and thought it would prolong the war by inciting the South even further. In his view, the president's missive was the "absurd proclamation of a political coward," something he hoped the people at home would remember when Election Day rolled around.[62]

The combined tensions of the elections, the preliminary proclamation, the suspension of habeas corpus, and the draft proved too much for some Democrats, and they rebelled. In Hartford City, Indiana, Blackford County sheriff Andrew Brickley and twenty-one other men were accused of inciting and participating in a riot on October 6 to prevent the draft. Brickley apparently had argued with the local enrolling officer and provost marshal on the day of the draft over who should supervise the proceedings. When the sheriff said he would have nothing to do with the conscription, the assembled crowd assaulted the officers and threatened to kill them. The rioters tore up the records, destroyed the lottery wheel, and chased the officers out of the court- house. Witnesses said Brickley was not involved in the riot itself and even intervened to protect the federal officers. But one federal officer believed that the riot had been planned ahead of time to prevent the draft and that Brickley had not acted quickly enough to quash the mob.[63]

Republicans entered the fall elections with considerable political baggage. Lincoln's armies were not doing well, he had suspended con- stitutional rights, his agents were arresting dissenters—some of them prominent men in their communities—he had put the popular McClellan on ice, and he had taken the huge and controversial step of emancipat- ing the slaves in occupied areas of the South. Former Democratic con- gressman John McKeon of New York recited these actions as proof that the Republican leadership had "seized the reins of power and threaten to involve themselves and their country in one common ruin, by their imbecility and corruption." While the Republicans whittled away at civil liberties, shoeless Southern conscripts were overrunning Union troops and even threatened the capital. In Connecticut, anonymous conservatives issued a pamphlet saying that with the Emancipation Proclamation, Lincoln was pandering to the "insane fanaticism" of the abolitionists, at great cost to the rest of the nation. The proclamation "erected an almost impassable barrier between the North and South," they wrote, and would "disgrace our country in the eyes of the civi- lized world, and carry lust, rapine and murder into every household of the slaveholding states."[64]

The first wave of the fall voting came in October, when Indiana, Ohio, and Pennsylvania held their elections. Extremists in both parties were gaining influence while the center eroded. The Republicans did not fare well at the polls. In Indiana, the Democrats took control of the legislature; there and in the other states, the Democrats won most of the House seats. The results left everyone in the White House "blue," one of Lincoln's secretaries wrote. Some of the men in the army were as upset as administration officials or maybe more so. Henry C. Gil- bert, a Michigan soldier, wrote his wife that given the number of "trai- tors" in the North, the army's chances for winning the war were poor. "If some of them could be made to stretch a rope [i.e., hanged] it would be better for the country," he said.[65]

The political misery continued for the Republicans in the Novem- ber contests. Democrats picked up the governorships of New York and New Jersey and gained control of the statehouses in New Jersey and Illinois. The setbacks were even bigger for the Republicans at the na- tional level, where Democrats gained thirty-two seats in the House of

Representatives. The delegation went Democratic even in Lincoln's home state of Illinois. "There has never been so great a revolution of public feeling. Everything two years ago was carried by the Republicans, but now radicals have ruined themselves and abolitionism," a Democratic partisan in New York wrote. Lincoln's old friend Orville Hickman Browning blamed emancipation and the suspension of habeas corpus, and told the president that they were "disastrous" for the Republicans because they gave the Democrats so much ammunition. Lincoln did not respond. The newly elected governor of New York, Horatio Seymour, thought the Democratic roll was only beginning. "Our people are not yet half educated as it respects the value of their Institutions," he said, adding that it took a lot of tyranny to make a mule value its freedom. William Jarvis in Connecticut did not share Seymour's big ideas about liberties, but he pronounced the election the "beginning of the end of the utter downfall of Abolitionism."[66]

But, as historians James M. McPherson and Allan Nevins have pointed out, the election results are somewhat deceptive. Democrats did well only in areas where they traditionally had been strong, and at the national level their gains in the House were the smallest of any minority party's in an off-year election in nearly a generation. Michigan, California, and Iowa all went Republican. A shift of two thousand votes in Pennsylvania and three thousand in Ohio would have changed the results in each of those states. Moreover, the Republicans picked up five seats in the Senate. "If the election was in any sense a referendum on emancipation and on Lincoln's conduct of the war, a majority of Northern voters endorsed these policies," McPherson argues. The men in the Executive Mansion came to the same conclusion. The week after the election, the *Washington Daily Morning Chronicle* carried an editorial that one of Lincoln's aides probably wrote. The people supported the war "to the bitter end," the anonymous writer claimed. Because of that support, Democrats had to sustain Lincoln and his war policies, including taxes, the imposition of martial law, arresting and imprisoning "domestic traitors," and the Emancipation Proclamation. Any failure to back the president "would be insubordination, mutiny."[67]

Most Democrats did not realize it, but they already were losing ground among the soldiers. The antiwar wing was alienating the troops, who believed that the Copperheads' comments undermined their ability to carry out the war successfully. "It is a common saying here that if we are whipped, it will be by Northern votes, not by Southern bullets. The army regard the result of the late elections as at *least* prolonging the war," an assistant surgeon in the 13th Iowa wrote. For the men in blue, the election outcome was a terrible jolt to the system. "My hope is almost gone," wrote a major with the 14th Indiana who had also lost respect for the government because of the preliminary Emancipation Proclamation and McClellan's dismissal earlier that year. "It looks like patriotism and decency had deserted the people, and conservatism and common sence had deserted the administration. The people have voted their sympathies for the rebellion, and the President has taken away the strongest hope of the army." The Copperheads became a negative reference point for many Yankees. They responded by reconsidering their political loyalties, and a slow but irreversible change began to take hold in the army. Over the next few months, increasing numbers of soldiers strayed from the Democratic Party and lined up behind Lincoln. A few days after the November election, a Wisconsin soldier observed to his wife that "the Army makes converts of all the democrats or there is but few of them Enlists." This shift would have profound effects on politics for years to come.[68]

With the election over, Lincoln dismissed McClellan on November 7 and replaced him with Ambrose Burnside. McClellan had refused Lincoln's direct orders in early October to give chase to Lee. While McClellan waited for the government to outfit his men with more uniforms, shoes, and equipment, the Confederacy's most dashing cavalryman, Jeb Stuart, swept through southern Pennsylvania, occupying Chambersburg overnight. McClellan hemmed and hawed until the end of the month, when he finally crossed the Potomac. He spoke vaguely about an advance but never informed his superiors as to what exactly he had in mind. Exasperation overcame Lincoln's reluctance to sack a man so popular with the troops. He dropped the ax. McClellan's excessive caution was his undoing, Lincoln said privately.[69]

The president still had reason to be optimistic, but the undercurrent of despair remained among the Northern public, especially in the uncertain days after McClellan's dismissal. Mattie Blanchard of Foster, Connecticut, wrote to her husband, Caleb, who was off with the 18th Connecticut Volunteers: "The more I see and hear the less confidence I have in our ever haveing peace restored to us again I think these United States will be a divided land when the fighting ceases if that ever is and I think it will soon for I think they have got most tired of it." It was not just military losses that contributed to the malaise; it was emancipation as well. The *Boston Pilot*, which earlier had admired Lincoln and blamed the South for the war, now editorialized that "secession is a necessary consequence of abolitionism. . . . What could the South do but declare for separation, when its chief property was violently threatened to be taken from it?"[70]

Some Confederate sympathizers regarded the ebbing support for the war as an opportunity to advance their cause. A Cincinnati man wrote to a like-minded Hoosier to inquire about how many men in his town sympathizers could count on, presumably to fight for the Confederacy either through mainstream military methods or through a guerrilla operation. The anonymous writer said he was part of a group that wanted to reinstate the "old Democratic party" by making a compromise that would be acceptable to the South. The aim of this organization, he explained, was to extend slavery to all the states "and ultimately form an Empire," slavery not being "Congenial to a Republic." If his conspiracy failed, France would take Mexico and put Prince Napoleon on the throne. At that point, the Confederate States would ask to be annexed to Mexico, thereby forcing the Union to fight France, England, and Mexico in addition to the Confederacy.[71]

This had been a year of trial for Unionists. Treated to a string of victories in the early spring, they saw the fortunes of the army sour in the late spring and over the summer. Despair among the public gave the Peace Democrats a new constituency: people who were prepared to end the war whatever the cost. Their strength, which had been building over the summer with each federal failure on the battlefield, increased exponentially when Lincoln issued the preliminary Emancipation Proclamation, a document that only seemed to confirm the worst suspicions of conservative Democrats. Meanwhile, cooling public ardor translated into slumping enlistments, forcing the government to adopt a pseudo-draft to fill the army's ranks. In fulfilling the law's demand that all eligible males be enrolled, the size and reach of the government expanded to dimensions never before experienced in American life. This new bureaucratic apparatus was particularly effective at rooting out dissenters. Arrests rose accordingly in late summer, giving the Copperheads yet another argument against the government and its policies. Having found issues that resonated with the disillusioned and the conservative, Peace Democrats gained a following that translated into political success in the fall elections. While Northerners at home and on the front lines fretted about the future, the military situation was about to take another turn for the worse.

3

When Will This Cruel War Be Over?

NEW DISASTERS ARRIVED with the change of seasons, making the winter of 1862–63 the bleakest period of the war yet. Military setbacks coupled with opposition to the Emancipation Proclamation stirred new levels of discontent in the Union. Rumors that the Northwest was preparing to break away from the East were broadly reported and widely believed. Enlistments dried up, prompting the Congress to adopt a new draft law, which in turn generated even more dissent. Copperheads, it became clear, were unwilling to grant Lincoln any unusual powers with which to fight the war. Conservative Democrats could not see, much less acknowledge, the danger that secession and the Confederacy posed to the Union. Furious at the lack of support from Peace Democrats, soldiers swore to avenge themselves when they returned home. Amid this turmoil the administration suffered a serious political wound when a rogue general arrested a former congressman for speaking against the government. Although men who loudly opposed the administration had been subject to detention for nearly two years, this was a new low. The arrest raised concerns even among Republicans about the government's ability to wield power responsibly. And as that drama played out, the Army of the Potomac suffered another crushing defeat.

The Army of the Potomac appeared to enter a new era on November 7, when General Ambrose E. Burnside took command. He wasted little time before acting. On November 15 Burnside moved his men forty miles from Warrenton, Virginia, to Falmouth. Fredericksburg lay just across the Rappahannock River, ripe and inviting. To attack, though, the Yankees would first have to figure out a way to cross the river. The plan was to build pontoon bridges, but foul-ups with the order for pontoons put Burnside behind schedule in attacking the city. More important, the delay gave Lee plenty of time to mass his forces on the high ground behind and south of the city. Ignoring the profound disadvantages that the terrain presented, Burnside decided to move on the city on December 13.

The assault was a disaster. About 12,600 Yankees were killed, wounded, or captured. Most of the casualties took place near the foot of Marye's Heights, a steep hill protected at the bottom by a sunken road and a rock wall. Confederates hid behind the wall and shot mercilessly at the bluecoats, who tried seven times to cross a bare, four-hundred-yard field that sloped between a canal ditch and the heights. The Union efforts were in vain. Hardly a single federal made it within twenty-five yards of the wall. Many of the wounded were left on the field overnight and froze to death.

Reaction in the North was swift and furious. Editors on both sides of the political fence were quick to call the battle a disaster. "Who is responsible for this terrible repulse?" demanded *Harper's Weekly*, usually a bastion of Republican sentiment. The hearts of loyal Northerners were filled with "sickness, disgust, and despair." The "obstinacy and incapacity" of the nation's leaders neutralized the best efforts of the people, the magazine declared in an unusually harsh commentary, and the war did not seem even close to ending. Northerners "have borne, silently and grimly, imbecility, treachery, failure, privation, loss of friends and means, almost every suffering which can afflict a brave people. But they can not be expected to suffer that such massacres as this at Fredericksburg shall be repeated." If the situation did not improve, the country was headed for a military dictatorship, *Harper's* predicted.[1]

The Democratic press was equally critical. "The truth may as well be told—the finest army that ever trod the earth, possessing superior arms, large and small, and with all the appliances and resources of war at command, has suffered a decided repulse at the hands of a half naked, half starved, half armed foe," the *New York Herald* said. Calling on Lincoln to clean out his cabinet and the War Department, the paper warned, "This fearful and useless slaughter of our brave young Union soldiers at Fredericksburg has kindled the new element of wrath in the seething currents of public opinion which President Lincoln cannot safely disregard." In Boston, the *Pilot* reflected the feelings of many in the North when it said that such a calamity never would have happened under McClellan. "Can [Lincoln] ever make atonement for his unaccountable blunder?" it asked, speculating that he sacked the general to hand out a political plum, or maybe to "satisfy the fanaticism of that herd who have pestered him since his election—the herd inflicted with the disease called 'Nigger on the brain.' "[2]

Average citizens were outraged, too. "The public is of course filled, not only with grief, but indignation, at such a useless sacrifice, in an attempt which military men, whose opinions I hear quoted, pronounce little short of madness," Boston lawyer William H. Gardiner II wrote. "My confidence is terribly shaken. So is everybody's. Things have never looked to me so black as at this moment." In Connecticut, a father who already had lost one son to the war agonized over the "criminal miscalculations" of the generals. The men at Fredericksburg had been "led into traps with no human probability that they could by any means succeed, to be shot down by hundreds and thousands. Must it be? Where does the awful responsibility rest?"[3]

The feelings in the army were even worse than among the civilian population. General John White Geary, a Democrat, suspected that his superior officers—many of them also Democrats—were up to no good. "Were it not for treason in our own army this wicked rebellion would have been, doubtlessly, long ago crushed," he complained to his wife. Oliver Wendell Holmes Jr. was so demoralized that he concluded that the Union would never beat the South. "The Army is tired with its hard, & its terrible experience & still more with its mismanagement & I think before long the majority will say that we are vainly working to effect what never happens—the subjugation (for that is it) of a great civilized nation," he wrote his sister. He later assured his father that he was not "wavering in my belief in the right of our cause" so much as in the ability of the army to succeed.[4]

For people who already opposed the war, Fredericksburg was further proof of the futility of the Union war effort. "I hope we shall soon conclude that this is not the way to mend a broken union," an antiwar Iowan noted in his diary. Burnside's generalship and the changing command of the Army of the Potomac were the leading topics of criticism among dissidents. The battle was what one could expect when promoting a "mudsill" like Burnside up against the "most accomplished men of the day," a Connecticut Copperhead wrote. "Davis is a great man, a Statesman and Solider; as Gladstone called him 'the founder of a Nation.'" Many people in the North—and not just peace men—wondered when the president would come to his senses and recall McClellan to his old command.[5]

The news out of Mississippi was not as maddening as Fredericksburg, but it was no more promising. Grant was trying to get down the Mississippi River to Vicksburg, but his supply lines were vulnerable, and the rebels took advantage of that. Compounding Grant's difficulties, the Confederates had artillery and entrenchments on high ground, while the Yankees were trying to wade across the swamps and sandbars of the

Mississippi Delta. Grant's efforts of the late fall failed, and at the end of December he returned to his old camp twenty miles north of Vicksburg. Ever determined, he tried five different ways that winter to cross the Big Muddy and get at Vicksburg, but each effort proved futile.

The events of December gave the Copperhead press more ammunition for proclaiming the war to be a waste of life and treasure. "It has been a year of blood and plunder—a year of carnage and conflagration—a year of imbecility, falsehood, and corruption—a year of bastiles, persecution and tears—a year of despotism, pride and vain glory—a year of sorrow, desolation and death," the Columbus, Ohio, *Crisis* editorialized. "It closes in despondency and despair." Similar sentiments were repeated all over the North.[6]

The year did not close entirely in despondency and despair, though. On the last day of 1862, news came that Union general William S. Rosecrans and the Army of the Cumberland were engaged in a fight at Stone's River in central Tennessee. Early on, the battle looked as though Rosecrans had lost, but, putting his own safety at risk, he rode the lines and rallied his men. The fight, which lasted until January 2, was among the war's worst, and the victory came at a high cost: Union forces lost nearly a third of their men to death, wounds, or capture. But they had won. Desperate for good news, Lincoln wrote a relieved telegram congratulating Rosecrans: "God bless you, and all with you! Please tender to all, and accept for yourself, the Nation's gratitude for yours, and their, skill, endurance, and dauntless courage." Relief was most palpable in the lower Midwest, where Unionists thought the victory neutralized plots to create a Northwest confederacy. "We stand upon a volcano, with a crust so thin, that only a spark will explode it," an Indiana man said.[7]

While "Old Rosie" and his men were fighting it out in Tennessee, the Emancipation Proclamation went into effect on January 1, 1863. Although the proclamation had been circulating since late September, its enactment stirred doubts even among War Democrats. The *New York Herald*, which steered an independent course politically, called the measure the "last card of the abolition Jacobins." Copperheads were apoplectic. In the House of Representatives, Clement Vallandigham of Ohio argued that "if this Union cannot endure 'part slave and part free,' then it is already and finally dissolved." The Constitution itself had created "the perfect and eternal compatibility" of a nation that could embrace both the free and the enslaved. Indeed, Vallandigham said, "in my deliberate judgment, a confederacy made up of slave-holding and non-slave-holding States is, in the nature of things, the strongest of all popular governments." In the New York State Assembly, Gilbert Dean warned that Union troops might simply refuse to fight for a cause whose purpose now seemed to be to turn the South into "a jungle like those of Africa, or of converting the whole region ... into a Golgotha of the white race for the imaginary good of creating there a Paradise for the negro." The editor of the *Niles Republican* in Michigan declared that "a more lame and impotent conclusion was never arrived at before. Literally, the mountain has labored and brought forth a mouse."[8]

Some publications regarded the preliminary Emancipation Proclamation as a threat designed to bring the Confederacy to heel. If it was, Southerners were not frightened enough to acquiesce, and the permanent Emancipation Proclamation went into effect January 1, 1863. (*Nick-Nax*/Courtesy of HarpWeek LLC)

Antiabolition sentiments were evident all across the North. In Sugar Ridge Township, Indiana, James Ferguson grumbled that he saw no hope for peace in the foreseeable future "nor a ray of hope for constitutional freedom for the *white* man under Federal Abolition rule." In other parts of the country, wavering Democrats came rushing back to the party fold in response to the Emancipation Proclamation and war losses. "The people here are getting all right, democracy is getting very popular," a Nebraska man wrote. "Men who were in favor of the war, extermination, emancipation, arbitrary arrests and all other unconstitutional measures ... are now loud in their denunciation of the administration in almost every respect." Some Democrats regarded abolition as a sure sign of treason. "The men that meddle with slavry is not loyal to there government," a pair of Indianans wrote a relative.[9] Widespread fears in Ohio that freedmen would flood the North and depress wages prompted the legislature to discuss amending the state constitution to bar blacks from entering the state. In upstate New York, the *Albany Atlas and Argus* claimed that freed slaves, impoverished and often lacking skills, were bound to become a long-term economic burden on taxpaying whites. "Are the white working men of this country willing to bind this heavy yoke around their necks, and entail it upon their children?" it asked. Objections to emancipation were so pervasive throughout the North that they were set to music:

> "De Union!" used to be de cry—
> For dat we went it strong;
> But now de motto seems to be,
> "De nigger, right or wrong!"[10]

Some of the men in uniform were as disgruntled as the people at home that abolition was now an explicit and official war aim. "The Soldiers are geting vary tiered of this buisness   they begin to see thare is too much negro in it," a Hoosier wrote. A sergeant in the 9th New Jersey said that when soldiers knew they were fighting to restore the Union they were confident of their success, but "we have never been successful since the emancipation proclamation ... and there is scarcely a man in the ranks of our army who approves of it."[11] Many men were deserting in protest, he and others reported to the people at home. Private John Harpin Riggs wrote his father in Seymour, Connecticut, that he no longer wanted to fight. "When I enlisted I came to defend the flag and to keep the union as it was but they have turned this war into a niger war and I want to get out now as soon as posable." Riggs threatened to "poke the boyonet through" any "black devils" who got in his way. "Many here (in the army) are almost frightened out of their wits for fear the proclamation will ruin us and say so boldly. Even officers say so in presence of the soldiers and secesh," an Indiana officer wrote.[12]

On the other side of the debate were the soldiers who were prouder than ever to be part of Lincoln's army. Corporal George E. Fowle of the 39th Massachusetts had not been an abolitionist before joining the army in the summer of 1862. Now, he said, "I am glad more than ever that I enlisted sence I have read the President's Proclamation because I think the fight is freedom or slavery." A private from Paterson, New Jersey, said he was proud to be "fighting for freedom." He hated the South more each day as he watched slaves bearing the scars of the lash seek safety behind Union lines. "It will make any man with sense to cry out against the South," he said.[13] General Geary, though a Democrat, supported the proclamation but worried about the political consequences for Lincoln. "I fear our country is on the verge of anarchy and despotism. God save us individually and, our country from the treason which surrounds us on every hand." As for the grumbling among his compatriots, one Indiana private airily dismissed it as part of the general complaining in which soldiers engaged.[14]

Copperhead leaders tried to leverage the dissatisfaction among civilians and soldiers by redoubling their assaults on the Emancipation Proclamation. Their argument was based on constitutional principles, but it was wrapped in racist rhetoric designed to appeal to people's basest fears. In a pattern that was already becoming evident, though, Copperheads would only criticize, not offer a workable alternative. Peace Democrats called repeatedly for the end of war but remained silent on the devilish details. Did peace mean granting the Confederacy its independence? Did it mean reuniting but maintaining slavery? If the nation returned to the *status quo ante bellum*, none of the issues that drove the country to civil war would be resolved. The only suggestion that some conservatives offered to solve the nation's problems was the Crittenden Plan that the Congress had rejected in the winter of 1861. Copperheads refused to concede the military advantages the Emancipation Proclamation gave the Union. Although they continued to criticize the proclamation for the rest of the war, they offered no proposals on what to do with the slaves who already had been freed under the Emancipation Proclamation or who had freed themselves by fleeing to Union lines. Nor did they suggest how the Union might compensate for the loss of manpower if Copperheads succeeded in purging the army of black soldiers. Nevertheless, their attacks on the administration were gaining a new audience with each disaster in the field.

Throughout January, talk was spreading across North and South of a further split in the Union. Rumor had it that the Northwest was ready to secede—by force, most likely. New England, with its abolitionists, along with the bankers and industrialists of New York and Philadelphia, had been frequent targets of abuse from Westerners even before the war. The draft, which Westerners believed fell more heavily on them than on the rich Easterners who could legally buy their way out of conscription for three hundred dollars, only increased tensions between the sections. Now, in the middle of winter, the imposition of the Emancipation Proclamation and the army's losses gave new currency to the idea of a Northwest confederacy. At the end of January, Copperhead representative George H. Pendleton of Ohio warned the House that Northwesterners were under a growing impression that "they have been deliberately deceived into this war . . . under the pretense that the war was to be for the Union and the Constitution, when, in fact, it was to be an armed crusade for the abolition of slavery." His home state was rumored to be on the brink of secession. In Illinois, people worried that the KGC was ready to "have us bound 'hand and foot' and the state handed over to the Southern Confederacy." An attempt was made on Indiana governor Oliver P. Morton's life as he walked out of the statehouse one night.[15]

The crisis was most intense in Indiana. The Knights of the Golden Circle in that state were supposedly plotting to depose the governor, seize the state arsenal and its fifteen thousand arms stored there, and establish a new confederacy of the Western states. Many observers thought Indiana's departure was imminent, especially given the makeup of the new legislature, whose members were "rampant, furious—crazy, almost, in their opposition to the War and to the State and National Governments."[16] Democrats responded to these claims by accusing Governor Morton of being paranoid. Besides, they pointed out, Republicans had formed their own secret societies, namely the Union Leagues. Republicans raised the stakes when they refused to attend an early session at which the legislature elected the U.S. senators.[17] The Democrats in turn claimed the legislature did not have a quorum and refused to hear the governor's annual message. When soldiers and officers in the field passed a series of resolutions reminding lawmakers of their duties, Democrats accused them of interfering with state politics and berated Republicans for slandering Democratic army officers. The rest of the session was spent in such fierce partisan bickering that the legislators never passed the appropriations bills needed to keep the state running. Morton executed an end run around the Democrats in June, refusing to convene them in a special session to pass the spending measures. The General Assembly did not meet again until January 1865. In the meantime, Morton raised money through extralegal means to keep the state running. He borrowed money from a New York bank, accepted financial aid from the War Department, and appealed to Republican counties and individuals for loans and donations. Morton entrusted the money to a specially created finance department since the state treasurer was a Democrat and was unlikely to condone Morton's fund-raising methods. This inflamed conservative Democrats even more. One man, referring to the governor, said:

[He] is a lowflung demagogue, and will try and have the State proclaimed and placed under martial law, as his party only knows how to govern by *force*. The abolitionists have no sense, and, when they get power, act more like lunatics than reasonable creatures. They all labor under the disease which now afflicts the country and threatens the ruin of its liberties, viz. "Yankee on the brain."

The political situation in Indiana was so bad that historian Kenneth Stampp has argued that constitutional government collapsed in that state between 1863 and the end of the war.[18]

Not everyone believed that Copperheads were as serious a threat as Morton and other Republicans claimed. A. B. Johnson of Utica, New York, dismissed these reports as "ghost stories." "Could these fallacies be dispelled, our people would readily become peaceful & that such fallacies have to be propogated & encouraged is a great proof of the unnatural character of the war:—it began in error & is maintained by a maintenance of error," he said. "We are destroying ourselves to avoid a prospective imaginary destruction—committing suicide to avoid an imaginary murderer." The South, on the other hand, had every right to leave the Union so far as he was concerned. The region was committing nothing but "a repetition of what Great Britain experienced when she lost her American Colonies."[19]

Whether there was any truth to the rumors that the Northwest was about to split off is impossible to tell, and, in many ways, the truth is beside the point. What is most important is that many contemporaries heard these stories, believed them, and made decisions based on that belief. Among those who got wind of these tales and found them credible were highly placed politicians. A correspondent confidently assured New York governor Horatio Seymour, "Movements on a large scale are being made *west* that will tell powerfully on the state of our country and cause the insane party at Washington to tremble." More important, stories about the West's impending secession reached the presidents of both the Confederacy and the United States. Jefferson Davis delighted at these reports and predicted that the West would soon leave the Union. "And thus," he said, "we see in the future the dawn—first separation of the north West from the Eastern States, the discord among them which will paralyze the power of both;—then for us future peace and prosperity." Lincoln confessed his alarm over the developments at home. "These are dark hours," Senator Charles Sumner wrote on January 17. "The President tells me that he now fears a 'fire in the rear'—meaning the Democracy, especially at the Northwest—more than our military chances. But I fear that our army is everywhere in a bad way. I see no central inspiration or command."[20]

Only three days after Sumner wrote about this exchange with Lincoln another disaster befell the Army of the Potomac. On January 20 General Burnside set out to regain the initiative near Fredericksburg by crossing the Rappahannock and hitting the Confederate flank. The night after the Yankee troops started their march up the river, rain began to fall. Roads turned to muck and the army bogged down in what became known as the "mud march." Two days after leaving, the men returned to their camps. The disgraced general resigned his command, but morale in the Army of the Potomac plunged nonetheless. According to one Union soldier, the lack of leadership in that command proved everything opponents of the war said. Another soldier told his brother that the war was no longer worth fighting because the Confederacy was so much better prepared for battle than the North. In addition, he thought Lincoln was "a Scamp . . . a coward and a Scoundrel" who was afraid to make a decision.[21]

The mud march marked a new low in Northern civilian confidence as well. "We will never close this war honorably under such a state of affairs," an exasperated War Democrat told his soldier son. In an echo of the Illinois soldier's remark above, he believed that the Confederates had more initiative to fight than the Yankees did. "The Rebels know *'it's neck* or *nothing'* with them, and they are exerting every nerve, while (with the exception of some of our western & South western troops) nothing has been gained on our part, to *make* and *unmake* commanders of 'the Army of the Potomac.' " A Democratic businessman in Norton, Connecticut, with a son in the army thought the time had come to strike a negotiated peace and to restore the Union with slavery. Disgusted at the role New England abolitionists had in the war, sickened by the loss of two hundred thousand Northern men, and worried about the rising financial cost of the fighting, he insisted: "*I am not a Traitor*. I am not disloyal to the Government and Constitution of the Union States. . . . Can you say we are traitors, for quietly, calmly, but firmly resolving to make a determined effort to stop this gigantic family Quarrel, by conciliatory measures[?]" Believing that only General McClellan could bring military success to the North, a number of Democratic newspapers called for his return.[22]

In New York City, a group of prominent men led by telegraph inventor Samuel F. B. Morse met February 9 and formed the Society for the Diffusion of Political Knowledge. This group would become the intellectual arm of the Copperhead movement, developing a coherent argument in opposition to the administration (though never a workable alternative vision for running the country or the war). Unlike many Copperhead politicians and antiwar men in various communities, the Society for the Diffusion of Political Knowledge tended at first to steer away from ad hominem attacks, instead stressing states' rights and constitutional issues. The Constitution, Morse said in the organization's first pamphlet, was not like "India-rubber, to be stretched in one direction in time of peace and in another direction in time of war." Morse, who had been president of a proslavery group when the conflict broke out, maintained that the crisis did not warrant the war powers Lincoln was invoking. The inventor said he was not out to undermine the government, which he thought had been commandeered by the abolitionists, but to remove this administration from office in the next election. Although the group initially set an intellectual tone in its pamphlets, the society had abandoned the high ground by 1864, when it was reprinting speeches that were as vituperative as anything else coming off the Copperhead presses.[23]

Unnerved by the rising opposition to the war, government officials steeled themselves for some kind of uprising. But it did not come—not that winter, at least. Instead, there was a backlash against the Peace Democrats. Angry Unionists increased their denunciations of the Copperheads and held more meetings in support of the war. Governors experienced a boost in correspondence informing them of disloyal activities in their states. And, one observer believed, Democratic leaders themselves toned down their rhetoric because they feared the consequences of disunion, West and South. "The wrath of loyal people is pretty nearly up to the exploding point. There will be a general smashing of them (copperheads) pretty soon," a Cincinnati man wrote.[24]

The election results of 1862 had surprised the soldiers. Now, word of rising antiwar sentiment quickly reached the front lines, and soldiers were outraged. Given the privations, disease, and discomfort they suffered, not to mention the peril that battle presented, bluecoats deeply resented any lack of support for their efforts. Further fueling their animosity, a growing number of soldiers believed that conservatives were extending the war by speaking against it. "It is only the encouragement held out to rebels of 'Peace on any terms' by [Copperheads] that is now protracting this war. Rebbel prisoners acknowledge that the only encouragement that they receive at present is from the North," an Indiana sergeant said. "If the North would present to the rebels a bold and united front and give them to understand that they could expect no other conditions than an unconditional submission to the laws and Constitution of the United States . . . this war would not last two months." In a comment that appeared repeatedly through much of the rest of the war, one Hoosier said that "one enemy in the rear is to be feared more than ten before us. The Souths great hobby is to divide the north. They told us that it as their belief that eer another year the East and west would be divided. And their papers harp on in continualy." "I have heard a great many soldiers say that they would fight willingly as long as the North is united," a member of the 12th Michigan wrote to his local paper, "but when it is divided they say they will through down their arms and fight no more. They say they did not enlist to fight both North and South."[25]

Even though their personal contact with conservatives was minimal, soldiers from rural New England—where Peace Democrats were far rarer than in the Northwest or the urban East—held as much contempt for the Copperheads as anyone else in the army. The "hellish imps of the Jeff Davis persuasion," as Vermont private Wilbur Fisk called them, "are doing more to contribute to our defeat and ruin, than if they enlisted under the banner of treason, and fought us face to face in the open field." He was struck by the similar arguments that the Copperheads and the rebels mounted against the government. "The points most prominent in both are always 'abolition' or 'nigger,' 'Lincoln's tyranny' 'State rights' etc., blaming the North and excusing the South."[26]

By late winter 1863, soldiers blamed Copperheads for any number of problems. John J. Barney, a corporal from Wisconsin, complained to his brother that he had expected full support from people in the North, "but now instead of helping us they even protect deserters and *help* them desert." The only reason men deserted was because some of the Northern press was "howling about the emancipation proclamation and fighting to 'free niggers' "—just the excuse some men needed to wriggle out of the army. Barney's fury at the Copperheads' perfidy took on a violent edge: "I would like to help mob some such papers as the News and those of like stamp. . . . I want to come North and kill *one half* of the Democrats there just to show how the soldiers appreciate their efforts to comprimise a peace, bought at the price of eternal dishonor of the North." His sentiments were broadly shared in the army. Samuel Merrill, lieutenant colonel of the 7th Indiana, wrote that his men were itching for a fight with those who did not stand behind them. "We are all distressed with reports of the state of affairs at home and the men are panting to return and take vengeance on those who are encouraging our enemies. There will be terrible work if any of the regiments have to be called from the field to suppress riots." Caleb Blanchard of the 18th Connecticut thought Copperheads should be shot for treason. They were encouraging the rebels by trying to thwart the administration and then were "puting the sword [in our backs] while the rebels are shooting us in front." If the Copperheads kept on with their activities "it will not be safe for them to show their faces when the union patriots get back. . . . If they would onely go into the rebel ranks we should know where to find them."[27]

Surprisingly, some soldiers defined themselves as Copperheads. Several of the officers of the 20th Massachusetts, for instance, proudly claimed the term. Their political leanings ran from out-and-out Southern sympathizers to the more conservative strand of Constitutional preservationists. It is difficult to know how these soldiers reconciled their political beliefs with their status as U.S. Army officers, but their participation in the war was probably predicated on a commitment to the Union. Most dissidents, after all, insisted on their abiding loyalty. Copperhead beliefs were rare in the army, though. Soldiers who harbored anything but full support for the war earned the rebukes of their comrades. A private in the 9th Indiana briskly told one of his acquaintances who thought the Northwest should align itself with the Confederacy that such talk was "little less than treason." Another private dismissed antiwar men as lazy—a damning accusation in a nation where the work ethic was an article of faith. Soldiers who enlisted expecting an easy time of it, he said, were "very apt to convert . . . into violent copperheads" when faced with hard marching and bad food. "But they are not the rule, they are exceptions, and there is hardly enough of them to make a decent exception."[28]

Even though some soldiers agreed with the idea of conciliation, most thought the decision-making would and should take place at the business end of a gun. "I think there is only two roads to peace, one is to conquor the rebels and force them to submit the other is to let them go, all the talk about compromising with them is mere nonsense and is not worth the thought of an intelligent man," Private Edward F. Hall of Exeter, New Hampshire, told his wife. Hall believed that even if Democrats gained control of the government, the Union still would have to fight the war. In the meantime, he was fed up with "those who find more fault with the administration than with the rebellion itself."[29]

American men had grown up in a world where differences were settled in political forums.[30] So it was natural for the soldiers to think in political terms as one way of ridding the nation of the peace advocates. Many bluecoats became long-distance political activists, generally on behalf of the Republican Party and its candidates. Blanchard, the Connecticut soldier, told his family that he hoped the people at home would not elect "those unprincibeld villains" to office. Women should take some initiative in the political arena, too, spurning men who voted for antiwar Democrats and spitting on them if disapproval were not enough. As for those Democrats already serving in the army, "they almost disspise the name," he said. Letters from soldiers denouncing the conservatives seemed to have some effect in parts of the country. In the area around Toledo, administration critics who had been quite "fiery" in their "speeches and effusions" fell nearly silent, one woman said. She admonished her brother in the 11th Ohio to remember, though, that "the enemy in the rear is a more dangerous one than that in front" and that the Copperheads would remain quiet only until they detected weakness in the army and the government.[31]

If the newfound resolve among the soldiers dampened the opposition, it did nothing to improve the morale of the population at large. Public despondency was in evidence, once again, at the enlistment offices. Very few men were volunteering for the army, even though towns and counties already were beginning to tax their citizens so they could boost the bounties they had started offering the summer before. Lincoln, who had quietly begun accepting African Americans into the army the previous summer, now publicly and heartily advocated having black men in blue, reasoning that they were the North's greatest untapped resource. The integration of the army came at the displeasure of some white soldiers.[32] "My opinion of 'nigger' soldiers has not risen very high, when the U.S. Government gets so hard pushed, that she feels compelled to take these confounded niggers to fight her battles, it better sell out to the first bidder," a Rhode Island artillery sergeant said. Copperheads, naturally, found the practice to be highly objectionable. "We of the west surely think this most degrading and miserably hemilitating on the part of our government. . . . It seems to be the policy of our congress men to be radical, more radical, most radical," a Clark County, Indiana, man wrote.[33]

Conservatives had other reasons to worry about bringing black men into the ranks of the army. They feared that military service would be a Trojan horse for racial equality. They argued that black men could not take orders efficiently—an odd position, given the Copperheads' support for slavery, an institution that was predicated on the assumption of compliance. Peace Democrats also argued that blacks did not have the courage to fight. "It is impossible to make a whistle out of a pig's tail," the Cleveland Plain Dealer editorialized. The threat of racial equality implied in African American service successfully stirred up many Democrats in the North. "We have some pride about us and will never assent to negro equality," said "Bertrand" in a letter to a Michigan newspaper. "If ever the Anglo Saxon American citizen forsake their manhood so far as to come on a level with the 'American citizen of African descent,' we will deserve to be forsaken by our Maker forever."[34]

Conservatives routinely tried to capitalize on racial fears, and African American soldiers offered a new avenue of threat. Publisher William Reed editorialized that they would lead to the complete breakdown of the social order in the South. The worst of his scenarios was that "negro women are to have the white women of the South—the gentle matrons and pure virgins—to do their menial work." Other peace men warned that accepting blacks into the army would promote slave uprisings in the South, an alarming proposition to a group that believed fervently the war could stop immediately if only the parties could meet at a negotiating table. Paradoxically, when the slaves did not rise up en masse against their masters and the Confederacy, Copperheads blamed them for prolonging the war.[35]

Allowing African Americans to serve in the army had the remarkable effect of politicizing the black population in a way even emancipation had not. An African American man in New Milford, Connecticut, wrote the governor—the first time he had ever done so, he said—to insist that blacks had to be in the army to help save the country. Democrats, Abraham J. Morrison said, were sure that the South "can never be concered [conquered] by the northern abolitionist and therefore have no desire to fight but to stay at home and vote peace men." Republicans had no choice but to turn to the black man to fight. "True it may seem that the treatment [blacks] received at the hands of the American people is enough to make us disloyal, but not so . . . ," he said. "We Sir do consider this to be our country rite, or wrong, if not yet wright, we trust in a higher and more glorious power to make it, God has already sent his servant Abraham Lincon to manage things to his glory and we have seen his hand writing in the afaires of this guilty nation."[36]

But black soldiers and white veterans could not fill the army's maw. The nine-month men conscripted the previous summer were about to end their enrollments, as were the two-year men who had signed up when the war broke out. Lincoln had to resort to a real draft—not the pseudo-conscription of 1862, but a full-fledged conscription. The army needed more men than volunteering or that proto-draft could produce. On March 3, 1863, Lincoln signed the Enrollment Act that made every man who was able-bodied, between twenty and forty-five, and a citizen or an immigrant who had applied to become a citizen subject to the draft. Each congressional district in the country would have to send a proportionate number of men into the army, either through volunteering or through drafting. Representative Samuel S. Cox of Ohio tried to stymie Lincoln's effort to allow blacks into the army by amending the bill, but his attempt to ensure that only white men would be enrolled failed.[37]

What became clear by the time the conscription bill was enacted was that Copperheads were so ideologically driven that they were blind to the threat that the war posed to the nation. Senator James A. Bayard of Delaware was typical of the conservatives' inability to acknowledge the depth of the crisis when he insisted that the bill was unconstitutional because it undermined the state militia system and therefore left states unable to counter any aggression by the federal government. Bayard was aware that his opposition would draw fire from the prowar faction, but he insisted he was defending the higher objectives of the nation—aims that superseded winning the war. "I differ from honorable Senators as to what constitutes the life of the nation," he said. "*In my judgment, the life of a free people consists in the preservation of their liberties, not in the extent of their dominion.*" To conservatives, this opposition may have been principled, but it also hindered the war effort. Whether Peace Democrats *intended* to do so remains unclear. There is no direct evidence in the archives. Obstruction was often the outcome, though. Vallandigham, for instance, could not help but erode morale and support for a draft by insisting on the House floor that it would only prolong a war "for coercion, invasion, and the abolition of negro slavery by force. Sir, the conscription of Russia is mild and merciful and just, compared with this." To his way of thinking, passing such a bill was nothing short of admitting that Northerners opposed the war.[38]

Constitutional objections notwithstanding, Lincoln needed men to prosecute the war. The real object of the Enrollment Act was to stimulate volunteer enlistments. One of the big inducements for men to sign up was a bounty—which could reach a thousand dollars in areas where state and local officials supplemented the federal bonus. But if that was a carrot, a stick was also involved. The draft was to be held in any congressional districts that did not meet their quotas through volunteering. The specter of a draft generated disaffection on its own, but the law contained two other provisions that created still more enemies for the administration. The measure allowed conscripts to avoid service either by paying a three-hundred-dollar commutation fee—good only for that draft cycle—or by hiring a substitute. Both practices brought bitter charges that the struggle had become a "rich man's war but a poor man's fight." In Columbus, Ohio, the *Crisis* called the Enrollment Act a "monstrous enormity." The fact that the law would distinguish between rich and poor was a "scandal" that made a mockery of the Declaration of Independence's claim that all men were created equal, the paper editorialized. The law "only carries out the abolition theory of equality without distinction of color."[39]

Resistance to the new law was visible everywhere, and it was not limited to peace advocates or even just to Democrats, as historian

Robert E. Sterling points out. James B. Fry, the provost marshal, later attributed negative reaction to the "great repugnance" Americans felt about the draft, seeing such a measure as "obnoxious to a free people." Fry acknowledged that outright conscription was "a novelty contrary to the traditional military policy of the nation." A newly combative environment emerged, pitting some Northerners against their own government. A parody of the previous summer's popular ditty, "We Are Coming, Father Abraham, 300,000 More," illustrates the changed mood:

> We're coming, ancient Abraham, several hundred strong
> We hadn't no 300 dollars and so we come along
> We hadn't no rich parents to pony up the tin
> So we went unto the provost and there were mustered in.

The *New York Herald* tried in vain to stanch public disillusionment with the law, regardless of its defects. The paper reminded its readers that they had a duty to sustain the president and that his new powers brought new responsibilities that would "make him more prudent with regard to whom he entrusts commands."[40]

Alienation was not the only by-product of the new law. The measure required that a federal provost marshal and board of enrollment be installed in each congressional district in the country. The districts were then subdivided so that local enrolling officers could pull together comprehensive lists of eligible men, drawing on information obtained through personal visits, polling lists, assessment rolls, and payroll records. The enrolling officers were supplemented by investigators and law enforcement officers, who were paid on a contractual basis. This new army of agents dramatically increased the federal presence in— and observation of—communities, and that amplified tensions between the government and some of its citizens even more. Arguing against the bill, Vallandigham warned his colleagues in the House that every district in the country "is to be governed—yes, governed—by this petty satrap—this military eunuch—this Baba—and he may even be black— who is to do the bidding of your Sultan, or his Grand Vizier." The *Chicago Times* believed the seventy-five thousand nonmilitary men who were enforcing the draft would be put to better use as conscripts. "The government would thus secure a ready-made army, with the advantage that every individual member thereof is in favor of a 'vigorous prosecution of the war,' " the paper said in an editorial. Then the administration could leave everyone else alone.[41]

Conscription produced men, but they did not necessarily make good soldiers. Commutation and substitution prompted less wealthy men to desert, historian Judith Lee Hallock asserts. Bounties retarded enlistments by luring men away from poorer areas into counties, cities, or towns that paid better bonuses. This led to such widespread fraud that there was a name for it: bounty jumping. Men would enlist, claim the bounty, and leave the area without ever showing up for muster. Often they would go someplace else, enlist, take the money, and run again. Substitution ratcheted up bounty prices, thereby increasing the temptation for men to defraud the system.[42]

Conscription under Lincoln was at best only a qualified success. Of the 76,829 men who were called up, only 46,347—60 percent—actually served. According to one comprehensive study, more men dodged the draft than paid commutation fees or hired substitutes. The situation became graver as the war continued. In the July 1863 draft, 13.5 percent of the men whose names were drawn failed to show up at their draft boards for examination. In March 1864, the figures rose to 24 percent; in July 1864, when morale bottomed out, the rate of draft dodging was 28.5 percent; and in December 1864, when the last draft was held, about one-fifth of those called to serve did not report. On average, more than 20 percent of the men whose names were pulled avoided the draft by never reporting for their exams.[43]

As they had the previous summer, men who were subject to the draft beat a path to doctors' offices. "There are very few enrolled or drafted men who do not claim disability of some kind, and of course demand exemption," Dr. Benjamin P. Morgan of Rutland, Vermont, said. Some men would cut off fingers or toes or knock out their own teeth to avoid conscription. Others would put sand or cayenne pepper in their eyes or irritants such as lye on their skin to fake diseases. "We feel as if we were among the lame, blind, dumb, and halt," an Urbana, Illinois, medical examiner observed dryly.[44]

Veteran volunteers wholeheartedly supported the new conscription law. It showed a spirit of resolve in a way that the Militia Act the previous summer had not, and it bypassed the militias completely, focusing instead on a national army. On the anniversary of Lincoln's inauguration, Private Aurelius Lyman Voorhis of the 46th Indiana wrote in his diary: "President Lincoln has now been in office two years and what a tremendous responsibility has rested upon him and is likely to rest upon him during the remainder of his term. Without doubt he is the right man in the right place and every loyal man should support him with their hands and voice." Shenanigans such as draft dodging and bounty jumping enraged veterans in the field, many of whom had volunteered early in the war and received a mere twenty-five dollars upon enlistment, with the promise of seventy-five dollars to come upon

Attention! "Avoid the Draft."

Buy our patent boots and shoes to escape the draft. They produce a perfect limp that will deceive the enrolling officer. Shanks, patentee and only manufacturer

☞ Ten thousand pairs sold in one week! ☜

Military-age men devised all kinds of schemes to avoid conscription. This cartoon presents an ingenious idea to persuade a draft board that a man was lame. (*Yankee Notions*/Courtesy of HarpWeek LLC)

honorable discharge (or death). Men who evaded the draft—legally or illegally—"are fighting against their country and against their God—fighting in the service of Satan and Jeff Davis and they are fools if they think they shall win in the end," a Vermont private said.[45]

The Enrollment Act amplified the ill will that Peace Democrats felt toward the government, even as it benefited them. Conservatives at all levels loudly challenged the measure's constitutionality, and this time some Republican stalwarts joined them in protest. Horace Greeley, editor of the *New York Tribune*, privately told Secretary of War Stanton that conscription was "repugnant" to Americans and could not be carried out "except at great peril to the free States. . . . Drafting is an anomaly in a free State; it oppresses the masses." He urged Stanton either to rescind or modify the law. The draft, though, was another windfall for the Copperheads on the order of the Emancipation Proclamation. It drove people into the fold, and like those who had bolted from the war ranks the previous fall, those who joined the peace side now became a permanent part of the antiwar coalition.[46]

Open defiance to the administration's policies was almost commonplace, especially in the form of desertion. Some families, fed up over the Emancipation Proclamation and the mounting death toll, advocated it. A McDonough County, Illinois, resident wrote to his nephew in the 16th Illinois: "Richard take a fool's advice and come home if you have to desert. . . . You will be protected—the people are so enraged that you need not be alarmed if you hear of the whole of the Northwest killing off abolitionists." Files of federal prosecutors are filled at this time with cases of parents being prosecuted for encouraging their sons to desert or dodge the draft, or harboring them once they did. Deserters sometimes enjoyed the complicity of local authorities. In Marshall, Illinois, a judge arrested a sergeant who had detained a group of deserters and charged the sergeant with kidnapping. Upon learning of the case, a furious major general telegraphed Stanton that he planned to rearrest the deserters, arrest the judge on charges of harboring and protecting deserters, and free the sergeant. Bands of deserters roaming the countryside became an increasing problem in parts of the Northwest. In Clark County, Illinois, where armed deserters roamed and the KGC was managing a resistance movement, a frightened local wrote Governor Richard Yates: "In God's name what is the end to be? . . . Danger is brewing." Meanwhile, Canada was experiencing an immigration overflow. So many men had run to that country that "the laboring people in Canada are obliged to come to Mich to get work," a Michigan woman wrote.[47]

The draft was not the only measure that offended Democrats who opposed Lincoln's war policies. The same day that Congress approved the Enrollment Act, it passed another bill that gave Lincoln the right to suspend habeas corpus anywhere in the United States. The law provided for some accountability by forcing military authorities to release prisoners upon the orders of a judge. Historian James G. Randall argued that if the overall effect of this law was harsh, it was mitigated by the ease with which a prisoner could be released. Prisoners often were let go after simply taking an oath of allegiance. Others were freed because of ill health or poverty. If the detention was precautionary, no charges were filed, or the arrest was made without "suitable authority," prisoners generally were released with little difficulty.[48]

The symbolic impact of the measure was clear, however. "In effect, the act made Lincoln a veritable, if benevolent, dictator until the rebellion was quelled," one historian has commented. The *World*, which had been a War Democrat paper but was gradually becoming more conservative, argued that the Constitution allowed habeas corpus to be suspended only in the event of a foreign war with invading armies, not in what the writer called "an ordinary war."[49] Copperheads were nearly frantic over what the president was doing. An Ohio man thought the government's aim was to "stifle the voice of an oppressed and downtrodden people, from speaking out every where . . . against the mad and *insane* policy of the Administration in prosecuting a war of vengeance and of hate against the people of the South and establishing upon the ruins of the Republic, a despotism, more odious than has ever disgraced the civilization of any age of the world!" Some men believed that the Lincoln government would "sooner see every man cut down on the field than see a nigger in bondage," as one Buckeye wrote. "I would to day if I had the power put every nigger in bondage and have the Constitution as it was not as it is."[50]

Fueled by the disasters of the armies over the winter and the actions of Congress and the administration, the Copperheads' strength was growing. In Connecticut, the peace faction took over the state's Democratic Party and ran one of its own, Thomas H. Seymour, for governor. Republicans thought his election would be a travesty. It would be "a more severe blow to the Conn troop in this department then would be the capture of Washington by Stonewall Jackson," Lieutenant Colonel Joseph Selden wrote home. Seymour's deputies responded by trying to soften their candidate's positions, but Seymour refused to cooperate. In a public statement, he wrote that the idea that the North could reunite the Union by attacking the cities of the South was a "monstrous fallacy." War would bankrupt the country, he said, and leave "its brave men on both sides consigned to hospitals and graves, a spectacle for the reproach and commiseration of the civilized world." Peace Democrats argued that they were the true defenders of the Constitution while Lincoln's actions were threatening to make a mockery of the document. The outcome was close, but the Republicans prevailed. Incumbent governor William Buckingham won with less than 52 percent of the vote and a margin of victory of fewer than three thousand votes.[51]

Elsewhere in the North, the increasing boldness of the Peace Democrats continued to rankle loyalists. An Ohio man wrote to General

Burnside, who now commanded the Army of the Ohio in Cincinnati, complaining that Copperhead women were allowed to sing "their cursed Secesh Songs" on steamers. He urged the general either to order such displays stopped "or authorize the traveling public to take such cases in hand." Soldiers were more and more concerned about the home front. "I am beginning to fear that the people of the North are going to prove themselves unworthy and unfit for a free government. I am beginning to fear, that there is not enough of patriotism and high *moral sense* in the mind & heart of the Nation to save it from Anarchy and ruin," Captain John R. Beatty of Minnesota wrote his fiancée. Soldiers were now banding together in opposition to the peace ranks. "Coperheadism has brought the soldiers here together more than anything else. Some of the men that yoused to be almost willing to have the war settled any way are now among the strongest Union soldiers we have got," Corporal Enoch B. Lewis of the 101st Ohio said. One conservative paper rejected the accusations that dissidents were Southern sympathizers by reminding its readers that the people making such charges "are laboring under the influence of a negro monomania." Their great fear of Copperheads stemmed "from the fact that they have colored 'snakes in their boots.' "[52]

While civilians were battling it out behind the lines, the armies prepared for the spring campaigns. On the Confederate side, Lee had high hopes for the fighting season. "If successful this year, next fall there will be a great change in public opinion at the North. The Republicans will be destroyed & I think the friends of peace will become so strong as that the next administration will go in on that basis. We have only therefore to resist manfully," he wrote his wife. On the Union side, the Army of the Potomac had yet another new commander, General Joseph Hooker. He was a man prone to excess in his speech, his drinking, and his penchant for women. Lincoln decided to take a chance on him anyway. "I am not quite satisfied with you," he warned his new general. The president had heard credible reports that Hooker had said the government needed a dictator. "Of course it was not for this, but in spite of it, that I have given you the command. Only those generals who gain successes, can set up dictators. What I now ask of you is military success, and I will risk the dictatorship." Hooker quickly got to work, improving the food for the men and the sanitation in the camps. He tightened up discipline and doled out more leaves. Morale in the ranks started to rise. Hooker thumped his chest and announced, to the humble Lincoln's great discomfort, that he headed "the finest army on the planet." But Hooker had yet to be tested in his new command. Antiwar men viewed the developments within Union and Confederate armies with a sense of resignation. "The armies are growing restive," Iowa attorney Charles Mason observed from Washington, where he was working at the time. "The harvest time of death is again coming round."[53]

In Ohio, meanwhile, Burnside continued to wreak havoc on the Union cause. After two terms in Congress, Vallandigham had been gerrymandered out of his seat and failed to win reelection in the fall. To Burnside's disgust, Vallandigham received a hero's welcome when he returned home to Dayton in March after wrapping up his business in Washington, D.C. Burnside could not abide Vallandigham's subsequent speeches. Fed up with statements he considered traitorous, Burnside issued General Order No. 38 on April 13. "Treason, expressed or implied, will not be tolerated in this department," he announced. Anyone who acted in such a way as to benefit the Confederates would be arrested immediately, tried as a traitor or spy, and executed or banished if found guilty.[54]

Vallandigham quickly saw an opening to embarrass the government. He traveled to Mt. Vernon, Ohio, where, on May 1, he laced into the administration, accusing it of misleading the people about the goals of the war. Burnside's orders were usurpation and a violation of the First Amendment, he said, and he encouraged the audience to disobey them. As he spoke, and with Vallandigham's full knowledge, one of Burnside's agents, wearing civilian clothes, leaned against the speaker's platform and took notes.[55] Burnside had had enough. Without checking with his superiors, he ordered Vallandigham arrested for violating General Order No. 38. In the wee hours of May 5, 150 soldiers arrived at Vallandigham's Dayton home. Dressed in his nightshirt, the former congressman had just enough time to shout a warning to other Copperheads in his neighborhood before the troops broke down his front door. After allowing him to dress, the soldiers hauled Vallandigham to a train and clapped him into prison in Cincinnati.

Ohio representative Clement Laird Vallandigham was the most infamous Peace Democrat in the nation. Union general Ambrose Burnside made him a martyr when he arrested Vallandigham and tried him in a military court, which found him guilty and sentenced him to spend the rest of the war in a military prison. Lincoln tried to cool the situation by banishing Vallandigham to the Confederacy. (*Harper's Weekly*/Courtesy of HarpWeek LLC)

The next morning a mob gathered in front of the *Dayton Journal*, the city's Republican paper, and set the offices on fire. Burnside responded by declaring martial law in all of Montgomery County. A military tribunal composed of eight officers found the former congressman guilty and sentenced him to spend the remainder of the war in federal prison. Vallandigham maintained his innocence and asked for a jury trial. He said in his statement to the court that he had been arrested and tried without due process. Unmoved, the court sent him to prison.[56]

War Democrats and even Republicans expressed doubts about the government's actions in the case, but conservatives were furious. "Every reader of every nation and tongue will be astounded at the arrest of a private *American* citizen, in his own country, upon such charges as are developed in this trial, and that by *military* authority . . . ," the *Crisis* of Columbus said. "If the people cannot discuss public measures, hear speeches, read such papers and documents as they desire, then all idea of a republican form of government is at an end." In New York, the *World* called the arrest a "high-handed assumption of despotic power."[57]

Feelings ran just as high among ordinary peace men as they did among the elites. Vallandigham was "a *patriot*, and statesman" who had warned of the "rapid strides of despotic power to crush out the last spark of civil liberty," one conservative said. Now Vallandigham's predictions were coming to pass. "He had pointed out with prophetic & patriotic fervour, the horrors, of an international war and its fatal, and crushing influence to destroy and corrupt the public morals & private virtues of the people," and that was happening, too. His arrest was "in utter defiance of all law, and without warrant." From New York, Governor Horatio Seymour said the congressman's incarceration "brought dishonor upon our country." The arrest violated the Constitution in several ways, Seymour said: freedom of speech, protection against search and seizure, passing sentence without a trial "save one which was a mockery." If the sentence were upheld, the rights of all Americans had been overthrown and military rulers would henceforth reign. In this environment, he suggested, thoughtful Northerners had to reconsider their backing of the administration. "Having given it a generous support in the conduct of the war, we now pause to see what kind of government it is for which we are asked to pour out our blood and our treasures." This remarkable comment, which itself seems to shade into troublesome speech, went unremarked on by government officials.[58]

Just as many of his followers did, Vallandigham considered himself a martyr, writing "Bastile" as the return address in his correspondence from prison and penning such melodramatic lines as this: "As to my fate, I am wholly unconcerned—prepared for any fortune—

imprisonment, exile—death." But he was also a smart politician, and he saw his case as one that would force the administration to defend its "abominable doctrines." He set about writing prominent Democrats to round up support. "We of the West must now depend largely upon you of New York & New Jersey who are *free*. Stand by us and we will by you," he wrote Manton Marble, editor of the *World*.[59]

Democrats in Albany, New York, met in front of the state capitol on May 16 to protest Vallandigham's arrest. Speakers attacked the administration for suppressing free speech and freedom of the press, suspending habeas corpus, barring trial by a civilian jury, and denying the supremacy of civil law over military justice. Participants adopted a series of resolutions which Democratic congressman Erastus Corning sent to Lincoln along with a statement underscoring the gathering's "hearty and earnest desire to support the Government in every Constitutional and lawful measure to suppress the existing Rebellion." Their arguments did nothing to sway Lincoln, who replied June 12 with a letter that read like a court brief in which he justified Vallandigham's treatment. According to Lincoln's reading of the Constitution, certain actions that would not otherwise be constitutional became legitimate under the extraordinary circumstances of rebellion, invasion, or a major threat to the public's safety.[60] In a similar letter to Ohio Democrats, Lincoln wrote:

> You claim that men may, if they choose, embarrass those whose duty it is, to combat a giant rebellion, and then be dealt with in turn, only as if there was no rebellion. The constitution itself rejects this view. The military arrests and detentions, which have been made ... have been for *prevention*, and not for *punishment*— as injunctions to stay injury, as proceedings to keep the peace.

Lincoln said that the Ohio committee's attitude encouraged desertion and resistance to the draft. He promised to release Vallandigham if the majority of the panel's members would agree to the following propositions: that a rebellion existed in the United States that threatened to destroy the Union, and the only way to put down the revolt was through military force; that none of the Ohio men would do anything to impinge on the military's effectiveness or its ability to muster men; and that each man would do all he could to support the men in arms and to pay, feed, and clothe them. The committee turned down Lincoln's offer. This exchange was another of Lincoln's astute political moves, because it demonstrated the Copperheads' unwillingness to acknowledge the peril that confronted the Union and their refusal to assist with the war effort.[61]

Burnside had put the president in an embarrassing and politically compromising position, though, and Lincoln wanted to avoid making a hero of Vallandigham. This was a touchy situation. If Lincoln ordered the congressman's release, he would appear to be undercutting his commanders. If he allowed the congressman to spend the rest of the war in a military prison, he would make Vallandigham a hero to the opposition. The problem thus posed, the president hit on a classically Lincolnian solution, one as pragmatic as it was amusing: banish the nation's most high-profile Southern sympathizer to the Confederacy. As it turned out, the rebels did not want Vallandigham, either. When a federal officer and a Confederate colonel met May 25 under a flag of truce to discuss the transfer, the colonel refused to take the congressman off the federals' hands. The Yankees took care of the problem by dumping Vallandigham and his valise near a rebel picket in the area of Murfreesboro, Tennessee. Having written and memorized a statement, Vallandigham recited it to a bewildered private: "I am a citizen of Ohio, and of the United States. I am here within your lines by force and against my will. I therefore surrender myself to you as a prisoner of war."[62]

Unsure of what to do with him, the local commander forwarded Vallandigham to headquarters in Shelbyville. General Braxton Bragg welcomed him to "the land of liberty" without checking with his superiors in Richmond. But Secretary of War James A. Seddon withdrew the hand of hospitality, telegraphing Bragg on May 30 that if Vallandigham claimed to be a loyal American citizen, the Confederate States of America would either charge or parole him as an "alien enemy." Seddon would allow Vallandigham to go to Wilmington, North Carolina, he added. Vallandigham took him up on the offer. Twenty-four days after arriving in the Confederacy, he caught a blockade runner for Bermuda, where he boarded another ship for Canada. He spent the next year in Windsor, Ontario, where he could look out his sitting room window and see Detroit and the U.S. gunboat *Michigan,* which was moored in the middle of the river with its guns trained on his residence, according to a visiting reporter. But if Vallandigham was gone, he was hardly forgotten. Republicans had not yet heard the last of the gentleman from Ohio.[63]

Before Vallandigham left the Confederacy, he met with the head of the Confederate Bureau of Exchange, Robert Ould. According to a clerk in the War Department who saw Ould's account of the meeting, Vallandigham said that if the Confederacy could hold out for another year the Peace Democrats would "sweep the Lincoln dynasty out of political existence." Vallandigham also said he and other Copperheads wanted only to reunite the country. If that could not be done, he might favor recognizing Southern independence. Any reconstruction in which the South did not voluntarily participate "would soon be followed by another separation, and a worse war than the present one," Vallandigham said.[64]

Vallandigham's belief that the South would even consider rejoining the Union resulted in a decidedly mixed reception for him from the Confederate press. The newspapers took him at his word that Lincoln was a despot and a tyrant, that civil liberties were a dead letter in the North. All of this vindicated the Confederate position and was a propaganda boon. That did not make Vallandigham a friend or an ally to Southerners. To the contrary, his insistence that the Union return to the *status quo ante bellum* made him "a mortal enemy." The Confederates did not want to reunite with the North; they wanted their independence. John Moncure Daniel of the *Richmond Examiner* was so suspicious of Vallandigham that he regarded the former congressman as an "earnest agent for [the Confederacy's] political annihilation." Mary Boykin Chesnut, who traveled in Richmond's highest political circles, was more diplomatic in her diary: "He will never help us against his own people, of that we may be sure." By the time Vallandigham left the country, most Southerners were glad to see him go.[65]

Lee, who could be a shrewd politician, regarded Peace Democrats as allies, not enemies. He was so distressed by Southern coverage of the Vallandigham affair that he even wrote a letter to Davis suggesting that the Confederate press pipe down in the interest of war aims. The most effective way of weakening the enemy "is to give all the encouragement we can, consistently with the truth, to the rising peace party of the North." This support should not bother with making any "nice distinction" between those who sought unconditional peace and those who favored it as a way of restoring the Union. Confederate opinion makers should focus just on undermining Northern support for the war, not the details of what it wanted from peace talks.[66]

Lee's political concerns notwithstanding, Southern editors had hit on a central problem with the Copperhead movement at large. Conservative Democrats—at least those who were not outright Confederate sympathizers—assumed that an appeased South would hasten back to the arms of its former country. But the war had become so violent and so bitter that few Confederates regarded this as a palatable option. They wanted their independence. In misreading white Southern opinion, the Copperheads were rather like Lincoln in the first year of the war, when he constructed his national strategy on the belief that the Confederacy was packed with Unionists who would join the Northern cause if given half a chance. Lincoln came to recognize the folly of that

belief, but Vallandigham and the other Peace Democrats clung mul-
ishly to their notion that the South would return to the Union if the
North would only let it. They could not see that by the time Vallandigham was delivered to rebeldom, white Southerners were long since
committed to having their own country, and thousands of men were
dying toward that end.[67]

While the Vallandigham drama was playing out, Hooker led the
Army of the Potomac into battle for his first and last time. The fight
came at Chancellorsville, a rural crossroads in the Wilderness west of
Fredericksburg, and it proved to be a disastrous one. Hooker "lost his
nerve" from the first skirmish on May 1. A bad situation became worse
for the Yankees on May 3, when a ball hit a post that Hooker had been
leaning against and knocked him nearly senseless. Despite being stunned,
Hooker refused to surrender control of his men. The wily Lee completely
took advantage of the unstrung general in what is widely considered to
be his greatest and most daring battle. Hooker withdrew from the field
on May 6, having suffered seventeen thousand casualties.[68]

Upon hearing the news, Lincoln turned ashen—the French-gray
shade of the wallpaper, in fact—and was the "picture of despair," according to a journalist who was in the room at the time. "My God! My
God! What will the country say!" he exclaimed. It said nothing good.
The *World* compared the loss to that at Fredericksburg, where another
incompetent general led his men to slaughter. Like many other Democratic papers in the North, it once again called for McClellan's rein-
statement. The bleak mood so permeated the nation that even its music
assumed a dark tone. "When This Cruel War Is Over" became a standard in the North: "Weeping, sad and lonely, hopes and fears how
vain!/When this cruel war is over, praying that we meet again."[69] The
song penetrated the public consciousness so deeply that for more than
a year thereafter, letters from the home front routinely asked, "When
will this cruel war be over?"

The loss at Chancellorsville was another body blow to morale in the
Army of the Potomac. Major Henry Abbott of the 20th Massachusetts,
never an ally of the administration, was sputtering for McClellan's return: "I should think the whole nation would cry out for McClellan."
He regarded Lincoln and Halleck as "caterpillars on the commonwealth.
. . . It certainly seems as if it were impossible for abolitionists to stop
lying & doing all they can to injure this army," he told his mother. In
New Jersey, the *Bergen Democrat* called the loss a "dreadful reverse"
and urged its readers to pray "to stop the dreadful carnage, and the
inhuman merciless butchery which is desolating the land and disgrac-
ing civilization."[70]

The armies of the West did nothing to improve morale at home and in the field. Rosecrans was idle in Tennessee, as he had been since his victory at Stone's River. Grant tried twice in May to take Vicksburg, but without success. In late April, his men had moved far south of Vicksburg on the western bank of the Mississippi before crossing the mighty river. Once in Mississippi, Grant moved east to the state capital, Jackson. There the federals made a hairpin turn and started for Vicksburg from the east. Grant moved relatively easily through the interior of the state, handily beating the rebels that confronted him, but he still could not take Vicksburg. Faced with entrenched Confederate troops, he suffered sharp defeats there on May 19 and again on May 22. Grant had no choice but to dig in for a siege. Union morale continued its springtime swoon.

Nevertheless, an important change was coming over the army. Many men who had resisted the idea of fighting for emancipation or for having blacks in the ranks were changing their minds. For some men, this change of heart was an equal and opposite reaction to the vehement opposition of Copperheads to emancipation. Others came to realize that black men in uniform increased the Yankees' manpower, or that emancipation kept foreign powers out of the fray. Still others, after seeing slavery up close during their travels through the South, decided that freedom for slaves was a desirable goal. It dawned on a handful of federals that their own careers could advance if they became officers in black units. Whatever its genesis, this change in attitude was sometimes startling to those at home. "We hear that you have enlisted with the Nigger service for the term of 5 years if such is the fact, your *Stomach* has become quit *strong* compared with its condition whilst you were at home," an Ohio Democrat wrote his soldier son. "You give some evidence of the fact in Marys letter for you speak of recruiting '*Contraband*.' it must be a *fancy business* compared to that of staying with common white men '*sic transit Gloria* &c.' "[71]

While positions on emancipation as a war aim could cause friction between soldiers and the people at home, an insoluble rift had developed by late spring over politics. Soldiers, whose anger at Copperheads had grown steadily over the winter and early spring, were now prepared to terminate longstanding relationships over what they perceived as disloyalty to the Union and to themselves. After several of his men became upset after receiving letters from their Copperhead friends, an Indiana sergeant helped them compose this response:

> Your letter shows you to be a cowardly traitor. No traitor can
> be my friend; if you can not renounce your allegiance to the

Copperhead scoundrels and own your allegiance to the Government which has always protected you, *you are my enemy*,
and I wish you were in the ranks of *my open, avowed,* and *manly*
enemies, that I might put a ball through your black heart, and
send your soul to the Arch Rebel himself.

One of the men asked the sergeant, Orville Chamberlain, to word it
more strongly for a letter that was going to his brother. "I tell you the
army is *loyal*, and it will remain so," Chamberlain told his own friends.
"The only effect of the labor of the copperheads is to *abolitionize* it. The
soldiers are and will be patriotic, hopeful, and determined in their Efforts to suppress treason wherever and whenever they meet it."[72]

Peace Democrats had made a powerful enemy in the soldiers. The
men in the field suffered from exposure, fear, and boredom. Their lives
were in almost constant jeopardy from battle or disease. But the Peace
Democrats offered little more than lip service in the way of support for
the men in blue. Soldiers had good reason to believe that conservatives were not behind them at all. Even as it became obvious that the
war was to be a protracted affair, reactionary Democratic politicians
refused to vote for measures that soldiers thought would help them
win the war more quickly, such as the conscription bill. To the contrary, Copperheads seemed to be urging men to avoid joining the army
altogether. Frustrated and angry, soldiers would soon begin to avenge
the disrespect of the peace men.

4

The Battle Behind the Lines

THE ENROLLMENT ACT CHANGED THE NATURE OF DISSENT in the North. Until the law passed, armed opposition to the war was scattered and generally weak. Earlier objections to government power most often took the form of speech targeting such abstract ideals as liberty, rights, and the meaning of republicanism. Emancipation was a more direct threat, but protest tended to be limited to the working classes, who feared for their jobs, and to people who had never had moral qualms about slavery. Conscription, with its potential to touch every white male citizen between twenty and forty-five, was different. The states had been responsible for all the earlier efforts to raise men, including figuring out how to meet the quotas that the Militia Act had laid out. Under the Enrollment Act, the draft was a national effort operated by the federal government, which was willing to bring its resources to bear to enforce it. As a result, the year following the adoption of the Enrollment Act was the most chaotic of the war, at least on the home front. The year broke down into three phases. The first was the most deadly, when resistance to the draft resulted in insurrection in some Northern communities, including the Union's largest metropolis, New York City. In the second phase, resistance moved from the streets to the political arena. Here the Copperheads were turned back, but despite their trouncing at the polls, Lincoln continued to experience political problems—mostly from within his own party. By the time strife took hold of the upper levels of the Republican Party, the rest of the country had entered a third phase. Having had time to reflect on the previous summer's victories at Gettysburg and Vicksburg, many Northerners were confident that the spring of 1864 would be the last of the war.

This year of whipsaw emotion opened in the spring of 1863 with large parts of the nation furious over the possibility of conscription.

The situation in some counties neared anarchy, with enrolling officers being favorite and readily available targets. In Democratic Holmes County, Ohio, a group of men stoned an enrolling officer eleven days after Vallandigham was banished to the Confederacy. A provost marshal who arrived a week later to arrest the assailants was waylaid and forced at gunpoint to free his four prisoners. The state then had to send four hundred soldiers into the county to put down the uprising and arrest the four suspects again.[1] In Dunkard Township, Pennsylvania, a group of men surrounded the enrolling officer and forced him out of town. A local draft official predicted that three other towns in Greene County would be "troublesome."[2] In Bedford County, Pennsylvania, the enrolling officer was in a panic. Four men told him the draft law was unconstitutional, "and if they were drafted they would use powder and lead. The same night my saw-mill was set on fire and burned to ashes. . . . I have declined to make the enrollment for the reason that I think that my family and the balance of my property would not be safe. . . . I would not risk my life and property and make the enrollment for $1,000 [pay]." The barn of another enroller was torched. In Lebanon, Wisconsin, the enrolling officer, a farmer with six children, was shot as he made his rounds. He was hit thirty-seven times in the neck and back with squirrel shot.[3]

These officers were lucky compared to their colleagues in Indiana. In June two enrolling officers were killed in an ambush in Rush County, and a third was shot to death in Sullivan County. "I am informed that the Union citizens almost consider themselves as abandoned to the mercy of bands of outlaws who are led by desperate men," the agent based in Terre Haute told his superiors after one murder. Opponents of the draft stole completed enrollment forms—which included the names, ages, and physical descriptions of potential draftees—in Owen and Clay counties, and men in several other places vowed the enrollers' paperwork would never leave the area. Conrad Baker, the local assistant provost marshal, thought the situation was dire. He reported that as many as fifteen hundred men from Sullivan and Greene counties met regularly for military drill and had warned enrolling officers "that if they went on with [their work] they must do so at their peril." Rumor had it that the antiwar faction was ready to tear up the local railroad tracks. If the government sent troops, they had better be prepared for a battle, Baker said. Enrollment was not to be easy anywhere in his area. Around Linton, "it appears to be a preconcerted agreement among the Opposition to answer no questions but heap on Uncle Sam's Officers all the insults they are masters of." In a biblical allusion, Baker wrote that the seven devils "Christ cast [out] of the *possessed* have taken up their abode with every one of them." Local roughs warned one enrolling agent for the district that if certain men were drafted he would be killed.[4]

Assaults and other violent acts began to erode the army's ability to raise men. Across the country, enrolling officers resigned in fear, while other men refused even to accept the job when it was offered to them. By the end of the war, the Provost Marshal General's Bureau's casualties stood at thirty-eight killed and sixty wounded. A dozen others suffered damage to their property. These figures do not include the losses that various army companies and regiments took while they were supporting the provost marshal's work. The danger that this work posed was a serious disincentive to civilians who were asked to undertake the job. The difficulty of hiring and retaining enrolling officers impeded the army's ability to muster enough men to maintain troop strength, but intimidation had another cost. In areas where the threats against local agents were considered serious enough, the army often sent troops to quell any disorder, siphoning off valuable manpower from the front lines.[5]

Indiana was the most tense and violent state in this fraught period. Feelings there ran so high by mid-June that even women were subject to abuse. When Copperheads met in the Butlerville schoolhouse and put butternuts on the American flag, a local woman snatched the nuts from Old Glory and prevented the meeting from moving forward. Her beau, whom she jilted after learning he was a Copperhead, shot at her six times, hitting her once in the leg and wounding her badly. In Brown County, one man named his son for Jefferson Davis, and another man said that "he wisht that tha [they] would evry won of grants men git kild befour tha tuck vicksburg." Butternuts were threatening to resist the draft with force, a local man told his soldier son, or, as he put it, "doo there fiting At home." In the town of Bergetts Corner, Peace Democrats reportedly went into churches and dared Unionists to take off the butternut pins that the Copperheads wore. Then after church they shot their weapons among women and children.[6]

As resistance rose, officers in the provost marshal's bureau started to describe dissenters in new kinds of language, those of class and nativism.[7] The "lower classes" had threatened resistance in Madison, Wisconsin, the local provost marshal wrote. In Indiana, the troublemakers in Sullivan and Greene counties were "generally exceedingly ignorant and are completely under the control of a few leaders who keep them excited and inflamed to an intense degree by all sorts of stories about Government oppression, outrage &c." A similar dynamic was said to be taking place in Welles County, where "a few unscrupulous men are now poisoning the minds of the ignorant, with all kinds of stuff."[8] Miners in Schuylkill County, Pennsylvania, who refused to subject themselves to either the enrollment or the draft were immigrants under the influence of native-born locals, according to the local provost marshal. Natives, whom he regarded as "more intelligent than the miners (who are for the greater part men of foreign birth tho citizens)," were trying to leverage the miners' resistance to the draft into hostility against the government.[9]

Robert E. Lee continued to monitor the political situation in the North and tried to think of ways to turn the growing disillusion to the Confederates' advantage. This was a side project that would occupy him for the next two years. "It is plain to my understanding that everything that will tend to repress the war feeling in the Federal States will enure to our benefit," he wrote President Davis. "I do not know that we can do anything to promote the pacific feeling, but our course ought to be so shaped as not to discourage it." As he penned those words, Lee was on the march. His men had crossed the Potomac River and moved into the rich farmland of Pennsylvania. The locals were terrified, and rumors about where he was headed spread across the state. With both armies heading in the general direction of Gettysburg, that town's blacks and its white men took flight, leaving mostly women and children to deal with the fury of what would be the war's deadliest battle. The *La Crosse Democrat* took no pity on terrified Pennsylvanians. Northern soldiers had been looting and vandalizing Southern homes, it observed, and "what is sauce for the goose is sauce for the gander."[10]

Neither Lee nor George Gordon Meade, who replaced Hooker as commander of the Army of the Potomac on June 28, intended to fight at Gettysburg. But when two Confederate brigades stumbled into John Buford's cavalrymen on July 1 west of town, the battle began anyway. The encounter was ferocious the first two days as the armies wrestled over the farms and orchards and rocky hills. Then Lee, his confidence still soaring in the wake of his stunning victory at Chancellorsville, struck on a plan he was certain would break the Yankee line. He sent three divisions under Generals James Johnston Pettigrew, Isaac Trimble, and George Pickett across nearly a mile of gently rolling but treeless fields to attack the bluecoats at the center of their line. Like the Confederates at Fredericksburg, the Yankees were safely ensconced behind a stone wall. They easily turned back the men in gray, inflicting enormous losses in the process.[11]

The story of the entire battle was one of incomprehensible loss: Meade suffered more than 23,000 casualties, including 3,155 killed in action. More than 2,000 of his wounded later died. If that was bad, Lee's story was worse. He lost 28,000 men, a third of his army. Meade infuriated Lincoln by not pursuing Lee's crippled army out of Pennsylvania, but for the first time in a long while, the Army of the Potomac scored a clear Union victory.[12]

There was more good news for the Union. While Meade was slugging it out in Pennsylvania, Grant finally broke through the siege at Vicksburg, taking the city on July 4 after months of effort. If any accomplishment could raise Northern spirits more than Gettysburg could, it was the taking of Vicksburg, the Gibraltar of the Mississippi. When Port Hudson fell four days later, the Mississippi River was open to Union traffic all the way from New Orleans to the Big Muddy's headwaters in Minnesota. It was thrilling news and portended a turning point for the Union's fortunes. The end of the war, the *New York Herald* announced, was "near at hand." One Indiana soldier said that when he heard about Grant's victory at Vicksburg, "I fear I should have kicked off my boot heels had I been at a dance."[13]

The excitement of two big, back-to-back victories did not last for long. New York City had been seething for months—years, really—with tensions over race, politics, labor relations, and class.[14] By the spring of 1863, the Irish were simmering about the draft and worried that African Americans would steal their jobs. Their fears may have run counter to the facts of the situation. Over the course of the war, the black population of the city dropped 20 percent, although it is impossible to know whether the exodus was already taking place at this time.[15] In any event, white Democratic politicians and newspapermen saw the white men's fears as an opportunity to attract them to the Democratic Party. They stoked racial strains with repeated reminders to white laborers that blacks were competing with them for employment.[16] New York's Democratic governor, Horatio Seymour, further inflamed Irish anger by attacking the draft and the administration. In a statement that drew tremendous criticism after the riots, Seymour told a Fourth of July crowd that action on the part of the people was sometimes justified. Ten days after the Confederates limped out of Gettysburg, New York City exploded in draft riots.[17]

In this volatile climate, it did not take much to spark an uprising. The trouble started the morning of July 11, a Saturday, when government officials held a draft lottery uptown in the Ninth District.[18] The draft, as historian Iver Bernstein points out, put into sharp relief three fundamental tensions with which New Yorkers had been grappling for several years: "relations between the wealthy and the poor, between blacks and whites, and between the city and the nation"—that is, local versus federal power. That night, complaints about conscription echoed through New York's lower-class bars, in private homes, and through the streets. A resolution submitted to the governor shortly thereafter "in the name of 350,000 working men" argued that conscription was a "monarchical principle & a sin." Its burden fell on the poor twice over: first by drafting them and then, if they were killed or maimed, by forcing their families into begging. Because of the potential consequences for those living on the edge financially, only the rich should be drafted. No mob law could be as "outrageous" as the draft law, the resolution concluded. Many New Yorkers may have disagreed with that statement after experiencing the anarchy of the riots.[19]

The draftees stewed over the weekend, and violence began in earnest on Monday when members of a fire company smashed the draft wheel in the provost marshal's office and then set the building ablaze. By noon the mobs had killed an enrolling officer who tried to persuade the firemen to douse the flames. The city was largely defenseless against the growing violence. Most of the troops normally stationed in the city had been sent down to Gettysburg, leaving only a few companies of soldiers and the local police to quell the mob. Over the course of the day, targets shifted from those associated with the draft to symbols of power, including police officers, the well dressed, government offices, and homes of rich Republicans. The city's business came to a standstill as the violence swelled. This was the riot's first phase.[20]

One or two priests implored the mob to stop its mayhem and had some success, but their influence was limited. "Rough fellows (& some equally rough women) . . . were tearing up rails, cutting down telegraph poles, & setting fire to buildings," wrote John Torrey, a prominent scientist who worked at the Assay Office on Wall Street. He raced home to protect his black servants. The crowd soon visited his house near Columbia University and asked if any Republicans lived there. "The furious bareheaded & coatless men assembled under our windows & shouted aloud for Jeff. Davis!" Torrey managed to stave them off, but later in the day he took a walk and found the mob surrounding a neighbor's home, intending to set fire to it. "The family were all out, entreating the scamps to desist, as 'they were all Brackenridge democrats & opposed to the *draft.*' "[21]

By Tuesday morning the riot was moving into its second phase. At that point, the mob's principal goal seemed to be theft, according to the chief mustering officer in the city. "City is in an intense excitement. Business all suspended. Rioting in almost every ward in the City," Colonel Robert Nugent telegraphed Colonel James B. Fry, the nation's provost marshal general. "It is a Spontaneous movement. There Seems to be no organization. It is principally for plunder." The composition of the crowd had changed. It was now mostly Irish and Catholic in-

HOW TO ESCAPE THE DRAFT.

Harper's Weekly was outraged over the New York draft riots. This cartoon pits a heroic black man and frightened child against a mob of Irish immigrants. One interesting aspect of this presentation is that the rioters are depicted in the kind of highly racialized caricature more often reserved for African Americans. (*Harper's Weekly*/Courtesy of HarpWeek LLC)

dustrial workers and laborers. They hated the Lincoln administration and were deeply resentful of emancipation and its implications. The crowds quickly turned on the city's well-known Republicans and then the blacks, who bore the brunt of the hordes' fury.[22]

By the end of the day the rebellion had moved fully into its third phase, transformed from an uprising against the draft to a full-fledged race riot. Packs of protesters targeted the Colored Orphan Asylum on Forty-third Street and Fifth Avenue, where they would not allow fire engines through to save the building or its occupants. From there, witnesses

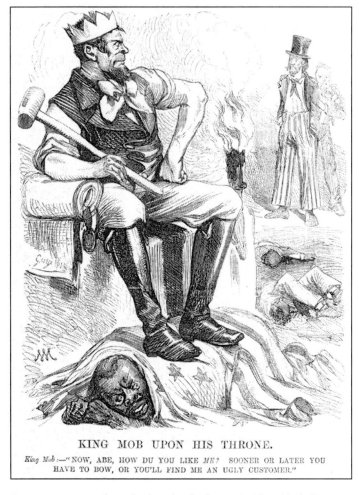

KING MOB UPON HIS THRONE.

King Mob :—"NOW, ABE, HOW DU YOU LIKE *ME?* SOONER OR LATER YOU HAVE TO BOW, OR YOU'LL FIND ME AN UGLY CUSTOMER."

Some cartoonists thought that the draft riots in New York City put Lincoln on the defensive, especially given his commitment to African Americans, who were a major target during the melee. The disturbance in Gotham and elsewhere had no effect on Lincoln's policies. (*Fun*/Courtesy of HarpWeek LLC)

reported, the mob started breaking into one house after another in search of African Americans. "Where a negro family was found they would rob them, then burn the house & beat them till they were almost killed," schoolteacher Samuel Morehouse wrote. "Finally they commenced hanging the negro men." Morehouse saw a black man hanged from a lamppost. Only the arrival of troops saved the man's sister from a similar fate, but that came at the cost of eight or ten lives. "I was not sorry to see them fall," he wrote of the dead rioters.

Morehouse, who spent a great deal of time on the streets during the uprising, said the insurgents "to a man have expressed themselves Democrats, believing this land is for white men & saying negros shall not divide it with them."[23]

He was not alone in blaming political leaders for the insurrection. Another New Yorker believed that disloyal political leaders were behind the rioting, which had exploded beyond the Copperheads' control. In a letter to Connecticut governor William A. Buckingham, this Gothamite accused New York governor Horatio Seymour of ordering only blanks to be fired from cannons. The city's frustrated mustering officer likewise blamed Democrats for the violence:

> The authorities in Washington do not seem able or willing to comprehend the magnitude [of] the opposition to the government which exists in New York. There's no doubt but that most, if not all, of the Democratic politicians are at the bottom of this riot, and that the rioters themselves include, not only the thieves and gamblers that infest this metropolis, but nearly every one of the vast democratic majority which has so constantly been thrown, at every election, against the administration.

Considering "the depraved and desperate character of these men," their hostility to the Lincoln administration, the "inflammatory harangues" of the New York press, and the "copious supplies" of alcohol, he wrote, "you will easily appreciate the difficulties of enforcing the Draft." However, the *Chicago Times,* one of the conservatives' leading voices, deflected the blame. It called the draft unconstitutional and made the unsupported assertion that seceded states were being blocked from rejoining the Union.[24]

By midweek the police, the few troops in the city, and the mob were engaged in a full-blown battle. The soldiers opened fire on the civilians with a cannon, killing twenty-seven. Gangs of thieves wandered from home to home, threatening to burn the houses unless the occupants gave them money. Down at the Assay Office the bureaucrats armed themselves. Some were "spoiling for a fight," Torrey wrote. The men inside the building had twenty-five rifles loaded and mounted on a gun carriage, along with four cannons, bombs crafted out of ten-pound shells, and projectiles filled with sulfur dioxide gas. The mayhem ended July 17, after hundreds of troops arrived from Pennsylvania to put down the riot. The government never declared martial law in the city, a decision Bernstein credits for sustaining the "legitimacy of Republican [Party] rule" not only in the city but also throughout the nation.[25]

As the New York riot played out, officials across the North feared that uprisings would break out in their districts. The most jittery were those whose states abutted New York. Local provost marshals sent a flurry of letters to their superiors asking for direction. From Washington, Colonel Fry's staff coolly told them to protect the records under their care at all costs. Some, such as the officer in Camden, New Jersey, whose protective detail had been sent to New York to help quell the riot, were told to have a staff member sleep in the office every night, make triplicates of the enrollment lists, and stash them in safe places as a precaution against theft or destruction. Devoted to administering the draft and providing the army with men, Fry seemed to regard his men's paperwork as more important than their lives.[26]

The officers, especially those in the East, had good reason to worry both about their records and about their lives in the days after the New York riot. In Boston, the cradle of abolitionism, Irish immigrants bitter about the Emancipation Proclamation launched a riot July 14. The fracas began when a provost marshal got into an argument with a woman at her North End home and arrested her. Her screams drew a crowd, and the mob assaulted the officer. The governor called in three companies of troops to quell the crowd, which was full of women and boys. The soldiers fired a cannon on a crowd trying to break into the Cooper Street armory, killing several people. The insurrection ended that same day, thanks mostly to the highly visible deployment of soldiers, but not before several people were killed by cannon fire as they tried to break into the Cooper Street armory.[27] In Fairfield, Connecticut, a group of men celebrated the riots in New York on its first day and then launched a rebellion of their own. A woman wrote her husband that the crowd was made up mostly of Irish men and boys who cheered for Davis and shot at the yards of Republicans. Riots also struck Portsmouth, New Hampshire; Rutland, Vermont; Wooster, Ohio; and Troy, New York. Violent resistance to the draft became so common that July that the nation seemed to be on the brink of revolution behind the lines. General John Geary could hardly believe what was happening. "Sometimes I think either I am crazy, or else a great many people are," he wrote. "There seems so little patriotism among the people at home, the country appears scarcely worth preserving, but on this subject I will say nothing for the people will think I am a fool."[28]

The turmoil in the North was so intense that it caught the attention of influential men abroad. Richard Cobden, a former member of Parliament, wrote his old friend Charles Sumner that the greatest danger facing the North that summer was not the Confederates but the Union's own politicians, especially the Copperheads. Cobden said he would not be surprised if the politicians tried to compromise with the South to take it back, slavery and all. Such an event would "cover with shame the partisans of the North throughout the world," Cobden said, "and justify the opponents of the war everywhere." Worse still, "it would leave the question to be settled by a similar process of blood by another generation."[29]

It hardly seemed as if the chaos in the North could get worse, but it did. At the same time that the riots gripped New York, the Confederate cavalry raider John Hunt Morgan carved a path through Indiana and Ohio, terrifying the residents of those states. In some neighborhoods, Morgan's actions were so specifically targeted that locals could only surmise that their Copperhead neighbors had briefed his men. From Georgetown, in southern Ohio, Margaret White Taylor wrote her husband that most of the men cleared out of the area when they heard Morgan was on the way, leaving only women and a few Southern sympathizers who could not defend the town. The raiders sacked stores and stables and

> took just what they wanted. . . . When they went to Levi Jacobs store he threw open the door and said "walk in gentlemen and help yourselves." One of the fellows asked him his politics. He said a butternut. They bowed and said they wanted nothing of him. They asked which were the abolition stores, and one of our citizens took it upon himself to show them.

The anonymous citizen apparently was not the only local to help Morgan. The raiders said two of the locals stayed in camp with them, presumably to fill them in on the area, and Taylor thought several other local men were following Morgan's troops to provide them with information. Witnesses in other areas said Morgan had no use or respect for Copperheads. In New Pennington, Indiana, his men kidnapped a merchant after ransacking the man's store and carried him about five miles away. When they found out he was a Butternut they put him on an old horse and sent him home, reportedly telling him that "they did not want any such cowardly villains that was a traitor to their country." In still other parts of the West through which Morgan passed, the threat of Confederate raiders had an entirely unexpected effect given the strains of the previous two years: It brought neighbors together.[30]

Morgan and several of his men were captured July 26 near Lisbon, Ohio, Vallandigham's birthplace. He was sent to the state penitentiary in Columbus. (Morgan's imprisonment proved to be short. He and a number of his men dug their way out on November 27.) The effects of his July rampage through Kentucky, Indiana, and Ohio were felt for some time. At least ten Cincinnati residents, men and women, were tried on charges of helping Morgan in his raid and of freeing prisoners from military custody. They also were accused of conspiring to spring three hundred prisoners, Morgan included, from the penitentiary. None of the defendants was convicted. Despite the damage Morgan inflicted and the fear he inspired, his raids generated little sympathy among the soldiers for the civilians who had been in his path. "Im not sorry that something has occured to wake up the people a little. it may tend to convert a few Coperheads," a member of the 57th Indiana wrote.[31]

By the end of July, most of the violence at home had played itself out, but small local skirmishes continued to erupt. In a bizarre episode in Clark County, Ohio, a female Peace Democrat was rushed at church by four or five other women. Her crime: wearing a butternut pin, which the women tried to remove. The unnamed victim "heroically defended herself . . . and came out of the conflict sustaining no injury, except that some of the ribbons were torn from her bonnet," the local paper reported.[32]

The riots in New York made a deep impression. Unionists became even more suspicious about Peace Democrats and their activities. Federal officials were so concerned about Congressman Daniel Voorhees of Indiana, a lieutenant of Vallandigham's, that they had a secret agent working on a case against him. The provost marshal in Terre Haute, Captain R. W. Thompson, worried that his superiors were preparing to arrest the congressman. Although Voorhees's speeches were "of a most objectionable character," Thompson did not think the government could prove that Voorhees had suggested outright that his followers resist the draft. Moreover, Thompson believed that Voorhees and his followers were "doing more good than harm to the Union cause" by splitting their own party and driving propertied men into the arms of the Republicans. Thompson feared that if Voorhees were arrested, it would unify the Copperheads and violence would ensue. This was a particular concern in Sullivan County and part of Green County, where Unionists were "so far in the minority that they would be completely at the mercy of this class, & many of them even now are in danger. It would be cruel to have them further exposed." Thompson urged his superiors to leave Copperhead leaders alone and concentrate on arresting draft resisters instead.[33]

One notable disturbance remained, and it took place in a town where Lincoln and Stephen A. Douglas had held one of their famous debates in 1858. During the riot-filled summer of 1863, Coles County, Illinois, was bitterly divided. The western part of the county, anchored by the town of Mattoon, was Republican; in the eastern portion, the heavily Democratic Charleston, where Lincoln and Douglas squared off, was the leading community. The political divisions in Coles County ran deep and took on a personal dimension. Democrats who visited Mattoon in the summer of 1863 were "continually assaulted, mobbed, and stigmatized as copperheads, secessionists, & c.," the Copperhead *Chicago Times* reported. On August 1, Democrats decided to make a statement by descending on Mattoon. Thousands of armed men joined in a procession three miles long. A pair of Democratic congressmen, John Rice Eden—who, earlier in the war, privately expressed his fear that the administration's "miserable policy . . . will end in the total ruin of the country"—and James Carroll Robinson, urged members of the crowd to protect their liberty "at all hazards, even to the bitter end," according to the *Times* account. Democrats, the newspaper said, were prepared to defend their rights "forcibly with the cartridge-box. . . . [W]hen all peaceful means fail, the democracy are ready and armed to maintain those rights as their fathers won them." Robinson and other party leaders continued to stir Democratic sentiments the next month, accusing the government of plotting to keep Democrats from voting. Their duty, Robinson told a rally, was to resist and to *"wade through blood knee deep* to the ballot box" if they had to. The *Shelby County Leader* warned that if the people decided that the government was operating in a way that would destroy the foundations on which it was created, "there will remain that INALIENABLE RIGHT OF REVOLUTION." Republicans responded with this ditty: "Butternut Britches and Hickory Poles, Democrats, Democrats, Damn their souls."[34]

Tensions were still high in the area when the 54th Illinois received a leave early in 1864 as a bonus for reenlisting. The regiment's presence—in fact, the part its men played in starting the riot—made the Illinois uprising different from those that had taken place in the East the previous summer. The furloughed soldiers in Mattoon entertained themselves that winter by forcing Democrats, including a local judge, to their knees to take an oath of allegiance. Once again, the *Chicago Times* urged Democrats to protect themselves, even to resort to lynch law. Its advice was "REPRISAL—RETALIATION IN KIND—for every outrage. Only by following this advice will the law of the land be re-established." If Democrats did not fight back, their party would quickly be annihilated, the paper warned. In early March soldiers on leave severely beat two Democrats in Charleston, and on March 26 they attacked and disarmed two other Democrats.[35]

March 28 was court day in Charleston. Congressman Eden was in town, as were Charles Henry Constable, the judge who had been humiliated in the streets of Mattoon, and Democratic sheriff John Hardwicke

O'Hair. Democrats from Coles and Edgar counties had met secretly before court day to determine how to defend their rights. "By God," one man swore, "we have taken all we are going to take from the soldiers." They rumbled into town March 28 with weapons stashed in the hay or among the other goods they had loaded on their wagons. Other conspirators had pistols tucked into their coats or pockets. Warned of the possibility of violence, Eden canceled the speech he was scheduled to give and worked his way around the courthouse square urging men to go home before it was too late. His efforts were of no use. Exactly what happened is unclear, but something took place between a young Democrat and a soldier, and shots quickly were exchanged between them. Within moments, the firing in the square was so intense that the bullets took the bark right off the trees around the courthouse. Among those shooting at the boys in blue was Sheriff O'Hair, who also had helped plan the ambush. For two hours, soldiers and area Republicans shot and slugged it out with the conservatives. Finally reinforcements arrived from Mattoon and the riot was over. Six soldiers, two Copperheads, and a Republican were dead. Fifteen suspects were sent to Fort Delaware, near Philadelphia, where they spent seven months in prison without trial.[36]

In what had become a standard response to violent episodes, the Copperhead press refused to hold Peace Democrats responsible for the uprising. To the contrary, the *Chicago Times* wrote, riot was "the natural and inevitable fruit of the lawlessness of abolitionism and for whatever comes of it abolitionism will be responsible." The paper called for a general crackdown on soldiers' "lawlessness." It also believed that the revolt might have been good for the country by showing abolitionists that they could carry their "atrocities" just so far. Moreover, the uprising was a warning to military commanders that they should not turn their soldiers loose among a population of "quiet, peaceful, and unoffending people."[37]

That last major riot remained in the future, though. At the moment, in the summer of 1863, loyalists remained agog at the growing influence of the Copperheads. This was nowhere more true than in the ranks. A private in the 83rd Ohio spoke for many of his companions when he wrote a letter home reflecting on all the hardships he and his friends had undergone and expected to go through in the future. "I can willingly do it all, if we can but conquer the Rebels. And when we are enduring all this, to see men at home living in style opposing us with all their might—it creates a feeling within our breast which, if we were permitted to execute, would not be good for their general health." This interest in doing grave physical harm to the conservatives, either now or once the war was over, was one widely shared among the bluecoats.[38]

Lincoln rarely responded to Copperhead attacks, but he made an exception in late August, when he sent a speech to an old friend to be read at a gathering in Springfield. This was a full defense of his policies, written with the logic of a successful lawyer and the occasional soaring rhetoric that signaled Lincoln was appealing not only to the Springfield crowd but to the nation at large. He began by confronting his critics directly. "You desire peace; and you blame me that we do not have it." As he saw it, the nation could achieve peace three ways. The first was by suppressing the rebellion. This seemed obvious. The second was to "give up the Union." This, too, was obvious, and Lincoln opposed this choice. "Are you for it? If you are, you should say so plainly," he said. The third alternative was compromise, and Lincoln did not see any deal that would reunite the nation as being possible at this point. The Confederate leadership had signaled no interest in coming to terms, and "all charges and insinuations to the contrary, are deceptive and groundless," the president said. The only real choice, then, if one sincerely wanted to save the Union, was to keep fighting. Then Lincoln turned to the Emancipation Proclamation, whose constitutionality had been vociferously challenged. He dismissed such arguments, citing his powers as commander in chief. Besides, "slaves are property. Is there—has there ever been—any question that by the law of war, property . . . may be taken when needed? And is it not needed whenever taking it, helps us, or hurts the enemy?" Some commanders—men who were no friends of abolitionism, incidentally—had told him that emancipation was the greatest blow the Union had dealt the rebels to date. Then Lincoln subtly challenged the Copperheads' manhood. "You say you will not fight to free negroes. Some of them seem willing to fight for you; but, no matter." Go ahead and fight for the Union, he urged the Copperheads; once the Union had been saved, they could refuse to fight for emancipation. History would always be on the side of freedom, though, and peace men would live to regret their actions, he suggested. "There will be some black men who can remember that, with silent tongue, and clenched teeth, and steady eye, and well-poised bayonet, they have helped mankind on to this great consummation, while, I fear, there will be some white ones, unable to forget that, with malignant heart, and deceitful speech, they strove to hinder it." These remarks, powerful though they were, did not dent the opposition in the slightest.[39]

The chaos behind the Union lines was irresistible to Confederates and their sympathizers in the North, and plans to take advantage of the upheaval started to appear on Jefferson Davis's desk in the fall of 1863. George P. Kane, the former police marshal in Baltimore, informed Davis from Montreal that he was planning an expedition to capture the ports of Milwaukee, Chicago, and Detroit. His aim was to destroy all the shipping, thereby paralyzing the lake commerce and spurring peace sentiment in Wisconsin, Michigan, Illinois, and Iowa. He suggested that Davis and his generals plan simultaneous raids on Erie, Pennsylvania, and on Buffalo, New York, which he also thought should be burned. Then he asked for money and veteran officers to carry out the scheme. Kane also proposed rescuing Confederate prisoners held at Johnson's Island in Sandusky Bay, Ohio, the only part of the proposal that he actually moved forward on. His attempt failed after one of his followers ratted out the mission. Other plots to free prisoners swirled through the upper levels of the Confederate government, but Kane's proposal progressed further than most.[40]

Unaware of these plans but keenly aware of the implications of home-front strife, Northerners at home and in the field started asking pointed questions about loyalty. The Union could "smash the Confederacy all to atoms in a very short time" if its men would only do the right thing and pitch in, Private Wilbur Fisk of the 2nd Vermont wrote in his home-town newspaper. Instead, the country had to resort to conscription, which produced draftees who "are more trouble to us than they are worth." Their "courage consists chiefly in daring to desert," Fisk wrote, while Confederates "shame us" with their "dogged perserverance."[41]

Accusations of disloyalty did not come from soldiers alone. A man backing Vallandigham's opponent in Ohio told his cousin, a Vallandigham partisan, that there was a "special part of [hell] fitted out for just such men as you are." From Nebraska, J. D. Morton wrote his son: "This is the last time I shall mention the subject of politics war or our country to you either in writing or conversation, without *you* request it." He was not happy with his boy, who he thought had been so blinded by Republicans that his allegiance to the nation was in doubt. "I think . . . that you are like Ephraim of old joined to your *Idol* and that Idol is party which overrides all love of country & gives the party the whole party & nothing but the party!"[42]

With elections approaching, by early fall 1863 the political realm rather than the streets once again became the principal venue for registering discontent. In Ohio, home of the most widely followed race of the season—Clement Vallandigham's bid for governor—Peace Democrats hoped to use widespread dissatisfaction with the war as a way to persuade people that the time for a negotiated peace had arrived. Their approach looked especially promising after the Union defeat at

Chickamauga, Georgia, in September, a loss that even the commander on the field characterized as a "severe disaster."[43] Running from his personal Elba of Windsor, Ontario, Vallandigham was a deeply divisive figure, even among Ohio Democrats. But after Burnside had turned him into the nation's most famous political martyr, he was irresistible to partisan loyalists. "No one felt like organizing a movement against an exile & a victim," Congressman Samuel S. Cox explained. Vallandigham was certain that if the Democrats got into power, the South would rejoin the Union. He held this belief with an almost religious fervor and despite considerable evidence to the contrary. As Vallandigham laid out his plans for putting the Union back together, he thought the Democrats had to "restore the constitution & liberty to ourselves & put down radicalism. This is the key note to our policy," Vallandigham told *New York World* editor Manton Marble, who was a War Democrat at the time. Pressing the war was not an option in Vallandigham's view. "Be silent, if you please, as to the war," he told Marble, "but, for God's sake, not more 'rigorous prosecution.' "[44]

Ohio Copperheads built their state campaign around national issues, arguing that the war was not about reunion but about abolition. They pointedly asked white men why they were dying for blacks. Such arguments resonated with a particular audience. One man wrote to his son, then serving in the 120th Ohio, that the "Abolition Party" did not like Vallandigham and would not approve of anyone who did not "fall down and worship a Nigger." He loved his country, he insisted, but "I want the union as it was and the Constitution as it is." The abolitionists, on the other hand, had no respect for the Constitution as far as he could tell. They wanted to draft a new document and abolish slavery, and those goals seemed to him to constitute the entire platform of the Republican Party.[45]

Ohio congressman Samuel S. Cox, a moderate among the Peace Democrats, said Buckeyes nominated the notorious Clement Vallandigham for governor because they saw him as a martyr. Cox later blamed Vallandigham, among others, for the loss of his own congressional seat. (*The Old Guard*/Courtesy of HarpWeek LLC)

Emancipation was the first item on a lengthy list of the conservatives' grievances. Other items included Lincoln's suspending habeas corpus and creating provost marshal's districts throughout the country, the imposition of military law on civilians such as Vallandigham, the creation of greenbacks and a mounting debt, the Enrollment Act, the suppression of the press and dispersal of public protests, African American troops, and confiscations of the property of people suspected of helping the Confederates. "Within two years we have all witnessed those things, and I have often been obliged to ask myself, 'What land do I live in?' " former postmaster general James Campbell told a group in Scranton, Pennsylvania. The former lieutenant governor of New York, clearly responding to Republican claims that Copperheads were traitors, told a Batavia audience that Democrats were defending the very foundations of the country. The experiment of free government "consists in determining whether a people will permanently abide by the laws of a written constitution. . . . It is when adversity comes upon us—when temptation allures or necessity exists, that restrictions in organic laws are in danger of being violated."[46]

Other issues surfaced as well. Antiwar men tried to resurrect the East-West divide, arguing that if the war continued, "the great monstrosity" that was New York City would so dominate the Union that "we will find ourselves . . . instead of freemen with personal rights, and free States with sovereign rights, stript of every last badge of self-government." The only solution to these outrages, one peace man after another said, was to stop the war. Immediately.[47]

The conservatives' use of wedge issues such as emancipation made some Northerners nervous. Rumors abounded that if Vallandigham won, Ohio would have its own civil war. The *Chicago Times* dismissed that as humbug. If violence were to stem from the election, it would be at the Republicans' initiation. The paper subtly equated Ohio's situation with the 1860 presidential race, the South's subsequent secession, and war, insisting, "The rebellion is simply an appeal from ballots to bullets." Unlike the Republicans, the *Times* said, Democrats knew how to deal with dissent lawfully; look at how long the nation had Democratic leaders and yet no war. Vallandigham, it said, "would demonstrate that a rebellion could be subdued without trespassing upon the constitutional rights of those who were obedient to law, or punishing by illegal and despotic action those who defies and insulted its authority."[48]

Democrats thought the soldier vote could tip the race in their favor, a belief that underscored how wildly out of touch they now were with the soldiers' sentiments. Most Ohio soldiers were embarrassed and outraged at Vallandigham and his seconds. They loathed the former congressman. He had not honored Major Robert Anderson for his stand at Fort Sumter, thanked the Yankees at Bull Run for their contributions, or supported a pay raise for soldiers in 1862. "Do you think the soldiers will vote for a man that they hate worse than the rebels?" one man wrote home. In a sentiment regularly expressed by the bluecoats, he added, "We know that just such men as Vallandingham is keeping up this war ... by keeping it up is causing all this misery." Soldiers filled the mails with bilious letters railing against the former congressman, equating a vote for him with one for the Confederates. Many of the federals threatened to come home and even the score with any of their old neighbors who cast ballots for Vallandigham. (Threats like this often were not idle; one discharged Hoosier, for instance, boasted that he had "cracked" two or three Butternuts since he had been home and expected to keep doing so "as long as there is any fools enough to acknowlage the same in my presents.")[49]

Democratic soldiers who remained loyal to their party paid for their fealty in the form of strained relationships with their comrades. One Ohio soldier warned that if any man in blue were caught voting for Vallandigham, he "would better be dead than living. The boys would cut him to pieces if they find out who does it." Many men bowed under the "damnable pressure" of their peers and either voted Republican or stayed out of the fray. Democrats faced an added difficulty in keeping abreast of their party's positions because they rarely received any Democratic literature. Commanders had banned treasonable pamphlets from circulating, and some officers took that directive to mean that no Democratic campaign materials or speakers whatsoever were welcome in the camps. This interpretation embittered some Democrats in the ranks. One complained to a former congressman that the abolitionists had fabricated all kinds of lies designed to "poison the minds of the soldier against their Democrat friends, calling them butter nuts, southern sympathisers, the enemy of the soldier." The Republicans were bent, he said, on "destroying and anihylating the power of the Democratic influence that is felt by them from the Democrats of the army."[50]

Vallandigham went down in flames in the October 13 election, losing by more than a hundred thousand votes. The soldier vote was so lopsided as to be almost laughable: 95 percent of the buckeyes in blue voted for John Brough. From Wisconsin, editor Brick Pomeroy consoled his fellow Democrats by saying, "They have found the ballot too weak for the strong arm of military power." Vallandigham remained a martyr for the cause, Pomeroy wrote, assuring his readers that "history will do him justice, for 'time at last sets all things even!' " In Pennsylvania, another Copperhead candidate for governor, George W. Woodward, lost—but in this race only by about fifteen thousand votes. Soldiers proved especially crucial in this latter contest by mobilizing in favor of the sitting governor, Andrew G. Curtin. They also had the assistance of War Democrats, who joined with the Republicans to push back against the Copperhead tide.[51]

The letters that soldiers wrote home may have played a more important role even than their votes in the Democrats' fall losses, and in this sense, too, soldier attitudes were starting to change. Given their experiences and sacrifices, some soldiers began to see themselves as better judges on political issues than civilians. "People at home have no idea of how well posted and how interested the solider is in the political questions of the day," an Indiana soldier wrote after the election. "My impression is that the majority of soldiers are much better qualified now to decide on political questions than they were at home." The people at home had reasons to vote against Vallandigham beyond the soldiers' hatred of him. The Union armies' successes over the summer and fall, high wheat prices, and a general sense of prosperity among the civilians all contributed to Vallandigham's trouncing. Nevertheless, the soldiers' growing sense of knowing what was best for the nation was an important change that was working its way through the army.[52]

Lincoln was deeply relieved at the election results, especially at Vallandigham's defeat, which he read as a referendum on the war. "Glory to God in the highest. Ohio has saved the Union," he telegraphed Governor David Tod. Lincoln's sentiments were shared by many in the North. A Washington resident thought the election results gave "new heart and energy" to Union men and, he hoped, "a death blow to traitors, north as well as south." One Buckeye thought Vallandigham's defeat so monumental as to be the turning point of the war. "The crisis of the Rebellion has passed," he said. "The Valindigham rebuke was the climax: public sentiment is coming into the preper chanel   there is no need of fear or doubt as to the conclusion of the trouble. it may require considerable time yet but the end must & will come by & by."[53]

Some Peace Democrats took the loss badly, fearing that now the war would last indefinitely. "There is no hope for a termination of the war until we have been much more severely punished *for our sins*," Charles Mason, the Iowa lawyer, wrote. Others regarded Vallandigham's defeat as nothing more than a minor setback. A Salem, Massachusetts, Democrat refused to believe the public had renounced Democratic principles, despite the election results. Vallandigham himself tilted toward this view, attributing his loss to unfortunate timing. "Honest & wise men would see that it is not anyman's opinions on the war, but the *season* that is against the Democracy. It is a bad year for us." In Boston, the *Pilot*, whose audience was Irish Catholics, wavered in its commitment to the conservative line. The Republic had to be preserved, it

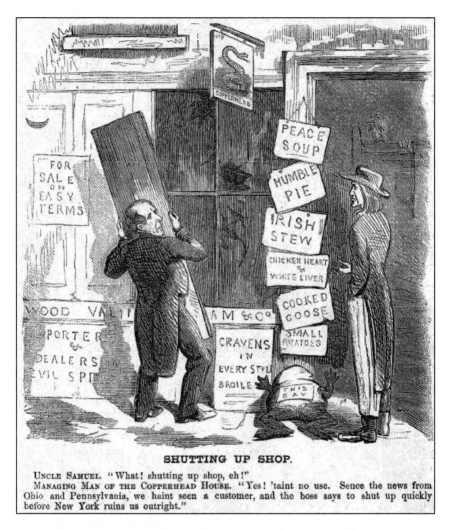

SHUTTING UP SHOP.

UNCLE SAMUEL. "What! shutting up shop, eh!"

MANAGING MAN OF THE COPPERHEAD HOUSE. "Yes! 'taint no use. Sence the news from Ohio and Pennsylvania, we haint seen a customer, and the boss says to shut up quickly before New York ruins us outright."

Some Republicans hoped that the humiliating losses that the Peace Democrats suffered in the 1863 elections would prompt them to close up business. The Copperheads saw their defeat as a temporary setback and looked ahead to fight another day. (*Harper's Weekly*/Courtesy of HarpWeek LLC)

editorialized, even if that meant crushing the South. "We are sorry to urge subjugation, but '*needs must*,' " the editors said, an opinion that sounded distinctly more like what one would expect from a War Democrat than from a committed Copperhead.[54]

Shortly after the elections, Lincoln went to Gettysburg to dedicate the national cemetery. Copperheads, still smarting from the elections, received his address with contempt. The *Chicago Times* wrote bitterly that "the cause for which the soldiers died was that the nation might 'have a new birth of freedom'; that the old government, and the old Union, and the old constitution, might die, and be supplanted by new ones." The editors thought Lincoln "did most foully traduce the motives of the men who were slain at Gettysburg. They gave their lives to maintain the old government, and the old constitution and Union." The *Times* of London, a steadfast critic of the president, wrote, "One is really tempted to think Mr. Lincoln cannot have been himself when he penned so grotesque a production." The comment circulated in the American press for months afterward.[55]

Although the fall elections put Lincoln in good stead politically, Confederates continued to scheme for ways to take advantage of divisions within the North. Senator Herschel V. Johnson of Georgia wrote a private letter to Jefferson Davis noting that more than a million votes were cast against the Republicans, with Democrats looking particularly strong in the Northwest. "Is this not evidence of a very strong hostility to Lincoln? It is true, I have no doubt, that they profess to be for the war and a restoration of the Union. But I am well satisfied, that if Lincoln could be defeated—or the candidate of his party—in the next presidential election, it would end the war and lead to peace." Johnson suggested that the Confederate government get a jump on the 1864 elections by posting a secret agent in Canada to encourage Northern conservatives and to help them organize more quickly and efficiently. The success of the Peace Democrats, he argued, would pave the way for a negotiated settlement to the war. The Confederate Congress agreed with Johnson and in January approved a $5 million appropriation for a secret service, $900,000 of which went to operations in Canada.[56]

Word of the Confederate venture in Canada quickly reached official ears in the North. The provost marshal's office in Detroit had particularly good information about plans that were hatching across the river, and the acting assistant provost marshal there regularly reported rumors of Confederate plans to attack from the north. Lieutenant Colonel B. H. Hill wrote on November 9, for instance, that rumors were circulating that the Southerners were targeting the gunboat *Michigan* along with Union prison camps at Chicago and Johnson's Island. Secret agents in Canada could draw on two thousand escaped prisoners, sympathizers, and refugees to man the action, Hill estimated. Other intelligence indicated that the rebels were fitting out a steamer in Canada to attack Johnson's Island, free the prisoners, and then move on Buffalo. Hill's reports, which proved to be accurate, set off a flurry of activity. Militia and active-duty troops moved to protect the most vulnerable parts of the northern border, and federal officials sent a series of warnings to governors, mayors, and Canadian officials. The quick response apparently foiled the plot, although the Confederates reportedly said they would only postpone the mission, not scrub it permanently. By November 16 all seemed quiet.[57]

In the West, the army got to work after the elections. In Tennessee, the Army of the Cumberland had been stalled since the fight in September at Chickamauga. Rosecrans was immobilized after that battle, and the situation was grim for the Union men. The troops, who were relying on a tenuous line for supplies, were going hungry. Lincoln grew impatient with the army's lack of movement and in mid-October put Grant at the head of all the armies between the Appalachian Mountains and the Mississippi River. One of Grant's first orders of business was to replace Rosecrans. Then he put together a plan to establish a more secure supply line. Those problems disposed of, Grant turned his attention to Chattanooga. He launched an attack November 24 and that day seized Lookout Mountain, which towers over the city from the southwest. The real drama came the next day, though, when the same men who had suffered such a humiliating defeat at Chickamauga stormed up Missionary Ridge on Chattanooga's eastern flank in an impromptu assault. Against all odds, the Yankees scoured the Southerners out of their trenches and drove them off the hill.

The battle helped end the year on a high note for Unionists, marking yet another change in attitude in the North. With winter upon them, many Northerners had time to reflect on the year's efforts and began to savor the meaning of their victories at Gettysburg, Vicksburg, and Chattanooga. Seward, the secretary of state, conveniently overlooked the strife of the summer when he wrote that the nation had enjoyed good spirits ever since Grant's victory at Vicksburg and Meade's at Gettysburg in July. There was no doubt that Northerners were again confident in the stability of the government, as Seward put it, and were upbeat about the prospects for the spring campaign. Even some hardened conservatives were optimistic—for them. "The ignorance and incompetency of scores of Generals have been redeemed by the heroism and glorious valor of private soldiers, who have always fought the best when fighting impossibilities," the *La Crosse Democrat* editorialized. Other Copperheads remained pessimistic. The *Chicago Times* dismissed any hope for peace by the Fourth of July as "delusive." Ever since the war's beginning, the public had been fed upbeat "pabulum" about the state of affairs. The war could be finished today "by the complete restoration of the Union and the honorable adjustment of our difficulties, had we men at the head of affairs who understand the position and are equal to its demands."[58]

Despite the happy returns in the fall elections and rising public confidence, Lincoln's political future remained uncertain. As 1864 opened,
disaffected Republicans talked publicly about putting up a different
candidate for the presidential election in November. Anger came mostly
from the Radical wing of the party, where abolitionists thought the
president had not done enough to help the slaves or to punish white
Southerners for leaving the Union. The two men who were the most
likely successors to Lincoln were Salmon Chase, the treasury secretary, and John C. Frémont, a general who had tried in vain to declare
emancipation in Missouri in 1861 and resigned in 1862. The main question was whom the abolitionists would support. They were divided.
Wendell Phillips favored Frémont, much to the consternation of William Lloyd Garrison, who worried that a split among abolitionists would
divide the Republican Party. Lincoln had problems, Garrison acknowledged, but he begged his followers to keep the big picture in mind.
"Incidental errors and blunders are easily borne with on the part of
him who, at one blow, severed the chains of three millions three hundred thousand slaves," he wrote. Phillips was unmoved. His American Anti-Slavery Society adopted a resolution saying its members saw
"no evidence" that Lincoln was working to guarantee the perpetual
freedom of African Americans.[59]

Of the two men challenging Lincoln early in the year, Chase was the
more aggressive. Upset by Lincoln's announcement in December 1863
that he would offer amnesty to Confederates who took an oath of loyalty to the Union, Chase's supporters—Radical Republicans—organized
and printed a vituperative pamphlet denouncing the administration.
Senator John Sherman, General William T. Sherman's brother, sent it
out to leading Republicans and newspapers of all political stripes. The
backlash against the pamphlet was immediate. Some of Sherman's
constituents in Ohio thought it was a Copperhead ploy. Others wrote
that it was unbefitting the senator to be involved in such a thing.
Sherman quickly backpedaled, lamely claiming that the material had
been mailed through his office either by mistake or some "fraudulent
design."[60]

As Sherman sought to distance himself from the controversial pamphlet, another circular appeared. Though it was not so nasty, the second pamphlet, like the first, observed that it was unlikely that Lincoln
would be reelected, especially if the Democrats had a strong nominee.
Both documents argued that Lincoln's tendency to compromise, along
with his "weak and vacillating" nature, could make the war last so
long that the national debt would "become a burden too great to be
borne." In a statement striking for its similarity to Copperhead allega-

tions, the Radicals' Pomeroy Circular, as the second publication was known, said that Lincoln could win only by manipulating the patronage system. Even to run for a second term was virtually un-American, it said, noting that no president had been reelected since Andrew Jackson. Chase, it concluded, had "more of the qualities needed in a President during the next four years than are to be found in any other candidate"—including the incumbent. The two pamphlets created a furor among Lincoln's many supporters, and Chase paid the price. Republican legislatures or conventions in fourteen states, along with the Republican National Committee, adopted resolutions in support of the president. Chase was finished as a candidate.[61]

Frémont's campaign started to unravel at the end of May, when a group of abolitionists convened in Cleveland to nominate him as a rump candidate. The convention lost all legitimacy when it was discovered that Democrats had infiltrated the group promoting Frémont. Nevertheless, his candidacy limped along until September, when he decided to withdraw. By that time, according to historian T. Harry Williams, Republicans began to realize that if Frémont continued, the party could be badly divided. Rather than carry on a hopeless campaign against Lincoln, Williams claimed, Frémont's supporters cut a deal with the president: remove Frémont's nemesis, Montgomery Blair, from the cabinet in exchange for Frémont's withdrawal.[62]

Another historian, Charles R. Wilson, has a different account. He argues that Frémont tried to withdraw in such a way as to favor the Democrats, but when George B. McClellan, the nominee, did not respond, Frémont simply withdrew. If there was a backroom bargain, it did not involve Frémont, who said bitterly that he considered the Lincoln administration "politically, militarily, and financially a failure." Williams's and Wilson's accounts share a single glaring shortcoming: Neither man considered what was happening on the battlefield. By early September, military victories had turned Lincoln into a political juggernaut. Frémont did not stand a chance against him. As long as the armies continued to win, Lincoln was invincible.[63]

That was far in the future, though. For the moment, Democrats chortled at the Republicans' infighting. Some of them were so certain that Lincoln would not be nominated for a second term that they began planning their strategy on the assumption that they would face a candidate other than Lincoln come the fall. One proposal, advanced by Congressman James E. English, was not to "agitate the negro question any more" and risk having the Democrats be viewed as proslavery. The suggestion made little headway. Democrats were becoming so confident of their chances in the fall that the *Chicago Times* had to remind its readers that the Republicans were likely to pull themselves together because they had too much to lose in the way of power and patronage to allow the party to rend itself asunder. The paper's one consolation was that it hoped voters were paying attention to what Republicans said about each other and taking it to heart as the truth.[64]

While the presidential drama played out, sporadic violence erupted in parts of the heartland. Over the winter of 1864, mobs, often spearheaded by soldiers on leave, sacked the offices of half a dozen newspapers in the West. Among the targets was the *Dayton Daily Empire*, which the exiled Clement Vallandigham had once owned. Violence was not limited to furloughed soldiers, though. In Monroe Township, Indiana, Copperheads surrounded the home of a woman who—on their dare— had snatched a butternut pin off the chest of one of them and refused to give it back. After considerable negotiations, she sent a child out bearing part of the pin, and the standoff was over. Tensions did not always result in violence. Sometimes hard feelings were enough. When a man in Williamson, New York, died, a townswoman commented with relief, "That makes one less *copperhead*."[65]

Lest the Lincoln administration grow too quiescent vis-à-vis Confederate scheming, reports continued to flood in from Detroit all winter about rebel and Copperhead plotting across the river in Windsor. Detroit was a target for the torch. Bands of men were preparing to burn steamships at Cincinnati, Pittsburgh, St. Louis, Louisville, and New Orleans. A lieutenant colonel reported that Democrats in Detroit regularly crossed the river to Windsor to visit Vallandigham and other Copperheads.[66] At least part of the intelligence was correct. A small group of Democrats traveled to Canada in February to ask Vallandigham to help them form a mutual protection society and a political counterweight to the Republican-sponsored Union Leagues. Vallandigham agreed to become the supreme commander of the new group, the Sons of Liberty. Frank Klement, the historian who delved deeply into this and other secret societies spawned by the war, concluded that the Sons were nothing more than a paper tiger. Vallandigham never convened a meeting or issued a directive, Klement pointed out. In a thoughtful and well-researched piece, however, Robert Churchill convincingly argues that both the Sons of Liberty and the danger they posed were real. The founder, Indianapolis printer Harrison H. Dodd, had elaborate plans to take over arsenals, free rebel prisoners, and lead Indiana, Illinois, Kentucky, and Missouri out of the Union. Dodd accepted money from the Confederate government in exchange for a promise to cooperate with the Southern army and spring Southern prisoners of war.[67]

It was not a real challenge for Dodd to organize the Sons of Liberty. Many communities had secret mutual protection groups that Democrats had formed earlier in response to military arrests and the draft. Five thousand members strong, they were not the benign groups that Klement insisted they were. Instead, they were well-organized cells that could, and did, gather on short notice. In Sullivan County, Indiana, they passed resolutions vowing to "resist the draft, by force of arms, if necessary, because they were not willing to submit to the government. They decided that the conscript law was unconstitutional and they would not obey it," according to a witness's statement. "In order to prevent the draft they resolved to prevent the enrollment of the townships of that county, even to the extent of taking the lives of enrolling officers, if they could accomplish it no other way." More moderate members of the Sons of Liberty were prominent Democrats who probably did not know of Dodd's larger scheme but had their own plots working. Worried that the Lincoln administration would somehow monkey with the November election, they were girding for a military response to such an event if it came to pass.[68]

Dodd's was only one of many conspiracies that attracted the attention of federal officials. In Columbus, *Crisis* editor Samuel Medary and eight other Peace Democrats were believed to have a plan for springing Confederate prisoners from Camp Chase and the Ohio Penitentiary in Columbus and from McLean Barracks in Cincinnati. Medary, a former territorial governor of Minnesota and later Kansas, was indicted and arrested for his alleged role in May 1864 and charged with conspiracy against the Union. He died before he could stand trial. Charges against the others were dismissed for lack of evidence in 1866. Whether there was truth to the allegation or whether Union authorities were trying to intimidate Medary into silence is impossible to say.[69]

In the House of Representatives, conservative congressmen continued to rail against the administration. In March, Daniel Voorhees of Indiana announced that he was witness to "the melancholy spectacle" of watching "a free government die." When they assumed office in 1861, Republicans had no interest in maintaining the peace, he said. Instead, "they invoked the storm which has since rained blood upon the land. They courted the whirlwind which has prostrated the progress of a century in ruins." Then Voorhees really let loose. "They danced with hellish glee around the bubbling cauldron of civil war and welcomed with ferocious joy every hurtful mischief which flickered in its lurid and infernal flames."[70]

Amid the steady drip of treason allegations, this kind of talk was eroding the reputation of the Democratic Party. Then Ohio Democrat Alexander Long opened the floodgates. On the House floor, he announced that the Emancipation Proclamation, confiscation, and other administration programs had crushed any possibility for the country to be reunited. "The Union is lost, never to be restored . . . and I now believe that there are but two alternatives, and they are either an acknowledgment of the independence of the South as an independent nation, or their complete subjugation and extermination as a people; and of these alternatives I prefer the former." Republicans tried to have Long expelled for his blasphemy but had to settle for a vote of censure instead.[71]

War Democrats were nearly as uncomfortable with Long's message as the Republicans were—and more tainted by it because of their party affiliation. War Democrats had been moving away from the peace men for some time, but talk like this was driving a wedge deep into the Democratic Party. The distrust was not solely—indeed, not even primarily—on the part of the war men. Many of the nation's leading Copperheads had no love for or confidence in War Democrats and were not shy about saying so. "When I contemplate, the cowardice, treachery, and duplicity of many of our leading and prominent men, professing to be democrats, Yet, acting with, and apologizing for the infamous wrongs of the Republican party, I almost despair of the Republic, and the Capacity of the people for free Govt," an Ohioan wrote Vallandigham. Charles Mason, the West Point–educated Iowa attorney, saw little hope in

Ohio representative Alexander Long set off a political firestorm when he said it was time to recognize the Confederacy as an independent nation. The House censured him for his position. (*The Old Guard*/Courtesy of HarpWeek LLC)

following normal political channels to achieve Democratic goals. "It makes me sick at heart to see the high handed measures of those in power. It is now almost certain that we must submit or resort to violent remedies."[72]

The divisions forming in the party were very upsetting to the party stalwarts, the men whose primary interest was in regaining power. Although he often shaded into Copperhead talk by this time, *World* editor Manton Marble did not entirely embrace the cause. The reasons were pragmatic. Any man who ran on a peace platform, including

McClellan, "is doomed to an utter rout at the polls. There ends all hope of Union & of the old form & spirit of Govt." Marble and others like him had an alternative and more politically viable plan: run the strongest candidate for the post, win the presidency, and then put measures into place that would bring about an immediate peace.[73]

The cracks within the party extended from the parlors of the elites in New York and Washington to the sitting rooms of the rank and file in Illinois and Wisconsin. Soldiers were writing increasingly vituperative letters home about the Democrats in general and the Copperheads in particular. The Yankees had come to regard peace men as cowards who were content to stay home and throw rocks at the government and the cause.

Family members who had different politics from those of their soldier boys felt their wrath. John Herr, an enlisted man in the 94th Ohio, was furious with his sister when she started dating Butternuts. He would rather be dead than hear such news, he told her, and then accused her of caring more for her friends than her brothers in the service. His mother bore the real force of his anger, though, after she wrote what he thought to be treasonable sentiments. "I am no respecters of persons when I talk about butternuts. . . . I shall never want to see any of my relations that worked against me while I was in the surves. . . . When I study over it makes my blood run cold to think that all the relations I have are working against my interest and their own." He reminded his mother that she had left Germany to get out from under a despotic government, but said it now seemed that she was dissatisfied with a free government. "You would better go back to germina again and live there we are fighting to maintain our wrights that our fourfathers fought bled and died for and the butternuts are working all they can to destroy them," he concluded.[74]

The hatred evident in the soldiers' commentary sometimes surprised family members, especially those who were Democrats and had believed their sons or brothers to be loyal partisans as well. "I rather think you have changed very much in your Politics since you went to the war judging from your last letter you wrote," John Glenn's brother wrote. John used to be virulently opposed to the Republicans and verbally attacked them at every political meeting he attended, William Glenn recalled. Now he was cutting off family members whom he believed to be Peace Democrats. John Glenn even hoped to vote for Lincoln, a turn that astonished and disappointed his brother, who nevertheless stressed to John that he was no Copperhead.[75]

Despite the threats from within his own party and the upheaval behind the lines, Lincoln's focus remained on the military situation. He decided to move Grant to the East in March 1864, making him general in chief of all the armies and granting him the rank of lieutenant general, a level only George Washington had reached before. Unionists were delighted. "The Administration has got the right man in the right place now. *Mark my words when Grant moves the Army of the Potomac he will whip the Rebels and down goes the Rebellion,*" an Illinois man wrote. Eastern soldiers were particularly impressed with their new commander, who "appears to be winning golden opinion for his modesty and unpretentious demeanor," according to the *New York Herald*. Administration critics were similarly optimistic. "The country, under these circumstances, is full of hopeful anxiety. . . . Failure is possible; but

GRANT TURNING LEE'S FLANK.

Certain that this meant the end of the war, Northerners were delighted in spring 1864 when U. S. Grant moved east to take command of all the armies. They turned against the tenacious general when horrible losses seemed to yield no results. (*Harper's Weekly*/Courtesy of HarpWeek LLC)

success and triumphant victory are among the strong possibilities," the *Boston Pilot* observed. Even Major Henry Abbott of the 20th Massachusetts, who rarely approved of the administration's decisions, endorsed Grant's promotion. "I feel pretty sure we shall be victorious at last," he wrote his mother. Grant probably was not a genius, he said, "but still if he has only as much shrewdness & character as he is supposed to have, with the immense resources which he can command, I feel that it is pretty safe."[76]

Grant and Lincoln forged a strong partnership, in large part because Grant understood what Lincoln wanted and was willing to execute it. That Grant had "unlimited power," thanks to the president, was obvious even to soldiers on the line. That Grant had "shrewdness enough" to see what needed to be done was a pleasant surprise. What the president had asked his generals for repeatedly over the past two years was to pursue the Confederate armies rather than Confederate strongholds such as Richmond. Grant's predecessors ignored Lincoln's strategy, but Grant shared the vision and acted quickly on it. "Lee's army will be your objective point. Wherever Lee goes, there you will go also," the general instructed Meade.[77]

Grant's promotion notwithstanding, it appeared to some Northerners as though the army was doing nothing in the early spring of 1864. Massachusetts resident William Gray Brooks, a solid supporter of the Lincoln administration, confided to his diary: "The state of the country looks gloomy. A time of depression. The rebels seem so determined not to be conquered or give up." But the Army of the Potomac was recharged by its new commander, fresh from his successes in the West. "Never in a war before did the rank and file feel a more resolute earnestness for a just cause, and a more invincible determination to succeed, than in this war; and what the rank and file are determined to do everybody knows will be done," a veteran from Vermont wrote. The time had come to destroy the Confederacy and its peculiar institution. "We have as a nation yielded to their rapacious demands times enough."[78]

Many Northerners thought this would be the last wartime spring, but this was not a nation united. Northern neighbors were pitted against each other, and soldiers were pitted against civilians. Unionists' fears of conspiracy were more elaborate—and, they now believed, well founded—than ever before. Rather than concentrating on the upheaval that had taken place in the year since the Enrollment Act passed, however, most loyalists chose to build on the victories at Gettysburg and Vicksburg and look forward to imminent victory. In their optimistic frame of mind, they overlooked the strife within the Republican Party. Lincoln was their man, and they, like the soldiers, moved into the fighting season with high morale and confidence in their leaders.

5

The Summer of Lincoln's Discontent

LINCOLN SAILED INTO MAY 1864 in reasonably good shape politically. In the heartland, where conservative Democrats enjoyed the greatest support, people seemed frustratingly content with the state of the nation, or so the Peace Democrats thought. "Feel very sadly   People do not seem as bitter as I expected to find them but still there is enough of political rancour manifest," attorney Charles Mason wrote upon returning to Iowa from Washington. But May proved to be yet another turning point in the fortunes of Lincoln and the Copperheads. The machinations to replace Lincoln with Chase and the violence in Charleston, Illinois, were harbingers of trials to come. Lincoln's most difficult months lay ahead of him, and the reason was the usual one: the failures of the Union armies.[1]

Northerners who thought they had seen the worst the Army of the Potomac had to offer with Fredericksburg and the mud march faced a new series of losses that cost a staggering number of lives. Predictably, more men sought ways to evade the draft or to desert once they were mustered in. As spring turned to summer, tempers rose with the temperatures. With a new call for men and veterans returning from the front, violence once again plagued many communities around the North. Losing armies meant declining civilian morale, and low spirits for the public meant high hopes for the Copperheads. Leading Peace Democrats were more vocal than ever in their calls for an end to the war, and they enjoyed widespread and increasing support of their efforts. Even leading Republicans, fearful of a tremendous beating at the polls in November, begged Lincoln to find a way to make peace.

The military situation was the catalyst that plunged the public mood from cautious optimism in the spring to abject despair in the summer of 1864. Grant had long enjoyed the full support of the president. Since arriving in the East in March, Grant had set about executing a strategy that Lincoln had been imploring his generals in the East for three years to follow: Forget about Richmond as a target and pursue the rebel army instead. Grant's plan was to use all the Northern armies in tandem to pin down the rebel forces and then demolish them. He sketched out his design to his generals in early April. His orders to Meade were clear, concise, and lethal: Chase Lee's army and crush it. Borrowing a phrase from the president, Grant wrote that the armies not directly involved in skinning "can hold a leg."[2]

Grant's plan quickly ran into what the German military theoretician Carl von Clausewitz called the "friction" of war—"the force that makes the apparently easy so difficult"—and what looked like a good plan on paper rapidly began to go awry under the real-life pressures of execution. In the trans-Mississippi West, Nathaniel Banks made the first move in mid-March and headed toward Shreveport, which he envisioned as a jumping-off point for sending troops into Texas. It was a fool's errand. After losing a battle forty miles outside Shreveport, the Yankees retreated back to New Orleans, arriving there too late in the spring to make a move on Mobile—an important element of Grant's master plan. Banks was removed from command and reassigned to his old job as military administrator of Louisiana. The Army of the Gulf spent most of the summer lolling around New Orleans.[3]

Sherman's army fared somewhat better as it moved from Chattanooga toward Atlanta. Sherman's practice in this campaign was to slip around the Confederates again and again, avoiding any direct confrontation that would cost the lives of thousands of men. At least that was his strategy until he reached Kennesaw Mountain, Georgia, on June 27. The battle there was the old story about the dangers of a frontal assault and its ugly consequences. Sherman took about three thousand casualties in the June 27 fight but kept moving south. "War," one of his officers wrote home, "is simply assassination." By July 10, Sherman was at Peachtree Creek on the outskirts of Atlanta. At that point Jefferson Davis intervened and yanked Joseph E. Johnston from command, replacing him with the one-armed, one-legged Texan, John B. Hood. Hood attacked Sherman on July 20, and their armies spent much of the next eight days fighting for control of the city. Sherman could not force Hood out of town, nor could he cut the Confederate's supply lines, so he chose to shell the city while he settled into a siege and waited for an opening. A promising campaign appeared to have ended in an embarrassing stalemate for the Yankees.[4]

If the events in the West were humiliating, those in the East were nothing short of disastrous. Franz Sigel was run out of New Market, Virginia, on May 15 by a group of Confederates that included 247 cadets from the Virginia Military Institute. The loss cost General Sigel his job. Farther south, Benjamin Butler moved too slowly up the James River to take the barely protected Richmond. Instead, his dawdling gave an inferior force an opening to trounce him May 16 at Drewry's Bluff. More than 4,100 Union soldiers were killed, wounded, or captured in the debacle. Grant's idea of coordinating the movements of all the Northern armies was starting to look like yet another dud for the federal war effort, and morale at home waned correspondingly. "What is all this for?" a Washington, D.C., man asked in a letter. "Is Richmond worth the heccatombs whose blood Deluge it? Wats this for to free a degraded race who are already threatening to take the country. Who are so puffed up by those Abolitionists as to imagine the Country already belongs to them."[5]

Butler's and Sigel's losses left the burden of winning the Eastern theater to Grant, and he demonstrated what his dogged plan could achieve in the hands of a competent general. His first opportunity came May 5 when Lee surprised him in the Wilderness a few miles west of Chancellorsville. The Wilderness was well named. Its dense thicket of trees and brush made fighting exceedingly difficult and even more dangerous than battle usually was. Soldiers had a hard time seeing through the tangle—not to mention the gun smoke—and wound up shooting at their comrades. Regiments stumbled the wrong way through the woods. Confusion reigned. And then the true horror of this battle developed. Bullets and shells set the underbrush ablaze, and hundreds of screaming, wounded men perished in the flames. The nightmarish contest looked like a loss for Grant, who took more than seventeen thousand casualties. A brigadier general hustled up to Grant and informed him that he knew from past experience what Lee would do, which was to "cut us off completely from our communications." Exasperated by the defeatist mindset of the Army of the Potomac's officers, Grant snapped: "I am heartily tired of hearing what Lee is going to do. . . . Go back to your command, and try to think what we are going to do ourselves, instead of what Lee is going to do." Rather than accept defeat and retreat as previous commanders had, Grant—"the pitiless little man," as one historian called him—pressed on after Lee.[6]

This was the first sign that a new day had dawned over the Army of the Potomac. In the past, commanders had withdrawn after a defeat.

Grant simply kept pushing south. Two days after the Wilderness, he caught up with the rebels at Spotsylvania, and another grisly battle followed over the next week and a half. This time, the Confederates made a serious mistake. Thinking that Grant was gone, they pulled their artillery from an area called the "mule shoe," named for the U-shaped trench that exposed Southern troops not only from the front but from the sides as well. It was a mistake; the federals had not pulled back. The next day, May 12, the federals slammed into the salient. The eighteen hours that followed featured some of the hardest and goriest fighting of the war, with gruesome hand-to-hand combat in the trenches and on the parapet. The area came to be known as "the bloody angle" for the clubbing and bayoneting that took place there. The Federals took about 6,800 casualties to the rebels' 5,000.[7]

The *Chicago Times* declared this bloodbath a great victory and said the Union should leverage it by suing for peace on the terms of the Crittenden Plan. This move "would not be more magnanimous than politic," it insisted. If the Confederates rejected the offer, the North would have lost nothing, and the option remained open to change the terms of the offer. The newspaper challenged self-proclaimed Unionists to take the plan seriously, asking, "Do you want the Union restored, gentlemen?" If Northerners did not accept the terms Crittenden proposed in 1861, the editors could only conclude they were not Unionists but "Garrison and Whiting Unionists"—abolitionists—whose "'loyalty' is not to the Union but to the theories of these men."[8]

Undeterred by the savagery at Spotsylvania, Grant continued to push south. He wanted to get between Lee and Richmond, but Lee had the advantage of interior lines—that is, he was closer to the city and therefore could move faster—and he beat Grant to the outskirts of the capital. On June 1 Grant pulled up to a lonesome crossroads called Cold Harbor. It was an inhospitable refuge indeed for the federal force. The night before the June 3 charge on the Confederate entrenchments, the fight was so obviously going to be desperate that Union men wrote their last letters and their names and next of kin on pieces of paper and pinned them to the inside of their jackets. "June 3. Cold Harbor. I was killed," one soldier wrote. The diary containing this grim entry was found on his body after the battle. This last in the war's series of murderous frontal assaults was, not surprisingly, a slaughter. About seven thousand federals were killed or wounded in less than an hour—this in addition to the five thousand Grant had lost between June 1 and June 12. Grant later wrote that he "regretted" the assault on the Confederates' breastworks, saying it "seemed to revive [Confederate] hopes temporarily; but it was of short duration. The effect upon the Army of the Potomac was the reverse."[9]

The violence and gruesomeness of Grant's Virginia campaign stunned the North. "There is death at the heart of this glory & greatness. This war is murder, & nothing else. and every man who gives a dollar or moves his finger to aid is an aider & abettor of murder," a New York Copperhead wrote. "My heart is sick of this horrible carnage. I long to see the time when we can stand up before the people and call these infernal deeds by their right names." One congressman wrote that he didn't think Grant was even a credible general. "I don't think he shows skill in hurrying so many into death & agony. . . . Is it butchery, or—war?"[10] Even members of Lincoln's cabinet were shocked. "It seems to myself like exaggeration when I find that in describing conflict after conflict in this energetic campaign, I am required always to say of the last one that it was the severest battle of the war," Seward wrote. Navy Secretary Gideon Welles believed that the public remained confident in Grant, but "the immense slaughter of our brave men chills and sickens us all. . . . There is heavy loss, but we are becoming accustomed to the sacrifice." Still, the bloom on Grant's rose was beginning to fade in Welles's estimation. "Grant," he said, "has not great regard for human life." Lincoln remained unreservedly supportive, though. "My previous high estimate of Gen. Grant has been maintained and heightened by what has occurred in the remarkable campaign he is now conducting," he assured a group of prominent New Yorkers.[11]

Grant ignored his critics. With Lincoln's steadfast backing, the general continued to dog Lee, chasing him in mid-June to the outskirts of Richmond. Lee dug a line at the edge of Petersburg, and repeated assaults on the Confederate trenches failed. On June 18 Grant dug in for a siege. This did not please many civilians in the North, but soldiers—especially the veterans—saw the advantage of patience. "I suppose folks at home are in a dreadful hurry to have us take Petersburg," a Massachusetts soldier wrote, "but if we can lay here during the hot weather and cut their railroads and siege them out rather than to charge and lose thousands of men, I for one shall be better satisfied."[12]

From May 5, when he launched the battle in the Wilderness, to early July, Grant racked up more than sixty-four thousand casualties. "It has been nothing but attack—attack—assault—assault through jungles & swamps against positions of which we knew nothing," McClellan's brother Arthur wrote him from the front. "I believe that sixty thousand men have been uselessly slaughtered. Even your bitterest enemies cannot fail to see, though they do not acknowledge, how completely you have been vindicated." Neither he nor most other Northerners appreciated the effect these losses had on Southerners. Confederates were awed by the fact that the North could absorb such casualties and still keep fighting. "When Grant has ten thousand slain, he has only to order up another ten thousand and they are there—ready to step out to the front. They are like the leaves of Vallombrosa," a South Carolina woman noted.[13]

Northerners, on the other hand, were horrified at the loss of life. The columns of names—men dead, men wounded, men missing—that newspapers across the country printed each day brought a new nickname to "Unconditional Surrender" Grant: "Grant the Butcher." John McElwee, the Copperhead editor of the *Hamilton True Telegraph* in Ohio, was apoplectic over the losses the general was taking. He urged his readers to try to keep more men from entering the "slaughter pens of those Federal butchers whom courtesy calls Generals."[14] In Boston, the *Post* accused Republicans of a "sickening flow of partisan delusion," portraying the army's setbacks as successes in order to "create capital" for itself. C. Chauncey Burr, editor of the *Old Guard,* pulled out all the stops, calling Grant "the death's head of a whole people." "What is the difference between a *butcher* and a *general*?" Burr asked. "A butcher kills animals for food. A general kills men to gratify the ambition or malice of politicians and scoundrels." While a hangman executes men for their crimes, the general's business is "to slaughter thousands of innocent men, with whom neither he nor society has any grounds for quarrel." Generals, he concluded, "kill for the sake of killing." The *Chicago Times* concluded that the staggering toll "ought to bring before the people the true character of the contest which is now raging, and also its barrenness."[15]

As casualties mounted and one army after another stalled, Lincoln's political fortunes evaporated. Even before the debacle at Cold Harbor, the impresario of New York's Republicans, Thurlow Weed, wrote privately that Lincoln's chances of reelection were nil. An observer in Iowa wrote that if Lincoln did not do something soon to turn the tide militarily and to stave off further challenges from within the party, conservative Republicans were likely to defect to the Copperheads. In fact, one group had already split from the Republican Party. Things were no better on the left end of the spectrum. A collection of Radical Republicans met in Cleveland at the end of May to nominate John C. Frémont for president.[16] In May, Frémont's nomination had seemed like a quixotic effort by a group of malcontents. Now it was gaining steam.

Meantime, the Peace Democrats were stepping up their attacks on Lincoln and the Republicans. The *Old Guard* was in the vanguard. "In the name of *liberty*, the people have been arrested contrary to all law, and immured in military bastilles. In the name of the Constitution, the

Constitution has been stricken down," editor Burr wrote, working himself into a rhetorical lather.

> In the name of laws, the laws have been violated. In the name of freedom, the *habeas corpus* has been destroyed. In the name of *humanity*, a grand scheme of robbing and murdering the people of the South has been urged by the Abolitionists. Under the pretence of saving the Union, these bloody-minded scoundrels have been doing their utmost to destroy it.

These were the themes that Copperheads had been hammering away at for nearly three years, but they had a new urgency given the extraordinary losses in the Army of the Potomac and the coming presidential election.[17]

The public's dismay over the horrible losses marked the third phase of the Copperhead movement. Motivated by a horror over the loss of life, both Republicans and Democrats moved into the antiwar column. Unlike those who were in the first two phases, these recent converts were not ideologically driven hard-liners. They did not use the same kind of rhetoric the Copperheads did, and in fact, even to call them Copperheads would be a misstatement. These newcomers simply wanted the bloodletting to end. Because they were people who responded to the headlines, they were particularly fickle. They gave the hard-liners tremendous force and influence over the summer, but as soon as the Union fortune's turned, so did they—as the Democrats would find out to their dismay.

Despite the many doubts about Lincoln's future by the time Cold Harbor ended, he was easily renominated just a few days later at the National Union Party convention—the Union Party being the name the Republicans had taken for this election to demonstrate their inclusionary outlook. In this spirit, they nominated Andrew Johnson, a Tennessee Democrat, for vice president instead of the sitting vice president, Hannibal Hamlin of Maine. They also adopted a platform that called for war to cease only on terms of the Confederacy's unconditional surrender, demanded the "utter and complete extirpation" of slavery from American soil, and recommended a constitutional amendment banning slavery. Despite the unanimous support for Lincoln at the convention, everyone knew he was in trouble. Lincoln himself seemed to recognize that his nomination could not be read as any sort of universal acclamation, even among Unionists. He told the National Union League that he took his nomination as a "personal compliment. . . . I have not permitted myself, gentlemen, to conclude that I am the best man in the country; but I am reminded, in this connection, of a story of an old Dutch farmer, who remarked to a companion once that 'it was not best to swap horses when crossing streams.' "[18]

The Copperhead press was thoroughly disgusted with Lincoln's re-nomination. "May Almighty God forbid that we are to have two terms of the rottenest, most stinking, ruin-working smallpox ever conceived by fiends or mortals, in the shape of two terms of Abe Lincoln's ad-ministration," the La Crosse, Wisconsin, *Democrat* wrote. In its usual take-no-prisoners prose, the newspaper said that Lincoln's goal was to reach the top of his "monument of skulls . . . his heap of national ruin." Elsewhere, editors dismissed Lincoln's chances of success. "Lincoln stock is not worth any more in this community, than Chase's Green-backs, which is now about fifty cents on the dollar," the Niles, Michi-gan, newspaper observed.[19]

Individual Copperheads started to petition George McClellan, Lincoln's likely opponent in the fall, to consider running as a peace man. Many leading conservatives obviously had not pieced together the implications of McClellan's own participation in the war. Details such as a war record notwithstanding, some peace men thought Little Mac was the only man in the country who could campaign success-fully for president on a platform demanding an immediate halt to the fighting. Some of his correspondents promised that if he ran as a peace candidate he would receive thousands of votes more than if he ran as a war candidate. Others disagreed strenuously. The *Cincinnati Enquirer* urged delegates to the Democratic national convention not to support any candidate who did not endorse peace. Brick Pomeroy, the reac-tionary editor of the *La Crosse Democrat*, publicly took McClellan to task for not marching on Washington after he was dismissed in 1862 and taking the president and cabinet prisoner. "He would have done a good thing for the country and could have had any office in the gift of the people. This was the golden moment he neglected to improve," Pomeroy wrote.[20]

Lincoln's political position deteriorated further in July, and once again the Union's military fortunes were responsible. Confederate gen-eral Jubal Early shocked Northerners when he stormed down the Shenandoah Valley on July 6 into Hagerstown, Maryland, which he virtually held hostage until the local population could come up with $20,000 as restitution for damage the bluecoats had wrought on the Shenandoah Valley. Three days later, Early was in Frederick, where he levied a $200,000 fine on local authorities. By July 11 Early had ad-vanced to Silver Spring, the very gates of Washington, D.C. When an assault on the city appeared to be a losing proposition, Early torched the home of Postmaster General Montgomery Blair and slipped back across the Potomac. The *Boston Post* took advantage of the moment to remind its readers of the administration's incompetence and to demand that Lincoln fire his entire cabinet immediately. Welles, the navy secretary, was hardly more sympathetic as he poured out his frustration in his diary: "The waste of war is terrible; the waste from imbecility and mismanagement is more terrible and more trying than from the ravages of the soldiers. It is impossible for the country to bear up under these monstrous errors and wrongs." While the *New York Herald* agreed that the incursion highlighted the ineptitude of the administration, it said that the only calamity as bad as the capital falling into the hands of the enemy was the ammunition such an event would give the Copperheads. The *Herald* predicted that if Washington were sacked, the Copperheads would "seize the occasion for stirring up their adherents to arms and lighting the fires of a Northern insurrection at a hundred points at once across the continent." The *Herald* was right about the conservative response. The *La Crosse Democrat* observed: "Patriotism is played out. . . . All are tired of this damnable tragedy. . . . Each hour is but sinking us deeper into bankruptcy and desolation."[21]

If May had been the cruelest month, July was rapidly turning into the most humiliating. Early had penetrated the North earlier in July—only the third time Confederates had been able to do so with any force—and had nearly made it into the capital city. Now, at the end of July, his cavalry turned up in Chambersburg, Pennsylvania. When residents there refused to meet General John McCausland's demand for half a million dollars, the general—on Early's orders—had the city burned to the ground. This was not the only setback that July 30 held for the Union. In Petersburg, catastrophe struck. Earlier that month, a Union colonel had talked Burnside, back in the East again after the Vallandigham mess, into what seemed like a good idea: break the Confederate line by digging underneath the rebel trenches and blowing them up. The Union had just the troops for the job, a regiment of Pennsylvania coal miners. They dug five hundred feet and packed eight thousand pounds of gunpowder under the rebels. The initial plan was to blow up the tunnel and send a division of black soldiers through to spearhead the attack. Meade and Grant got cold feet the day before the attack, though, and pulled the African Americans in favor of white troops. Both generals had concerns about the readiness of the blacks and about being accused of using them as cannon fodder if the plan went awry. Their concerns proved well founded. When the charge blew, things went badly and then some. Some of the white troops stood and gawked at the thirty-foot-deep hole. Others ran into the crater the blast had created rather than around it. The

Confederates quickly recovered, pulled up artillery pieces, and shot at the men trapped in the enormous cavity. One of the federals' commanding officers stayed in the rear bracing himself with rum he had cadged off a surgeon. By the time the black soldiers went into the battle, the fight had turned into a chaotic and confused mess, and they became targets of a human turkey shoot.

This latest blow appalled the North, and the participation (or nonparticipation) of black troops gave the antiwar press a new avenue for attacking the government. Several Copperhead papers accused Burnside of having gone into such a sulk after the black troops were removed from the lead position that he refused to take charge when the mine exploded. The *New York World*, by now firmly in the antiwar column, claimed that Burnside's apathy cost the lives of 4,500 Union men. "The Negro mania has been as mischievous in the conduct of the war, as it has been in and is in politics," the Philadelphia *Age* said. If military decisions and promotions were based "not upon deeds of gallantry, but in devotion to the Negro-equality dogma of a political party, then no man can tell where the demoralization of our army will end, or what calamity the future has in store for it."[22]

More generally, the debacle once again brought questions of the officer corps' competency to the fore. The *Boston Pilot*, a Copperhead paper, wrote, "It begins to look to many folks in the North that the Confederacy perhaps can never really be beaten, that the attempts to win might after all be too heavy a load to carry, and that perhaps it is time to agree to a peace without victory." Welles confessed that the fiasco at the Crater "has been disheartening in the extreme." The episode called Grant's skills into question, even in the highest quarters of government. Deeply shaken, the navy secretary wrote that Grant and Sherman together made a single competent general, but with the two of them now operating in different parts of the South he wondered if Grant was "not equal" to the job. He feared that thousands of young men had "poured out their rich blood" in vain over the past three months. "A blight and sadness comes over me like a dark shadow when I dwell on the subject, a melancholy feeling of the past, a foreboding of the future. A nation's destiny almost has been committed to this man, and if it is an improper committal, where are we?"[23]

Some soldiers joined civilians in these sentiments. A New York private, Newton B. Spencer of the 179th, was so frustrated that he wrote a letter to the editor of an upstate newspaper, the *Penn Yan Democrat*, in which he criticized the government and the army leadership at the Battle of the Crater. General Meade, he said, was "the most complete military charlatan that has worn a Maj. General's stars." The real problem, though, was "the abolition mania for employing 'nigger' soldiers. . . . It was to glorify the sooty abolition idol that upon a division of raw and worthless black paltroons was devolved the most important task of the whole conflict." He begged Northerners to "come down to the rescue of this army at once . . . or else effect an honorable peace by negotiators." Army officials who read the letter concluded that it aided and comforted the enemy, and they court-martialed him. Spencer said he did not realize he was not allowed to criticize the army in writing; he was only trying to encourage people of the North to send reinforcements to the army quickly. The court found him guilty of showing disrespect and contempt for Meade and of conduct prejudicial to good order and discipline. He was publicly reprimanded and fined eight dollars a month for the next six months.[24]

Grant, always unflappable, and his loyal lieutenant, Sherman, remained confident in their plan. But the public simply saw two armies bogged down outside of Petersburg and Atlanta. From early May to the end of July, the Union had taken a hundred thousand casualties. Many observers thought the nation had paid a dear price and had received nothing in return. "If it were not for the interest I felt in the fate of the slaves, and the hardly inferior interest in the removal of that stigma of slavery from your character as a free Christian community, I should turn with horror from the details of your battles, and wish only for peace on any terms," Richard Cobden wrote Senator Sumner from England. "As it is I cannot help asking myself—whether it can be within the designs of a merciful God that even a good work should be accomplished at the cost of so much evil to the world." Many on the American side of the Atlantic shared his opinion.[25]

It was not just the military situation that was looking grim by now. After three years, parts of the North were starting to buckle under the weight of war. Violence returned to the home front with the summer heat. In Chester, Illinois, a town near the Missouri border, bushwhackers burned a flour mill and a barn and tried to kill a local citizen, according to an adjutant stationed in Randolph County. Several men were arrested and tried, but—according to a government agent—packed juries acquitted them. A traveling salesman was so worried after a trip through Illinois that he wrote the army's Northern Command upon arriving home. "I regret to see throughout this beautiful Western country, a state of feeling existing & based upon political opinions, which leads one to anticipate a more sad change than would be caused by a revolution at the ballot box—among neighbors and those, who of old, were friends, there exists a feeling of enmity, hatred & general conduct bordering almost upon insanity."[26]

In some Northern towns, Democrats decided to protect themselves from violence and the possibility of arrest by forming freeman's protective unions. These were more dangerous than the militias that had been around since the beginning of the war. They explicitly held Republicans in the neighborhood responsible for anything that might happen to a local Democrat. Neighborhood Republicans would be punished in the event of attacks or arrests, and any officials involved in these activities would be targeted for retaliation. When Unionists in La Crosse, Wisconsin, threatened to burn down the offices of Brick Pomeroy's *Democrat,* he was not shy about threatening retaliation, even in print.

> When this office is destroyed, a hundred buildings in this city will keep it company. Matches are cheap and retaliation sweet. If anyone wants a little riot, they shall have a big one—one to last them forever. When they ignite the match, let us apply the torch. . . . If the Administration supposes that it can go much further in its course of lawless violence upon personal rights, it and its leading supporters may rue the day when these deeds of despotism began. Such blows were never given without producing and justifying blows in return.

As so often was the case where threats of violence were concerned, most mainstream Democratic leaders and levelheaded Copperheads averted their eyes while the most reactionary Peace Democrats reveled in such vituperation.[27]

In the late spring and summer of 1864, the three-year terms of service for many men expired. Thousands of veterans came home for good, but a significant portion reenlisted. Those who reupped were rewarded with furloughs home. The unintended consequence of this action was the arrival of soldiers bent on obtaining revenge against those whom they considered more hated enemies than even the rebels: the Copperheads. "Men are assaulted, men are threatened, men are shot, property is molested & there is danger by exposure of property *or person* while a train of armed troops hurry along the RR as random shots are fired through the car windows, killing & maiming live Stock," an Illinois man reported. Conservative Democratic newspapers were ripe targets in many communities. A company from an Iowa regiment ruined an editor's type and drove him from the county in retaliation for his calling a murdered comrade of theirs a "Lincoln hireling." A group of soldiers from the 22nd Illinois sacked the office of the *Egyptian Picket Guard,* destroying or damaging the type, press, and building of the "notoriously disloyal sheet." Area Copperheads rallied later in the day in support of the newspaper, but because the soldiers already had left, they could do nothing but cheer Jefferson Davis and Clement Vallandigham and threaten the few Republicans in the neighborhood. Nevertheless, the local adjutant was rattled enough to ask his superiors to send four or five hundred soldiers to his aid.[28]

The widespread involvement of soldiers in harassing, threatening, or assaulting citizens marked an important shift. For two years soldiers had responded to the antiwar Democrats with increasing levels of frustration and fury. Given the hardships they had suffered—bad food, sickness, exposure to the elements, boredom, terror, and sorrow— their bitterness toward the Copperheads was understandable. To this point, though, the soldiers' anger had been confined mostly to letters. "If the Copperheads and Peace men succeed in carrying out their principals, *we will have war as long as there is a single square foot of land* in the North *that dare call itself a free soil,*" an Iowa soldier wrote. Soldiers had long written about their wish to hurt or kill Butternuts, but now their fantasies took on an increasingly morbid tone. "I hope by the fourth of July that the men who composed the rebel cabinet will be hung so the buserds will have feed on their flesh," a Wisconsin infantryman wrote. He had the same hope for the Copperheads, whom he supposed were feeling "down in the mouth" at the moment about what he regarded as Grant's successes. The war, he added, "is to be put down now."[29]

Gruesome threats of how soldiers would deal with the Peace Democrats were not the only change civilians saw in their Yankees. The dual experiences of battle and travel had brought many soldiers who once may have harbored doubts about the Union cause or abolition into Lincoln's corner. "You are a ware I *was* a great friend of the Southerner before this war. I looked upon him as possesing finer qualities than our Eastern men; now much as I yet dislike in many of the New Englanders I must acknowledge I would much prefer to live among them than in such society of ignorance as is plain to be seen in every town and neighborhood in their 'Sunny South,' " an Illinois soldier wrote home.[30]

Meanwhile, talk of conspiracies began to reach a crescendo. This was especially true in the West, where suspicions about Butternut activities had run rampant since the war broke out. Government agents from nearly every state west of the Appalachians reported rumors that Copperheads were preparing some sort of violent uprising. In Ohio, Indiana, and Michigan, the most common report continued to be that the antiwar forces were colluding with the Confederates on a plan that involved their taking over a prisoner of war camp, freeing the rebel soldiers, and then laying waste to the nearest city. These reports were so prevalent and came from so many different parts of the country that it is nearly impossible to believe something was not afoot.[31] Moreover, the reports came from local military agents and were addressed to either the state or the national command. These reports were not for public consumption, and their authors had nothing to gain from them politically. In fact, many of the local officers reported the rumors reluctantly, saying that they would not normally pass the stories along but were doing so at this time because they were so pervasive and the officers believed there was something to them. While the case is certainly not airtight, their convocations suggest that Klement was overzealous in asserting that rumors of conspiracy were nothing more than allegations concocted by Republicans who thought they could do better at the polls if the public was frightened.[32]

Whether these plots were rumor or fact, Indiana was unquestionably the hotbed of conspiracy theories and quite possibly of conspiracies themselves. By late winter and extending all through the summer, Republicans were charging that while all Democrats were not traitors, "certain it is that every traitor is a Democrat." As early as June the state adjutant general, Henry B. Carrington, wrote that tensions were reaching a boiling point. Rural Copperheads in the state were openly declaring their intent to resist the draft and stop the war and were repairing their rifles in preparation for some sort of outbreak. A shop in Indianapolis reportedly sold ninety revolvers in a single day to disloyal men. The word on the street was that someone would release the rebel prisoners at the first sign of disturbance. Carrington had faith in the loyalists of Indiana but feared that their lethargy, combined with the boldness of the Copperhead leadership, could lead to serious problems for the state.[33]

Something did turn out to be rotten in the state of Indiana. The state was probably the most fertile ground for the Order of American Knights and its progeny organization, the Sons of Liberty. The latter group in 1864 claimed eighteen thousand Hoosiers among its members. The state's adjutant general reported that it was organized in forty-four of the state's sixty-nine counties and was using the state Democratic Party as a front for its activities. The main principles of both organizations revolved around states' rights, especially as they were articulated in the Virginia and Kentucky Resolves of 1798. Republicans portrayed the secret societies as being representative of the Democratic Party as a whole, even though most mainstream Democratic organizations called for peace on condition of reunion. The founder of the Order of American Knights, Harrison H. Dodd, played right into the Republicans' hands by hatching a scheme to liberate the prisoners at Camp Morton in Indianapolis, seize the arsenal in the capital, and then launch an insurrection. The Indianapolis uprising was supposed to link to a larger effort to overthrow the government and forge a Northwest confederacy, or to have the Old Northwest join the Confederate States of America.[34]

At this point his plot ran into problems that characterized the entire antiwar movement: shoddy organization and loose lips. These were endemic in the Copperhead movement, and in Dodd's case he had only himself to blame: He had told everything to an agent of Governor Morton and Carrington, having assured the man that he was one of the few people Dodd trusted completely. While pods of reactionary Democrats certainly did exist as small local militias, and while some of them surely had an eye on creating mayhem—be that by assaulting enrolling officers, attacking local Unionists, or overthrowing the state government—there is little to suggest their networks extended beyond the adjoining county. Even in cases where Copperheads crossed county lines there appears to have been only a minimum of coordination. Dodd's plan was unique in that it had serious aspirations as a regional uprising. But his conspiracy illustrates another difficulty the Sons of Liberty and other "secret" societies had, namely, their lack of secrecy. Union sympathizers throughout the war reported such activities as Copperhead meetings and militias drilling in the woods, and government agents easily penetrated the most suspicious cells.[35]

A Carrington spy blew the whistle on Dodd several weeks before the planned August 16 insurrection. Carrington and Governor Morton opted not to act on the information, though, and the sixteenth came and went without an uprising. Four days later, responding to a tip that Dodd was receiving arms from New York, military authorities raided his printing shop and found four hundred revolvers and a considerable amount of ammunition. The find gave the Republicans a field day: Finally, they had proof of a Copperhead conspiracy to stage a coup. Dodd was arrested in early September and put on trial for treason despite the rather flimsy evidence against him. During the trial, he escaped from his unguarded quarters and fled to Canada. A specially appointed military commission listened to the judge advocate pronounce constitutional liberties "dead for the time being" and necessity "the sole law," and proceeded to find Dodd guilty in absentia and sentence him to hang. Three of Dodd's accomplices, including Lamden P. Milligan, also were found guilty and sentenced to hang. A fourth was sentenced to hard labor for the rest of the war.[36]

Dodd's scheme may be the best documented, but it was not the most ambitious. That accolade goes to another Sons of Liberty plot whose object was to overthrow the Lincoln government. According to a letter dated August 12 to Jefferson Davis, the Sons' grand council met in Chicago that month and agreed on a plan to capture Indianapolis, Louisville, St. Louis, and Rock Island simultaneously. The plot was contingent on the Confederate government's sending troops into Kentucky and Missouri. The conspirators needed help in those two states because the Sons of Liberty were not as strong there as in Illinois and Indiana, the letter said. The organization was well positioned in the latter two states, the author said, because its men could organize and operate under the guise of being active members of the Democratic Party.[37]

While this particular scheme may have been fanciful, the Confederates had a great deal to gain if the Copperheads' secret societies, especially those in the Northwest, could mount any sort of insurrection. In the hopes of fomenting some sort of rearguard action in the North, Davis had sent four men to Canada to stir up trouble. They had several goals: to arrange for escaped Confederate prisoners to get back south, to subsidize newspapers in the North for propaganda purposes (an effort that failed), and to coordinate efforts with groups such as the Sons of Liberty. One of the agents, Jacob Thompson, who had served as secretary of the interior under President Buchanan, met on June 11 with Vallandigham, who by that time was the supreme commander of the Sons of Liberty. Vallandigham made a friendly overture by initiating Thompson into the organization. Although the two men disagreed as to the ultimate aim of the war—reunion or independence— Vallandigham was open to talking about the possibility of fomenting a revolution in the Northwest with an eye to creating a Western confederacy. Subsequent conversations with other leaders of the Sons of Liberty led to yet another plot to seize the governments of Illinois, Indiana, Ohio, Kentucky, and Missouri. This was to be a three-pronged attack involving Confederate soldiers who had escaped from Northern prison camps and were now in Canada, prisoners still held in the camps, and the Sons of Liberty, which would administer the states once they had fallen. The idea was for the prisoners to rise up spontaneously, fight their way out of their garrisons, and go to federal arsenals that Confederate agents were to have seized. Having armed themselves, the rebels would link up with the Sons of Liberty's fighting force and, at the very least, create enough of a commotion to force Lincoln to transfer a significant number of troops north to stamp out the insurrection. The Davis government was satisfied enough with this plan to spend $500,000—no mean sum, considering the financial straits of the Confederacy at this point in the war—to pay for guns for the Sons of Liberty and for transporting its members to key locations. Vallandigham denied any involvement in the scheme, but the Confederates with whom he was talking insisted in later years that he was fully aware of the plot. In fact, his return to Ohio and his expected arrest there were to be the signals for the start of the uprising. That idea fizzled, though, when federal authorities refused to arrest him after he reentered the country in mid-June.[38]

Foiled, the Confederates cooked up a Plan B: stage a coup during the Democratic Convention, due to be held in July. That plot, too, was stymied when the Democrats decided to postpone the meeting. A third plan intersected with Dodd's conspiracy for August 16, the one that never came off. A fourth scheme involving laborers in New York also failed to materialize. Representative Benjamin Wood, who was also the publisher of the *New York Daily News,* had gotten wind of "the storm impending and about to burst in the West" and offered to help. The workingmen of New York could be rallied at a moment's notice and be persuaded to help throw off "the yoke of the tyrant," he said. Clement C. Clay Jr., the Confederate agent, leaped on the possibility of sparking another riot in New York as a diversionary measure. Thompson sent Wood a check for $25,000 to buy arms. As the machinations progressed, conspirators in the West thought they should stage a series of rallies to "prepare the public mind." The first, in Peoria, was a success. But the air quickly went out of many men who supported a coup when they concluded in mid-August that they could beat Lincoln by legitimate means at the ballot box. Thompson wrote Judah P. Benjamin, the Confederate secretary of state, that members of the Sons of Liberty were losing their nerve.[39]

All of this conniving went on against the backdrop of war, which remained a relentless consumer of men. Nothing stopped the army's need for more soldiers. So, despite all the troubles on the home front, Lincoln on July 18 issued his third call for men. This draft, to be held September 5 if the quotas were not met, was rather different from its predecessors in that a new law barred commutation as an option for avoiding service. Lincoln's request for half a million more men was a tremendous burden on already depleted communities. In the West, labor shortages and inflation had driven wages up to four hundred dollars a year for a farmhand, twice what a laborer's salary had been before the war. The lucrative pay was just one reason it was more difficult than ever for the government to pry men away from their homes. Many Northerners had come to share the opinion that thousands of lives had been wasted, not just in Grant's Virginia campaign but over the entire course of the war. A Democratic editor summed up the feelings of many Northerners, terming this round of drafting the "Lottery of Death."

Another called it "The Slaughter Pen" and concluded that "The Want of Brains Must Be Made Up By Numbers." One Democratic soldier thought this call was political suicide. If it was true that the president was asking for half a million more men, "Lincoln is deader than dead," he wrote. Lincoln reportedly told friends who worried about the impact the draft would have on his reelection that the people of the North needed to understand that he meant to crush the rebellion militarily. Whether he won or lost in November, raising men now was an essential component of Union victory. "We must lose nothing even if I am defeated," Lincoln insisted.[40]

With so many young men dying on battlefields, the tensions around conscription rose to new heights in some communities. In New York, where the draft riots of the previous summer were still fresh in people's minds, some speculated that whole cities would have to be placed under martial law for conscription to take place. There was talk in some quarters that the Terror of the French Revolution was sure to be visited on the North if the government insisted on carrying out the draft. This kind of fear may have been new to the Eastern cities, but it had long since become part of the emotional landscape in parts of the West. "I Shall not be Surprised to hear at any moment of an outbrake of the moste terrible and bloody character not equaled any where since the days of the French Revolution. I shall regret to see it but I fear it is coming," an Indiana man wrote. A provost marshal in central Illinois reported that guerrillas, bushwhackers, and other men claiming to be Southern sympathizers were banding together into gangs to rob, murder, or torch any target as soon as the time was right. Iowa's Republican governor was convinced that two-thirds of the Democrats in his state were disloyal and that thirty-three thousand men were actively involved in secret Copperhead societies, mostly along the Iowa-Missouri border, where guerrillas staged occasional incursions. He issued a proclamation barring Iowans from offering asylum to any Missouri resident who had fought against that state's Unionist government. In Indiana, Governor Morton received warning that draftees along the state's southern border were so enraged that African Americans were allowed to enlist that they had joined guerrilla forces and were ready to take revenge at any time on Union men. This rich irony of this situation—draftees protesting against those whose voluntary enlistment meant there would be fewer men conscripted—underscores the obsession that Copperheads had about race, even when the actions of African Americans benefited the antiwar crowd's personal interests.[41]

As another draft loomed, recruiters had an increasingly difficult time meeting their quotas. Eligible men from all over the North once again fled to Canada. It is impossible to know how many went there, although enrolling agents from across the North and private individuals often mentioned the phenomenon in their correspondence. The far West was another destination for men on the run from the provost marshal's agents. Flight was only one option available to those who wanted to avoid conscription. Doctors across the country reported outbreaks of mysterious illnesses among draft-age men that tended to disappear as soon as the local quota was filled. In some areas, resistance was more aggressive. A group in Hamilton, Ohio, vowed that *"by force and with arms,"* it would resist any efforts to enforce the draft in Butler County. It also urged other Americans who opposed the continuation of the war to prepare to do likewise.[42]

Concerns about the consequences of a draft reached to the highest levels. General Halleck wrote Grant that combat troops would probably have to be pulled from the field to contain the violence he expected to break out on the home front and to keep the Copperheads under control. Grant would have none of it, saying that governors would have to respond to any problems with their own militias. "If we are to draw troops from the field to keep the loyal states in harness it will prove difficult to suppress the rebellion in the disloyal states," he wrote. Lincoln concurred. Like Grant, he said, "neither am I willing" to send battle troops to defend the hearth. "Hold on with a bulldog grip," he told Grant, "and chew and choke as much as possible."[43]

The need to fill quotas pushed many communities to adopt creative solutions. In upstate New York, some townships recruited blacks from Kentucky and Tennessee and paid them bounties. More common were the efforts of towns and counties to attract volunteers by raising bounties to new highs. Rochester, New York, for instance, spent more than half a million dollars on this call alone to induce men to enlist. Some of the North's elites were disgusted that filling the ranks had become a mercenary proposition. "Patriotism and love of the cause are supplanted to a large degree, as a motive of filling our armies by the mercenary spirit of making money out of the operation," Ohio's governor observed. Veteran soldiers were even more disapproving of the ways communities were trying to fill—or dodge—their obligations. One angry soldier from Connecticut wrote a newspaper to criticize the way Northeastern states conducted themselves. "When the government issues a new appeal for men, the great effort in New England seems to be to prove by Yankee 'ciphering' that it has been already met, not to supply what it demands—to furnish excuses not soldiers," he wrote.[44]

The resistance to the July 1864 call is evident in the numbers. In the first two rounds of drafting after the 1863 Conscription Act passed,

slightly more than half the congressional districts in the country fell
short of volunteers and had to resort to a draft. Now, to meet the quotas for Lincoln's July request, more than three-quarters of the congressional districts had to conscript men. Draft dodging was another sign
of resistance, and it reached epidemic proportions. In March 1863, only
Wisconsin, Michigan, New York, and Pennsylvania had rates of draft
dodging that exceeded 20 percent. The problem was relatively localized. By July 1864, though, draft dodging had turned into a national
crisis, spreading to large parts of Maine, New Jersey, Ohio, Illinois,
Minnesota, Maryland, West Virginia, Kentucky, and Missouri. These
nine states accounted for 57.7 percent of the men who failed to report
during the bloody and discouraging summer of 1864. Moreover, draft
resistance had spilled out of areas with large Catholic or immigrant populations or cities near the Mason-Dixon line and become commonplace in
Yankee strongholds like rural Michigan and upstate New York. Proximity to Canada or the South may have induced men in those areas to evade
conscription in higher numbers as draft dodging rose. For thousands of
civilian men of a certain age, any commitment they once may have had
toward the Union cause waned as the casualty lists grew longer.[45]

Resistance to the draft at home had important repercussions in the
field. Men who signed up just for the bounties or those who hired themselves out as substitutes were more likely to desert once they were
mustered into the army. Moreover, a community's support and degree
of unity for the war effort appears to have had a direct influence on a
soldier's decision to desert. This would explain why both immigrants,
whose ties to the country were sometimes weak, and men from large
cities, where one could hide easily, had higher desertion rates than soldiers from rural areas. In any case, desertions skyrocketed in 1864, averaging 7,333 per month compared to 4,647 per month in 1863 and
4,368 in 1865.[46]

The combination of wartime casualties, defeats, and the draft placed
extraordinary pressure on the people at home. Peace proposals looked
more and more appealing. The editor of the *New York Tribune*, Horace
Greeley, had been strongly supportive of Lincoln as recently as June.
Within a month, however, he had become desperate for peace. On July
5 he received a note from an acquaintance asking him to come to Canada
to meet with three Confederate representatives and engage in peace
talks. In fact, none of the Southerners was in Canada on a peace mission. All three were secret service agents whose real directive was to
recruit men to engage in terrorist acts against the North, manipulate
the gold market, and foment disruption in the Union. The unsuspect-
ing Greeley took the bait. Two days later he wrote Lincoln "to remind

you that our bleeding, bankrupt, almost dying country . . . longs for peace—shudders at the prospect of fresh conscriptions, of further wholesale devastations, and of new rivers of human blood." Pleading for the president to invite the Southerners to Washington for negotiations, he informed Lincoln that there was a "widespread conviction that the government and its prominent supporters are not anxious for Peace and do not improve proffered opportunities to achieve it." This impression, he warned, was certain to hurt Lincoln in the coming election unless the president acted quickly. Besides, the possibility of securing a "just peace" now could "save us from a northern insurrection."[47]

Exasperated with the editor, Lincoln told Greeley to go to Niagara Falls and follow up on the matter himself. If Greeley could find "any person anywhere professing to have any proposition of Jefferson Davis in writing, for peace, embracing the restoration of the Union and abandonment of slavery, what ever else it embraces," he should bring the man to Lincoln, who would assure the Confederate safe passage through the North. "I just thought I would let him go up there and crack that nut for himself," he told Senator James Harlan of Iowa. Lincoln sent along one of his personal secretaries for the trip in case anything came of the meeting. But the prospects of any negotiation quickly fell apart when the Confederate agents disclosed that they had no authority to engage in peace talks. They suggested that they could go to Washington and then to Richmond, where they were sure to gain the permission they needed to negotiate. Greeley returned home a national laughingstock. James Gordon Bennett, editor of the *New York Herald*, called his rival a "nincompoop without genius."[48]

Greeley's adventure helped Lincoln in one important way: It gave the president an opportunity to make his terms for peace absolutely clear. In a July 18 message addressed "to whom it may concern," he wrote: "Any proposition which embraces the restoration of peace, the integrity of the whole Union, and the abandonment of slavery . . . will be met by liberal terms on other substantial and collateral points." The inclusion of emancipation was a crucial point and one that would resurface as an issue only a month later. For Lincoln, emancipation was as important as reunifying the divided nation if there was any hope for peace. Lincoln was skeptical that the Confederates would agree to any deal that did not recognize their independence. His hunch was dead on. About the same time Greeley was involved in his peace parley, a Northern journalist and a federal colonel met with Jefferson Davis to see what he had to say about stopping the war. Davis abruptly put an end to the two men's efforts when he announced that the Confederacy would keep fighting *"unless you acknowledge our right to self-government.*

We are not fighting for slavery. We are fighting for INDEPENDENCE, and that, or extermination, we *will* have."[49]

Ignoring their own president's intransigence, the three Confederate agents in Canada wrote an open letter venting their indignity at Lincoln's comments: If any Confederates still believed peace was possible, Lincoln's "To Whom It May Concern" missive would "strip from their eyes the last film of such delusion" and strengthen their resolve to continue on with the war. Whether they intended to or not, the agents' response struck a deep chord with Peace Democrats in the North as well. In Columbus, Samuel Medary of the *Crisis* wrote that their letter "has done more to kill off the War Democrats than any one thing that has happened." One of the agents, Clement C. Clay Jr., wrote Secretary of State Judah Benjamin that the Democratic press was denouncing Lincoln. The effect of his letter, he said, was "consolidating the Democracy, dividing the Republicans and encouraging the desire for peace. Many prominent politicians of the U.S. assure us that it is the most efficient instrument for stopping the war that could have been conceived or expected."[50]

Peace was not to be had, though, at least not then. The pressure on Lincoln was intense, but it still had not reached its apex. That would come in August, when Lincoln was on the ropes and embroiled in the greatest crisis of his career. By early August the stage was set for the crucible moment. The most powerful of the Union armies were stalled in front of Petersburg and Atlanta, and the commander of all the armies, Grant, was virtually a public pariah. The enormous losses of the late spring had plunged the nation to a new depth of mourning. Demands for peace went unmet, and Lincoln's resolve was looking more and more like stubborn inflexibility even to some of his supporters. Confederates and the most reactionary of the Copperheads took advantage of the gloom to plot their most fantastic schemes to date, although none panned out. More politically astute peace men focused their attention on the coming convention and to November, when they were sure their candidate would return to the Executive Mansion. Men in Lincoln's own party had turned against him, and even the Republican operatives who were supposed to be his champions thought he was doomed. But the war was not yet over, and the presidential campaign had not yet begun.

6

The Rise and Fall of the Copperheads

As July turned to August, tensions at home showed no sign of easing. The precarious summer of 1864 merely pressed on. The country was shrouded in gloom, which gave the Peace Democrats the greatest political might they had yet known. But in exercising that power, they laid the foundation for their own undoing. The difficult summer also boosted rebel hopes for fomenting a revolt that would finally prompt the Northwest to secede from the Union—only to learn that the Copperheads who had talked so brashly balked when it came to dying for their beliefs. In this desperate and unsettled environment, Lincoln had to make a decision that would define him and possibly ruin him politically; that decision was the bravest and boldest of his career. Then came September, which was the month of redemption for Lincoln and the Unionists. Sherman took Atlanta, and Sheridan started working his way through the Shenandoah Valley. Two weeks after Lincoln's fateful decision, his opponent, George McClellan, was faced with his own moment of truth, when he had to decide how to stand up to his own party. Unlike Lincoln, though, McClellan was not up to the challenge. Union military successes turned the tide for Lincoln, doomed the Copperheads, and threatened the Democratic Party at large.

In the heat of midsummer, Lincoln was in trouble, and he knew it. Conservative Republicans and moderates of both parties were abandoning him. Even the party leadership—members of Congress and his own cabinet—appeared to be heading for the exits. His attorney general freely expressed the opinion that the country's greatest need was a "competent leader." Radical Republicans, outraged that the president had pocket-vetoed the Wade-Davis Bill that outlined a plan for congressional reconstruction, sounded like Copperheads when they vented their spleen in early August to the *New York Tribune*. They accused Lincoln of usurping power by administering reconstruction himself and wrote, "If he wishes our support he must confine himself to his executive duties—to obey and to execute, not make the laws."[1] Lincoln's cool response: "Well, let them wriggle." In New York a group of disaffected Republicans met to plan a second party convention to be held September 28 in Cincinnati. The men who attended that meeting would decide whether Lincoln or a more viable politician would be their candidate. The *Tribune*, which had been one of the Republicans' leading organs, endorsed the convention. Greeley, its editor, flatly declared: "Mr. Lincoln is already beaten. He cannot be elected. And we must have another ticket to save us from overthrow." Republicans should find someone "who commands the confidence of the country, even by a new nomination if necessary."[2]

Thurlow Weed, New York's Republican Party boss, had been pessimistic about Lincoln's chances as far back as late spring. His assessment had not improved in the intervening months. He bluntly wrote Seward in August that Lincoln's reelection was widely regarded as an "impossibility. . . . The People are wild for Peace." The secretary of state responded privately by writing that the military campaigns then under way seemed "alarmingly protracted" to the public, regardless of how successful they were. If he were to believe the papers and the information coming to him from such veteran politicians as Weed, "one might well believe that the people are deeply despondent, that their resolution is failing, and that new and menacing distractions are imminent." Despite the alarms clanging from every corner of the nation, Seward believed that no antiadministration movement was formidable enough to oust Lincoln and that Americans were too smart to throw in their lot with a revolutionary crowd. If the voters exercised their best judgment in the coming election, he said, the war would and could be brought to a proper conclusion. But even Seward could not resist the melancholy tendencies of the public: "I am not altogether able to dispel this popular gloom from the region of my own mind," he admitted.[3]

Seward's hopes notwithstanding, support for the president continued to deteriorate. Henry J. Raymond, editor of the *New York Times* and chairman of the Republican Party, wrote privately of a nationwide conviction "that we need a change, that the war languishes under Mr. Lincoln and that he *cannot* or *will* not give us peace. . . . The country is tired & sick of the war & is longing for peace." Raymond believed Northerners would "scorn and scout any peace that involved disunion" but would welcome any proposal that involved reunification, whether the deal protected emancipation or not. Meanwhile, people were beginning to suspect that the president "is fighting not for the Union but for the abolition of slavery."[4]

For their part, Copperheads continued hammering away at the themes that had become their rhetorical centerpieces: the financial and human costs of the war, the suspension of habeas corpus, the presence of the draft, the fact that this had become a war of emancipation. Lincoln was a tyrant who had only contempt for the Constitution. In Philadelphia, the Copperhead newspaper *The Age* accused Yankee civilians of having only four concerns on their minds: how to profit from the war, how to prolong the fighting, how to dodge the draft, and how large a percentage of his earnings a man would have to spend to buy a substitute. Given the military disasters of recent months, peace was an ever-present theme for the conservatives. "God's curse is upon the land," a Pennsylvania publisher wrote on August 6, which Lincoln had designated as a day of humiliation and prayer. "Does it become us to acknowledge the truth, and pray for forgiveness of God for any and every part we may have taken in upholding the sins and abominations of this wicked administration . . . to put on sack-cloth and retrace our steps[?] . . . Oh, God, give us Peace! . . . Stop this bloody hell-devised carnage." Brick Pomeroy of the *La Crosse Democrat* took to calling Lincoln the "widow maker." The only exception was when he referred to the president as the "orphan maker." Pomeroy said any man who voted for Lincoln was "a traitor and a murderer." If Lincoln was reelected, Pomeroy wrote, "we trust some bold hand will pierce his heart with dagger point for the public good." Surprisingly, Pomeroy was spared arrest for advocating assassination.[5]

Conservatives also opened a new line of argument, assuring skeptics—in the face of entirely contrary evidence—that the Confederates were eager to reach a peace accord. In a triumph of vague rhetoric, New Jersey governor Joel Parker assured a crowd in Freehold that "influential men recently expressed a willingness to talk over our difficulties, without prescribing independence of the confederacy as an ultimatum. I believe the Southern people are tired of war. We can judge their feelings by our own."[6]

Race had always been a potent issue for the Copperheads, and in the weeks leading up to the Democratic convention, racist claims became an increasingly prominent theme. The *Age* reminded its readers that "fanatical Abolitionism" was to blame for starting the war. The whole idea of emancipation was foolish, it argued, because "slavery was established on this continent for wise purposes in the Divine mind—to make it the nursery of civilization, for which, in His own good time, should be taken the instruments through which benighted

Africa was to be colonized, civilized, and Christianized." Blacks, including slaves, were treated better in the former United States than anywhere else in the world, the paper said, and the happiest black was one whose subjugation was "most complete."[7]

One reason race took on a new prominence in Copperhead rhetoric was the appearance the previous Christmas of an anonymously written pamphlet called *Miscegenation: The Theory of the Blending of the Races, Applied to the American White Man and Negro*. Written in the voice of an abolitionist, the seventy-two-page tract actually was the handiwork of the managing editor and a reporter from the *New York World*.[8] Marshaling the kind of scientific language that racists often used to "prove" the inferiority of blacks, the authors argued that miscegenation—a word the writers had made up from *miscere*, Latin for "to mix," and *genus*, "race"—was the foundation for human progress. The Civil War's "final fruit" was to be the "blending of the white and black," the pamphlet said. It went on to target a particular population that seemed, to the Yankee mind, ideal for this intermixing: the Irish. "Wherever there is a poor community of Irish in the North they naturally herd with the poor negroes. . . . [C]onnubial relations are formed between the black men and white Irish women . . . pleasant to both parties, and were it not for the unhappy prejudice which exists, such unions would be very much more frequent." Clearly this was aimed at driving a wedge further between the already alienated Irish and the Republicans. Emancipation, the pamphlet assured its readers, meant amalgamation, and the Republican Party was "the party of miscegenation."[9]

The pamphlet *Miscegenation* had a goal beyond inflaming tensions between the Irish and the Republicans, and that was to mock the abolitionist community. The idea was to fool emancipationists into believing the work was written by one of their own and endorsing it publicly, thereby marginalizing them further in the public mind. Several abolitionists took the bait, but others, suspecting a setup, were more guarded in their reactions. Abolitionists were not the only people who were gulled. The most sensational responses came from conservative Democrats, who pounced on the tract as evidence of the administration's perverse and hidden agenda. Representative Cox of Ohio gave a lengthy address on February 17 in the House. Abolitionists and Republicans "used to deny, whenever it was charged, that they favored black citizenship; yet now they are favoring black suffrage in the District of Columbia, and will favor it wherever in the South they need it for their purposes." This and other evidence "ought to convince us that that party is moving steadily forward to perfect social equality of black and white, and can only end in this detestable doctrine of—

miscegenation!" The most extreme peace men thought Cox did not go far enough in decrying racial mixing. In New York, the editor of the *New York Weekly Day-Book (Caucasian)* concluded that miscegenation was the inevitable result of emancipation. "Every man . . . opposed to 'slavery' is of necessity in favor of amalgamating with negroes," Dr. J. H. Van Evrie wrote. The *La Crosse Democrat* took this as an opportunity to needle the abolitionists when it supported sexual relations between them and African Americans: "It may be hard on the niggers, but it will be the making of the abolitionists. Anything to make them loyal, or to breed them to minding their own business. Even a cross with yaller dogs would improve some of them mightily." Not surprisingly, no prominent Copperheads ever discussed or even acknowledged the fact that racial mixing was well established in American life, having taken place for generations on Southern plantations.[10]

Cox's speech was printed up as a pamphlet and reprinted in the Democratic press, which put it into broad circulation. The address set off a firestorm of discussion in political circles and the newspapers, but the Copperhead press was especially vitriolic. Reactionary papers started regularly printing accounts of African American men and white women engaging in sexual relations—something that they had done on occasion before *Miscegenation* appeared but that became far more common after the pamphlet's publication. Black soldiers came under particular scrutiny, and the Democratic press accused them of numerous incidents of rape, murder, and arson. The *Chicago Times* reported that when an African American regiment left town in May, a "vast throng of especial admirers" saw them off. "White women were there in attendance to bid farewell to black husbands, around whose necks they clung long and fondly!" Even normal interactions on the street were interpreted as evidence of miscegenation. "Filthy black niggers, greasy, sweaty, and disgusting, now jostle white people and even ladies everywhere, even at the President's levees," the *New-York Freeman's Journal and Catholic Register* reported. When Lincoln suggested that only family ties should be stronger than those uniting working men, the *Jeffersonian* of West Chester, Pennsylvania, declared that the president was pushing the amalgamation agenda by lumping together white and black laborers. The laboring classes needed to be more aware of the threat of miscegenation because they had far more to lose from emancipation than the "non-producing classes" of professional men, the conservative press warned. "The producing classes, the mechanic, laborer, etc., had better cut the throats of their children at once than hand them to 'impartial freedom,' degradation and amalgamation with negroes," the *Day-Book* advised.[11]

By summer, Van Evrie, editor of the *Day-Book*, had come up with a new term to describe what he saw as the natural order of the universe: *subgenation*, "the natural or normal relation of an inferior to a superior race." This scientific-sounding explanation gave Van Evrie a springboard to engage in the kind of inflammatory racial rhetoric that the Copperheads employed so often. "*The equality of all whom God has created equal (white men), and the inequality of those He has made unequal (negroes and other inferior races) are the corner-stone of American democracy, and the vital principle of American civilization and of human progress,*" he wrote. "We should announce that the grand humanitarian policy of progressive and civilized America is to restore subgenation all over the American Continent."[12]

As always, these racist arguments had a highly receptive audience. With the presidential race nearing, the stakes were higher than ever. Democrats were ready to reassume what they believed was their rightful claim to the government's highest office. Even some soldiers endorsed this way of thinking—not only because they did not agree with what was happening on the battlefield, but also because they had not come to terms with emancipation and still resented the change in war aims. "I am in hopes that we shall get rid of Old Abe the devlish old ful, and his imbicle cabinet, this fall. A change of men may save us, and I hope to see the Democrats carry every thing. I'm one my self. I'm no nigger worshipper," a New York soldier wrote a friend. But this was a minority view among the men in the field; most by now applauded the proclamation as a legitimate war measure.[13]

Despite the threat that emancipation posed to his political career, Lincoln remained unwilling to abandon the freedmen. In a letter dated August 17, he explained his reasons. First, he said, he had made them a promise, the promise of freedom. Lincoln could not "escape the curses of Heaven, or of any good man" if he broke that promise as soon as it appeared expedient to do so. Besides, thousands of black men now wore a blue uniform, and their presence in the army was crucial to the Union's success. If he announced that he would no longer insist on emancipation, those men would desert immediately, and, Lincoln asked, who could blame them? "Why should they give their lives for us, with full notice of our purpose to betray them?" Finally, the president reminded his correspondent, a Democratic editor in Green Bay, Wisconsin, that no Confederate official had made any overtures about restoring the Union under any conditions. In a comment that seems directed to Copperheads and wavering conservatives of both parties, Lincoln wrote: "Shall we be weak enough to allow the enemy to distract us with an abstract question which he himself refuses to present as a practical one?" To this point in the letter, Lincoln appeared to be foursquare behind emancipation. Then he muddied the waters. It is unclear whether this was because Lincoln wanted to leave his options open, because he wanted to smoke out Davis, or because he was genuinely uncertain. Whatever the case, he appeared to step back from his adherence to emancipation as a condition for peace. "I repeat this now," he wrote, perhaps with the conservatives in mind again. "If Jefferson Davis wishes, for himself, or for the benefit of his friends at the North, to know what I would do if he were to offer peace and re-union, saying nothing about slavery, let him try me." Davis never did. And Lincoln, for whatever reason, never mailed the letter.[14]

With pressure growing for Lincoln to sue for peace and with his political fortunes on the wane, the Republican National Committee met in New York on August 22. The tidings were grim. Reporting to Lincoln on the gathering, Raymond told him that if the election were held that day, he would lose such linchpin states as New York, Pennsylvania, and Illinois; he would be lucky to carry Indiana and nearly every other state. "The want of military successes, and the impression in some minds, the fear and suspicion in others, that we are not to have peace *in any event* under this Administration until Slavery is abandoned" were at the root of Lincoln's political troubles, Raymond said. "In some way or other the suspicion is widely diffused that we can have peace with union if we would." This last sentence is notable because it indicates how deeply the military losses had seared the nation's consciousness, how far the conservatives' rhetoric had penetrated the public mind, and how deep the yearning was for peace by this time.[15]

Raymond then made a request that was astonishing, coming from the chair of a party founded on antislavery ideology. He begged the president to put together a commission and offer Davis a deal: peace *"on the sole condition of acknowledging the supremacy of the constitution."* In other words, emancipation would not be a precondition. This was a gambit. Raymond's calculus was that Davis would reject the offer out of hand, thereby dispelling the "delusion" so many Northerners had that peace could easily be had if only Lincoln would turn his back on the slaves. Just three days before Raymond wrote his letter, Lincoln once again had rejected this notion of trading emancipation for peace, saying that if he agreed to such a swap he would be "damned in time and eternity for doing so." But upon receiving Raymond's letter, Lincoln waffled. His uncertainty here suggests that he had not been deceptive in his August 17 letter to the Green Bay editor. So often sure-footed in his decisions, Lincoln was struggling with what to do. Emancipation rested on one side of the scales, and his own future—and possibly that of a reunited nation—on the other. On August 24 Lincoln drafted a memo to put Raymond's plan into play, authorizing him to meet with Davis and proposing an immediate cease-fire based on the restoration of the Union. All other questions would be dealt with later. Then the president changed his mind. He rejected Raymond's plan within twenty-four hours of writing the memo, telling the editor that "sending a commission to Richmond would be worse than losing the Presidential contest—it would be ignominiously surrendering it in advance." He would not abandon freedom for the slaves in return for an immediate end to the war. He would rather be right than president.[16] It was Lincoln's greatest moment.

Lincoln made this choice believing he would not be president for much longer. Based on information he was receiving from Republicans across the country, newspapers, and meetings with average Americans, this politically astute president thought he had little hope of winning the race in November. On August 23, the day after Raymond wrote his bleak report on the meeting of Republican leaders, Lincoln wrote a memo to his cabinet. "It seems exceedingly probable that this Administration will not be re-elected," the memo said. "Then it will be my duty to so co-operate with the President elect, as to save the Union between the election and the inauguration; as he will have secured his election on such ground that he can not possibly save it afterwards." He asked each member of his cabinet to sign the memo without ever seeing its contents.[17]

It turned out Lincoln had good reason to suspect that his presumptive successor would not save the Union. At almost the same time Lincoln was asking his cabinet to sign his memorandum, George B. McClellan, the likely Democratic nominee, was meeting with a St. Louis businessman named James Harrison. Although McClellan publicly supported the war effort, Harrison's account of the meeting depicts a man who was more malleable in his convictions. In a letter to a friend, Harrison said he found the general to be "a strong peace man." McClellan told Harrison that he intended to call an immediate armistice if he was elected, bring together a convention of all the states, and "insist upon exhausting all and every means to secure peace without further bloodshed." He would not wait for the Confederates to call for peace: "We should make the call first," McClellan said.[18]

Coincidentally, the same day Lincoln bowed his head to the political fates, the Union's fortunes—and, by extension, his—began to turn. This would only become apparent as events unfolded. The first of three military victories that would bail out his foundering ship came courtesy of the navy. The story had begun three weeks earlier, on August 5, at Mobile Bay. Admiral David Farragut took fourteen wooden ships, four ironclads, and 5,500 soldiers into the bay, which was about thirty miles south of Mobile. After a harrowing trip through a mined entrance, the Yankee ships battered their Confederate counterparts to win the fight on the sea. Winning the fight on the land, which meant taking the three forts that protected the bay, was up to the army, and this was the job that finally was completed the day Lincoln wrote his fatalistic memorandum to his cabinet. The capture of the bay sealed the Confederates' Gulf Coast from blockade runners.

The capture of Mobile Bay made headlines but did little to allay the despair that gripped the country. Government officials also had reason to be concerned that the "fire in the rear," as Lincoln had once called it, was about to turn into a conflagration. Reports had come into state capitals and Washington all summer about threats of uprisings. By August those reports had turned into a torrent. Armed bands of deserters and delinquent draftees had banded together in Cambria and Columbia counties in Pennsylvania, leaving the local provost marshal overwhelmed and too demoralized to counteract them. Union men in the region were so scared of the dissidents that they were switching sides, "preferring their comfort to their principles." Indiana remained in a state of near anarchy. More than two hundred armed and mounted men roamed Sullivan and Greene counties in the southwest part of the state robbing the homes of Union men, looking for money and guns. The state adjutant general believed the bandits were operating at the behest of Andrew Humphrey, a candidate for state representative who was urging locals to be armed and ready to resist the draft "at all hazzards." A federal official in Milwaukee predicted there would be riots there if the army did not send a significant number of men to help.[19]

Government officials and Republican appointees were not the only people alarmed about what was happening at home. One Iowa woman whose husband had volunteered for the army complained that the military had taken most of the loyal men from her area, leaving loyal families prey to the local Copperheads. Peace Democrats taunted the soldiers' families and told them they hoped the men would not live to come home. They also threatened to burn her property. "I live in fear of them so much so that I take my three children and go from home to stay nights," she said. Another Hawkeye wrote her father: "O everything is so sad and anxious. When will the good time come. . . . We have not only an open foe to contend with, but a secret foe at home in our very midst, rebel sympathizers, peace men traitors, copperheads, or whatever you may term them, are daily plotting treason, to overthrow the government. O how sad it is to think of it."[20]

Such fears were not as fantastic as Klement and later historians have portrayed them. After Dodd was arrested in Indianapolis in mid-August, the Confederates and Sons of Liberty hatched yet another plot to free Southern prisoners of war and take over Northern cities. The latest incarnation of this scheme targeted Chicago and the Democratic convention. Under this plan, seventy Confederate soldiers who had escaped to Canada would infiltrate the city, where they were supposed to be met by fifty thousand Copperheads. The rebels gave the Sons of Liberty leaders money to cover transportation costs and arms; a Chicago man had received enough to outfit the two regiments of revolutionaries he claimed to have at the ready. Once the Confederates and their Copperhead allies were in Chicago, five thousand Southerners imprisoned at Camp Douglas were somehow supposed to break out—in all the variations on this plan, it was never clear how they were to spring themselves—and seize weapons from the federal arsenal. When the signal was given, Confederate sympathizers across the North were to rise up, cut telegraph and railroad lines, free rebel soldiers from other prison camps, and try to take over governments all over the Northwest.[21]

Huge crowds came to Chicago for the convention—more than one hundred thousand by some estimates. Alerted to the possibility of trouble, the army also arrived in force, and that seems to have unnerved the revolutionaries from the Sons of Liberty. They were "appalled by the actual demand for overt action against armed forces," one of the Confederate agents, Captain John B. Castleman, recalled years later. The Sons balked when the rebels asked them to take Camp Douglas; they apparently had not understood when they signed up that the project might involve loss of life, specifically, their own. That was the end of the Chicago conspiracy.[22]

The Confederates tried to salvage something of their scheme by asking for a detachment of men to liberate the prison camp at Rock Island and overrun the arsenal in Springfield. That proposal also met resistance. Copperhead commanders suggested postponing the coup attempt until after the presidential election. Their mission completely frustrated, the rebel conspirators blamed the Sons of Liberty for the fiasco. This was the last gasp for any sort of viable Copperhead conspiracy. Local plots would continue to simmer in parts of the Northwest, but the threat of a revolutionary uprising in the North was over.[23]

Amid these machinations, the Democrats finally met. The convention originally had been scheduled for July 4, but military losses and declining morale had led party leaders to believe their cause could only gain strength if they bided their time before meeting. Now, in late August, they could wait no longer. The leadership had played its hand well. By the time the convention opened, the national mood was decidedly dark: "vacillating and despondent," was the way Seward described it. A Democratic newspaper in Boston accused Lincoln of his own scheming: It said that the military could claim no successes and that Lincoln and his advisers were withholding news of military losses and making up reports of advances to remain in power. Peace Democrats were quick to play on the bleak national sentiment. Henry Clay Dean of Iowa told a crowd gathered on a Chicago street that Lincoln and his armies had *"failed! Failed!!* FAILED!!! FAILED!!!!" The loss of life "has never been seen since the destruction of Sennacherib by the breath of the Almighty and still the monster usurper wants more men for his slaughter pens." Ever since Lincoln, "the usurper, traitor, and tyrant," had come to power, Republicans "had shouted war to the knife, and the knife to the hilt," he said. "Blood had flown down in torrents, and yet the thirst of the old monster was not quenched. His cry was for more blood."[24]

Democrats may have been united in their opposition to the administration, but they did not arrive in Chicago of one mind on other issues. A deep rift had developed over the summer as to who should carry the party banner in November. Copperheads had no interest in a man whose reputation was as a War Democrat—a man like McClellan, the frontrunner, who supported the war and many of Lincoln's policies, though not that of emancipation. McClellan's certain nomination was predicated on the belief that he would draw thousands of votes from soldiers in the field.[25] Even though he was politically viable and shared conservatives' opposition to emancipation, McClellan was too moderate for the peace faction. In July a splinter group of Philadelphia hard-liners tried to nominate Millard Fillmore or Franklin Pierce, both former presidents, as the party candidate. The effort went nowhere, but peace men across the North nodded in approval. Congressman Alexander Long of Ohio bluntly wrote that a War Democrat was not electable. The problem, as he saw it, was the war faction's lack of support for an immediate end to the carnage. "If we can Succeed in getting a peace platform and peace candidate at Chicago all will be well, but if McClellan is put upon us all is lost," he said. The *Old Guard's* editor, C. Chauncey Burr, had fretted early in the summer that "no true Democrat will support this war another hour."[26] Now he worried openly that McClellan would be the nominee just because he was available. The Democrats needed a peace man who had never participated in the "stupendous abominations that have destroyed us," Burr argued. Other conservatives thought the nation had finally caught up to them in their desire for an end to war. Lieutenant Charles Medary, the soldier son of the Columbus, Ohio, *Crisis* editor, wrote, "As the winds of peace are blowing favorably . . . it is best not to nominate any man who has any war in him." Still others thought the Democratic Party should show no weakness in its commitment to its values. "Peace men must rouse themselves, sweep away the War leaders of the Democracy, nominate a candidate for President who shall bear upon his banner Peace and Subgenation . . . [and see to] *the adoption by the North of the Confederate Constitution!*" Van Evrie of the *Day-Book* argued. But the Copperheads, though highly influential in the party, could not sway the majority of their party away from the Young Napoleon. McClellan enjoyed broad support with the public and most especially—or so the Democrats thought—with the soldiers. His popularity, along with his military credentials, gave him the lock on the nomination. Conservatives were left to find other ways to advance their beliefs.[27]

The Copperheads were surging in power. Their point of view was gaining increasing credibility in the public mind, and their strength within the party was beyond question. Mainstream Democratic leaders could not afford to ignore them or offend the peace wing, but they worried about its rogue tendencies. Samuel Barlow, the party chairman, wrote the editor of the *New York World* that he hoped New York governor Horatio Seymour, who had been named president of the convention, would be able to control the peace men of the West.

Seymour, a conservative who was more moderate than, say, Vallandigham, needed to persuade his fellow Copperheads that "our only safety, lies in success, and . . . with McClellan, peace is certain." Peace had to be the central focus if the Democrats hoped to win, he said, and conservatives needed to know that the party at large was hearing their message and adopting at least parts of it. Once the Copperheads understood that they were not being overlooked, the party leadership could draft a platform that would appeal to anyone who opposed Lincoln.[28]

New York governor Horatio Seymour moved back and forth between being a War Democrat and a Peace Democrat. (*Harper's Weekly* / Courtesy of HarpWeek LLC)

Then there was the issue of the vice presidential candidate, Barlow said. He needed to be chosen carefully so that his presence would not weaken the ticket. A border-state man might do, he said. "If our friends [the Peace Democrats] are wise, and do not absolutely throw away success, I have no doubt of our ability to elect McClellan and to restore the Union."[29]

The convention opened August 29 with a broadside from William Bigler, a former Pennsylvania governor and senator. He set a tone of negativity that would characterize the entire gathering. "After more than two millions of men have been called into the field, on our side alone, after the land has been literally drenched in fraternal blood, and wailings and lamentations are heard in every corner of our common country, the hopes of the Union, our cherished object, are in nowise improved," he told the crowd. In a pointed reference to the aims of men like Dodd who sought a coup, Bigler said the only solution to the nation's woe was the "overthrow, by the ballot," of the Lincoln government. Then the Democrats would "directly and zealously, but temperately and justly . . . bring about a speedy settlement of the national troubles on the principles of the constitution and on terms honorable and just to all sections." Unlike Lincoln, he promised, the Democrats would lay down no preconditions for peace, not even that of reunion. Although Bigler went on to discuss reunion as though the Confederates wanted it, his comments very nearly suggested that he was ready to settle for peace without reunion. This was the kind of speech that would leave a strong whiff of defeatism (read: lack of patriotism) about the party in the coming weeks.[30]

On the second day, Governor Seymour of New York spoke to a crowd that spilled out onto the streets along the Wigwam, where the convention was held. He accused the Republicans of gross mismanagement and stubbornness that threatened the future of the nation. "They will not have Union except upon conditions unknown to our constitution; they will not let the shedding of blood cease, even for a little time, to see if Christian charity, or the wisdom of statesmanship may work out a method to save our country," he said. "This administration cannot now save this Union if it would. It has, by its proclamations, by vindictive legislation, by displays of hate and passion, placed obstacles in its own pathway which it cannot overcome and has hampered its own freedom of action by unconstitutional acts." Two things made this speech noteworthy. First was Seymour's assertion that the country was beyond saving, at least by Lincoln. Second was Seymour's absolution of the soldiers. The failure of the government was not due to "the want of courage and devotion on the part of our armies" but because of the

Lincoln administration. The remark is worth noting not for its content but for its timing. Seymour was the first Democratic official to directly acknowledge the contributions of the soldiers over the past three and a half years, and he did not take the stage until the convention was halfway over. The fact that soldiers were largely ignored as a topic of conversation in Chicago was not lost on the men at the front. They would allude to this slight bitterly as the election grew nearer.[31]

The most damning—and lasting—product of the convention was the party platform. Despite Barlow's hope that Seymour would rein in the Copperheads and the party would craft a moderate platform, the leadership wound up putting Vallandigham in charge of the platform committee and stocking it with other Copperheads. This was an acknowledgement of the conservatives' burgeoning power and an effort to keep them in check. But for all the good their platform did McClellan and the Democratic Party, the leadership might as well have tied the general into a sack filled with rocks and thrown him into Lake Michigan. Barlow, a moderate war man, might have been able to head off the disastrous decision to assign Vallandigham to draft the platform, but he had refused to attend the convention on the grounds that his presence would only make McClellan's other, more conservative managers jealous. Barlow had deputized Samuel Tilden to keep Vallandigham under control, but Tilden was a conciliatory man, and the ideologically driven outlaw from Ohio easily steamrolled him.[32]

The platform opened with a refutation of Republican policies. The Constitution, it said, had been "disregarded in every part, and public liberty and private right alike trodden down [and] the material prosperity of the country essentially impaired." It went on to accuse the administration of purposely and purposefully trying to prevent a restoration of the Union and of exercising "extraordinary and dangerous powers" that the Constitution never granted. The most controversial plank termed the war a "failure," demanded "immediate efforts" to end hostilities, and called for a convention to cobble together a treaty and restore peace "on the basis of the Federal Union of the States." The statement was frustratingly imprecise. Would such a convention be held with individual states, some of which had indicated an inclination to end hostilities, or with the Davis government, which presumably was less willing to end the war without winning independence? Was reunion an absolute precondition for such talks? What were Democrats prepared to concede in return for peace? Rejecting emancipation would be the most likely concession, but what about the Union itself? Once again, the Copperheads ignored the Confederates' oft-stated interest in continuing as an independent nation. They also refused to address the Southerners' claims that secession was among their rights under the Constitution—a point some in the rebel press were quick to pounce on after the platform became public. Vallandigham was unmovable in his commitment to the platform's suicidal depiction of an unsuccessful war and the call for peace. If the platform was not adopted, he said at the convention, he would leave the party and perhaps "go further still" if the Democrats tried to alter it. It is hard to know what Vallandigham meant by this, but the party needed to keep the conservatives in the fold and under control. Vallandigham's bluff, if it was indeed a bluff, worked. The members of the convention adopted the entire platform with only four dissenting votes.[33]

On the third day of the convention, the Democrats nominated McClellan. The groundswell for him was so strong that even the most committed Copperheads—men such as Vallandigham, Fernando Wood, and Connecticut's former governor Thomas Seymour—fell in line. The peace wing, which had advanced Seymour as a candidate until he said he was not interested, was rewarded for its loyalty with the number two spot on the ticket. (The fact that the position went to a conservative was yet another acknowledgment of how influential and powerful the peace wing had become.) George Pendleton, a Buckeye whose family originally hailed from Virginia and who was one of the country's most hard-line Copperheads, was the unanimous choice for vice president. Pendleton had gained notoriety among Unionists by voting against such war measures as increasing the size of the regular army, revenue bills, the greenback bill, and conscription. Like the platform, Pendleton's candidacy would taint McClellan in the weeks leading up to the election and would divert Democratic efforts away from promoting McClellan to doing damage control instead.[34]

The convention was the high-water mark for the Copperheads. They failed to secure the nomination for Thomas Seymour as they had hoped, but they succeeded in getting one of

The vice presidential nomination of Peace Democrat George Pendleton demonstrates how powerful the Copperheads had become within their party. (*The Old Guard*/Courtesy of HarpWeek LLC)

their own on the ticket. Their leader, Vallandigham, ran the committee that drafted the party platform, and the platform—and thus the party— bore their imprimatur boldly. Their input was more than just a sop that mainstream Democrats threw them; it was a necessary political concession to the conservatives' broad appeal within the party. They were so strong now that they posed a real challenge to the war wing of the Democratic Party. Lusty cheers inside the Wigwam greeted the plank that most reflected their ideals. Helped by the dismal performance of the army, many of their ideas had seeped so far into the party consciousness that even weary War Democrats sounded themes that the peace men had been expounding for more than three years. This moment was the Copperheads' apex. Paradoxically, their success in Chicago left an impression of defeatism that ultimately cost McClellan and his party dearly.[35]

When the convention broke up August 31, most Democrats returned home from Chicago feeling highly optimistic. They extolled McClellan in terms approaching the heroic and delighted over the party platform. "Proclaim the old watch cries of Peace, and Union, the Constitution and Freedom," the *Detroit Free Press* trumpeted. "Away with the gag, with all the manacles with which the present administration has endeavored to bind Liberty. Let the giant awake and burst his bonds. . . . Let every patriot fall into the ranks of the army of Liberty."[36]

Republicans, on the other hand, were indignant over what had taken place in Chicago and especially about the platform. "My ire was considerably aroused by reading the extracts of speeches at the Chicago Convention, worse 10 times worse than Rebel speeches for they are turning *traitors base dishonest traitors* to their country in this her time of peril," a Michigan woman wrote her husband, who was in Sherman's army. "As much as I desire peace and your return I do not want it until it can be a righteous and lasting one." Like many other Republican publications, *Harper's Weekly* seethed that the platform had "no word of righteous wrath against the recreant citizens who have plunged the country in the blood of civil war" and did not censure the Confederacy. Instead, it freely branded the government that was defending the Union as "tyrannical and despotic." "There is not a word in it that can cheer any soldier or sailor fighting for his country; not a syllable that stirs the blood of a patriot," *Harper's* went on. "It is craven, abject, humiliating. It confesses the defeat of the Union cause, and covertly implores the mercy of *Jefferson Davis* and his crew." Democrats defended themselves against such charges of treason by turning the tables and blaming the Republicans for secession. The *World,* for instance, charged that abolitionist—that is, Republican—invective against the South had driven that section out of the country. Democrats would not repeat that mistake by including antagonistic speech in their platform, it declared.[37]

The men at the front were furious over the platform's terming their efforts a failure. Anyone who would support such a platform by voting for a Democrat "is more detrimental to the country and more beneficial to the rebellion than if they placed themselves actively in arms side by side with the rebels in the field," General Benjamin Butler told Raymond. Moreover, soldiers were deeply offended that in Chicago the Democrats had hardly mentioned them or their sacrifices. The Republican platform, on the other hand, had explicitly thanked Union soldiers and sailors for their service. Soldiers began to flood the home front with angry letters explaining why civilians should vote for Lincoln.[38]

To the extent that there was an official response to the Democratic convention, it came from Seward in a stump speech in New York. (At the time, tradition held that presidential candidates never hit the hustings on their own behalf.) "I think you will agree with me that the Richmond democrats and the Chicago democrats have lately come to act very much alike," he told the crowd. Confederates and Democrats shared three goals: to declare an armistice, nominate a candidate who supported the armistice and a peace convention, and keep Lincoln from being re-elected. Seward dismissed the Copperheads' concerns. On the subject of civilian arrests, he said the government could hardly be expected to let spies and traitors roam free while waiting for more states either to be invaded or to secede. Copperheads walked the streets uttering treasonous statements with the aim of being arrested just so they could complain that they had been denied their right of free speech, he said. As for the draft, the administration would not allow "the ship to be scuttled" without calling all hands, even if that meant resorting to conscription.[39]

Lincoln obliquely responded to Democratic criticisms in a letter turning down an invitation to speak in Buffalo. "Much is being said about peace; and no man desires peace more ardently than I. Still I am yet unprepared to give up the Union for a peace which, so achieved, could not be of much duration. The preservation of our Union was not the sole avowed object for which the war was commenced. It was commenced for precisely the reverse object—*to destroy our Union.*" His goal when the war began had been to preserve the Union, and that had never changed, he said. "Any substantial departure from it insures the success of the rebellion. An armistice—a cessation of hostilities—is the end of the struggle, and the insurgents would be in peaceable possession of all that has been struggled for." He defended his policy regarding freedmen, saying that any course other than the one he had followed would deprive the nation of the blacks' assistance. His comments here were similar to those he had made a year earlier in his letter to the Springfield gathering. "We can not spare the hundred and forty or fifty thousand now serving us as soldiers, seamen, and laborers. This is not a question of sentiment or taste, but one of physical force . . . ," Lincoln said. "Keep it and you can save the Union. Throw it away, and the Union goes with it. Nor is it possible for any Administration to retain the service of these people with the express or implied understanding that upon the first convenient occasion, they are to be re-inslaved."[40]

Republican characterizations of the platform and the Democrats were downright charitable compared to what black newspapers had to say about them. A letter to the *Christian Recorder* depicted the Democrats as an "old, defunct party" that sought to "regain power and bring back those good old days, when they moved, at the sound of their master's whip, to catch the panting fugitives fleeing to the North." Democratic aims should not be taken lightly, the writer warned. "If that party succeeds in the election of its candidate and assumes the Government, every black man may prepare to be deprived of every right which he now enjoys, and the race may also look across the ocean for a place of asylum."[41]

Republicans and African Americans were not the only people upset at the outcome of the convention. Many War Democrats disapproved of Pendleton's presence on the ticket and resented the fact that the platform denounced neither the rebellion nor the rebels. Given their more moderate tendencies, though, the disgruntled War Democrats refused to do anything that might undercut the party. Not given to compromise, the Copperheads likewise were disgusted at what had happened in Chicago. "I am displeased with the platform & nominee McClellan," J. Sterling Morton wrote in his diary. "They will both be beaten & ought to be. I am for Peace, Peace Platform & Peace Man on it & so we would deceive no one who is for war as the only means of restoring the Union. Peace *might* restore it. War cannot & war makes disunion."[42] Letters poured in to leading Peace Democrats from followers who accused them of selling out to the war men. One New Yorker wrote to Governor Horatio Seymour to say that he and the other party leaders had guaranteed Lincoln's reelection by putting up McClellan. "I think Sir that you will realise before long that the nomination of McClellan at chicago by the democratic leaders was the greatest blunder of their lives."[43]

True to form, Copperheads were willing to resort to destructive means to make their point. A group that included Vallandigham, George Pugh, Edson Olds, and Medary of the *Crisis* met in Columbus on September 14 and decided to break with the Democratic ticket. They called for a convention in Cincinnati on October 18 and invited Copperheads from throughout the Northwest to attend. Vallandigham later changed his mind and decided to back the McClellan ticket in the interest of party unity, but the rump convention met anyway. It was a bust, and for all the usual reasons. Lack of leadership and an inability to agree made a hash of the meeting, which disbanded in chaos. In a separate but equally embarrassing display of no confidence, Alexander Long (the censured congressman) and William M. Corry met with other peace-at-any-price men in Cincinnati. They issued resolutions denouncing McClellan, defending slavery, and proclaiming the war "wholly unconstitutional." With McClellan's policies being "identical" to Lincoln's, "we have before us two candidates, but no choice," the convention said. They nominated Long as their presidential candidate, but he declined the honor. Like many other men in this splinter group, he refused to cast a vote for president in November.[44]

Confederates watched all this closely. As true believers, the Sons of Liberty were "totally demoralized" by McClellan's nomination and the disclosures about and arrests of Dodd and his compatriots in Indiana, the Confederate agent Thompson told Judah P. Benjamin. "The feeling with the masses is as strong as ever. They are true, brave, and, I believed willing and ready, but they have no leaders," he said. Davis received intelligence from the North directly. Writing on the New York City mayor's letterhead, Samuel Anderson told him on August 30 that even though he had doubts about McClellan and his insatiable ambitions, he was sure the Young Napoleon would be "enthusiastically elected." Assuming McClellan was elected, he "would submit propositions to you which it would be difficult to reject," Anderson reported. "The alternative, I do not doubt, would be war *with a united North.*" John B. Jones, a Maryland-born clerk in the Confederate War Department, wrote in his diary: "The next two months will be the most interesting period of the war; everything depends upon the result of the Presidential election in the United States. We rely some little upon the success of the peace party." He greeted the Democrats' platform with a great deal of pleasure. "I think the resolutions of the convention amount to a defiance of President Lincoln, and that their ratification meetings will inaugurate civil war," Jones wrote.[45]

Other rebels were less optimistic that the Democrats would advance their cause. North Carolina businessman Edward Jenner Warren wrote a friend that he saw "no prospect of peace" in the Democratic platform. Because it recognized "no peace men, no supporters of the constitution, no enemies of Lincoln & despotism outside of 'the Democratic Party,' " Warren saw only the "most conclusive proof that the North will never consent to a separation." Robert Garlick Hill Kean, head of the Confederate Bureau of War, regarded McClellan as a candidate much more dangerous to the South than Lincoln. "He would constantly offer peace and reconstruction on the basis of the Constitution, which would rapidly develop a reconstruction party in the South," Kean wrote in his diary.[46]

Then came Atlanta. Sherman's victory there made a mockery of all the Democrats' speeches, their vice presidential candidate, and most of all their platform. Their much-delayed convention could be the worst-timed event in American political history. Sherman's final assault on Atlanta began August 25, four days before the Democrats arrived in Chicago. He swung to the south of the city, a move that flummoxed the rebels. At first General John Bell Hood thought he had succeeded in driving the Yankees from Atlanta, and he began to celebrate its liberation in missives to Richmond. By the time he realized his mistake, it was too late. Sherman beat Hood on August 31 at Jonesboro. Unwilling to continue an engagement, the Confederates slipped out of the city the night of September 1–2, torching everything of military value as they left. "Atlanta gone. Well—that agony is over," Richmond resident Mary Boykin Chesnut wrote in her diary. "No hope. We will try to have no fear."[47]

When the news arrived, the mood in the North made a 180-degree turn. Despair gave way to cheerful—almost giddy—confidence. "Old Abe's Reply to the Chicago Convention. Is the War a Failure?" a headline in the *St. Paul Daily Press* read. The usually curmudgeonly *New York Herald* adopted a completely different tone with Sherman's victory. "The fall of Atlanta has produced a general impression throughout the country that the end of the war is near at hand," it editorialized. "We believe that within the sixty days grace to Jeff. Davis allowed by the Richmond journals that city will be purged of the rebellion. In the meantime the present political situation in the North will destroy the last hope of the rebel leaders of a successful Northern Presidential diversion in favor of a disunion peace." The *New York Times* was jubilant, calling the victory "of such wide scope, such far-reaching result, such indisputable importance" that the country could do nothing but glow in exultation. "What infamy it is that at such an hour croakers should be croaking, and Copperheads hissing, and men actually contemplating a disgraceful surrender to this thrice-accursed rebellion."[48]

The consequences of the victory in Atlanta were not lost on Lincoln, who thanked Sherman and his men profusely. Nor were the connotations lost on Democratic leaders. While McClellan wrestled with his acceptance letter, Manton Marble, who was in charge of publicity for

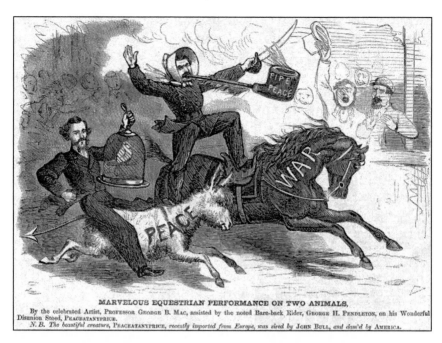

MARVELOUS EQUESTRIAN PERFORMANCE ON TWO ANIMALS,
By the celebrated Artist, Professor George B. Mac, assisted by the noted Bare-back Rider, George H. Pendleton, on his Wonderful Disunion Steed, Peaceatanyprice.
N.B. The beautiful creature, Peaceatanyprice, recently imported from Europe, was sired by John Bull, and dam'd by America.

The Democratic platform saddled prowar presidential candidate George B. McClellan with a strongly worded peace plank. Though McClellan tried to distance himself from it, he was unsuccessful. This cartoon calls his masculinity into question as he tries to straddle the issue. McClellan's running mate, the Copperhead George Pendleton, rides a white donkey named Peaceatanyprice. Note the shape of that donkey's tail. (*Harper's Weekly*/Courtesy of HarpWeek LLC)

the party, privately urged the general to keep up his army connections as a way of offsetting the damage that the peace plank had inflicted. "You know how the platform hurts us there & how confidently Mr. Lincoln counts upon the ambition of the Army officers & the votes of the soldiers to assist in his re-election," Marble wrote. Other high-ranking Democrats were less optimistic. They knew their party would be dead on arrival in November.[49]

Across the country, support for McClellan cratered. The *World* tried to make the best of the situation when it noted that "happily for General Sherman . . . his fame will ere long be in the hands of a sound, constitutional, and conservative administration." The paper was whistling in the graveyard. Whatever enthusiasm McClellan had generated at the convention seemed to vanish—quite literally, almost overnight— with Sherman's victory. The mood of the country was so changed that even volunteering picked up. "The spirit of the crusades is revived. . . . I am wondering whether the furor for McClellan has not expended itself in his nomination," a bewildered Iowa Copperhead said. "McClellan stock is not quoted at all . . . ," a Republican in Indiana wrote. "Prospects generally are becoming brighter and brighter every day for the Union cause. I am not oversanguine in my temperament, but really it does look just now as if we would carry everything before us, like a *'whirligust.'* " Some conservatives remained oblivious, though. "The nomination of George B. McClellan, by the Chicago Convention, is the death-knell to the abolition party," the *Boston Pilot* blustered. The war had yielded disastrous results: a "deranged" currency, inflation, a policy that would "exalt a degraded, inferior race into equality with the white race," assaults on the rights of property and personal security, and a death toll that "surpasses the wildest dreams of the gloomiest alarmist." Atlanta apparently never registered with the editors.[50]

Democratic editors sourly maintained that a vote for Lincoln was a vote for the draft. This argument made enough of an impact as the country was waiting for its next round of conscription that Republicans implored Grant to write a note supporting the draft. He did, saying that waiting for a draft was worse than the event itself and that "the enforcement of the draft and prompt filling up of our armies will save the shedding of blood to an immense degree." Concerns about draft-related violence appear to have been ill-founded in this newly exuberant era. Provost marshals in even the most recalcitrant districts reported that the Copperheads were stricken "with an air of vacant purpose," meaning that the worst problem enrolling officers were likely to face was not active resistance but flight to Canada.[51]

Although the mantle of despair was shifting from the Unionists to some conservatives, hard-liners in the West were not dead yet. James Guthrie of Kentucky, a former treasury secretary, demanded an immediate halt to hostilities and a guarantee to Confederates of "their rights in the Union under the Constitution." Jefferson Davis was a friend of his, and, he assured an audience in Indiana, "the South are for peace." Elsewhere, violence continued to simmer. In Green County, Indiana, a man issued a proclamation saying that within thirty days of the coming draft "every union family in the county shall leave or be hanged until they are *dead dead*!!" In Ohio, ambushers fired at two deputy provost marshals in Van Wert County. One of the marshals had his horse shot out from under him. Federal deputies and Unionists in that county received several threats to their life or property, and loyal civilians were so scared they would not leave their homes. Meanwhile, the Sons of Liberty reportedly were meeting nightly and vowing "to a man" that they would resist the draft. Resistance in Van Wert County ended only when the army sent a detail of men. After that, "not a man could be found that was willing to resist the Officers in delivering the notices. . . . Resistance in the Fifth District was squelched and the Resisters had vanished," the provost marshal boasted to his superiors.[52]

As the North celebrated Sherman's triumph, McClellan was busy writing his letter accepting the Democratic nomination. War Democrats saw this as Little Mac's opportunity to repudiate the peace plank that, it was becoming clear, was a serious liability. "I need not tell you how bitterly I am disappointed by the want of wisdom manifested at Chicago. Their second resolution looks as if it had been concocted to destroy their own candidate," George Ticknor Curtis wrote Little Mac. But the damage was done, and McClellan had to walk a fine line in accepting the nomination. If he blatantly rejected the plank, he risked alienating the Peace Democrats, who were an important and influential part of the party. Embracing the document, however, would drive away Unionist moderates of both parties who had been drawn to his candidacy. McClellan's task would have been difficult in the best of times, but he had to act now in the excited days after Atlanta. As *Harper's Weekly* put it, the general needed "an extraordinary exercise of the skill of the most accomplished equestrian simultaneously to ride two horses going different ways." McClellan proved not to be so good a rider.[53]

Early versions of McClellan's letter show him to be highly conciliatory to the South as long as the Union was restored. By the time he wrote his sixth and final draft on September 8, though, Sherman had captured Atlanta, and the Republicans were capitalizing on the peace plank. McClellan's writing therefore took on a more precise and much less mollifying tone. Peace on the basis of reunion was the primary theme to emerge from McClellan's final letter. Lest his point go unnoticed, McClellan said nine times in his relatively brief missive that the Union had to be preserved. That was the only reason the North had gone to war in the first place, it should continue to be the nation's only war aim, and it was the "indispensable condition" of any settlement, he said. Although McClellan sounded conciliatory toward the rebels in the early drafts of his acceptance letter, he took a much harder line in the final product. If the Confederates disagreed with his conditions, "the responsibility for ulterior consequences" would be on their heads. In an obvious effort to appease soldiers offended by the Chicago platform, he wrote that it would be unconscionable for him to negotiate a peace on any other terms: "I could not look in the face of my gallant comrades of the Army and Navy, who have survived so many bloody battles, and tell them that their labors, and the sacrifice of so many of our slain and wounded brethren had been in vain—that we had abandoned that Union for which we have so often perilled our lives." Without saying so publicly, McClellan was desperately try-ing to divorce himself from Vallandigham's plank. Privately, he told Congressman Samuel S. Cox that he could not run on the platform "without violating all my antecedents—which I would not do for a thousand Presidencies."[54]

McClellan's second theme was that under his administration the Southern states could rejoin the Union with their constitutional rights fully and immediately restored. This was in contrast to Lincoln's exist-ing system of Reconstruction, which demanded that seceded states earn the trust of the Union before they could return as full and equal part-ners. States' rights was a tricky issue, one that had vexed the nation since the time of Adams and Jefferson. Although slavery was the rea-son for this war, leading Southerners and Copperheads had wrapped that ugly institution in the shiny rhetoric of states' rights. McClellan's vague talk about states' rights had the potential to inflame Northern-ers' fears as much as his peace talk had the potential to calm them. On the other hand, McClellan's references to constitutional rights could be read as code for a return to slavery. The general had never hidden his opposition to the Emancipation Proclamation, and indeed had ad-vised Lincoln not to free any slaves, despite the military advantages that move might bring.[55]

McClellan's final draft received mixed reviews. *Harper's* perceptively read the document as "confused and verbose: wanting both the manly directness of the soldier and the earnest conviction of the patriot." War Democrats greeted the letter with a sense of relief. Peace Democrats were disgusted. "You have witnessed the base truckling, and betrayal of the Dem party at Chicago in the nomination of McClellan," a friend of Pendleton's wrote him. John Allen Trimble noticed that McClellan did not endorse the platform but instead took issue with "the only saving clause of that remarkable document." A committed opponent of the war since its outbreak, Trimble was enraged. "Think you that the people will submit to such a glaring and gratuitous fraud upon their rights and fran-chises as am [American] citizens[?]" he asked Pendleton.[56]

The good news was turning into a flood for Lincoln. First Farragut took Mobile Bay. Then the Democrats nominated Pendleton and drafted the peace plank. Sherman captured Atlanta. Now, in mid-September, the Democrats were flustered and sniping at one another, and Lincoln's Republican challengers scattered. Chase, who had not been a serious contender for months but had remained in the wings as a fallback can-didate, was neutralized for good September 23 when Lincoln ousted Chase's archrival in the cabinet, Postmaster General Montgomery Blair. Chase could no longer capitalize on divisions within the administra-tion. Frémont withdrew his nomination the day after Blair's resignation was accepted because he feared that, even with the military's change of fortune, Republican infighting could lead to a McClellan victory in November. Given McClellan's hostility toward emancipation, that scenario was unthinkable to the abolition-minded Frémont.[57]

The news for the Democratic Party and for the Confederacy only got worse as September's end neared. General Philip Sheridan started moving through the Shenandoah Valley on September 19 and did not stop until mid-October. Along the way Sheridan broke Jubal Early's rebel command and ravaged the food stores and livestock of the area. He promised to "go on and clean out the Valley," which supplied both Lee's and Early's armies. "The destruction of the grain and forage from [Harrisonburg] to Staunton will be a terrible blow to them. . . . When this is completed the Valley, from Winchester up to Staunton, ninety-two miles, will have but little in it for man or beast."[58]

The result thrilled the North. Hugh McCulloch, a Hoosier who would become treasury secretary in 1865, wrote his wife: "There scarcely ever

By the beginning of October 1864, when this was published, it was clear to many in the North that the activities of the various Union armies had finally cut the heart out of the rebel war effort. The title of this cartoon was particularly descriptive: "The Monster Rebellion Beaten Out Flat." (*Frank Leslie's Budget of Fun*/Courtesy of HarpWeek LLC)

was a greater change effected in the public mind than has taken place since I was in Indiana. The Chicago Platform an[d] successes in the field have put a new aspect upon our public affairs. The rebellion is staggering under the blows." Lincoln was sure to be reelected "by a triumphant majority," McCulloch predicted. "He is more hated & feared by the rebels, than any other man & his election will crush out their remaining hopes of success by means of divisions in the north." Party leaders were so dispirited that Marble of the *World* declined to editorialize on Sheridan's exploits, although they were covered at length in the news pages. By late September, Republicans were boasting about their anticipated victories in the war and at the polls while Democratic candidates begged party leaders for money to organize their efforts and fend off their opponents.[59]

The combination of Mobile, Atlanta, and the Shenandoah Valley was a terrible blow to the Confederates, and some Southerners gave up their greatest hope for independence—McClellan's election. "Lincoln will walk all over the course," the head of the Confederate War Office predicted on September 25. Josiah Gorgas, the chief of Confederate ordnance, agreed that Union successes at Mobile and Atlanta doomed the Democrats in the November elections. John Jones, the War Department clerk who regarded the election as the most important harbinger of the Confederacy's future, said Southerners stopped caring about the outcome. They blamed McClellan for engineering his own demise by not coming out firmly in favor of peace and indicating a willingness to recognize Confederate independence. Soldiers noticed the shift in Southern morale. "I have heard the rebels say that their main hope now was help from the north"—that is, the Democrats, an Indiana soldier wrote. "I believe the election of Old Abe would tend more to close the war now than any thing else."[60]

With the arrival of fall, Lincoln and the Republicans appeared poised for success. Lincoln had weathered the summer through his own mettle. (Certainly he had enjoyed little support from his advisers.) In the face of enormous pressure to sue for peace, to sell out emancipation, Lincoln had refused—at considerable risk to his career. To be sure, the Democrats helped Lincoln enormously. With their peace plank and Copperhead nominee for vice president, the Democrats had hurt themselves irreparably. In writing his tortured response to the platform, McClellan had demonstrated that he was nothing close to Lincoln's equal in either moral fortitude or political prowess. But the moments of crisis that both Lincoln and McClellan faced were not the primary factors that would determine the election.[61] The most important factor was the success or failure of the Union military.

"Faction in Civil War Is Unmitigated Treason"

MAINSTREAM DEMOCRATS HAD MADE A TERRIBLE MISTAKE in ceding such control to the peace wing at the convention. The Copperheads, who were so strong at the end of August, turned into a political millstone for McClellan and the rest of the party. By allowing the peace wing to write the party platform and install Pendleton as McClellan's running mate, the party gave the Republicans the chance to tar them as disloyal, an opening the Republicans capitalized on again and again. No matter how hard Democrats tried, they could not rid themselves of what the Republicans repeatedly referred to as "the smell of treason on their garments." The man at the top of the ticket further stymied the Democrats' attempts to regain traction. McClellan absented himself from the political game, cloistering himself instead in his New Jersey home. He refused almost all public appearances and often declined to meet important politicians in private, preferring to correspond with them instead. Tainted and leaderless, the Democrats hit the shoals in the October elections and the rocks in November. McClellan suffered a humiliating defeat at the hands of a man he had once ridiculed as "the *original gorrilla*," losing even the soldier vote he presumably had locked up. The soldiers, it turned out, wanted to see the war through to its conclusion.[1]

Sherman's capture of Atlanta and Sheridan's continuing victories in the Shenandoah Valley left many Northerners—soldiers in particular— certain that the end of the war was in sight. "The last hours of the Rebellion are drawing nigh," a Yankee surgeon in the Shenandoah Valley wrote his wife. "God has struck terror into the heart of our foes, and we are driving them everywhere before us. Upon the right, upon the left, in front and all around, rises that unmistakable cheer of victory!"

An Iowa soldier also thought the war was nearing its conclusion, but he admitted having suggested that before and therefore said it now only with great caution. He knew one thing for certain: He did not feel like fighting any more until the presidential election was settled. "If the north is going to be divided and McClellan elected, we have already done enough for nothing. All our labor and fighting and suffering will then be for nothing; all the blood that has been shed and the lives that have been lost will be in vain." This impression would spell the doom of McClellan and the Democrats at the polls that fall.[2]

The campaign rhetoric in the fall of 1864 recapitulated most of what conservatives had been saying for the past three years. Pamphlet after pamphlet, editorial after editorial pounded away at Lincoln for his "usurpations" and tyrannical aspirations, for the imprisonment of dissenters, for the draft, for the bloodshed, for the financial cost of the war and the new tools the administration employed to pay for it, and for emancipation. The one area in which the War Democrats seemed to bear the most influence was in insisting over and over again that they wanted the country to be reunited. (The Copperheads had been saying that, too, just not as emphatically.) As usual, however, the details for a peace plan were conspicuously absent. Most Democrats insisted that they wanted the "Union as it was," suggesting that reunification was a necessary precondition for ending the war. But most never defined what they meant by the "Union as it was." Some conservatives alluded repeatedly to the Crittenden Plan, but this was hardly a universal call. A Democratic peace probably would have included slavery, but would the issue of slavery in the territories be resolved? Would the Fugitive Slave Act still be on the books? Would Southerners again control much of the government?[3] How would they square this return to the *status quo ante bellum* with the enormous losses the Union had suffered during the war?

Among the vaguest of the Democrats' arguments was what they meant by states' rights. Presumably it meant that the Southern states, once they rejoined the Union, were free to continue the peculiar institution, although the Democrats, for once, did not put this in their party platform. Rather than defending the right to own slaves, they focused instead on white supremacy. But the issue remained: Did a belief in states' rights mean that Democrats considered secession legal? This was a vexing question, and one that was at the very heart of the war. The framers of the Constitution had never stipulated what ratifying the document meant. Was the Union a voluntary association that the parties—that is, the states—were free to join or leave as they saw fit? Or was it a permanent compact? Again, the Democrats never went into specifics. That did not mean the question, with all its nuance, was lost on the voters, espe-

The Copperheads were more inclined to speech than action. Here conservative Democrats are depicted as jawboning a bored Jefferson Davis, offering him nearly anything he wants. Note Democratic presidential candidate George B. McClellan on the left. (*Harper's Weekly*/Courtesy of HarpWeek LLC)

cially the soldiers whose lives were at stake over the issue. States' rights, an Indiana volunteer wrote, carried with it the right of secession. Secession had led to the collapse of political edifices and ultimately to anarchy. He had to conclude, then, that the only kind of secession with any redeeming value was that of the slave from his master.[4]

As political pamphlets flooded the North, those from the Democrats resorted again to virulently racist arguments. One leaflet was devoted entirely to miscegenation, which, the author claimed, "was a part of the original purpose of the Abolitionists." "If this is 'human progress,' the world may well pray to remain stationary," he wrote. Jeremiah S. Black, a former attorney general and secretary of state, argued that Republicans had used the war powers section of the Constitution "to rob the white man of his property and bestow it on the negro. . . . You can degrade the white man to the level of the negro—that is easily done—but you cannot lift the negro up to the white man's place." A Democratic campaign song put these appeals to racial superiority to music. One ditty went:

Abe, Seward, and Greeley, Chase, Beecher, and Co.,
Made very loud pretensions to Freedom, you know;
"Free men" and "Free speech," "Free homes," were
    their cry!
And now for every BLACK MAN *freed twenty* WHITE
    MEN *die.*[5]

Claims like these made little headway among most voters. This is
not to say that Northerners had suddenly put aside their prejudices,
but many of them had come to realize how important African Americans were in the war effort. Yankees—many of whom had witnessed
slavery during their time in the army and were impressed by the black
soldiers they saw—especially found the proslavery argument to be
offensive and were largely unmoved by it. After these years of war,
only a man "entirely blinded by party prejudice" or one who was "im-
minently dishonest and traitorous" would refuse to attack slavery, a
Hoosier soldier said. "For however we may try to avoid the fact, slavery . . . is the cause of all our troubles." Moreover, he said, a free government could not rest partially on an economic system that included
slave labor.[6]

The Republican Party and several semi-independent publication
societies ginned up the presses to attack the Democrats. The publication societies, most notably the New England Loyal Publication Society and the New York Publication Society, printed hundreds of
thousands of pamphlets and broadsides and sent them to newspapers,
Union Leagues, and soldiers. Some of the material was targeted for
specific audiences, including the Irish, farmers, or Midwesterners. One
pamphlet, for instance, warned Germans that laborers could not expect to have any rights if the Democrats, with their Southern allies,
were elected. "If you would have masters set up over you . . . vote for
McClellan. Would you retain your equal rights as citizens of a free country, vote for Lincoln, who has been an honest working man like your-
selves."[7] In addressing themselves to specific constituencies, the
Republicans seemed to be far more organized than the Democrats. Then
again, the Republicans had managed to bury their differences for the
fall campaign, whereas divisions between the war and peace factions
of the Democrats were apparent for anyone to see.[8]

Although the Democrats tried to maintain the offensive, their copper-
tinged platform and Pendleton's presence on the ballot repeatedly set
them on their heels. The presence of such extreme views in the platform and a Copperhead candidate on the ticket appalled and frightened Unionists—including moderate Democrats—and opened the

entire party to accusations of treason by the Republicans, who called the opposition a party of "Dixie, Davis, and the devil." The imputation stuck in the minds of many voters. "Our most dangerous public enemy is not Jefferson Davis with his army, but the party of malcontents at home—traitors represented by 'little Mac'clellan and Pendleton, H. Seymour, Vallandigham, Cox & Co.," New York lawyer George Templeton Strong said. For some soldiers, Democrats and Confederates had become synonymous. An Iowa soldier suspected the two were colluding to win the election. The Southerners, he expected, would "strain every nerve . . . to help McClellan and encourage the northern rebels." James Gordon Bennett, the nonpartisan editor of the *New York Herald*, suggested that the Democrats jettison Pendleton and replace him with a war man. The remark fell on deaf ears.[9]

Part of the Democrats' weakness stemmed from the head of the ticket. McClellan offered no leadership to counteract Republican claims. As was typical for presidential candidates of the time, McClellan remained aloof from the public campaign. Unlike Lincoln, however, McClellan also removed himself from the behind-the-scenes effort to secure his election. His unwillingness to engage, even privately, made him as vulnerable as the party itself to charges of disloyalty. When one particularly heated Republican speaker accused him of being "the leader of the Confederate forces," an allegation blatantly designed to rankle the former head of the Army of the Potomac, the general remained unmoved. His passivity in the face of a forceful enemy should not be surprising. His behavior during the political campaign resembled his habits in his military campaigns, where his tendency was to balk, stall, and ignore unsolicited advice.[10]

With McClellan on the sidelines, decision-making devolved to the party leaders, who realized they had a serious problem with Pendleton and the platform. William Aspinwall advised Samuel L. M. Barlow to make sure that Democrats celebrated Union victories as vigorously as the Republicans did to assure voters of the party's loyalty. August Belmont, the party chair, ordered Manton Marble in late October to publish "at once" letters in the *World* from Pendleton explaining his positions, along with copies of his speeches and his voting record. Belmont added that Marble should print extra copies of the paper and distribute them among the soldiers. In the published letters, Pendleton insisted "there is no one who cherishes a greater regard for the Union," but he said he opposed any policy that would prevent the government from being reestablished "upon its old foundations." He supported military appropriations "for the support and efficiency" of the army and navy, he said vaguely, but not when they were "loaded down with fraudulent items" for the benefit of contractors or were made "a stalking-horse for some abolition scheme." In addition to publishing the Pendleton pamphlet, Marble carried an editorial in the *World* saying that the only reason the Republicans were focusing on the vice presidential nominee was because McClellan's record was so well known and "so conspicuously invulnerable." Pendleton, the *World* insisted, was not a peace-at-any-price man, but believed force did not have to exclude conciliation and that that war should not be waged in such a way as to further alienate Southerners. But neither the editorials nor pamphlets carrying the same message did anything to stanch the damage Pendleton wrought on the ticket.[11]

Democrats tried to launch a counteroffensive by arguing that peace was impossible under Lincoln. "What was Abraham Lincoln by trade? A rail-splitter. What is he now? Union-splitter," a Democratic pamphlet called *The Lincoln Catechism: Wherein the Eccentricities & Beauties of Despotism Are Fully Set Forth.* For forty-eight years out of the sixty since parties were formed, Democrats had controlled the presidency, they pointed out, and in all that time no civil war had broken out. Once the Republicans, a sectional party, took control, the nation plunged into fratricide. That Lincoln and his party refused to sue for peace once war began, not to mention the way they trampled on civil liberties, was evidence of their treachery. One Democratic campaign song, "Fraternal Liberty," dedicated itself to this idea:

> All hail DEMOCRACY! All ye who would be free!
> It's base is COMPROMISE and PEACE, it's hope is
>   LIBERTY!
> But TRAITORS cry for BLOOD, reject all COMPROMISE,
> And style themselves "THE UNIONISTS," tho' Traitors
>   in disguise.
> But as THE UNION was, So shall it EVER be,
> The UNION of the North and South, FRATERNAL
>   LIBERTY.

These efforts failed to win converts and may have succeeded only in alienating moderate voters further.[12]

Although many leading Democrats seemed certain that Davis would accept a peace plan if one were offered, the matter was a subject of some debate within the party. Congressman James Guthrie of Indiana, claiming Jefferson Davis as a friend, insisted that the South was for peace. If the North would only offer those states their rights under the Constitution, they would quickly rejoin the fold, Guthrie said. Others, including John Van Buren of New York, said peace was impossible as long as Lincoln and Davis governed the warring nations. If the voters of the North jettisoned Lincoln, Southerners would soon overthrow Davis and his associates, Van Buren believed. As usual, though, neither Van Buren nor Guthrie nor any other prominent Democrat came forward with a plan that indicated what they were prepared to surrender in exchange for peace. The point was moot anyway. In early October, Davis announced again that he would not have any part in suspending the war "on any other basis than independence."[13]

Regardless of what Davis had to say, the Democrats' lack of specificity on terms was a source of great concern to soldiers. Whenever peace came, they wanted the war to be over for good. They worried that the Democrats, who said nothing in their platform about slavery and whose candidate did not support emancipation, would allow the Southerners to return to the Union with the peculiar institution intact. "Then we can fight them again in ten years," a soldier under Sherman's command wrote. "But let Old Abe settle it, and it is always settled." The confidence that Lincoln would see the war through to its end drew even men who otherwise did not care for him to the Republican tent. As one sailor wrote, "He is pledged to continue the war till a lasting peace is established."[14]

The *New York Herald* listened to the arguments of both sides and considered them with the cynicism its readers had come to expect. Though irreverent in tone, the *Herald* actually may have struck the least partisan balance of any newspaper in the country. "While we have no hopes of Paradise regained with this election, we have no fears of the destruction of the country with the success of either Lincoln or McClellan. Each is a failure," the paper editorialized. "Neither of them was the candidate of the leaders of his party. The choice, Old Abe or Little Mac, is rather a choice of evils than a choice of excellencies; but still, this way or that way, Lincoln or McClellan, it is the fixed resolve of the people that the rebellion shall be put down, that the Union shall be saved; and so it will be."[15]

Most people in the North were certain by early fall that Lincoln would prevail, but Confederates still held out hope for the Democrats generally and the Copperheads specifically. John Jones, the war clerk, recorded an incident in which soldiers broke up a Democratic rally in Ohio in early October. "This fire may spread, and relieve us," he said. At the very least, rebels could hope that a revolution or civil war would break out if the Republicans won. An uprising of that sort would require Lincoln to pull his troops out of the South, or so Jones liked to fantasize. Jefferson Davis was cautiously optimistic but not much more realistic. On October 6 he told an audience in Columbia, South Carolina, that he hoped the peace party, "if there be such at the North," would win the Northern election. Whichever party won, he told the crowd, it would learn that it was better to end the war and cut the South loose than to continue to fight.[16]

Some in the North agreed with the Southerners' assessment of Little Mac's chances. "McClellan seems to be in every bodys mouth here and I dont think there will be any doubt about his being our next President. The old soldiers of the Potomac Army are nearly all for him," an Illinois soldier wrote home. But this Yankee was ill-informed. Few men in the North and even fewer in the army subscribed to this belief a month before the presidential election.[17]

African Americans, who could not vote even in most Northern states, paid close attention to the campaign. At a national convention that met October 4 in Syracuse, New York, they declined to endorse either McClellan or Lincoln but made their position clear in their "Address of the Colored National Convention to the People of the United States," which said that the Democratic Party was the source of only "fierce, malignant, and unmitigated hostility. Our continued oppression and degradation is the law of its life, and its sure passport to power." The party, which "belongs to slavery," brought together the worst America had to offer, "and we need not expect a single voice from that quarter for justice, mercy, or even decency." A Democratic victory in November, the statement concluded, would be "the heaviest calamity that could befall us in the present juncture of affairs."[18]

Before the November election, however, came state elections in Ohio, Indiana, and Pennsylvania. These drew enormous attention because they were considered a foreshadowing of what the country could expect in the general vote—a poll of sorts in the days before public opinion polling. Ohio, which looked likely to swing Republican, was of the least concern to either party. Pennsylvania, by dint of its size and expected influence in the general elections in November as well as its proximity to the money, power, and press centers on the East Coast, was by far the biggest prize. The state could go to either party, but by early October, Democrats were wringing their hands at their chances. Despite repeated pleas for speakers and, more important, money, Democratic operatives felt as though they were slipping behind. One prominent Democrat declared the state a loss as early as October 6 because the national party had not done enough to support its candidates there.[19]

The Republicans trounced the opposition everywhere in the October 11 elections—a harbinger of the following month. In Indiana, Republican governor Oliver Morton was reelected, and his party picked up four congressional seats. Pennsylvania's twenty-four-man congressional delegation had been equally divided between Republicans and Democrats; the election made it fifteen to nine in the Republicans' favor. Moreover, the state legislative races went hard to the Republicans. In Ohio, Republicans enjoyed a landslide in the congressional elections, taking seventeen of the state's nineteen seats. The Democrats previously had held fourteen of the seats. Samuel S. Cox was among the congressmen who lost, and he wasted no time in pointing fingers. He wrote Marble that Vallandigham's reputation, a lack of support from the Crisis in Columbus, and shenanigans at the ballot box that kept the soldiers from voting for him were to blame for his defeat.[20]

Other Democrats saw broader problems and ominous foreshadowing in the October contests. James A. Bayard, a senator from Delaware with Copperhead leanings, looked at the results and concluded, "The jig is up & Lincoln [is] certain of re-election." The only way for McClellan to win in November would be for him to carry the army vote, but Bayard dismissed that possibility as "merely absurd." William Davis, whose brother John had lost his re-election bid in Indiana, regarded Lincoln's reelection as almost a "fixed fact," and he worried that if Lincoln did win in November, it would be the last election the country ever had. "He will be proclaimed Emperor long before his term expires," Davis predicted in the kind of doomsday language that conservatives were wont to use. Not that it mattered; this was what a majority of the people wanted, and it was what they deserved as far as he was concerned, since they had neither sense nor honesty enough to maintain a republican form of government.[21]

Inside the Executive Mansion, Republicans breathed a sigh of relief. John Hay, the president's secretary, thought the Indiana victory was especially important because it would bring Illinois into Lincoln's corner in the presidential election and would save Indiana from sedition and civil war. Lincoln was more relieved by the Pennsylvania results because Pennsylvania was a large and influential state that carried twenty-six electoral votes.[22]

Delight with the election results rippled through the Republican North. An Indiana soldier wrote, "Treason has received a blow from which it may not recover, and traitors slink away into their holes where they will have time to consider their meanness, their worse than sinful course, and perhaps repent if repentence is for such vile creatures, which to my mind seems rather doubtful." He proclaimed that Lincoln's reelection was now a "moral certainty." In parts of the South, the October results seemed to be further confirmation of the Confederacy's dwindling chances for survival. "The rebs here are much chapfallen at the disaster to their political friends in the North. They seem to consider it worse than a disaster in the field, and a death blow to their dearest hopes of success in their infamous secession schemes," General Geary wrote from Atlanta.[23]

Lincoln took advantage of the Republican victory at the polls to address Democratic allegations that he planned to ruin the government if he lost in November. There was some talk that if McClellan won, he should seize control of the government immediately to keep Lincoln from somehow hijacking it. "I hope the good people will permit themselves to suffer no uneasiness on either point," Lincoln assured a crowd gathered to celebrate Maryland's adoption of a new constitution that included emancipation. "I am struggling to maintain government, not to overthrow it. I am struggling especially to prevent others from overthrowing it." It was one of the very few times the president expressed any concern about the intentions of the Peace Democrats.[24]

The *New York Times* jumped on Lincoln's speech as a chance to mock the hard-liners. "Will not the Copperheads breathe freer, sleep sounder, and look less haggard and wretched after this? It is this that they have been in mortal fear of for the last six months," the paper editorialized. "They have talked about it all day and every day; dreamed about it every night and all night, and pondered over it on Sundays. It has interfered with their digestion; has made them bilious and atrabilious, and has brought some of them to the verge of suicide. All this misery has been for nothing." [25]

While maintaining publicly that he might lose the election, privately Lincoln was confident that he would not. In mid-October, he surveyed the political scene and figured he would take all but New York, Pennsylvania, Illinois, and the border states, to win the Electoral College 120 to 114. Elsewhere, although most Republicans had high hopes for the November election, some still harbored moments of doubt. Grant's political mentor, Representative Elihu Washburne of Illinois, wrote Lincoln on October 17 despairing of the possible outcome in his state. "Everything is at sixes and sevens; and no head or tail to anything. There is imminent danger of losing the State," he said. Lincoln had no time for such negativity. He thought Washburne had fallen victim to the Democrats' propaganda. "Stampeded," he scrawled on the envelope, and put away the letter.[26]

Meanwhile, the Confederates were still churning away at schemes to create chaos in the North. In mid-September they tried to execute a plan to capture the *Michigan*, a federal gunboat on Lake Erie, to release prisoners at Johnson's Island, who would then drop down to Columbus to free the prisoners at Camp Chase. They managed to capture two boats, but officers aboard the *Michigan* learned they had a Confederate spy on board and foiled the plot. The Southern agents in Canada were not done yet, though. In October, on the same day that Lincoln gave his speech pledging not to overthrow the government, twenty Confederates slipped across the border, robbed three banks in St. Albans, Vermont, and then tried to set fire to the town. The robbery was not so much for the money as to force the U.S. government to deploy troops along any borders vulnerable to raids. The incursion failed to do that. Nor did the arson plan work; all the rebels burned down was a shed. They succeeded in stealing about $220,000 and terrorizing the locals, however. Thirteen of the raiders were arrested as they fled into Canada, but Canadian authorities let the men go because they believed they had no jurisdiction to prosecute. These schemes ultimately were double negatives for the Confederates: They not only did nothing for the rebel cause, but they also pushed the Peace Democrats further into disrepute and hampered McClellan's chances for election.[27]

By the end of October, Democrats were disconsolate. Maria Lydig Daly, the wife of a War Democrat judge in New York City, could not believe what was happening. "Lincoln, a rail-splitter, and his wife, two ignorant and vulgar boors, are king and queen for now and candidates for election." Equally bad, the country was "at present ruled by New England, which was never a gentle or tolerant mistress." "There is scarcely any hope," Judge Charles Mason wrote even as he spearheaded McClellan's campaign in the Washington, D.C., area. "Still we must conduct ourselves as though success was within reach." One Democratic operative told Marble that victory would have been possible except for the influence of the Copperheads. "I have always felt . . . that just so long as the dead-weight of Vallandigham, Woods etc., had to be carried by the democracy just so long would it be sacrificed. The Chicago platform gave me a *chill* in the Convention when it was read that I still feel. Had it possessed any *life* our success would have been beyond a doubt." Unlike Republicans, Democratic leaders were reluctant to share their dark forecasts with the candidate. To the contrary, McClellan's incoming correspondence teems with letters full of hope and possibility.[28]

Some Democratic newspapers began to stretch the limits of plausibility, publishing almost any rumor that floated their way in an effort to stave off what appeared to be an inevitable Republican victory. The *Dayton Daily Empire* printed a story based on a private letter purportedly written by a highly placed administration official. The letter said that the South could not be vanquished until all its adult males were exterminated, which the official estimated would take another thirty years. Half to two-thirds of the Northern population—presumably the male portion—would have to be sacrificed to this end, the piece claimed. The *World* printed an article less than a week before the election saying that soldiers, who cast their ballots earlier than civilians, were voting for McClellan in droves and that many Republicans were jumping to the Democrats' side. Numerous soldier letters and the final tally contradict that claim, but the newspaper declared that Democratic success was "almost positive." Meanwhile, the *Old Guard* dismissed as rubbish the Republicans' claim that the rebellion was nearly over. "If we could believe Mr. Lincoln's telegraph, we have crushed it to death a thousand times," the *Guard*'s Burr said. Soldiers were totally demoralized by the fact that this had become a war for emancipation, he said. "The thought cuts through them like a knife. It rankles in their bosoms like a poison tainting the very fountain of life." As a result of Lincoln's policies, future armies would have to be entirely conscripted because no one would volunteer. "Unless there is a change in the entire aim and spirit of the war, the North has, we think, already exhibited, if it has not exhausted, its strength against the South," he said.[29]

As Election Day neared, other Democratic newspapers sounded almost like Republican publications with a twist. In Boston, the *Post* published a campaign edition that tried to reverse the accusations of treason. "The enemy in the front is scarcely less dangerous than the disguised one in the rear," it editorialized. "One is open and armed; and against his treason to the Union all are substantially united; but the enemy in disguise puts on the show of devotion to the Union to cloak his guilty treachery to that Bible of our Political Faith—the Constitution of the United States." In Ohio, the *Dayton Daily Empire* wrote that reunion was impossible, thanks to the administration's policies. Then, returning to more traditional Copperhead rhetoric, it added that continuing the war would only lead to Confederate independence, the disintegration of the Union, bankruptcy, civil war in the North, and a loss of liberties. "Step by step are Mr. Lincoln and his advisers traveling on, on to revolution and to despotism."[30]

The growing prospect of a big win liberated some normally staid Republicans to lash out at the Copperheads. "I would walk several miles to see [Horatio] Seymour duly and lawfully hanged—as convicted of treason," lawyer and diarist George Templeton Strong fantasized. "He is an avowed traitor—*traitoro-phile.*" In Indiana, Sarah Dooley wondered what the Copperheads would do after the war was over: "Crall in thare holes from whence they cam never return I expect and hope for I get more and more disgusted at them every day," she wrote her husband. "Just to think how they will work against thare own intrest but let them howl and spout thare doom is sealed and they will reap thare reward   I cannot i will not cauntnance them nor will I neighbor with them." Another Hoosier wrote: "It makes me shudder to think there are men at home, disposed to stir up civil war where our families are peacefully located. The extreme penalty of the law, and the extreme end of a rope should be their fate. What fools they are!"[31]

Although the political fate of Peace Democrats looked grim, localized resistance movements remained active throughout the North. About five hundred men banded together to resist the draft in Orange and Crawford counties in Indiana. An army officer in the town of Patoka, Indiana, arrested thirty-five men after they allegedly tried to murder the local sheriff and shot at a lieutenant in the state militia— presumably with the aim of resisting the draft. An enrolling officer in Ironton, Ohio, was shot at on two separate occasions, and a bullet struck his horse. A man in a nearby town who resembled the enrolling officer had his buildings burned down.[32]

The most serious resistance in the country emerged in a new place— Clearfield and Cambria counties in west central Pennsylvania—where 1,200 to 1,800 deserters, delinquent drafted men, and Copperheads reportedly organized and armed themselves to resist federal officers seeking to arrest them. The dissenters were so well organized that they were said to have a fort at Knox Township. After they killed a colonel sent to find a group of deserters and draft dodgers in Clearfield County, the government sent marksmen to flush out the resistors. On November 13 a company of soldiers surrounded a house filled with nineteen resisters and deserters. The troops killed the leader, "the notorious Tom Adams," and took eighteen prisoners. One soldier was killed in the fight. The local provost marshal assured his superiors that he would be sending out another company shortly and hoped to bring an end to the "terror and disgrace [in] that Section of the State."[33]

With the general election approaching, Lincoln's cabinet hit the stump. Seward returned to his hometown of Auburn, New York, during the fall to urge the locals to support the president. If Lincoln did not win it would mean the end of the republic, Seward suggested, none too subtly. The North had only two choices: continue the war and subjugate the rebels or abandon the effort completely. He dismissed the Democratic accusation that Lincoln had shifted the goal of the war from one for reunion to one for abolition. "Slavery is the mainspring of the rebellion," he explained, and the government therefore had to strike at it. Those who thought bringing Jefferson Davis to the bargaining table was better than continuing the war were political naifs. Davis would surely agree to an armistice and to peace talks, but he would never agree to reunite the country, Seward said. Consequently, anyone who insisted on divisive bickering over the president's policies posed a threat to the nation. "Faction in civil war is unmitigated treason," he declared bluntly.[34]

More influential on public opinion than the Republican leaders were the thousands of soldiers in the field, the overwhelming majority of whom favored Lincoln over McClellan. Countless numbers of them wrote their loved ones at home, reviling the Democrats and urging their friends and family to cast their ballots for Lincoln.[35] Their letters demonstrate how deeply the Copperhead platform had alienated the men who were supposed to be McClellan's natural constituency. "I am glad to see that you are getting waked up to the necessity of all electing Uncle Abe by an overwhelming majority. If you at home will do your share you may rest assured that the soldiers are all right," a New York soldier wrote. "I want peace as much as any other man, but not a *dishonorable* one," an army surgeon said. "We had better fight a year or two longer than submit to disgraceful compromises." Another call for half a million men would add enough soldiers to put the matter to rest within three months, he thought.[36]

Soldiers had other reasons to be angry at the Copperheads. Many thought the Democrats' activities had extended the war. "I could shoot one of them copperheads with a good heart as I could shoot a wolf. I would shoot my father if he was one," Private John Brobst of Wisconsin said. Other soldiers doubted that eligible men who had not yet served would ever engage in combat, even if they were drafted. "All that will fight are in the army doing battle for the *union*: The others are only Copperhead blowers, allways finding fault with every thing not done by their *party*." Mostly, soldiers became very angry when they thought about the Peace Democrats. One Minnesotan offered a typical assessment: "When I think how often I have risked my life in the terrible storm of Battle to put down this rebellion and Save the country the man who deliberately goes against me is my enemy—my bitter enemy—unlike any other enemy—I grow fierce—I feel ugly—Nothing I ever experienced could rouse me like that—It is like an attempt to disgrace me and then to encourage an assassin to kill me."[37]

Thousands of men who entered the army as Democrats crossed party lines to keep Lincoln in office. Indeed, the war turned many a Democratic soldier permanently into a Republican. One Buckeye who had been a lawyer in civilian life wrote that his change of heart would "set the republican party on their toes and the copperheads heels up" when he came home. The Peace Democrats had a great deal to do with his switch. "I won't have anything to do with any set of men opposed to the war. My entire and radical change has been progressing during the last four years." The wife of a Michigan soldier was surprised that he was "forsaking" the Democratic Party but not unhappy about the change. "Do you hold that the framers of the Chicago Platform that you so bitterly denounce are no longer Democrats?" Lebbie Trowbridge asked.

> It certainly is a base disloyal article and if McLelland was a loyal man he would refuse to have anything to do with a party that would adopt such a platform. Sheridan's late victories and the voices of Pa Ohio & Indiana will, I should think, make the *copperheads* hunt for a hole in which to hide their deformed heads when the other states shall unite with these three next month and speak in tones that will make traitors tremble.[38]

By this point in the war, soldiers generally enjoyed the political support of their families at home. Some family members were nearly as enthusiastic in condemning Peace Democrats as their soldier sons, husbands, and brothers were. "I think the leaders would sue for terms *now*, if it were not that they hope the copperheads will carry the next election, and then the Armistice which they (the Cops') promise, and finally the withdrawal of our armies and finally the acknowledgement of their independence," a Norwalk, Ohio, man wrote his son. But the rebels' hopes would be in vain because Lincoln was sure to sweep the election, he thought. Nothing but a severe military loss could elect McClellan. "It is humiliating, is it not? that we have a political party that depends upon the disaster of our army for success, but so it is, and the copperheads here and their friends the rebels in arms know it." While Union men celebrated the victories at Atlanta, Mobile Bay, and the Shenandoah Valley, "the 'Cops' look as sour and sullen as if the election had already gone against them. They know that every victory to our arms diminishes their chance of success, so they sneer at our victories and say that we can never conquer the south, and cowardly propose to let them go in peace."[39]

For the first time in recorded history, soldiers in the field were allowed to vote. Nineteen states sent ballots to the front. The army granted leave to soldiers from states that did not provide for absentee voting, especially such key states as Indiana and Illinois, where Democratic legislators had blocked efforts to allow absentee ballots.[40] Democrats worried—with good reason—that the soldiers' votes would lead to a Republican landslide (an indication that at least some Democrats were aware of the political change that had come over the army). Ruminating on the idea that "thousands of bits of paper" could bear the

responsibility for such great consequences, a Vermont private said military men would never vote for the Democrats. "Soldiers don't generally believe in fighting to put down treason, and voting to let it live,"
he said.[41]

This election was unique not only in that soldiers were able to participate as voters but also in that it was held at all. Holding a national
election in the middle of a civil war was something no country had
ever done. Until the election went off, Democrats remained skeptical
that it actually would be held. Lincoln was profoundly aware of the
significance of maintaining democratic institutions and customs. The
day after the election, he talked about the remarkable position in which
the country found itself:

> It has long been a grave question whether any government,
> not *too* strong for the liberties of its people, can be strong *enough*
> to maintain its own existence, in great emergencies. On this
> point the present rebellion brought our republic to a severe test;
> and a presidential election occurring in regular course during
> the rebellion added not a little to the strain.

The election could further divide and at least partially paralyze the
nation. Nevertheless, the contest had to go forward. "We can not have
free government without elections; and if the rebellion could force us
to forego, or postpone a national election, it might fairly claim to have
already conquered and ruined us."[42]

As Election Day neared, fears started to rise again in parts of the
North over the prospect of unrest. Rumors of conspiracies involving
Confederate refugees and Southern sympathizers circulated through
the major cities of the Union. Seward wrote to New York City's mayor
urging him to be vigilant, and General Benjamin Butler was sent to the
city with a "considerable force of troops." Chicago, which turned out
to be the target of yet another plot of the Confederates in Canada, was
also a concern. Cities were not the only rumored targets: Enrolling
agents from across the North reported hearing of plans to upset Election Day in their areas. In the end, though, the day passed without
incident.[43]

Little Mac went down to a crushing defeat, losing the popular vote
by ten percentage points to the commander in chief he had once dismissed as an "idiot."[44] He lost the Electoral College vote 212 to 21.
McClellan took only his home state of New Jersey along with Delaware and Kentucky, which the *New York Herald* pronounced as being
"as erratic in her movements as if guided by a drunken Bourbon leader,

brimful all the time of the real Old Kentucky Bourbon whiskey." Selected in part because of his perceived strength in the army, McClellan did even more poorly among the soldiers, despite the love they once had for him. Four out of five soldiers voted for Lincoln. Among California and Iowa soldiers, Lincoln won by a ten-to-one margin; among those from Vermont, Maine, Maryland, Ohio, and Wisconsin, the margin was five to one. The president would have won the election without the ballots from the men in the field, but they gave him a landslide victory and an incontrovertible mandate to continue prosecuting the war.[45] Their steadfast support for him even during difficult times also may have helped him with the civilian vote because the soldiers' input forced many Northerners to keep a more open mind toward the president, even if they did not like what was happening on the field or in the government. The soldier vote led to widespread Democratic allegations of fraud and charges that many of the men cast their ballots for Lincoln under duress, but James M. McPherson has concluded that the 1864 election was no more irregular than any other of the nineteenth century.[46]

Officers and enlisted men alike were ebullient. "We rejoice with the loyal citizens of the North that our country is not to grovel at the feet of Jeff Davis, but is going to fight out her own battles and suppress the rebellion, crush treason and Rebels, North and South, and restore the supremacy of our government, and be a nation free,—or a country lost," a regimental quartermaster from Ohio wrote. "I hope the friends of 'little Mac' are satisfied now," Democratic General Geary

Long Abraham Lincoln a Little Longer.

This dramatic illustration celebrates Lincoln's reelection with a visual pun on his height. (*Harper's Weekly*/Courtesy of HarpWeek LLC)

wrote his wife. "They certainly understand by this time that they are making a very large sized error and that their dogmas are not in keeping with the progress of the age." The Confederacy, he added, was "much crippled by the result." "I think that we give the rebels a good lick when we put old Abreham Lincoln in for Prsidend and i voted for him," one veteran boasted. Civilians were delighted, too. George Templeton Strong crowed that the election result was "the strongest testimonial in favor of popular institutions to be found in history."[47]

For many rebels, the election results were a clear sign that the end was near. Robert G. H. Kean, who ran the Bureau of War, wrote in his diary that Lincoln won by a far greater margin than anyone in the South had anticipated. As a result, the Confederates' spirits were considerably dampened, and their army a "good deal" depressed. Among Kean's greatest disappointments was that no violence attended the voting. For his part, ordinance chief Josiah Gorgas seemed conflicted: despairing on the one hand and belligerent on the other. "There is no use in disguising the fact that our subjugation is popular at the north, & that the war must go on until this hope is crushed out & replaced by desire for peace at any cost."[48]

For other rebels, the North's election results did nothing to clarify their fate. Jefferson Davis remained publicly defiant, insisting that no military success on the part of the Yankees could vanquish the Confederacy. Nothing could save the North from the "constant and exhaustive drain of blood and treasure which must continue until he shall discover that no peace is attainable unless based on the recognition of our indefeasible rights." The clerk John Jones, who was rather given to fantasy, at first speculated that Lincoln may have kept pressing the war only in order to be reelected; now that that had happened, perhaps there would be some relaxation of the war's "rigors." When the magnitude of Lincoln's victory sank in, though, he lost hope. "The large majorities for Lincoln in the United States clearly indicate a purpose to make renewed efforts to accomplish our destruction," he said.[49]

Lincoln seemed relieved—not just that he had won, but also that the elections had come off at all. "It has demonstrated that a people's government can sustain a national election, in the midst of a great civil war," he said. "Until now it has not been known to the world that this was a possibility. It shows also how sound, and how strong we still are. . . . It shows also, to the extent yet known, that we have more men now, than we had when the war began." The president extended the olive branch to the Democrats and asked his supporters to do the same. "Now that the election is over, may not all, having a common interest, re-unite in a common effort, to save our common country?"[50]

The loss left the Democrats in disarray. Right after the election, McClellan told Barlow that while he deplored the election results, "I feel that a great weight is removed from my mind." Shortly thereafter the general shipped out for Europe and remained abroad for two years, denying the Democrats their leading voice in opposing the administration. Recriminations began immediately. "It is fashion here to denounce and proscribe *me* in every way, and I am compelled to feel the persecution in more ways than one," wrote Philadelphian William B. Reed. In Indiana, the *Sullivan Democrat* was quick to blame the Sons of Liberty and the Organization of American Knights for the damage. "It may have been true that none but Democrats belonged to it, and that no others would have been received had they applied, but it is gross injustice to the Democratic party to hold it responsible for the sins of that secret organization," the newspaper complained. Moreover, it was unfair to hold all the members responsible for the "revolutionary, if not treasonable, designs of [H. H.] Dodd & Co."[51]

Manton Marble privately seethed at the outcome. "The coming calamities will teach even the North their bitter lessons; suffering pierces at last the most obdurate heart and finds some secret access at length to the most pervert understanding . . . ," he told McClellan. "The North in its secret soul is still stubborn and stiff—in its refusal of constitutional right to those who saw its temper and sought a lawless and wicked remedy, therefore the time is not ripe for our success. We must not despair of the Republic, yet how impossible it is to hope." Publicly, his paper, the *World*, wrote that the Democrats' chances were "almost hopeless" from the start because of the number of party members the Confederacy took out of the Union (this, exactly a week after gloating about almost certain victory for the party). Despair settled on Barlow, the chair of the Democratic Campaign Committee. "Under Mr. Lincoln, I see little prospect of anything, but fruitless war, disgraceful peace, & ruinous bankruptcy."[52]

Efforts to buck up partisans were for naught. "Patriotic men cannot excuse themselves from duty by madly saying 'let it go, all is gone, the administration has got us into it and cannot get us out, they are responsible,' " the *Niles Republican* reminded Michiganders. But the best strategy to many Peace Democrats seemed to be to keep their heads down. Across the country, they adopted a very low profile, knowing well where the election results left them. Given their earlier chest-thumping, though, they could not escape the examination of their neighbors even with relative silence. In Greenville, Illinois, Clara Gaskill noted that the Copperheads of Bond County were "all getting ashamed of themselves & say very little now." Strong, the New York City lawyer, wrote approvingly that "Copperheads talk meekly and well." Even with the situation at home settling down, soldiers remained unable to forgive the Copperheads. William Kepner of the 1st U.S. Veteran Volunteer Engineers refused to have anything to do with his Copperhead father and brother, whom he hated "wors than the rebels." He moved his possessions out of their house to get as far away from them as possible.[53]

Lincoln was a forgiving man and one not given to gloating. There were wounds to bind after the election, and Lincoln applied himself to the task in his annual message to Congress. He was pleased, he said, that regardless of how people voted, "the purpose of the people . . . to maintain the integrity of the Union, was never more firm, nor more nearly unanimous, than now." Although they had different ideas for how best to advance the Union cause, both presidential candidates agreed that the Union must reunite. This showed the nation and the world the "firmness and unanimity of purpose" that Americans felt.[54]

Lincoln's public interpretation of the election results did not mean he had forgotten how close he had come to losing the contest. During a cabinet meeting two days after the election, he pulled from his drawer the letter he wrote in August, the letter he had his cabinet members sign without ever seeing its contents. Lincoln opened it and read the contents to the assembled men. It was the letter in which he had said it appeared "exceedingly probable" he would not be reelected. Lincoln told his cabinet that he had assumed McClellan would win. His plan in that case was to see the general and work out a way in the months before McClellan's inauguration for the two to pool their resources—influence in McClellan's case and power in his own—to finish the war. Seward piped up: "And the General would answer you 'Yes, Yes,' and the next day when you saw him again and pressed these views upon him, he would say, 'Yes, Yes;' & so on forever, and would have done nothing at all." Lincoln responded, "At least I should have done my duty and have stood clear before my own conscience."[55]

The election of 1864 was a disaster for the Democrats, and the peace wing found itself humiliated. Having counted upon public disaffection for the war to advance their cause, Copperheads lost when military fortunes and public sentiment turned on them. Having called the war a failure, they could not justify their position when Sherman, Sheridan, and Farragut piled up key victories. Tarred as traitors, regardless of their actual positions on the war, Democrats were beaten at state polls in October and roundly thrashed in November. In fact, the stench of treason clung to the Democrats for years; nearly a generation would pass before another Democrat, Grover Cleveland, occupied the White House.[56] The pounding by the electorate was not the party's only problem. With McClellan out of the country, the party had no leader behind whom it could rally. Conservatives had never been organized enough to coalesce behind a single man, and now they were in such deep disrepute that they could not have swayed public opinion even if they did have a credible leader. The stunned and equally discredited War Democrats were thoroughly confused and did not have a man with high enough standing to criticize the administration effectively. As a result, Democrats had little leverage in national politics as the war wound down and Reconstruction geared up.

8

Defeated

THE ELECTION RESULTS MADE IT CLEAR that Northerners were in a fighting mood, and peace men responded by falling silent. Some of the most extreme continued to berate the administration loudly, and several editors who had been deeply critical did little more than tone down their rhetoric. But most of the nation's leading Copperhead politicians simply faded into the background. The silence of the peace wing fell even more deeply when William Tecumseh Sherman marched through Georgia and then the Carolinas, endeavors that more than ever indicated the war was nearly over. The most obvious change took place at the community level, where the Peace Democrats who had so frightened their neighbors over the previous three and a half years suddenly went mute on the subject of politics. The Copperheads had nearly disappeared from the scene by the time Lincoln was assassinated, when suspicions about their involvement in the plot briefly rose. Despite their relative quiet in the months since the election, the Copperheads had been neither forgotten nor forgiven for their actions.

Sherman had spent Election Day reviewing the 1860 census, identifying the most prosperous counties in Georgia. With Lincoln reelected, Sherman launched his march to the sea. It was a daring mission by any standard, and it electrified the North. Sherman cut himself off from his communications and supply lines and disappeared with sixty thousand men into the countryside. Northern and Southern newspapers alike were bewildered as to Sherman's whereabouts and his destination. Lincoln himself had no idea where the general was headed. He told Sherman's brother John, a senator from Ohio: "We have heard nothing from him. We know what hole he went in, but we don't know what hole he will come out of." The only way to tell where Sherman

might be was by following where telegraph communication ended. If
the lines were still live, that meant that Sherman's men had not arrived
yet to cut them.[1]

While Sherman made his way across Georgia, John Bell Hood moved
his troops into Tennessee, hoping to lure Sherman into chasing him.
The plan failed, so Hood turned his attention to intercepting the federals
under General John Schofield between Pulaski and Nashville, where
another thirty thousand Yankees were stationed. Schofield ducked
Hood and entrenched his men at Franklin, fifteen miles south of Nashville. Apparently having learned nothing from the experiences of the
Eastern armies, Hood insisted on a frontal assault on November 30.
His command was cut to pieces. Among the Confederates' 6,300 casualties were a dozen generals and fifty-four regimental commanders.
After the fight Schofield pulled back to Nashville, where he linked up
with the rest of George H. Thomas's army. Hood pursued the bluecoats
but was too weak to start a fight. Instead, he waited. After more than
two weeks, Thomas initiated an attack December 15 and crushed the
rebels. What was left of the Army of Tennessee hobbled back to Tupelo,
Mississippi, where many of its soldiers waited out the war.[2] In Richmond, Josiah Gorgas received the news and called the day "one of the
gloomiest in our struggle." The battle, he realized, had been a disaster
and left the Confederacy with only one army of any power—Lee's.[3]

Sherman's march through Georgia gave the war a new tone. This
had become a hard war, one involving civilians.[4] The Yankees were
not the only ones who played this game. The Confederates had long
been interested in creating havoc on the Northern home front. Their
agents had tried to manipulate gold prices, rob banks, and sponsor
uprisings in the Northwest. Now the Confederates turned to New York
City. Spies sneaked into the city and on November 25 set nineteen fires
in some of the city's most prominent hotels—including the St. James,
the Gramercy Park, and the Belmont House—along with Barnum's
Museum and Tammany Hall. The blazes, most of which were started
by lodgers soaking their beds with camphene and then setting fire to
them, were discovered quickly and extinguished, but the arsons were
deeply unsettling to New Yorkers.[5]

With Lincoln elected for another term and Sherman rolling along
toward the Georgia coast, Northerners had little question as to the
outcome of the war, and dissent faded from the public stage.
Vallandigham and his followers still railed against the administration,
but their commentary made little impact on the public, which was more
interested in when, not if, the war would end. General Geary called
the Copperheads "antiquated fossils." From Yellow Head, Illinois,

Sophronia Chipman wrote her soldier husband that one of his relatives had stopped by the week before Christmas but was subdued on the subject of politics. "He does not talk like a Copper head and I believe he is ashamed that he has ever been one," she reported. Even in the reactionary hotbed of Sullivan County, Indiana, the Copperheads were "caveing in" and submitting to the draft, the local provost marshal reported.[6]

Once good news started in the North, it seemed hard to stop. When Sherman reached Savannah on December 22, he sent Lincoln a pithy telegram: "I beg to present you, as a Christmas gift, the city of Savannah, with 150 heavy guns and plenty of ammunition, and also about 25,000 bales of cotton." Northerners were ecstatic. Even the *World* had words of praise for Sherman. Noting that Washington won the Battle of Trenton on December 26, the editors believed Sherman's achievement would go down in history to the same plaudits. They did not fail to remind their readers of the real objective of Sherman's march: "Would to God, that this coincidence, connecting this important and bloodless success alike with patriotic and Christian memories, might be the harbinger of PEACE, dating its dawn from the birthday of the PRINCE OF PEACE!" Like many other newspapers, Republican or Democratic, the *World* had little trouble with the destruction Sherman left in his sixty-mile-wide wake. Sherman estimated the damage to be "$100,000,000; at least, $20,000,000 of which has inured to our advantage, and the remainder is simple waste and destruction. This may seem a hard species of warfare, but it brings the sad realities of war home to those who have been directly or indirectly instrumental in involving us in its attendant calamities."[7]

Expectations in the North were soaring as the calendar rolled into 1865, and with good reason. The new year was only two weeks old when the Yankees captured Fort Fisher, a stronghold made of sand at the mouth of the Cape Fear River twenty miles below Wilmington, North Carolina. The victory, which involved the largest naval fleet of the war along with eight thousand army troops, was important because it closed Wilmington as the Confederacy's last blockade-running port of any size. The win also further disheartened Confederates. "The prospect is growing darker & darker about us," Gorgas wrote while suffering a short-lived case of the blues. As Southern hopes waned, Northern confidence continued on the upswing. Lincoln was one beneficiary, but Grant's stock may have been rising even faster. "The papers say there is strong talk of Peace measures about to be made But I expect if Grant has anything to do with it, it will be of the U S sort such as they secured at Vicksburg," an Illinois housewife wrote her husband in the 76th Illinois, alluding to Grant's first nickname, "Unconditional Surrender."[8]

Four days after Fort Fisher fell, Sherman ordered troops to start moving from Savannah into South Carolina. If the Confederates thought they had seen the worst Sherman and the Yankees had to offer on his march to the sea, they were wrong.[9] South Carolina was the cradle of the Confederacy. The federals, who had shown some restraint in Georgia, were decidedly not in a charitable mood where the Palmetto State was concerned. They blamed South Carolina for starting the war and were eager to avenge Fort Sumter. "The whole army is burning with an insatiable desire to wreak vengeance upon South Carolina. I almost tremble at her fate, but feel that she deserves all that seems in store for her," Sherman wrote while his men were still in Savannah. When they arrived in South Carolina, Yankee soldiers unleashed their pent-up anger. They made little distinction between public and private property, military or personal necessity. What they did not take they torched. The state capital, Columbia, suffered the worst damage, although it is likely that Confederate cavalry, slaves, and escaped prisoners were as responsible for the conflagration that broke out the night of February 17 as the newly arrived Union soldiers. On the coast, meantime, the North reached a major symbolic milestone when Charleston, home to Fort Sumter, surrendered February 18.[10]

Unconditional surrender was the term of the day. With peace sentiment now growing in the South, Davis appointed Vice President Alexander Stephens—an old friend of Lincoln's—and two other men in January to explore the possibility of ending the war between "the two countries." Lincoln agreed to meet with the commission to explore the possibility of bringing peace "to the people of our one common country." The semantic difference was pointed and intentional on Lincoln's part. He had never recognized the Confederacy as an independent entity, only as a group of states in rebellion, and he certainly was not going to change his approach now that the rebels were on the ropes.[11]

Lincoln and Seward met the Southerners on February 3 aboard the *River Queen*, which was docked at Hampton Roads, Virginia. No one other than the principals was in the room, so the only accounts are from the participants themselves. The meeting was calm, polite, and informal, but it yielded no peace. Lincoln told the Southerners that he would make no treaty or agreement with the Confederacy because that would recognize it as a separate power. For the same reason, he refused to negotiate with any state individually. Lincoln also told the commissioners that Congress had just adopted the Thirteenth Amendment, which abolished slavery, suggesting the rebel states would have to accept that once they rejoined the Union. Finally, Lincoln remained adamant that any peace would come only with the full restoration of the United States. Although Lincoln assured the commissioners that he would be lenient once peace was restored, they could not accept the proposal. Lincoln and Davis both remained too fastened to their positions, and Davis was not yet convinced his options had run out.[12]

The conference may have been a failure in terms of ending the war, but according to New Yorker George Templeton Strong, it made great headway in "silencing or converting" many Copperheads. Finally, it seemed, Peace Democrats had started to realize that the Confederates wanted independence, not peace. Having recognized that, many of them now believed there was nothing to do but fight until the South surrendered. Others remained as obstreperous as ever. Charles Mason wrote that some people thought the Confederacy was about to collapse. "They will be mistaken," he wrote in his diary.[13] Alexander St. Clair Boys, a devout Ohio Peace Democrat, told Representative W. W. Long that his opponents in Congress had proved disloyal to the principles of the Democratic Party and were "destitute of patriotism, courage, and every public virtue." Long was the only man in Congress to defend state sovereignty, and without state sovereignty, the government would cease to exist, in Boys's opinion. Alexander Long, the congressman who had been censured for his treasonous talk, told Boys he was convinced that the South would gain its independence. The "Northern beast" had to be defeated, and those who did not help the Confederate cause should be denounced as traitors.[14]

Despite their ever-darkening prospects, some Southerners continued to hold out hopes for success. Like Unionists in the North, they deeply resented any attempts at a negotiated peace. "Our only chance for peace lyes in our rifles, that will bring it after awhile, if we will only remain true to ourselves," a South Carolina planter turned soldier told his wife.[15]

While the armies were pressing forward on the military front, Lincoln was moving on the political front. At the top of his agenda was the Thirteenth Amendment, which permanently abolished slavery. Congressional Democrats had defeated the amendment the previous June, and as recently as December, Democrats were still arguing that if slavery was an acceptable institution for the people of the Bible, it should be an acceptable institution for the people of the United States. Lincoln was prepared to call a special session of the new Congress in March but opted instead to give the lame-duck Congress another chance to pass the amendment, saying that it was better to adopt it sooner rather than later. The House took him up on the offer, and the amendment came before it January 30. The timing of the vote was particularly awkward for the racist Copperheads in the House because the

Davis government was considering freeing slaves who joined the Confederate army. Samuel S. Cox, for one, was entirely baffled as to how to
handle the amendment in light of developments in the South. "If Davis
(as he will) rejects any *tender* of accommodation, & arms & frees (as he
is now doing, for he has 5 Regts of negroes all ready at Richmond,) his
negroes,—shall we be committed to voting against the amendts, when
Davis is at work freeing them?" he wrote Manton Marble. "Where will
it place us? . . . What object have I or you, looking to the near future, as
well as the remote,—in being tied to the body of Death? Is it for State
rights? . . . Is it for peace? No hope for that,—for that I would first
assume to be tried & jailed. No hope for Democratic ascendancy by
such votes, *as you know*."[16]

In spite of Lincoln's certainty that the measure would pass in the
incoming Congress, what this lame-duck Congress would do was
anyone's guess. As late as noon January 31, the day of the vote, no one
was sure how the roll call would go. The amendment passed by a vote
of 119 to 56, seven more than needed. Historian Michael Vorenberg
argues that the antipathy of the Peace Democrats toward the amendment drove moderate Democrats to support it. Moderates saw this as
a way of moving the party in a new direction. Once the vote was taken,
the men thronging the galleries burst into cheers and the ladies waved
their handkerchiefs, while Republican members of the House leaped
to their feet and clapped. In celebration, the House took the rest of the
day off and Washington reverberated with the sound of a hundred-
gun salute.[17] According to newspaper reports, Lincoln appeared at a
window of the Executive Mansion the next day and told the crowd
gathered below that the amendment was "a King's cure for all the evils.
. . . It winds the whole thing up. He would repeat that it was the fitting
if not indispensable adjunct to the consummation of the great game
we are playing. He could not but congratulate all present, himself, the
country and the whole world upon this great moral victory." Black
soldiers in the field did not see the amendment as finishing their work;
they saw it as beginning the next phase of their fight for rights. "Let us
all strive to show the world that we are worthy of our freedom, while
the detestable copperheads have been trying to make sensible people
believe that we were fit for nothing but slaves, and for blacking boots,
and waiting on them," a member of the 43rd U.S. Colored Troops wrote
the *Christian Recorder* from Richmond. "I have heard such talk down
here by some of our copperhead officers, but we must impute it to
their ignorance."[18]

The Confederacy's death rattle was all but audible. Richard Cobden,
the British businessman and politician who had kept close tabs on the

With the 1864 election behind him, Lincoln turned to making emancipation, which he had adopted as a war measure, permanent. The result was the Thirteenth Amendment, which abolished slavery for good. (*Frank Leslie's Budget of Fun*/Courtesy of HarpWeek LLC)

war from the far side of the Atlantic, wrote Sumner in March that "I cannot doubt that your *great* military operations are drawing to a close. The war is being driven into a corner." He advised his friend to disregard rumors that the European powers might yet enter into the war. "Nothing of the kind is now possible," he said, calling such reports "the purest fiction."[19] Confederates saw the end, too. "People are almost in a state of desperation, and but too ready to give up the cause, not that there is not patriotism enough to sustain it, but that there is sentiment of hopelessness abroad, a feeling that all our sacrifices tend to nothing, that our resources are wasted, in short that there is no leadership, and so they are ready to despair," ordnance chief Gorgas wrote. The federals could see the Confederates' growing sense of hopelessness. "Great events are to happen in a few days, and I want to be there to see the end. The end of the war will be the end of slavery, and then our land will be the 'Land of the free,' " wrote a twenty-three-year-old colonel who had been in every major battle the Army of the Potomac had fought.[20]

The Confederacy was not dead yet, though. The final scene began March 25, when Lee broke through a Union line east of Petersburg. The rebels overran nearly a mile of trenches before the Yankees wrested their works back. After a brief but costly—to the Confederates—fight April 1 at Five Forks, Grant decided the time had come to make a full charge on the rebels. The Southerners backpedaled all the next day before slipping out of Petersburg that night and marching west. Left undefended, the Confederate government ordered everything of military value burned—bridges, factories, arsenals, documents—and fled Richmond. A black cavalry regiment, the 5th Massachusetts, was among the first into the Confederate capital.

The state of the Confederacy gave some federals a chance to reflect on what had happened over the past four years. George Frush of Iowa wrote that in his part of the world "most of the copperheads have submited there necks to the yoake and they are Bound to ware it if it should gall them a little." The difference that peace and harmony made in his hometown of Abingdon was striking, he said. A year earlier the Copperheads had tried to stage some sort of rebellion during a church service because the minister was a Unionist. Frush made a habit of going to church armed with a revolver and at times a Bowie knife, and once was part of a guard detailed to protect the church. "About that time the cops had all left the church or in other words all the Dimocrats that used to Belong to the church left   they ware so Religious that they could not Bare to hear they minister Pray for the goverment or our soldiers." Over the past winter, though, conservative Democrats had decided "their race was run," and most of them had returned to the fold. General Geary wrote his wife about how pleased he was that he had joined the army rather than throw his lot in with "secret bands of traitors of the baser kind" who sought only to destroy the country. Some of their friends, he knew, could show their faces only among the peace men. "What will the iron pen of history say of them?" They might have more money than he, but their gain was ill gotten, *"with a traitor's name attached,* and a *traitor's doom awaiting,* to carry down a worthless fame to the grave, and be 'unwept, unhonored, and unsung.' " Geary's comments were melodramatic, but his sentiments were widely shared, especially by veterans.[21]

Grant chased Lee's hungry and exhausted men to Appomattox, capturing a fifth of Lee's thirty-five thousand troops in a single battle along the way. Lee, realizing he was surrounded and unwilling to scatter his men to become guerrillas, surrendered April 9.[22] Grant's terms were nearly that of unconditional surrender, but he paroled all captives and allowed the rebel soldiers to take draft animals home so they could start putting in their crops.

Veterans were jubilant. "Hip! Hip! Hurrah! General Lee surrendered yesterday. It was the greatest day that I ever saw," a corporal with the 141st Pennsylvania gushed. A veteran of the famed Iron Brigade wrote: "Has not April been to us a glorious month? Where are the men now who said that the army of the Potomac has never accomplished any thing?" But some veteran Copperheads, men who had argued so long for peace, were strangely unmoved at its arrival. "The war news grows less interesting" was Charles Mason's only comment.[23]

After so many years and so much hardship, a number of soldiers had come to have a strong bond with the president. Especially in the Army of the Potomac, the only army Lincoln was able to visit personally, soldiers noticed that Lincoln suffered as they did; his face showed the wear. On this particularly happy day, one private marveled again at Lincoln's presence. "Mr. Lincoln presides over millions of people, and each individual share of his attention must necessarily be very small, and yet he wouldn't slight the humblest of them all. . . . The men not only reverence and admire Mr. Lincoln, but they love him. May God bless him, and spare his life to us for many years."[24]

That was not to be. On April 11, two days after Lee's surrender, Lincoln gave an impromptu speech from a balcony of the White House. In it, he suggested that some black men should get the vote. In the audience was actor John Wilkes Booth, a Confederate sympathizer from Maryland who already had been plotting to kidnap the president. This latest turn in Lincoln's thinking enraged Booth, and his plan turned from a kidnapping plot to an elaborate assassination scheme involving not just Lincoln but Vice President Johnson and Secretary of State Seward as well. Five days after Lee surrendered, Lincoln went to Ford's Theater with his wife and another couple. Partway through the comedy *Our American Cousin*, Booth slipped into the president's box, shot Lincoln once in the head, leaped to the stage, and made his escape. The unconscious president was carried to a boardinghouse across the street and placed diagonally across the bed—the only way his long frame could fit into it. In another part of town, Lewis Powell stabbed Seward multiple times, badly injuring but not killing him. Another conspirator got cold feet and never even tried to carry out his mission against

FROM OUR SPECIAL WAR CORRESPONDENT.

"CITY POINT, VA., *April* —, 8.30 A.M.
"All seems well with us."—A. LINCOLN.

This editorial cartoon celebrates the end of the war by quoting Lincoln. The issue in which the illustration appeared was dated April 15, 1865, the day Lincoln died, which puts this in a rather different light. (*Harper's Weekly*/Courtesy of HarpWeek LLC)

Johnson. Meanwhile, much of Lincoln's cabinet had gathered in the room, along with Lincoln's son Robert, the Speaker of the House, and Senator Charles Sumner, who himself had nearly died nine years earlier when he was caned on the Senate floor by a Southern congressman. Mary Lincoln was so overwrought that a friend took her from the room, but Mary returned hourly to visit. It was in that company that Lincoln died at 7:22 the next morning. "Now he belongs to the ages," Secretary of War Stanton said.[25]

The nation was shocked. This was the first president in American history to be assassinated, and Lincoln had been killed less than a week after the moment of his greatest triumph. Confusion, anger, and sorrow gripped the North. That Booth had shot the president was common knowledge, but at whose behest? The Confederates'? The Copperheads'? Many soldiers wrote that if the war had still been going on they gladly would have retaliated upon the Southerners. "The soldiers are wild with rage to think that this great and good man who did so much for our land should be stricken down in the hour of victory," one officer wrote. The most common conspiracy theory was that Booth was acting on orders from the Davis administration.[26]

The Copperheads came under suspicion as well. One soldier was deeply distressed to think that thousands of Northerners would "*rejoice* at the dire calamity which has come upon this nation." Lincoln's old friend Orville Hickman Browning hardly knew whom to blame but said the consequences of the assassination "may be exceedingly disastrous to the Country. It must, necessarily, greatly inflame and exasperate the minds of the people, and, I fear lead to attempts at summary vengeance upon those among us who have been suspected of sympathy with the rebellion, and hostility to our government. This would be followed by anarchy and the wildest scenes of confusion and bloodshed, ending in military Despotism."[27]

As it was, however, they remained quiet. Americans began to realize what Lincoln had meant to them. Strong said he thought before Lincoln's assassination that people might appreciate him

> twenty years hence, but I did not suppose his death would instantly reveal—even to Copperhead newspaper editors—the nobleness and glory of his part in this great contest. . . . *Death* has suddenly opened the eyes of the people (and I think the world) to the fact that a hero has been holding high place among them for four years, closely watched and studied, but despised and rejected by a third of this community, and only tolerated by the other two-thirds.

Strong was certainly correct about the reaction of conservatives. Even such hard-core peace men as Chauncey Burr mourned the president's death. Burr wrote that he could not "disguise our conviction that the death of Mr. Lincoln is the greatest calamity to our country. It is generally believed that he had fully settled upon a policy which would speedily end our civil strife, and give rest to our bleeding land. . . . The blow was as blind as it was great in the enormity of its crime."[28]

Authorities finally found Booth on April 26 hiding in a barn in Virginia. As the building burned around the assassin, troops shot him to death. The other conspirators were caught, tried, and hanged. Even after the executions, suspicions remained as to the rebels' possible involvement in the plot to kill the president. However, belief that the Copperheads had a hand in the matter soon disappeared.[29] The fact that they came under scrutiny at all, though, suggests how deeply they had alienated Unionists. It also suggests to what extremes Unionists still believed, even with the war over, that Copperheads were willing to go. That "smell of treason" that the Republicans had talked about in the fall still clung to the garments of the Peace Democrats, and it would stick to their party for years to come.

IN MANY WAYS, THE COPPERHEADS were brought down not by external events but by their own weaknesses. They were never well organized. Although the leading conservatives were in contact, their discussions never resulted in a plan that would mobilize Peace Democrats across the nation. Proto-military and other Copperhead organizations existed at the local level, especially in the Northwest, but as with the national leaders, communication and organization among these cells was limited at best. Besides hurting the Copperheads politically, this lack of organization also meant that they never could mount an effective rejoinder to accusations of disloyalty. A credible response was especially important in the late summer and early fall of 1864, when the exposure of Dodd's plot in Indiana brought the question of treason to the fore and when Union victories in the field belied the peace platform. The Peace Democrats' insistence that they were loyal may have been true for many of them, but few Unionists believed them.

Rather than offer any alternatives to Lincoln's policies, the Copperheads acted only as naysayers and obstructionists. Their relentless and often ad hominem attacks helped to erode public confidence in Lincoln's government. The only suggestion they had was to end the war, but they never produced a realistic or concrete program to achieve peace. Nor did they ever acknowledge in any way the Confederates' repeated statements that they were not interested in peace if that meant surrendering their independence. More important, the Peace Democrats impinged on military strength at the front. By encouraging men to resist the draft or to desert, Copperheads had a direct effect on the army's ability to muster the men it needed to fight the war. Violent resistance also forced the army to spread its resources out behind the lines rather than concentrate them at the front.

The Copperheads' repeated claims that the war was a failure and a waste of men so alienated the soldier population that it had the contrary effect of mobilizing them against the Democrats. The politicization of military men contributed mightily to the conservatives' failure. Soldiers made no effort to hide their hatred for the conservatives. They thought that pronouncing the war a failure denigrated the sacrifices that they and their comrades had made. In an age when honor counted, this was an extreme insult in the eyes of the troops. Their stream of letters to their friends and relatives at home likely caused many civilians to pause before casting their lot or casting their ballot with the Peace Democrats—or Democrats generally. More important, however, the soldiers' continuing faith in Lincoln and the government buttressed the president and served as the foundation for his political resurrections after the bloody summers of 1862 and 1864. Their support of Lincoln in their correspondence sent an important message to the people at home: Lincoln would pull the nation out of the war and reunite the country.

The prospect of reunion was anything but clear at many points in the war. The nation at times looked as though it could split not just in two but perhaps into three different countries: North, South, and West. To this day, the Civil War remains the most treacherous period in the nation's history. Yet the Copperheads never recognized—or if they did, they certainly never acknowledged—the seriousness of the threat to destroy the United States. Their rigid ideology led them to focus on important constitutional issues but not to put those issues in the context of a greater danger. Their concern about and constant attention to civil liberties may well have kept the Lincoln administration from being more aggressive than it was, but the Copperheads were never willing to grant the president any quarter to deal with the crisis at hand. Finally, their narrow interpretation of the Constitution never allowed them to see how restrained Lincoln actually was in the way he dealt with dissidents.

Although the Copperheads bear much responsibility for their own demise, the war itself was the single most important factor in both their rise and fall. The antiwar men appealed to Northerners only when the public's hopes for victory faded. It is no coincidence that the peace faction was strongest at the moments when the army was suffering its worst defeats. Conversely, the Copperheads suffered their greatest setbacks when the Union armies won. By the end of the war, the Peace Democrats were men out of time. Committed to a belief system that extended back at least a century, they could not keep up with the economic, social, or political changes that the war and industrialization wrought. Beyond the obvious fact of emancipation, they seem not even to have recognized the massive shifts that had taken place between 1861 and 1865. Instead, by the end of the war they seemed to occupy a bubble world that had little connection with the society that was emerging. They preferred to hearken back to a simpler era, assuming that ever existed. Whether it had or not, that world was one that had little in common with the United States of 1865. While they looked over their shoulders, the nation at large moved into the future.

Abbreviations Used in Notes

CHS	Connecticut Historical Society, Hartford
CL	Clements Library, Ann Arbor, Michigan
CSL	Connecticut State Library, Hartford
IHS	Indiana Historical Society, Indianapolis
ISA	Indiana State Archives, Indianapolis
ISL	Indiana State Library, Indianapolis
LC	Library of Congress, Washington, D.C.
LL	Lincoln Library, Springfield, Illinois
LLIU	Lilly Library, Bloomington, Indiana
MHS	Minnesota Historical Society
NARA	National Archives and Records Administration, Washington, D.C.
NYSL	New York State Library Manuscripts and Special Collections, Albany
OHS	Ohio Historical Society, Columbus
SHSI	State Historical Society of Iowa, Iowa City and Des Moines

Notes

INTRODUCTION

Unorthodox spelling and grammar are common in letters and diaries from this era. Throughout this book, such errors are left as they were in the original.

1. Democrats had little better luck with the Senate, which they controlled for only ten of the sixty-four years between 1868 and 1932 (1879–81, 1893–95, and 1913–19). The Democrats performed better in the House of Representatives, whose control began to shift between the parties in 1875, a decade after the Civil War ended.

2. David Potter has made this argument for Lincoln most strongly, saying that, given Lincoln's attributes and Confederate President Jefferson Davis's weaknesses, "it hardly seems unrealistic to suppose that if the Union and the Confederacy had exchanged Presidents with one another, the Confederacy might have won its independence." David Potter, *The South and the Sectional Conflict* (Baton Rouge: Louisiana State University Press, 1968), 284.

3. Eric L. McKitrick, "Party Politics and the Union and Confederate War Efforts," in *The American Party Systems: Stages of Political Development*, ed. William Nisbet Chambers and Walter Dean Burnham (New York: Oxford University Press, 1967), 133–44. Mark E. Neely Jr. takes issue with McKitrick, though not entirely convincingly, in *The Union Divided: Party Conflict in the Civil War North* (Cambridge: Harvard University Press, 2002).

4. Charles H. Coleman, "The Use of the Term 'Copperhead' During the Civil War," *Mississippi Valley Historical Review* 25 (1938): 263.

5. Research on republicanism has burgeoned in the past generation. The most thorough work on the deep roots of this idea is J.G.A Pocock's *The Machiavellian Moment: Florentine Political Thought and the Atlantic Republican Tradition* (Princeton: Princeton University Press, 1975). For more on how these ideas played out in the United States, see John M. Murrin, "The Great Inversion, or

Court Versus Country: A Comparison of the Revolution Settlements in England (1688–1721) and America (1776–1816)," in *Three British Revolutions: 1641, 1688, 1776*, ed. J.G.A. Pocock (Princeton: Princeton University Press, 1980), 368–453; Drew R. McCoy, *The Elusive Republic: Political Economy in Jeffersonian America* (Chapel Hill: University of North Carolina Press, 1980); and Jean H. Baker, *Affairs of Party: The Political Culture of Northern Democrats in the Mid-Nineteenth Century* (Ithaca: Cornell University Press, 1983). Peace Democrats regarded the Constitution as "a formal set of rules," whereas Republicans saw it as "a living document that incorporated laws, customs, and practices," according to Baker. She also makes a fascinating argument that the kind of rhetoric the Copperheads used hearkened back to the kind that the Patriots used during the Revolution. "By placing their appeals within this antiauthoritarian tradition, Democrats conveyed a threat that is difficult to apprehend today," she writes. Baker, *Affairs of Party*, 152–53.

6. Reuben A. Kessel and Armen A. Alchian, "Real Wages in the North During the Civil War: Mitchell's Data Reinterpreted," in *The Economic Impact of the American Civil War*, ed. Ralph Andreano (Cambridge, Mass.: Schenkman, 1967), 13.

7. Roy P. Basler, *The Collected Works of Abraham Lincoln*, vol. 7 (New Brunswick: Rutgers University Press), 281–82.

8. Wood Gray, *The Hidden Civil War: The Story of the Copperheads* (New York: Viking Press, 1942); George Fort Milton, *Abraham Lincoln and the Fifth Column* (New York: The Vanguard Press, 1942.); Frank L. Klement, *The Copperheads in the Middle West* (Chicago: University of Chicago Press, 1960).

9. Carl Von Clausewitz, *On War*, trans. and ed. Michael Eliot Howard and Peter Paret (Princeton: Princeton University Press, 1984), 89.

10. Because one would naturally expect resistance in the border states, I do not consider what happened in Kentucky, Missouri, Delaware, or Maryland.

11. Edward L. Pierce, ed., *Memoir and Letters of Charles Sumner*, vol. 4 (Boston: Roberts Brothers, 1893), 114.

CHAPTER 1

1. Whether Lincoln baited the Confederates into attacking has been the subject of spirited debate among historians. See Charles W. Ramsdell, "Lincoln and Fort Sumter," *Journal of Southern History* 3 (August 1937): 259–88; Richard Current, *Lincoln and the First Shot* (Philadelphia: Lippincott, 1963), and Kenneth M. Stampp, *The Imperiled Union: Essays on the Background of the Civil War* (New York: Oxford University Press, 1980), 163–88, for opposing points of view on the question. Anderson formally surrendered the fort April 14.

2. *Crisis*, April 11, 1861.

3. *New York Herald*, April 13, 22, 1861.

4. William J. Jackson, *New Jerseyans in the Civil War: For Union and Liberty* (New Brunswick: Rutgers University Press, 2000), 37; Roland Swift to Mother, April 23, 1861, Swift Family Correspondence, folder 2, CSL.

5. Nina Silber and Mary Beth Sievens, eds., *Yankee Correspondence: Civil War Letters Between New England Soldiers and the Home Front*, A Nation Divided: New Studies in Civil War History (Charlottesville: University Press of Virginia, 1996), 56.

6. *Niles Republican*, April 20, 1861 (many thanks to Robert C. Myers of the Berrien County Historical Association for his extensive list of references from this newspaper); Frank L. Klement, *The Copperheads in the Middle West* (Chicago: University of Chicago Press, 1960), 109, 291, n. 7; James M. McPherson, *Ordeal by Fire: The Civil War and Reconstruction*, 3rd ed. (Boston: McGraw-Hill, 2001), 164.

7. "Mayor Wood's Recommendation of the Secession of New York City," www.teachingamericanhistory.org/library/index.asp?document=435. Thanks to my student Matthew Nagle for alerting me to this document.

8. *Dubuque Herald*, April 14, 1861; Emma Lou Thornbrough, *Indiana in the Civil War Era, 1850–1880* (Indianapolis: Indiana Historical Bureau and Indiana Historical Society, 1965), 103.

9. United States Census Office, *Statistics of the United States, 8th Census* (Washington, D.C.: Government Printing Office, 1866).

10. United States Bureau of the Census, *Population of the United States in 1860* (Washington, D.C.: Government Printing Office, 1864), xxix. For more on Minnesota during the war, see Kenneth Carley, *Minnesota in the Civil War* (Minneapolis: Ross & Haines, 1961). It is unclear what percentage of the German population in Wisconsin was Catholic, but Catholicism appears to be more important than being German. For instance, Minnesota, which attracted a number of Protestant Germans and Scandinavians, was far less contentious.

11. Key readings on republicanism include Pocock, *The Machiavellian Moment;* McCoy, *The Elusive Republic;* and Murrin, "The Great Inversion, or Court Versus Country."

12. Jefferson proved to be far more moderate as president than these beliefs would suggest—the result of his concern with maintaining constitutional stability, according to Richard E. Ellis. Moderate Jeffersonians went on to use the government to help organize and advance the settlement of the West and to build up American industry. Richard E. Ellis, "The Market Revolution and the Transformation of American Politics, 1801–1837," in *The Market Revolution in America: Social, Political, and Religious Expressions, 1800–1880,* ed. Melvyn Stokes and Stephen Conway (Charlottesville: University Press of Virginia, 1996), 150–57.

13. McPherson, *Ordeal by Fire*, 6; Norman K. Risjord, *The Old Republicans: Southern Conservatism in the Age of Jefferson* (New York: Columbia University Press, 1965), 1–9; Ellis, "The Market Revolution and the Transformation of American Politics, 1801–1837," 168–70. Jackson split badly with John C.

Calhoun, his vice president, who had written several years earlier in support of the right of secession and the veto power he believed states had over federal legislation. Calhoun reached his conclusions largely by drawing on the precedent the Virginia and Kentucky Resolutions provided.

14. Phillip S. Paludan, "The American Civil War Considered as a Crisis in Law and Order," *American Historical Review* 77 (1972): 1013–34.

15. Peter Ruffner to Joseph Lane, July 4, 1861, Joseph Lane MSS, LLIU; William Jarvis to William, January 8, 1861, William Jarvis Letters, box 1, CHS; John Niven, *Connecticut for the Union: The Role of the State in the Civil War* (New Haven: Yale University Press, 1965), 297–98.

16. Ch. O'Connor to James A. Bayard, July 2, 1861, Papers of Thomas F. Bayard, vol. 6, LC.

17. William H. Seward to Franklin Pierce, December 20, 1861, Papers of Manton Marble, vol. 2, LC; *Daily Chicago Times*, April 22, 1861.

18. William Jarvis to William, January 8, 1861, William Jarvis Letters, box 1; *Dubuque Herald*, April 13, 1861; John Campbell, *Unionists Versus Traitors: The Political Parties of Philadelphia; or the Nominees That Ought to Be Elected in 1861* (Philadelphia: N.p., 1861), 7, 10.

19. Amos Evans to Samuel Evans, March 28, 1862, Evans Family Papers, box 1, OHS; *New York Herald*, December 12, 1861.

20. Thomas H. Seymour to Edwin Stearns, September 15, 1861, Stearns Family Papers: Political Correspondence, box 6, folder AA, CHS.

21. Anonymous to Governor Richard Yates, n.d., Yates Family Papers, box 2, LL; Parker Earle and Charles Colby to Governor Richard Yates, n.d., 1861, Yates Family Papers, box 2; Union Bethel to Governor Oliver P. Morton, July 8, 1861, Indiana Legion Adjutant General, box 31, Warrick County Correspondence, ISA; Julius B. Curtis to Governor William A. Buckingham, August 23, 1861, Governor Buckingham: Incoming Letters, box 13, folder 9, CSL.

22. Jacob C. Adams to John G. Davis, December 8, 1861, John G. Davis Papers, box 4, folder 11, IHS.

23. Ollinger Crenshaw, "The Knights of the Golden Circle: The Career of George Bickley," *American Historical Review* 47 (October 1941): 23–50; William H. Templeton to John Williams, October 30, 1861, John Williams & Company Papers, box 6, LL.

24. For a book-length treatment of Klement's argument, see his *Dark Lanterns: Secret Political Societies, Conspiracies, and Treason Trials in the Civil War* (Baton Rouge: Louisiana State University Press, 1984). He argues his case more succinctly in *Lincoln's Critics: The Copperheads of the North* (Shippensburg, Pa.: White Mane Books, 1999), 15–19.

25. A. Becker to Isaac Crowe, July 1861, Isaac Crowe Papers, box 3, MHS.

26. Charles F. Cooney, "Treason or Tyranny? The Great Senate Purge of '62," *Civil War Times Illustrated* 18 (1979): 30–31; William Jarvis to William, October 15, 1861, Jarvis Letters, box 1, CHS; Charles J. Hoadley to Anonymous, Oct. 4, 1861, Hoadley Letter, CSL; F. D. Payton et al. to John Ingle Jr., August 16, 1861, John G. Davis Papers, box 4, folder 11.

27. Charles Mason, Diary, August 31, 1861, Charles Mason Collection, SHSI— Des Moines; Daniel A. Farley to John G. Davis, January 16, 1862, John G. Davis Papers, box 4, folder 12; G. R. Tredway, *Democratic Opposition to the Lincoln Administration in Indiana* (N.p.: Indiana Historical Bureau, 1973), 113–14.

28. *Cong. Globe*, 36 Cong., 1st Sess., Appendix, 43; Clement L. Vallandigham, *Speeches, Arguments, Addresses, and Letters of Clement L. Vallandigham* (New York: J. Walter, 1864), 211.

29. J. A. Cravens to William H. English, April 9, 1861, William H. English Papers, box 2, folder 15, IHS.

30. Heather Cox Richardson, *The Greatest Nation of the Earth: Republican Economic Policies During the Civil War* (Cambridge: Harvard University Press, 1997), 12–13.

31. Frank Klement, "Middle Western Copperheadism and the Genesis of the Granger Movement," *Mississippi Valley Historical Review* 38 (1952): 683–86; Emerson Fite, "The Agricultural Development of the West During the Civil War," in *The Economic Impact of the American Civil War*, ed. Ralph L. Andreano (Cambridge, Mass.: Schenkman, 1962), 48–54.

32. United States Bureau of the Census, *The United States on the Eve of the Civil War: As Described in the 1860 Census* (Washington, D.C.: U.S. Civil War Centennial Commission, 1963), 73; Fite, "The Agricultural Development of the West During the Civil War," 48–54; Klement, "Middle Western Copperheadism and the Genesis of the Granger Movement," 683–86. By the end of the war, prices for agricultural products were double or triple what they were in 1861, while freight rates for grain dropped slightly from 1861 levels and rates for livestock rose only marginally. Fite, "The Agricultural Development of the West During the Civil War," 55.

33. Klement, *The Copperheads in the Middle West*, 3–6; *New York Herald*, May 2, 1861. Inflation continued to be a significant problem throughout the war, averaging 13 percent from 1860 to 1865, and hitting highs of 25 percent per year in 1863 and 1864. Stephen J. DeCanio and Joel Mokyr, "Inflation and Wage Lag During the American Civil War," *Explorations in Economic History* 14 (October 1977): 314.

34. Clement L. Vallandigham, *Speech of Hon. C. L. Vallandigham, of Ohio, on Executive Usurpation* (Washington, D.C.: H. Polkinhorn, 1861), 4; *Crisis*, May 23, 1861; *Dubuque Herald*, July 9, 1861.

35. The *Merryman* case never made it before the Supreme Court. Instead, Taney, an appointee of President Andrew Jackson, made the ruling alone (in his capacity as the senior judge in Maryland's federal circuit court) and without ever hearing arguments on behalf of the government. Part of the reason there was not more public outcry about Lincoln's refusal to honor the decision is that Taney had deeply alienated the Northern public in 1857 with the decision he rendered in the *Dred Scott* case. Merryman was charged in July with treason, but he was released on bail and his case never went to trial. William H. Rehnquist, *All the Laws but One: Civil Liberties in Wartime* (New

York: Knopf, 1998), 26–40. For another account of *Merryman,* see J. G. Randall, *Constitutional Problems Under Lincoln,* rev. ed. (Urbana: University of Illinois, 1964), 161–63.

36. George H. Pendleton, *Speech of Hon. George H. Pendleton, of Ohio, in the House of Representatives, December 10, 1861* (N.p.: 1861), 7.

37. Randall, *Constitutional Problems Under Lincoln,* 121, 154–55; Mark E. Neely Jr., *The Fate of Liberty: Abraham Lincoln and Civil Liberties* (New York: Oxford University Press, 1991), 4–9.

38. Basler, *Collected Works,* vol. 4, 426–31.

39. *Crisis,* August 1, 1861; *Chicago Times,* September 24, 1861.

40. Vallandigham, *Speech . . . on Executive Usurpation,* 1, 8. A "no-party movement" had strong support from Republicans and a number of War Democrats. Some Democrats who supported this notion found themselves in the extremely odd position of saying that "no-partyism in no way meant that they supported the Republican party and its policies." Silbey, *A Respectable Minority,* 30–48.

41. Thornbrough, *Indiana in the Civil War Era,* 106; Frank Luther Mott, *American Journalism: A History of Newspapers in the United States Through 250 Years, 1690 to 1940* (New York: Macmillan, 1941), 341–42. The Union loss at First Bull Run sent Greeley into a deep depression. His enemies blamed Greeley for the disaster, and Greeley, "half crazed," suffered an attack of brain fever. On July 25 he published an editorial promising to refrain from criticizing any army movements and to support the administration's management of the war. Ibid.

42. *New York Herald,* July 23, 1861; *La Crosse Democrat,* July 29, 1861; *Niles Republican,* July 27, 1861.

43. *Niles Republican,* September 28, 1861; Stephen J. Buck, " 'A Contest in Which Blood Must Flow Like Water': Du Page County and the Civil War," *Illinois Historical Journal* 87 (Spring 1994): 4; Michael C. C. Adams, *Fighting for Defeat: Union Military Failure in the East, 1861–1865* (Lincoln: University of Nebraska Press, 1992).

44. Wilson's Creek occupied the Army of the West in August, and the navy kept busy with victories at Hattaras Inlet in August and Port Royal in November.

45. Reid Mitchell, "The Northern Soldier and His Community," in *Toward a Social History of the American Civil War,* ed. Maris A. Vinovskis (New York: Cambridge University Press, 1990), 79–85; Phillip Shaw Paludan, *"A People's Contest": The Union and Civil War,* 2nd ed., Modern War Studies (Lawrence: University Press of Kansas, 1996). For more on the veteran soldiers on both sides and their contributions to their respective causes, see James M. McPherson, *For Cause and Comrades: Why Men Fought in the Civil War* (New York: Oxford University Press, 1997).

46. Wm. B. Wedgwood, *The Reconstruction of the Government* (New York: John H. Tingley, 1861), 12.

47. Rehnquist, *All the Laws but One,* 46–47. The main target of enforcement in 1861 seems to have been opposition newspapers and their editors, but no

civilian was ever executed on charges of treason. Dean Sprague, *Freedom Under Lincoln* (Boston: Houghton Mifflin, 1965), chap. 14; Neely, *The Fate of Liberty*, 14–18.

48. Thomas M. Cook and Thomas W. Knox, eds., *Public Record Including Speeches, Messages, Proclamation, Official Correspondence, and Other Public Utterances of Horatio Seymour* (New York: I. W. England, 1868), 34–35.

49. Bray Hammond, "The North's Empty Purse, 1861–1862," *American Historical Review* 67 (1961): 2–10.

50. Richardson, *The Greatest Nation of the Earth*, 2–10.

51. Hammond, "The North's Empty Purse, 1861–1862," 10; Edward McPherson, *The Political History of the United States of America During the Great Rebellion* (Washington, D.C.: Philip & Solomons, 1864), 361.

52. Silbey, *A Respectable Minority*, 62–63 and 63n.

53. *Cong. Globe*, 37th Cong., 2nd Sess., 552; Buck, " 'A Contest in Which Blood Must Flow Like Water,' " 3; Montgomery Meigs, "General M. C. Meigs on the Conduct of the Civil War," *American Historical Review* 26 (January 1921): 292.

54. Emil Rosenblatt and Ruth Rosenblatt, eds., *Hard Marching Every Day: The Civil War Letters of Private Wilbur Fisk, 1861–1865*, Modern War Studies (Lawrence: University Press of Kansas, 1992), 1.

55. *Chicago Times*, November 26, 1861. In the spring of 1862, Major General David Hunter made a similar gaffe when he emancipated all the slaves in Georgia, Florida, and South Carolina—again, without checking with his superiors first. Lincoln countermanded that order, too, but the *Dubuque Herald* nevertheless cited the order as evidence that he had become a military despot and had committed treason. The editor, Dennis Mahoney, bemoaned the fact that Northerners were so lackadaisical about defending their liberties and declared that he had lost confidence in Americans' political virtue. *Dubuque Herald*, May 28, 1862.

56. Ernest A. McKay, *The Civil War and New York City* (Syracuse, N.Y.: Syracuse University Press, 1990), 112.

57. Colin M. Ingersoll to Thomas H. Seymour, March 21, 1862, Thomas H. Seymour Papers, box 5, folder 14, CHS; William Brindle to Joseph Lane, March 24, 1862, Lane MSS.

58. McPherson, *Ordeal by Fire*, 250–254.

59. Allan Nevins, *The War for the Union: War Becomes Revolution, 1862–1863* (New York: Charles Scribner's Sons, 1960), 111–14.

60. *Pilot*, May 17, 1862; *La Crosse Democrat*, April 30, 14, 1862.

CHAPTER 2

1. Nevins, *The War for the Union: War Becomes Revolution*, 43–44.

2. McPherson, *Ordeal by Fire*, 258. McClellan, who had both a prodigious capacity for self-pity and a martyr complex, wrote his wife that "no Genl ever labored under greater disadvantages, but I will carry it through in spite of everything." Stephen W. Sears, ed., *The Civil War Papers of George B. McClellan:*

Selected Correspondence, 1860–1865 (New York: Ticknor & Fields, 1989), 240.There is no evidence to back McClellan's allegation that the administration was trying to undercut him out of personal or political spite.

3. Basler, *Collected Works,* vol. 5, 184–85.

4. Nevins, *The War for the Union: War Becomes Revolution,* 118–23.

5. James M. McPherson, *Crossroads of Freedom: Antietam,* Pivotal Moments in American History (New York: Oxford University Press, 2002), 46–47; Nevins, *The War for the Union: War Becomes Revolution,* 140–43.

6. David W. Blight, ed., *When This Cruel War Is Over: The Civil War Letters of Charles Harvey Brewster* (Amherst: University of Massachusetts Press, 1992), 16.

7. McPherson, *Ordeal by Fire,* 260–64.

8. Michael Burlingame, ed., *With Lincoln in the White House: Letters, Memoranda, and Other Writings of John G. Nicolay, 1860–1865* (Carbondale: Southern Illinois University Press, 2000), 80; Orville Hickman Browning, *The Diary of Orville Hickman Browning,* ed. Theodore Calvin Pease and James G. Randall, vol. 1 (Springfield: Illinois State Historical Library, 1925), 563.

9. Joanna D. Cowden, "Sovereignty and Secession: Peace Democrats and Antislavery Republicans in Connecticut During the Civil War Years," *Connecticut History* 30 (1989): 49; Arnold Shankman, "William B. Reed and the Civil War," *Pennsylvania History* 39 (1972): 464; Thomas H. O'Connor, *Civil War Boston: Home Front and Battlefield* (Boston: Northeastern University Press, 1997), 117; *Dubuque Herald,* August 8, 1862.

10. Maria Lydig Daly, *Diary of a Union Lady: 1861–1865,* ed. Harold Earl Hammond, with an introduction by Jean V. Berlin (Lincoln: University of Nebraska Press, 2000), 143; Sallie Ross to James N. Hill, May 9, 1862, Hill MSS, LLIU.

11. M. Bradley to Governor Richard Yates, June 6, 1862, Yates Family Papers, box 6.

12. "A Deaf Mute" to Governor William A. Buckingham, June 19, 1862, Buckingham Incoming Correspondence, box 16.

13. Klement, *The Copperheads in the Middle West,* 27–28; Burlingame, *With Lincoln in the White House,* 82; Henry Barber to Brother, June 24, 1862, Henry Barber Papers, LL.

14. T. R. Eastman, July 25, 1862, Governor Samuel Kirkwood Papers, Correspondence: War Matters, 1858–88, SHSI—Des Moines; Governor's Letter Book: Military Record, August 20, 1861, to August 22, 1863, 182 and 224, SHSI—Des Moines.

15. McPherson, *Ordeal by Fire,* 273; Neely, *The Fate of Liberty,* 52; James W. Geary, *We Need Men: The Union Draft and the Civil War* (DeKalb: Northern Illinois University Press, 1991), 28–33; Margery Greenleaf, ed., *Letters to Eliza from a Union Soldier, 1862–1865* (Chicago: Follett, 1970), 8.

16. In the Army of the Potomac, senior generals and their followers tended to be Republicans who supported emancipation. The younger officers who supported McClellan were Democrats. T. Harry Williams, *Lincoln and His Generals* (New York: Vintage Books, 1952), 68.

17. Daly, *Diary of a Union Lady*, 157, 183; E. R. Abbott to Edwin M. Stanton, August 24, 1862, Turner-Baker Papers, RG M797, entry no. 2536, microfilm roll 67, NARA.

18. Neely, *The Fate of Liberty*, 52; Randall, *Constitutional Problems Under Lincoln*, 247; Geary, *We Need Men*, 27–34. During this trip, Vallandigham assured the state Democratic Convention that their own eyes could witness he was not, as his enemies would have it, the "extraordinary compound of leprous and unsightly flesh and blood ever exhibited. . . . You see that I am not quite 'monstrous,' as least, and bear no special resemblance to the beast of the Apocolypse, either in head or horns." Clement L. Vallandigham, *The Record of Hon. C. L. Vallandigham on Abolition, the Union, and the Civil War*, 9th ed. (Columbus: J. Walter, 1863), 127.

19. Nevins, *The War for the Union: War Becomes Revolution*, 163. For perceptive essays on the connection between soldiers and their hometowns, see Reid Mitchell, *The Vacant Chair: The Northern Soldier Leaves Home* (New York: Oxford University Press, 1993), chap. 2, and Paludan, "*A People's Contest*," chap. 1.

20. Those who favored conscription did not clearly lay out the reasons for their support, although the fact that the Confederacy had been drafting men for a year may have played a role in their thinking.

21. Thomas H. Seymour to Edwin Stearns, August 5, 1862, Stearns Family Papers: Political Correspondence.

22. William Platt to Governor William A. Buckingham, August 11, 1862, Buckingham Incoming Correspondence, box 17; Levi Hungerford to Governor William A. Buckingham, August 11, 1862, ibid.; Alpheus Parker to Hilon Adelbert Parker, August 15, 1862, Parker Papers, CL.

23. S. C. Brown to Major Levi C. Turner, August 12, 1862, Unmicrofilmed Turner-Baker Papers, RG 94, entry no. 697, box 20, NARA; Vincent F. Seyfried, "The Civil War in Queens County," *Long Island Historical Journal* 5 (1993): 153. The *Toledo Blade* reported on March 17, 1863, that nearly two thousand men had moved to Canada since the previous summer to avoid the draft. Hugh G. Earnhart, "The Administrative Organization of the Provost Marshal General's Bureau in Ohio, 1863–65," *Northwest Ohio Quarterly* 37 (1965): 98, n. 23.

24. Nevins, *The War for the Union: War Becomes Revolution*, 316.

25. Geary, *We Need Men*, 34. The only other bureaucracy that approached the same vastness by the end of the war was the network of assessors and collectors set up to collect the income tax that Congress had approved in 1861.

26. Accurate data about arrests are impossible to come by in the federal records, but a review of hundreds of files from the provost marshal's office at the National Archives leads one anecdotally to this conclusion.

27. Klement, *The Copperheads in the Middle West*, 19. The year after his arrest, Mahoney wrote a memoir of his experiences called *The Prisoner of State* (New York: Carleton, 1863).

28. Major Levi C. Turner to William Hildreth, August 14, 1862, vol. 1, Turner-Baker Papers, Letter Books, RG 94, entry no. 179. Many suspects were

released within a few months without ever appearing before a military or civilian court.

29. David L. Phillips to Edwin H. Stanton, September 4, 1862, Turner-Baker Papers, RG 94, entry no. 124, box 4.

30. Ibid.

31. Klement, *The Copperheads in the Middle West*, 20; Neely, *The Fate of Liberty*, esp. 232–35; Colonel Joseph H. Tucker to Major Levi C. Turner, September 2, 1862, Turner-Baker Papers, RG 94, entry no. 540, box 16.

32. Edward H. Battershill to Turner, September 5, 1862, Turner-Baker Papers, RG 94, entry no. 541, box 16; N. H. Watson to Turner, September 5, 1862, ibid.; Lyman Bradley to J. H. House, September 5, 1862, ibid. It appears from the dates of the letters that this was a coordinated campaign, but Turner nonetheless ordered Bradley discharged. Turner to Battershill, September 16, 1862, ibid.

33. Major Levi C. Turner to James B. Flagg, September 24, 1862, vol. 1, Unmicrofilmed Turner-Baker Papers, Letter Books, RG 94, entry no. 179. Nevins argues that moderation generally prevailed because no one was hanged for treason and less than $130,000 worth of property was confiscated over the course of the war. Nevins, *The War for the Union: War Becomes Revolution*, 204.

34. *Mass Convention of the Democracy and Conservative Citizens of Indiana* (N.p.: 1862), 17.

35. Klement, *The Copperheads in the Middle West*, 20–22.

36. The federal provost marshal's office, which was established in March 1863, was even more effective than its state-level counterpart. See chap. 3.

37. J. M. Dimack to Thomas H. Seymour, July 14, 1862, Thomas H. Seymour Papers, box 5, folder 18.

38. Burlingame, *With Lincoln in the White House*, 85.

39. *Facts for the People Relating to the Present Crisis* (N.p.: [Indiana] Democratic State Central Committee, 1862), 11; Frank R. Levstik, "The Toledo Riot of 1862: A Study of Midwest Negrophobia," *Northwest Ohio Quarterly* 44 (1972): 102–4. Rioting itself was not uncommon at this time. In the years before the war, riots were "a piece of the ongoing process of democratic accommodation, compromise, and uncompromisable tension between groups with different interests," according to the most thorough study of rioting in antebellum America. David Grimsted, *American Mobbing, 1828–1861: Toward Civil War* (New York: Oxford University Press, 1998), viii.

40. Frank Klement, "Sound and Fury: Civil War Dissent in the Cincinnati Area," *Cincinnati Historical Society Bulletin* 35 (1977): 100; Albon P. Man Jr., "Labor Competition and the New York Draft Riots of 1863," *Journal of Negro History* 36 (1951): 389–91.

41. Republicans, who controlled Congress, did not pay slaveowners in the territories because they believed that slavery had never existed legally there. Nevins, *The War for the Union: War Becomes Revolution*, 94.

42. Gideon Welles, "The History of Emancipation," *Galaxy*, December 1872, 538–42. Aware of the president's negotiations and the increasing cry in Wash-

ington to deal severely with Confederate slaveowners, McClellan weighed in on the subject July 7 with a remarkable letter to Lincoln, one that eventually became public. The war should not seek to "subjugate" Southerners, nor should it target civilians, he said. "Neither confiscation of property, political executions of persons, territorial organization of states or forcible abolition of slavery should be contemplated for a moment." If the government appropriated slaves, the owners should be compensated, he argued. "A system of policy thus constitutional and conservative, and pervaded by the influences of Christianity and freedom, would receive the support of almost all truly loyal men. " Sears, *The Civil War Papers of George B. McClellan*, 344–45.

43. Nevins, *The War for the Union: War Becomes Revolution*, 145–46; Basler, *Collected Works*, vol. 5, 336–38, 433–36; Welles, "The History of Emancipation," 543–55.

44. Depositions, August 27 and 28, 1862, Turner-Baker Papers, RG 94, entry no. 411, box 12.

45. Silber and Sievens, *Yankee Correspondence*, 63–64; Greenleaf, *Letters to Eliza from a Union Soldier*, 19. For more on soldiers' attitudes toward emancipation, see McPherson, *For Cause and Comrades*, chap. 9, and Bell Irvin Wiley, *The Life of Billy Yank: The Common Soldier of the Union* (Baton Rouge: Louisiana State University Press, 1993), 40–44.

46. Nevins, *The War for the Union: War Becomes Revolution*, 174–86.

47. George Templeton Strong, *Diary of the Civil War*, ed. Allan Nevins (New York: Macmillan, 1952), 251, 253; Daly, *Diary of a Union Lady*, 171.

48. Silber and Sievens, *Yankee Correspondence*, 68–69.

49. Joseph L. Harsh, *Taken at the Flood: Robert E. Lee and Confederate Strategy in the Maryland Campaign of 1862* (Kent, Ohio: Kent State University Press, 1999), 48–49, 57–58, 124–25.

50. McPherson, *Crossroads of Freedom*, 56–61; Clifford Dowdey and Louis H. Manarin, eds. *The Wartime Papers of R. E. Lee* (New York: Bramhall House and the Virginia Civil War Commission, 1961), 301.

51. McPherson, *Crossroads of Freedom*, 107–9, 4–8; Jeffrey D. Marshall, ed., *A War of the People: Vermont Civil War Letters* (Hanover, N.H.: University Press of New England, 1999), 104–6; McPherson, *Ordeal by Fire*, 306–9. By "combat deaths" I mean those killed in action and those mortally wounded.

52. *New York Times*, October 20, 1862.

53. Basler, *Collected Works*, vol. 5, 336–37.

54. "Letters of Richard Cobden to Charles Sumner, 1862–1865," *American Historical Review* 2 (1897): 308–9.

55. *Circleville Watchman*, n.d., quoted in Klement, "Sound and Fury," 102; Nevins, *The War for the Union: War Becomes Revolution*, 302; Margaret Bethauser, "Henry A. Reeves: The Career of a Conservative Democratic Editor," *Journal of Long Island History* 9 (1973): 39–40; *Illinois State Register*, November 5, 1962, quoted in Frank Klement, "Midwestern Opposition to Lincoln's Emancipation Policy," *Journal of Negro History* 49 (1964): 179. Reeves had a personal

interest in the subject of civil liberties, having been detained for a month in 1861 for treasonable speech. Bethauser, "Henry A. Reeves," 39–40.

56. David Snyder, October 4, 1862, Turner-Baker Papers, RG 94, entry no. 536, box 16; William Jarvis to William, September 23, 1862, William Jarvis Letters, box 2; H. B. Whiting to Thomas H. Seymour, September 29, 1862, Thomas H. Seymour Papers, box 5, folder 20. Allen was arrested October 15 on suspicion of discouraging enlistments and taken to Camp Chase in Columbus. Earl Bill to Turner, October 17, 1862, Turner-Baker Papers, RG 94, entry no. 536, box 16.

57. Nevins, *The War for the Union: War Becomes Revolution*, 308–9. For a full treatment of the Democrats' divisions, see Silbey, *A Respectable Minority*.

58. Basler, *Collected Works*, vol. 5, 536–37; Neely, *The Fate of Liberty*, 52–53; United States War Department, *The War of the Rebellion: A Compilation of the Official Records of the Union and Confederate Armies*, ser. 2, vol. 4 (Washington, D.C.: Government Printing Office, 1880), 358–59 (hereafter referred to as *O.R.*); Browning, *The Diary of Orville Hickman Browning*, vol. 1, 586–87.

59. Matthew Bulkley to Thomas H. Seymour, September 24, 1862, Thomas H. Seymour Papers, box 5, folder 20.

60. Thomas H. Seymour to Edwin Stearns, September 26, 1862, Stearns Family Papers: Political Correspondence, box 6, folder BB; Anonymous, *Copperhead Platform!* 2, 4; Nevins, *The War for the Union: War Becomes Revolution*, 302.

61. W. W. Dawson to Alexander St. Clair Boys, October 7, 1862, Alexander S. Boys Papers, box 1, folder 5, OHS.

62. Fitz-John Porter to Manton Marble, September 30, 1862, Marble Papers, vol. 3.

63. Samuel I. Glassey to Simeon Draper, November 5, 1862, Turner-Baker Papers, RG 94, entry no. 475, box 15.

64. John McKeon, *The Administration Reviewed* (New York: Van Evrie, Horton, 1862), 6–9; Anonymous, *Copperhead Platform!* (N.p.: 1862), 3.

65. Nevins, *The War for the Union: War Becomes Revolution*, 300; Burlingame, *With Lincoln in the White House*, 89; Henry C. Gilbert to Hattie Gilbert, October 16, 1862, Henry C. Gilbert Papers, CL.

66. Daly, *Diary of a Union Lady*, 195; Browning, *The Diary of Orville Hickman Browning*, vol. 1, 588–89; Horatio Seymour to Manton Marble, November 11, 1862, Marble Papers, vol. 3; William Jarvis to William, October 21, 1862, William Jarvis Letters, box 2.

67. McPherson, *Ordeal by Fire*, 319–20; Nevins, *The War for the Union: War Becomes Revolution*, 321; Burlingame, *With Lincoln in the White House*, 91–92. Another historian attributes the Democrats' success to the fact that so many Republicans stayed away from the polls. Silbey, *A Respectable Minority*, 145.

68. Mildred Throne, ed., "Iowa Doctor in Blue: Letters of Seneca B. Thrall, 1862–1864," *Iowa Journal of History* 58 (1960): 109–10; Elijah H. C. Cavins to Ann, November 9, 1862, Elijah H.C. Cavins Collection, box 1, folder 3, IHS; Robert Steele to Wife, November 8, 1862, Robert Steele Papers, folder 1, Wisconsin Historical Society, Madison.

69. Nevins, *The War for the Union: War Becomes Revolution,* 324–30; Browning, *The Diary of Orville Hickman Browning,* vol. 1, 590.

70. Silber and Sievens, *Yankee Correspondence,* 113; *Pilot,* December 13, 1862.

71. Anonymous to Abiah Hayes, October 19, 1862, Benjamin J. Spooner Collection, ISL.

CHAPTER 3

1. "The Reverse at Fredericksburg," *Harper's Weekly,* December 27, 1862;

2. *New York Herald,* December 16 and December 18, 1862; *The Pilot,* December 27, 1862.

3. William H. Gardiner II to Mary Gardiner Davis and William Nye Davis, December 24, 1862, William H. Gardiner II Letters, 1852–63, Massachusetts Historical Society, Boston; John W. Hinckson to Governor William A. Buckingham, December 19, 1862, Buckingham Incoming Correspondence, box 18.

4. William Alan Blair, ed., *A Politician Goes to War: The Civil War Letters of John White Geary* (University Park: Pennsylvania State University Press, 1995), 74; Anthony J. Milano, "The Copperhead Regiment: The 20th Massachusetts Infantry," *Civil War Regiments* 3 (1993): 48, 52. Geary switched parties after the war and was elected governor of Pennsylvania.

5. Charles Mason, Diary, December 15 and 16, 1862, Mason Collection; J. Cotton Smith to Thomas H. Seymour, December 28, 1862, Thomas H. Seymour Papers, box 5, folder 23.

6. *Crisis,* December 31, 1862.

7. McPherson, *Ordeal by Fire,* 331–34; Basler, *Collected Works,* vol. 6, 39; Isaac L. Beach to Dr. Charles M. Wetherill, January 10, 1863, Charles Mayer Wetherill Papers, folder 3, ISL.

8. *New York Herald,* January 3, 1863; *Cong. Globe,* 37th Cong., 3rd Sess., appendix, 52–60; Gilbert Dean, *The Emancipation Proclamation and Arbitrary Arrests!!* (Albany: Atlas & Argus, 1863), 8; *Niles Republican,* January 10, 1863. Representative George H. Yeaman of Kentucky had tried on December 11 to pass a resolution in the House saying that the proclamation was unconstitutional, but his effort was tabled. The House on December 15 adopted a responding resolution that the Emancipation Proclamation was, in fact, in accordance with the Constitution. The vote was 78 to 51. A year later, Peace Democrats again proposed a resolution calling the proclamation unconstitutional, but the measure was again set aside. McPherson, *The Political History of the United States of America During the Great Rebellion,* 229.

9. James Ferguson to John G. Davis, January 5, 1863, John G. Davis Papers, box 4, folder 14; James C. Olson, *J. Sterling Morton* (Lincoln: University of Nebraska Press, 1942), 125; William and K. R. Symmonds to Solomon E. Symmonds, February 22, 1863, John G. Davis Papers, box 4 folder 13.

10. Forrest G. Wood, *Black Scare: The Racist Response to Emancipation and Reconstruction* (Berkeley: University of California Press, 1970), 24, 19.

11. Ezra Bowlus to Samuel E. Williar, February 8, 1863, Ezra Bowlus Civil War Letters, folder 3, IHS; Alan A. Siegel, *Beneath the Starry Flag: New Jersey's Civil War Experience* (New Brunswick: Rutgers University Press, 2001), 92–93.

12. Silber and Sievens, *Yankee Correspondence*, 74; E. B. Allen to General Laz Noble, February 8, 1863, Adjutant General, Miscellaneous Civil War Correspondence, folder 8, ISA.

13. Greenleaf, *Letters to Eliza*, 19; Siegel, *Beneath the Starry Flag*, 93.

14. Blair, *A Politician Goes to War*, 56; Steven E. Woodworth, *Cultures in Conflict—The American Civil War*, Greenwood Press Cultures in Conflict Series (Westport, Conn.: Greenwood Press, 2000), 99.

15. George H. Pendleton, *Speech of Hon. George H. Pendleton, of Ohio, on the Enlistment of Negro Soldiers, Delivered During the Debate in the House of Representatives, January 21, 1863* (Washington: N.p., 1862 [1863]), 7; W. P. Nenfro to Governor Richard Yates, January 31, 1863, Yates Family Papers, box 10, LL. Republicans and Democrats alike believed that Western states shouldered more of the burden for supplying men. Indiana governor Oliver P. Morton, a Republican, wrote Provost Marshal James B. Fry to complain and to warn him that the perceived unfairness was starting to engender a bitterness that could be disastrous to the government. Governor Oliver P. Morton to Colonel James B. Fry, February 1, 1863, vol. 3, Letterbook of Oliver P. Morton, September 1863–December 1866, ISA; William Dudley Foulke, *Life of Oliver P. Morton*, vol. 1 (Indianapolis: Bowen-Merrill, 1899), 383–84.

16. Isaac L. Beach to Dr. Charles M. Wetherill, January 10, 1863, Wetherill Papers, folder 3.

17. Senators were elected by state legislatures into the early twentieth century, when a number of states adopted reforms that allowed for direct election of senators. Direct election was not nationally provided for until 1913, when the Seventeenth Amendment was adopted. In this case, the Indiana legislature had to decide on both senators at one time because the Senate had expelled Jesse D. Bright in February 1862 over allegations of disloyalty. For more on how senators were appointed, see www.senate.gov/artandhistory/history/common/briefing/Direct_Election_Senators.htm.

18. Kenneth M. Stampp, *Indiana Politics During the Civil War*, ed. Dorothy Riker and Gayle Thornbrough, vol. 31, Indiana Historical Collections (Indianapolis: Indiana Historical Bureau, 1949), 165, 173–85; Thornbrough, *Indiana in the Civil War Era*, 183–90; John Dowling to Son, March 1863, John Dowling Papers, box 2, folder 3, IHS.

19. A. B. Johnson to Thomas H. Seymour, March 2, 1863, Thomas H. Seymour Papers, box 6, folder 5.

20. S. Churchill to Horatio Seymour, January 28, 1863, Horatio Seymour Papers, 1764–1886, box 7, folder 39, NYSL; Dunbar Rowland, ed., *Jefferson Davis, Constitutionalist: His Letters, Papers, and Speeches*, vol. 5 (Jackson: Mississippi Department of Archives and History, 1923), 392; Pierce, *Memoir and Letters of Charles Sumner*, vol. 4, 114.

21. Rosenblatt and Rosenblatt, *Hard Marching Every Day*, 69; Sidney O. Little to Elvin Little, February 19, 1863, Sidney O. Little Letters, CL.

22. Andrew Evans to Samuel Evans, February 1, 1863, Evans Family Papers, box 1, folder 6; Silber and Sievens, *Yankee Correspondence*, 75–76.

23. "The Constitution" (New York: Society for the Diffusion of Political Knowledge, 1863); Carleton Mabee, *The American Leonardo: A Life of Samuel F. B. Morse*, revised ed. (Fleischmanns, N.Y.: Purple Mountain Press, 2000), 346–51. Other founding members of the society included August Belmont, the U.S. representative of the Rothschilds; Wall Street lawyer Samuel Tilden; George Ticknor Curtis of New York and Charles Mason of Iowa, both of whom worked as attorneys for Morse; and New York editors Manton Marble of the *World* and William C. Prime of the *Journal of Commerce*.

24. M.L.P. Thompson to Anonymous, February 24, 1863, M.L.P. Thompson Letter, OHS.

25. Benjamin F. Wiley to Sister, February 22, 1863, James B. Plessinger Papers, folder 2, ISL; Bergun H. Brown to Folks at Home, March 7, 1863, Bergun H. Brown Papers, IHS; *Niles Republican*, February 14, 1863.

26. Rosenblatt and Rosenblatt, *Hard Marching Every Day*, 54–55, 68–69.

27. Woodworth, *Cultures in Conflict*, 134–35; A. T. Volwiler, "Letters from a Civil War Officer," *Mississippi Valley Historical Review* 14 (1928): 511; Silber and Sievens, *Yankee Correspondence*, 114.

28. Thomas Prickett to Matilda Darr, February 23, 1863, Thomas Prickett Papers, folder 5, IHS; Earnhart, "The Administrative Organization of the Provost Marshal General's Bureau in Ohio," 37–38.

29. Silber and Sievens, *Yankee Correspondence*, 114–17.

30. Phillip S. Paludan thoughtfully explores the relationship between Americans and their government during this period in Paludan, "The American Civil War Considered as a Crisis in Law and Order," 1013–34.

31. Silber and Sievens, *Yankee Correspondence*, 77, 114–17; Nellie to Rudolph Williams, February 25, 1863, R. Williams MSS, LLIU.

32. Basler, *Collected Works*, vol. 6, 149–50; Earnhart, "The Administrative Organization of the Provost Marshal General's Bureau in Ohio," 53. I refer to integration here in a limited sense. Civil War regiments were segregated by race, though the officers of black regiments were white; black soldiers received lower pay, at least at this point in the war; and most African Americans were barred from the officer corps, surgeons and chaplains being the exceptions.

33. Silber and Sievens, *Yankee Correspondence*, 86; M. W. Rodman to James A. Cravens, March 1, 1863, Cravens MSS, LLIU. After seeing the all-black 54th Massachusetts in action in the summer of 1863, the artillery sergeant changed his mind. He wrote a cousin, "When you hear nay one remark that nigger soldiers will not fight, please request them to come down here and judge for themselves." Silber and Sievens, *Yankee Correspondence*, 86.

34. Wood, *Black Scare*, 27–28, 42–44; *Niles Republican*, April 14, 1863.

35. William B. Reed, *A Northern Plea for Peace: Address of the Hon. William B. Reed, of Pennsylvania* (London: Henry F. Mackintosh, 1863), 22.

36. Abraham J. Morrison to William A. Buckingham, March 2, 1863, Buckingham Incoming Correspondence, box 19.

37. McPherson, *The Political History of the United States of America During the Great Rebellion,* 261.

38. James A. Bayard, *Two Speeches of James A. Bayard of Delaware* (Baltimore: W. M. Innes, 1863), 4, italics his; Clement L. Vallandigham, *Speeches, Arguments, Addresses, and Letters of Clement L. Vallandigham* (New York: J. Walter, 1864), 459–60.

39. *Crisis,* March 4, 1863.

40. Robert E. Sterling, "Civil War Draft Resistance in the Middle West" (Ph.D. diss., Northern Illinois University, 1974), 658–61; Nuria Sales De Bohigas, "Some Opinions on Exemption from Military Service in Nineteenth-Century Europe," *Comparative Studies in Society and History* 10 (1968): 268; *New York Herald,* March 6, 1863; *Chicago Times,* October 13, 1863.

41. Randall, *Constitutional Problems Under Lincoln,* 248–49; Vallandigham, *Speeches, Arguments, Addresses, and Letters of Clement L. Vallandigham,* 457–58; *Chicago Times,* October 13, 1863.

42. Judith Lee Hallock, "The Role of the Community in Civil War Desertion," *Civil War History* 29 (1983): 125; Randall, *Constitutional Problems Under Lincoln,* 251; Rosenblatt and Rosenblatt, *Hard Marching Every Day,* 149–50. Hallock also argues that immigrants were more likely to desert than the native born. Hallock, "The Role of the Community in Civil War Desertion," 125–26.

43. These figures include data from Connecticut, Maine, Massachusetts, Rhode Island, New Hampshire, Vermont, New York, New Jersey, Pennsylvania, Delaware, Maryland, West Virginia, Ohio, Indiana, Illinois, Wisconsin, Michigan, Minnesota, Iowa, Kansas, Missouri, and Kentucky. Peter Levine, "Draft Evasion in the North During the Civil War, 1863–1865," *Journal of American History* 67 (1981): 817–21.

44. Peter T. Harstad, "Draft Dodgers and Bounty Jumpers," *Civil War Times Illustrated* 6 (1967): 29–32.

45. Randall, *Constitutional Problems Under Lincoln,* 247; Woodworth, *Cultures in Conflict,* 100; Rosenblatt and Rosenblatt, *Hard Marching Every Day,* 149–50.

46. Randall, *Constitutional Problems Under Lincoln,* 268n. Citing the federal government's power to declare war and raise armies, the lower courts disagreed with the Copperheads' interpretation of the Constitution and upheld the draft. The Supreme Court did not hear a case on the matter until 1917, when it ruled that the Selective Service Act was constitutional. Ibid., 252–56, 272–74.

47. Ronald C. White Jr., *The Eloquent President: A Portrait of Lincoln Through His Words* (New York: Random House, 2005), 197; Major General H. G. Wright to Edward M. Stanton, March 10, 1863, General Burnside's Telegrams, Part 1, RG 393, entry no. 3511; Uri Manly to Governor Richard Yates, March 7, 1863, Yates Family Papers, box 11; Elvira Aplin to George Aplin, March 16, 1863, Aplin Family Papers, CL.

48. Randall, *Constitutional Problems Under Lincoln*, 156, 165–66. As noted in chap. 1, the *Merryman* decision was the opinion of only one Supreme Court justice. To this day, the matter has never come before the full Court, although the Lincoln administration twice considered bringing a relevant case before it. Lincoln received "a sort of indirect sanctioning" of the suspension in the spring of 1863 with the *Prize Cases*. In these, the Supreme Court was inclined to support the president by ruling that Lincoln did not have to wait for Congress to declare war in 1861 before he initiated military action. Randall, *Constitutional Problems Under Lincoln*, 130–32 and 137n. For more on the *Prize Cases*, see Frank J. Williams, *Judging Lincoln* (Carbondale: Southern Illinois University Press, 2002), 65–66; Stuart L. Bernath, *Squall Across the Atlantic: American Civil War Prize Cases and Diplomacy* (Berkeley: University of California Press, 1970.

49. *World*, March 4, 1863.

50. John Allen Trimble to Horatio Seymour, March 17, 1863, John Allen Trimble Papers, box 2, OHS; Roger Long, "Copperhead Clement Vallandigham," *Civil War Times Illustrated* 20 (1981): 23.

51. Lieutenant Colonel Joseph Selden to William A. Buckingham, March 6, 1863, Buckingham Incoming Correspondence, box 19; Cowden, "Sovereignty and Secession," 48–49.

52. W. M. Armstrong to General Ambrose E. Burnside, May 13, 1863, Records of United States Army Continental Commands, Miscellaneous Records—Post of Cincinnati, Ohio, 1862–65, RG 393, entry no. 217, box 1, NARA; John R. Beatty to Laura Maxfield, May 27, 1863, John R. Beatty Papers, MHS; William D. Dillon, ed., "The Civil War Letters of Enos Barret Lewis, 101st Ohio Volunteer Infantry," *Northwest Ohio Quarterly* 57 (1985): 90; *Niles Republican*, May 23, 1863. Thanks to James M. McPherson for the Beatty and Lewis citations.

53. Dowdey and Manarin, *The Wartime Papers of R. E. Lee*, 438; Basler, *Collected Works*, vol. 6, 78–79; Hooker quoted in McPherson, *Ordeal by Fire*, 343; Charles Mason, Diary, March 21, 1863, Mason Collection.

54. *O.R.*, ser. 2, vol. 5, 480.

55. Ibid., 237; Klement, *The Copperheads in the Middle West*, 89–91.

56. Frank L. Klement, "Clement L. Vallandigham's Exile in the Confederacy, May 25–June 17, 1863," *Journal of Southern History* 31 (1965): 150–52; Long, "Copperhead Clement Vallandigham," 24.

57. *Crisis*, May 13, 1863; *World*, May 6, 1863.

58. John Allen Trimble to Samuel Medary, May 7, 1863, Trimble Papers, box 2; *New York Herald*, May 19, 1863.

59. Clement L. Vallandigham to Manton Marble, May 12, 1863, Marble Papers, vol. 4.

60. *Correspondence in Relation to the Public Meeting at Albany, N.Y.* (N.p.: n.d.); Basler, *Collected Works*, vol. 6, 260–69.

61. Basler, *Collected Works*, vol. 6, 300–306.

62. Klement, "Clement L. Vallandigham's Exile," 150–52.

63. Ibid., 154; *O.R.*, ser. 2, vol. 5, 959–60, 963; *Cleveland Plain Dealer,* September 29, 1863, rpt. in *Chicago Times,* October 2, 1863.

64. John B. Jones, *A Rebel War Clerk's Diary,* ed. Earl Schenck Miers (Baton Rouge: Louisiana State University Press, 1993), 229–30.

65. Frank L. Klement, *The Limits of Dissent: Clement L. Vallandigham and the Civil War* (New York: Fordham University Press, 1998), 203–4; Klement, "Vallandigham as an Exile in Canada," *Ohio History* 74 (1965): 158–63; C. Vann Woodward, ed., *Mary Chesnut's Civil War* (New Haven: Yale University Press, 1981), 451.

66. Dowdey and Manarin, *The Wartime Papers of R. E. Lee,* 507–9.

67. Mark Grimsley, *The Hard Hand of War: Union Military Policy Toward Southern Civilians, 1861–1865* (New York: Cambridge University Press, 1995), 7–11, chap. 4.

68. McPherson, *Ordeal by Fire,* 344–47.

69. Noah Brooks, *Washington in Lincoln's Time* (New York: Century, 1895), 57–58. Complete lyrics are available by typing in a title search at the Library of Congress's American Memory website, http://memory.loc.gov.

70. Robert Garth Scott, ed., *Fallen Leaves: The Civil War Letters of Major Henry Livermore Abbott* (Kent, Ohio: Kent State University Press, 1991), 178; Siegel, *Beneath the Starry Flag,* 101.

71. Andrew Evans to Samuel Evans, May 24, 1863, Evans Family Papers, box 1, folder 9. [*Sic transit Gloria mundi:* Thus passes away the glory of the world.]

72. Orville Chamberlain to Friends, May 31, 1863, Joseph and Orville Chamberlain Papers, box 1, folder 10, IHS.

CHAPTER 4

1. Kenneth H. Wheeler, "Local Autonomy and Civil War Draft Resistance: Holmes County, Ohio," *Civil War History* 45 (1999): 148–50, 153–54.

2. *O.R.*, ser. 3, vol. 3, 321–22, 321–22; Captain R. W. Thompson to Colonel Conrad Baker, June 18, 1863, Provost Marshal General's Bureau, Letters Received, Indiana District 7, 1863–64, RG 110, entry no. 5236, box 6, NARA.

3. *O.R.*, ser. 3, vol. 3, 324–25; Lieutenant Colonel William D. Whipple to Commodore Cornelius K. Stribling, June 1, 1863, Records of the United States Army Continental Commands, 1821–1920, Miscellaneous Records – Post of Philadelphia, Letters Sent, 1862–65, RG 393, entry no. 1360, NARA.

4. *O.R.*, ser. 3, vol. 3, 393–94; I. Codington to D. Toping, June 16, 1863, Provost Marshal General's Bureau, Letters Received, Indiana District 7, 1863–64, RG 110, entry no. 5236, box 6.

5. Colonel James B. Fry, *Final Report Made to the Secretary of War, by the Provost Marshal General, of the Operations of the Bureau of the Provost Marshal General of the United States,* vol. 2 (N.p.: 1866), 352.

6. Amanda Chittenden to Husband, June 17, 1863, Chittenden Papers, ISL; Jesse Handley to James Handley, June 29, 1863, Handley MSS, LLIU; Isaac

Dick to Governor Oliver P. Morton, July 29, 1863, Civil War Miscellany: Adjutant General, drawer 107, folder 84, ISA. Butternut pins were made of butternuts that had been cut in half and mounted.

7. Although a great many studies link ethnic and religious background to Copperhead beliefs, there is no broad scholarship on a link between class identity and the propensity to become a Peace Democrat. Grace Palladino deals with some of these questions, however, in her focused study of Pennsylvania coal miners. Grace Palladino, *Another Civil War: Labor, Capital, and the State in the Anthracite Regions of Pennsylvania, 1840–68* (Urbana: University of Illinois Press, 1990).

8. Lieutenant Colonel Charles S. Lovell to Colonel James B. Fry, June 2, 1863, Provost Marshal General's Bureau, Letters Sent, 1863–65, Wisconsin, vol. 1, RG 110, entry no. 6104, NARA; Captain R. W. Thompson to Colonel Conrad Baker, June 18, 1863, Provost Marshal General's Bureau, Letters Received, Indiana District 7, 1863–64, RG 110, entry no. 5236, box 6; J. R. Lefever to General Laz Noble, August 10, 1863, Miscellaneous Civil War Correspondence: Adjutant General, folder 13.

9. Lieutenant Colonel C. J. Ruff to Colonel James B. Fry, June 9, 1863, Provost Marshal General's Bureau, Letters to the Adjutant General, Pennsylvania Western District, 1864, vol. 1, RG 110, entry no. 3127, NARA. The Pennsylvania coal mines had more trouble than just the draft. Conscription came at a time of considerable labor unrest there, and owners were able to use the military's need for coal to call in provost marshals and the army to put down strikes, according to Grace Palladino. For a complete account, see Palladino, *Another Civil War.*

10. Dowdey and Manarin, *The Wartime Papers of R. E. Lee,* 530–31; *La Crosse Democrat,* July 7, 1863.

11. McPherson, *Ordeal by Fire,* 358.

12. Meade submitted his resignation upon learning of Lincoln's disapproval, but the president did not accept it. He was nevertheless upset at the general. In a letter he never sent, he wrote Meade: "I do not believe you appreciate the magnitude of the misfortune involved in Lee's escape. He was within your easy grasp, and to have closed upon him would, in connection with our other late successes, have ended the war. . . . Your golden opportunity is gone, and I am distressed immeasureably because of it." Basler, *Collected Works,* vol. 6, 328.

13. *New York Herald,* July 8, 1863; Bergun H. Brown to Mother, July 21, 1863, Bergun H. Brown Papers.

14. For a thorough account of the draft riots and how they fit into a larger story of New York politics at midcentury, see Iver Bernstein, *The New York City Draft Riots: Their Significance for American Society and Politics in the Age of the Civil War* (New York: Oxford University Press, 1990).

15. Man, "Labor Competition and the New York Draft Riots of 1863," 375.

16. Longshoremen went on strike in March and April over blacks joining them on the wharves. These dockworkers led columns of rioters when the draft riots broke out in July. Ibid., 377–400.

17. Eugene C. Murdock, "Horatio Seymour and the 1863 Draft," *Civil War History* 11 (1965): 133–38. Seymour may not have been as out of line as he appeared after the fact. Even Abraham Lincoln believed in "right of revolution" and had spoken on the subject before coming to office. As late as his first year in office, Lincoln wrote that violent resistance to the government was acceptable "when exercised for a morally justifiable cause." Basler, *Collected Works*, vol. 4, 249–71, esp. 426 and 434, n. 83.

18. The draft worked like this: After the enrollment lists were completed and if a draft was necessary to fulfill a congressional district's manpower obligation, the names of enrolled men went into a wheel. At a public gathering, a blindfolded man pulled names out of the drum. Conscripts were notified through newspapers combined with personal visits from a member of the local draft board, or, failing the latter, with a letter left at the draftee's last known address. Once he received news of his conscription, a man had to undergo a physical exam and then go before the enrollment board to see if he qualified for an exemption. When all the conscripts had completed this process, the board drew up a roster of inductees. Draftees then had ten days to pay a commutation fee, hire a substitute, or get their affairs in order and report for duty. Geary, *We Need Men*, 74.

19. Bernstein, *The New York City Draft Riots*, 8; M. Benedict to Horatio Seymour, July 16, 1863, Horatio Seymour Papers, box 7, folder 39.

20. Bernstein, *The New York City Draft Riots*, 18–23.

21. A. Hunter Dupree and Leslie H. Fishel Jr., "An Eyewitness Account of the New York Draft Riots, July, 1863," *Mississippi Valley Historical Review* 47 (1960): 476.

22. Colonel Robert Nugent to Colonel James B. Fry, July 15, 1863, Provost Marshal General's Bureau, Letters Sent by Chief Mustering Officer, New York Southern District, 1863–65, RG 110, entry no. 1360, NARA, 92–93.

23. Dupree and Fishel, "An Eyewitness Account of the New York Draft Riots," 476; Christina Ericson and Barbara Austen, "On the 'Front Lines' of the Civil War Home Front," *Connecticut History* 39 (2000): 155–56.

24. J. H. Almy to Governor William A. Buckingham, July 16, 1863, Buckingham Incoming Correspondence, box 20; Colonel Robert Nugent to Colonel James B. Fry, July 15, 1863, Provost Marshal General's Bureau, Letters Sent by Chief Mustering Officer, New York Southern District, 1863–65, RG 110, entry no. 1360, 113–16; *Chicago Times* editorial rpt. in *La Crosse Democrat*, July 17, 1863.

25. Dupree and Fishel, "An Eyewitness Account of the New York Draft Riots," 477–78; Bernstein, *The New York City Draft Riots*, 259.

26. Lieutenant Colonel Robert C. Buchanan to Captain R. C. Johnson, July 15, 1863, Provost Marshal General's Bureau, Letters Sent, New Jersey, 1863–66, vol. 1, RG 110, entry no. 2539, NARA.

27. William F. Hanna, "The Boston Draft Riot," *Civil War History* 36 (1990): 263–68. Estimates of the number of dead have swung between fourteen and twenty, but Hanna writes that the exact number is impossible to know because friends and family carried some victims away. Ibid., 268.

28. Ericson and Austen, "On the 'Front Lines' of the Civil War Home Front," 160; Blair, *A Politician Goes to War,* 107.

29. "Letters of Richard Cobden to Charles Sumner, 1862–1865," 312.

30. Margaret White Taylor to Thomas T. Taylor, July 16, 1863, Thomas T. Taylor Papers, box 1, folder 10, OHS; Kate Starks to Husband, July 15, 1863, Kate Starks Papers, ISL.

31. Kellee L. Blake, "Ten Firkins of Butter and Other 'Traitorous' Aid," *Prologue* 30 (1998): 290; Caleb R. Gill to Sister, July 26, 1863, George S. Johnson Papers, folder 1, IHS.

32. Clark County, Ohio, *Democrat* rpt. in *La Crosse Democrat,* September 11, 1863.

33. Captain R. W. Thompson to Colonel Conrad Baker, August 15, 1863, Provost Marshal General's Bureau, Letters Received, Indiana District 7, 1863–64, RG 110, entry no. 5232, box 5.

34. Robert D. Sampson, " 'Pretty Damned Warm Times': The 1864 Charleston Riot and 'the Inalienable Right of Revolution,' " *Illinois Historical Journal* 89 (1996): 109–10; Kenneth W. Noe, " 'The Conservative': A Civil War Soldier's Musical Condemnation of Illinois Copperheads," *Illinois Historical Journal* 84 (1991): 270.

35. Sampson, " 'Pretty Damned Warm Times,' " 111–12; *Chicago Times,* March 12, 1864.

36. Sampson, " 'Pretty Damned Warm Times,' " 113, 99–101.

37. *Chicago Times,* March 31, April 1, 2, 1864.

38. Joseph Orville Jackson, ed., *"Some of the Boys . . .": The Civil War Letters of Isaac Jackson, 1862–1865,* with a foreword by Bell Irvin Wiley (Carbondale: Southern Illinois University Press, 1960), 78–79.

39. Basler, *Collected Works,* vol. 6, 406–10.

40. Jefferson Davis, *The Papers of Jefferson Davis,* ed. Lynda Lasswell Crist, vol. 10 (Baton Rouge: Louisiana State University Press, 1999), 86 and n. 14; William C. Davis, *Jefferson Davis: The Man and His Hour, a Biography* (New York: HarperCollins, 1991), 515. The fact that the Confederates were considering ways to undermine the Lincoln government by sowing dissent was an open secret. Indeed, the *New York Herald* (July 24, 1863) warned Davis to "dismiss the idea that he has a great political conspiracy in the North moving for his support the sooner will the misery and the suspense of Davis and his fellows be ended."

41. Rosenblatt and Rosenblatt, *Hard Marching Every Day,* 151.

42. Arnold Shankman, " 'Soldier Votes' and Clement L. Vallandigham in the 1863 Ohio Gubernatorial Election," *Ohio History* 82 (1973): 97; Olson, *James Sterling Morton,* 123.

43. *O.R.,* ser. 1, vol. 30, pt. 1, 142. What no one at the time could know, of course, was that the battle would be the last major Southern offensive of the war.

44. Samuel S. Cox to Manton Marble, June 14, 1863, Marble Papers, vol. 4; Clement L. Vallandigham to Manton Marble, August 13, 1863, Marble Papers, vol. 5.

45. George M. Trowbridge to Lebbie Trowbridge, October 11, 1863, George Martin Trowbridge Papers, CL; John Vannest to Joseph Vannest, June 15, 1863, Joseph P. Vannest Papers, IHS.

46. James Campbell, *Speech of Hon. James Campbell, of Philadelphia, Delivered at Scranton, Pennsylvania* (Philadelphia: *The Age*, 1863), 1; Sanford E. Church, *Speech by Hon. Sanford E. Church at Batavia, October 13, 1863* (N.p.: 1863), 7.

47. Church, *Speech*, iv–v.

48. *Chicago Times*, October 6, 1863.

49. Shankman, " 'Soldier Votes,' " 90–97; Leo. D. Sirrania to Friend Monroe, November 22, 1863, Amos C. Weaver Papers, folder 2, IHS.

50. Milton Crist to Sister, August 7, 1863, Crist MSS, LLIU; Shankman, " 'Soldier Votes,' " 95, 98; John Vanhook to John G. Davis, October 29, 1863, John G. Davis Papers, box 4, folder 13.

51. *La Crosse Democrat*, October 22, 1863; Allan Nevins, *The War for the Union: The Organized War, 1863–1864* (New York: Charles Scribner's Sons, 1971), 171–72.

52. Shankman, " 'Soldier Votes,' " 99–104; Daniel Wait Howe, Diary, March 4, 1864, vol. 2, Daniel Wait Howe Collection, IHS.

53. Klement, "Vallandigham as an Exile in Canada," 165; Hugh McCulloch to Susan McCulloch, October 18, 1863, McCulloch MSS, LLIU; George M. Trowbridge to Lebbie Trowbridge, December 22, 1863, Trowbridge Papers.

54. Charles Mason, Diary, November 5, 1863, Mason Collection; W. D. Northend to Thomas H. Seymour, October 27, 1863, Thomas H. Seymour Papers, box 6, folder 14; Clement L. Vallandigham to Samuel S. Cox, October 28, 1863, Marble Papers, vol. 5; *Pilot*, November 7, 1863.

55. *Chicago Times*, December 2, 1863; White, *The Eloquent President*, 221.

56. Davis, *The Papers of Jefferson Davis*, vol. 10, 152–55, including n. 8.

57. *O.R.*, ser. 3, vol. 3, 1008, 1012–15, 1018–19, 1022–25, 1031–33, 1043–46.

58. George E. Baker, ed., *The Works of William H. Seward*, vol. 5 (Boston: Houghton, Mifflin and Company, 1884), 117; *La Crosse Democrat*, January 18, 1864; *Chicago Times*, January 28, 22, 1864.

59. O'Connor, *Civil War Boston*, 196–98.

60. Charles R. Wilson, "The Original Chase Organization Meeting and the Next Presidential Election," *Mississippi Valley Historical Review* 23 (1936): 62–65.

61. Ibid., 67–68; McPherson, *Ordeal by Fire*, 440–41.

62. T. Harry Williams, "Frémont and the Politicians," *Journal of the American Military History Foundation* 2 (1938): 191.

63. Charles R. Wilson, "New Light on the Lincoln-Blair-Frémont 'Bargain' of [1864?]," *American Historical Review* 42 (1936): 74–78.

64. James E. English to Edwin Stearns, February 15, 1864, Stearns Family Papers: Political Correspondence, box 6, folder DD; *Chicago Times*, March 1, 1864.

65. Sergeant Elliott Richmond to Lieutenant John J. Judy, January 21, 1864, Civil War Miscellany: Adjutant General, drawer 107, folder 83, ISA; Julia Maria Fish to Carlton Brewster Fish, March 13, 1864, Fish Family Papers, CL.

66. G. E. Johnson to Major General Heinzelman, January 26, 1864, Records of United States Army Continental Commands, 1821–1920, Northern Department, Letters Received, 1864–65, RG 393, entry no. 3349, box 2, NARA; Lieutenant Colonel J. R. Smith to Major Granville E. Johnson, February 22, 1864, and March 10, 1864, ibid.

67. Klement, *Dark Lanterns;* Robert Churchill, "The Sons of Liberty Conspiracy, 1863–1864," *Prologue* 30 (1998): 295, 301–2.

68. Churchill, "The Sons of Liberty Conspiracy," 295–97.

69. Reed W. Smith, *Samuel Medary and the Crisis* (Columbus: Ohio State University Press, 1995), 138–44. Although many editors went to jail for their editorials, Medary's arrest had nothing to do with anything he said in the columns of his newspaper.

70. Daniel W. Voorhees, *Speech of D. W. Voorhees, of Indiana, Delivered in the House of Representatives, March 9, 1864* (Washington, D.C.: Constitutional Union Office, 1864), 1, 8.

71. Alexander Long, *The Present Condition and Future Prospects of the Country: Speech of Hon. Alexander Long, of Ohio* (N.p: 1864), 8–9.

72. John Allen Trimble to Clement Vallandigham, January, 1864, Trimble Papers, box 2; Charles Mason, Diary, January 25, 1864, Mason Collection.

73. Manton Marble to James A. Wall, March 30, 1864, Marble Papers, vol. 6. Joel Silbey has written the best study on the cleavages in the Democratic Party during this time in *A Respectable Minority.*

74. John Herr to Sister, March 31, 1863, and to Mother, April 29, 1864, Herr Papers, Duke University, Raleigh. Thanks to James M. McPherson for the citation.

75. William Glenn to Brother, March 28, 1864, John F. Glenn Papers, LL.

76. Stroud Keller to John Glenn, March 27, 1864, Glenn Papers; *New York Herald,* March 31, 1864; *Pilot,* May 14, 1864; Scott, *Fallen Leaves,* 242.

77. Scott, *Fallen Leaves,* 244; *O.R.,* series 1, vol. 33, pt. 2, 828.

78. William Gray Brooks, Diary, March 23, 1864, William Gray Brooks Papers: Diary, 1863–68, Massachusetts Historical Society, Boston; Rosenblatt and Rosenblatt, *Hard Marching Every Day,* 207.

CHAPTER 5

1. Charles Mason, Diary, May 3, 1864, Mason Collection.

2. *O.R.,* ser. 1, vol. 33, 827–29; *O.R.,* ser. 1, vol. 32, part 3, 246.

3. Von Clausewitz, *On War,* 119–21, McPherson, *Ordeal by Fire,* 446–47.

4. Volwiler, "Letters from a Civil War Officer," 519.

5. A. W. Hearn to Willie, May 9, 1864, Bailhache-Braymen Family Papers, box 2, LL.

6. Horace Porter, *Campaigning with Grant* (New York: Da Capo Press, 1986), 69–70; Bruce Catton, *A Stillness at Appomattox* (Garden City, N.Y.: Doubleday, 1957), 92. The kind of uncertainty that this officer exhibited was common—perhaps endemic—among the Army of the Potomac's high command, according

to Michael C. C. Adams in *Fighting for Defeat: Union Military Failure in the East, 1861–1865* (Lincoln: University of Nebraska Press, 1992).

7. Confederate losses in this fight do not include those captured, for which estimates are not available.

8. *Chicago Times*, May 17, 1864.

9. McPherson, *Ordeal by Fire*, 455–56; Ulysses S. Grant, *Personal Memoirs of U. S. Grant*, ed. E. B. Long (New York: Da Capo Press, 1982), 444–45.

10. Sabin Hough to Thomas H. Seymour, May 15, 1864, Thomas H. Seymour Papers, box 7, folder 5; Samuel S. Cox to Manton Marble, May 14, 1864, Marble Papers, vol. 7.

11. Baker, *The Works of William H. Seward*, 128; Gideon Welles, *Diary of Gideon Welles*, vol. 2 (New York: W. W. Norton, 1960), 44–45; Basler, *Collected Works*, vol. 7, 374.

12. Greenleaf, *Letters to Eliza*, 117.

13. Arthur McClellan to George B. McClellan, June 27, 1864, George B. McClellan Papers, microfilm, reel 50, LC. Woodward, *Mary Chesnut's Civil War*, 640.

14. Blake, "Ten Firkins of Butter and Other 'Traitorous' Aid," 290. The federal government indicted McElwee for these and similar statements; the Supreme Court dismissed the case in 1869. Ibid.

15. O'Connor, *Civil War Boston*, 200; C. Chauncey Burr, "Editor's Table," *Old Guard*, July 1864, 189; *Chicago Times* editorial rpt. in *La Crosse Democrat*, June 25, 1864.

16. Thurlow Weed to Edwin D. Morgan, May 27, 1864, Edwin Denison Morgan Papers, 1836–83, box 13, folder 16, NYSL; Henry H. Wilson to Edwin D. Morgan, June 11, 1864, ibid., box 20, folder 10; Harold M. Dudley, "The Election of 1864," *Mississippi Valley Historical Review* 14 (March 1932): 504–5.

17. C. Chauncey Burr, "The Tricks of Tyrants," *Old Guard*, June 1864, 132–33.

18. 1864 Republican Party Platform; Basler, *Collected Works*, vol. 7, 383–84.

19. Frank Klement, " 'Brick' Pomeroy: Copperhead and Curmudgeon," *Wisconsin Magazine of History* 35 (1951): 112; *Niles Republican*, June 18, 1864.

20. David Sheean to George B. McClellan, June 21, 1864, McClellan Papers, reel 50; Anonymous to George B. McClellan, July 6, 1864, ibid.; Michael Vorenberg, *Final Freedom: The Civil War, the Abolition of Slavery, and the Thirteenth Amendment* (New York: Cambridge University Press, 2004), 143; *La Crosse Democrat*, June 14, 1864.

21. O'Connor, *Civil War Boston*, 201; Welles, *Diary of Gideon Welles*, vol. 2, 73; *New York Herald*, July 23, 1864; Klement, " 'Brick' Pomeroy," 112.

22. J. H. Hutter and Ray H. Abrams, "Copperhead Newspapers and the Negro," *Journal of Negro History* 20 (1935): 140–41.

23. O'Connor, *Civil War Boston*, 202; Welles, *Diary of Gideon Welles*, vol. 2, 91–92.

24. R. G. Merrill, "The Court-Martial of Private Spencer," *Civil War Times Illustrated* 27 (February 1989): 34–40.

25. "Letters of Richard Cobden to Charles Sumner, 1862–1865," 314–15.

26. T. C. Smithton to General Rosecrans, July 24, 1864, Records of United States Army Continental Commands, 1821–1920, Northern Department, Letters Received, 1864–65, RG 393, entry no. 3349, box 2; Charles Calahan to Major General Heintzelman, May 24, 1864, ibid., box 1.

27. Klement, " 'Brick' Pomeroy," 113.

28. Charles Calahan to Major General Heintzelman, May 24, 1864, Records of United States Army Continental Commands, 1821–1920, Northern Department, Letters Received, 1864–65, RG 393, entry no. 3349, box 1; Hubert H. Wubben, *Civil War Iowa and the Copperhead Movement* (Ames: Iowa State University Press, 1980), 168; T. C. Smithton to General Rosecrans, July 24, 1864, Records of United States Army Continental Commands, 1821–1920, Northern Department, Letters Received, 1864–65, RG 393, entry no. 3349, box 2.

29. Wubben, *Civil War Iowa and the Copperhead Movement*, 173; R. Matthew Perry to Brother, May 22, 1864, R. Matthew Perry Papers, Wisconsin State Historical Society.

30. John F. Glenn to Katy, June 6, 1864, Glenn Papers.

31. For a convincing account of a broad plot afoot in the West, see Stephen Z. Starr, "Was There a Northwest Conspiracy?" *Filson Club Historical Quarterly* 38 (1964): 323–41.

32. Klement makes this claim most forcefully in *The Copperheads in the Middle West* and *Dark Lanterns*. For a description of the Ohio plot, see Eugene Holloway Roseboom and Francis Phelps Weisenburger, *A History of Ohio*, Prentice-Hall History Series (New York: Prentice-Hall, 1934), 288.

33. Kenneth M. Stampp, "The Milligan Case and the Election of 1864 in Indiana," *Mississippi Valley Historical Review* 31 (1944): 43; Brigadier General Henry B. Carrington to Captain C. H. Potter, June 18, 1864, Records of United States Army Continental Commands, 1821–1920, District of Indiana, Letters Sent, 1864–66, RG 393, entry no. 218, NARA.

34. Thornbrough, *Indiana in the Civil War Era*, 215–18; Brigadier General Henry B. Carrington to Captain C. H. Potter, June 18, 1864, Records of United States Army Continental Commands, 1821–1920, District of Indiana, Letters Sent, 1864–66, RG 393, entry no. 218; Stampp, *Indiana Politics During the Civil War*, 231–49.

35. Stampp, "The Milligan Case and the Election of 1864 in Indiana," 47; Klement, *The Copperheads in the Middle West*, 175. For a more thorough treatment of these secret societies, see Klement's *Dark Lanterns*. This is a good source for basic factual information, but I wholly disagree with Klement's interpretation and conclusions about the danger these organizations posed to the government.

36. Thornbrough, *Indiana in the Civil War Era*, 215–18; Stampp, *Indiana Politics During the Civil War*, 231–49; Stampp, "The Milligan Case and the Election of 1864 in Indiana," 41. After the war President Andrew Johnson commuted the death sentences to life imprisonment. The case ultimately went to the Supreme Court as *ex parte Milligan*. In April 1866 the justices ruled that trying

civilians in a military court was unconstitutional while civilian courts were in operation. The prisoners were released immediately after the ruling, but prosecutors did not drop the charges until the next year. Thornbrough, *Indiana in the Civil War Era*, 218–20, including n. 76. For a complete account of the case, including full transcripts of the trial and the Supreme Court decision, see Samuel Klaus, ed., *The Milligan Case: Civil Liberties in American History* (New York: Da Capo Press, 1970).

37. Davis, *The Papers of Jefferson Davis*, vol. 10, 609.

38. Gray, *The Hidden Civil War*, 167–79. Vallandigham's return to Ohio is nearly as amusing as his departure. Wearing a cape and false beard, he snuck across the Detroit River and took a train to Hamilton. He made his first public appearance June 15. When Ohio governor John Brough telegraphed Stanton that Vallandigham planned to make a speech that day in Dayton, Stanton responded that in his opinion the former congressman should be arrested, but Seward intervened and blocked any action against Vallandigham. Smith, *Samuel Medary and the Crisis*, 141; *O.R.*, ser. 2, vol. 7, 371–72.

39. *O.R.*, ser. 1, vol. 43, pt. 2, 930–36. For a detailed account of the Confederate plots for the Northwest during the summer of 1864, see Oscar A. Kinchen, *Confederate Operations in Canada and the North* (North Quincy, Mass.: Christopher, 1970), chap. 3.

40. Wubben, *Civil War Iowa and the Copperhead Movement*, 161–65; Ray H. Abrams, "*The Jeffersonian*, Copperhead Newspaper," *Pennsylvania Magazine of History and Biography* 57 (1933): 26; Smith, *Samuel Medary and the Crisis*, 142; Dudley, "The Election of 1864," 511.

41. J. A. Valentine to Thomas F. Bayard, May 18, 1864, Bayard Papers, vol. 9; J. A. Cravens to M. W. Wines, August 6, 1864, Worden Papers, IHS; Captain Henry Asbury to Sen. Lyman Trumbull, May 19, 1864, vol. 1, Provost Marshal General's Bureau, Letters Sent, Illinois District 4, 1863–65, RG 110, entry no. 5631, NARA; Wubben, *Civil War Iowa and the Copperhead Movement*, 163–64; James H. McNeely to Governor Oliver P. Morton, June 13, 1864, Governor Oliver P. Morton Papers, microfilm, roll 8, ISA. Removing the commutation option proved to be an effective way of evening the burden of service across occupational and, presumably, class lines. See Geary, *We Need Men*, 147–49, esp. tables 9–11.

42. Gray, *The Hidden Civil War*, 180. Italics in original.

43. Bruce Catton, *Grant Takes Command* (Boston: Little, Brown, 1968), 353–54.

44. Donald Fisher, "1863: The First Year of National Conscription," *Rochester History* 53 (1991): 14–15; Levine, "Draft Evasion in the North During the Civil War, 1863–1865," 821; Roseboom and Weisenburger, *A History of Ohio*, 286–87; Niven, *Connecticut for the Union*, 92.

45. Levine, "Draft Evasion in the North During the Civil War, 1863–1865," 822–28. One unintended consequence of conscription was that the navy enjoyed surging enlistments as men looked for a way to avoid going into the army. Welles, *Diary of Gideon Welles*, vol. 2, 121.

46. Hallock, "The Role of the Community in Civil War Desertion," 125, 134; E. B. Long and Barbara Long, *The Civil War Day by Day* (New York: Da Capo Press, 1971), 714.

47. Edward Chase Kirkland, *The Peacemakers of 1864* (New York: Macmillan, 1927), 67–77; Basler, *Collected Works,* vol. 7, 435, text and n. 1.

48. Basler, *Collected Works,* vol. 7, 435; Kirkland, *The Peacemakers of 1864,* 80–81; McKay, *The Civil War and New York City,* 265.

49. Basler, *Collected Works,* vol. 7, 451; Kirkland, *The Peacemakers of 1864,* 85–96. Italics and capitals are as they appeared in Edmund Kirke's account of the meeting in the *Boston Evening Transcript* of July 22, 1864.

50. Kinchen, *Confederate Operations in Canada and the North,* 82–86.

CHAPTER 6

1. Browning, *The Diary of Orville Hickman Browning,* vol. 1, 676; Kirkland, *The Peacemakers of 1864,* 98–103. Historian Michael F. Holt has argued that Congressional Republicans adopted the same take-no-prisoners approach with both Democrats and Confederates: They simply refused to compromise or accommodate either group. Although Lincoln was able to work well with the Radicals and other Republicans on the whole, in this particular instance Holt's generalization could extend to the president as well. Michael F. Holt, "Abraham Lincoln and the Politics of Union," in *Abraham Lincoln and the American Political Tradition,* ed. John L. Thomas (Amherst: University of Massachusetts Press, 1986), 117.

2. Welles, *Diary of Gideon Welles,* vol. 2, 95; McKay, *The Civil War and New York City,* 267; Catton, *A Stillness at Appomattox,* 289.

3. Basler, *Collected Works,* vol. 7, 517–18; Baker, *The Works of William H. Seward,* vol. 5, 146–47.

4. Francis Brown, *Raymond of the Times* (New York: W. W. Norton, 1951), 259–60.

5. Hutter and Abrams, "Copperhead Newspapers and the Negro," 131–34; Abrams, "*The Jeffersonian,* Copperhead Newspaper," 279; *La Crosse Democrat,* September 5, August 29, 1864.

6. Joel Parker, *Speech of Governor Parker, at Freehold, N.J., Aug. 20, 1864* (N.p.: 1864), 8.

7. Hutter and Abrams, "Copperhead Newspapers and the Negro," 149, 131–34.

8. The pro-Confederate London *Morning Herald* disclosed just before the election that the pamphlet was a hoax and that two young Democratic journalists in New York wrote it. The two, editor David Goodman Croly and reporter George Wakeman, both died without ever being unmasked or publicly confessing to their authorship. Croly's wife privately admitted his role more than a decade after his death in 1889. Sidney Kaplan, "The Miscegenation Issue in the Election of 1864," *Journal of Negro History* 34 (1949): 284–337.

9. Ibid., 277–84.

10. Ibid., 286–301; *La Crosse Democrat,* February 29, 1864.

11. Hutter and Abrams, "Copperhead Newspapers and the Negro," 136–45; Kaplan, "The Miscegenation Issue in the Election of 1864," 318–21.

12. Kaplan, "The Miscegenation Issue in the Election of 1864," 314.

13. Rufus H. King to Isaac H. Vrooman, August 7, 1864, NYSL.

14. Basler, *Collected Works,* vol. 7, 499–502, including n. 1.

15. Brown, *Raymond of the Times,* 259–60.

16. Ibid., 260; Basler, *Collected Works,* vol. 7, 517–18, 514–15. Henry Clay originated the phrase "rather be right than president," and James M. McPherson has used it privately numerous times in describing Lincoln at this juncture. John Hay and John Nicolay, Lincoln's private secretaries, never believed that the president really planned to send Raymond south for a meeting with Davis; they thought he drafted this memo only to make Raymond "a witness of its absurdity." James M. McPherson, "No Peace Without Victory, 1861–1865," *American Historical Review* 109 (February 2004): 1–18.

17. Basler, *Collected Works,* vol. 7, 514.

18. Kinchen, *Confederate Operations in Canada and the North,* 93.

19. Richard I. Dodge to Brigadier General James B. Fry, August 10, 1864, Provost Marshal General's Bureau, Letters Sent, Pennsylvania Western District, 1863–66, RG 110, entry no. 3127, vol. 2, NARA; Brigadier General Henry B. Carrington to Captain C. H. Potter, August 9, 1864, Records of United States Army Continental Commands, 1821–1920, District of Indiana, Letters Sent, 1864–66, RG 393, entry no. 218; Lieutenant Colonel Charles S. Lovell to Colonel James B. Fry, August 9, 1864, Provost Marshal General's Bureau, Letters Sent, 1863–65, Wisconsin, RG 110, entry no. 6104, vol. 4.

20. Mary Peet to S. P. Adams, August 25, 1864, Provost Marshal General's Bureau, Acting Adjutant Provost Marshal General, Letters Received, Iowa, 1863–65, RG 110, entry no. 6356, box 1, NARA; Pa to Whiting, August. 31, 1864, Catharine Barker Papers, box 2, folder 3, SHSI—Des Moines.

21. Gray, *The Hidden Civil War,* 181–82.

22. Kinchen, *Confederate Operations in Canada and the North,* 67–70.

23. Ibid.

24. Baker, *The Works of William H. Seward,* 152–53; *The Chicago Copperhead Convention* (Washington, D.C.: Congressional Union Committee, 1864), 12.

25. This breach in the party had been developing for some time. For a full account, see Silbey, *A Respectable Minority.*

26. Alexander Long to Alexander St. Clair Boys, August 9, 1864, Boys Papers, box 1, folder 5; Irwin F. Greenberg, "Charles Ingersoll: The Aristocrat as Copperhead," *Pennsylvania Magazine of History and Biography* 93 (1969): 208; C. Chauncey Burr, "The Ultimatum of the Peace Men," *Old Guard,* July 1864, 163–64.

27. C. Chauncey Burr, "Gen. M'clellan's 'Availability' Examined," *Old Guard,* August 1864, 184–87; Smith, *Samuel Medary & the Crisis,* 142; Kaplan, "The Miscegenation Issue in the Election of 1864," 314–15.

28. Samuel Barlow to Manton Marble, August 21, 1864, Marble Papers, vol. 8.

29. Ibid.

30. Democratic National Convention, *Official Proceedings of the Democratic National Convention, Held in 1864 at Chicago* (Chicago: Times Steam Book and Job Printing House, 1864), 4. While most Democrats, including many Copperheads, insisted that reunification was a precondition for peace, some were willing to recognize Southern independence. Charles Ingersoll of Philadelphia believed the issue was one of form rather than substance. The North's actions, he said, already suggested its tacit recognition of a Confederate nation by sending flags of truce, exchanging prisoners, and even treating the Southerners as belligerents. Greenberg, "Charles Ingersoll," 210.

31. Democratic National Convention, *Official Proceedings of the Democratic National Convention, Held in 1864 at Chicago*, 23.

32. Stephen W. Sears, *George B. McClellan: The Young Napoleon* (New York: Ticknor & Fields, 1988), 371–73. Tilden himself was the Democrats' presidential candidate in the election of 1876. Tilden won the popular vote but not the Electoral College, where twenty votes were in dispute. A congressionally appointed panel finally cut what had become a Gordian knot and handed the election to the Republican, Rutherford B. Hayes. In exchange, Hayes agreed to remove all remaining Union troops from the South, thus ending Reconstruction.

33. Democratic National Convention, *Official Proceedings of the Democratic National Convention, Held in 1864 at Chicago*, 27–28; *Richmond Examiner*, September 5, 1864; Sears, *George B. McClellan: The Young Napoleon*, 373.

34. Allan Nevins, *The War for the Union: The Organized War to Victory, 1864–1865* (New York: Charles Scribner's Sons, 1971), 99–101.

35. A remorseful Barlow wrote McClellan several days after the convention that the peace wing seemed to have forgotten "that the real battle and the only hope of victory is at the polls in November and not in the Convention." Silbey, *A Respectable Minority*, 134.

36. *Detroit Free Press*, September 1, 1864; John Gibbons to Robert Gibbons, September 27, 1864, John Gibbons Letters, Wisconsin Historical Society.

37. Lebbie Trowbridge to George M. Trowbridge, August 31, 1864, Trowbridge Papers; *Harper's Weekly*, "The Chicago Convention," September 10, 1864; *World*, September 1, 1864.

38. Benjamin F. Butler, *Private and Official Correspondence of Gen. Benjamin F. Butler, During the Period of the Civil War*, vol. 5 (Springfield, Mass.: Plimpton Press, 1917), 748; Republican Party platform, www.presidency.ucsb.edu/site/docs/doc_platforms.php?platindex=R1864; Mary R. Dearing, *Veterans in Politics: The Story of the G.A.R.* (Baton Rouge: Louisiana State University Press, 1952), 22.

39. Baker, *The Works of William H. Seward*, vol. 5, 498–502.

40. Basler, *Collected Works*, vol. 8, 1–2.

41. *Christian Recorder*, September 10, 1864.

42. J. N. Baldwin to Manton Marble, September 5, 1864, Marble Papers, vol. 8; Washington Hunt to Manton Marble, September 8, 1864, ibid.; Olson, *J. Sterling Morton*, 129.

43. John Rees to Horatio Seymour, September 10, 1864, Horatio Seymour Papers, 1764–1886, box 7, folder 39.

44. Smith, *Samuel Medary and the Crisis*, 143; Klement, "Sound and Fury," 109; *Cincinnati Convention, October 18, 1864, for the Organization of a Peace Party* (N.p.: 1864), 16.

45. *O.R.*, ser. 1, vol. 43, pt. 1, 931–32; Jefferson Davis, *The Papers of Jefferson Davis*, vol. 10, 629–30; Jones, *A Rebel War Clerk's Diary*, 412, 416.

46. Woodworth, *Cultures in Conflict*, 153; Edward Younger, ed., *Inside the Confederate Government: The Diary of Robert Garlick Hill Kean* (Baton Rouge: Louisiana State University Press, 1993), 174.

47. Woodward, *Mary Chesnut's Civil War*, 642.

48. Gray, *The Hidden Civil War*, 189; *New York Herald*, September 12, 1864; *New York Times*, September 3, 1864.

49. Sears, *The Civil War Papers of George B. McClellan*, 599 n. 1.

50. *World*, September 3, 1864; Charles Mason, Diary, September 4, 1864, Mason Collection; William Henry Harrison Terrell to John T. Wilder, September 6, 1864, J. T. Wilder Papers, folder 2, ISL; *Pilot*, September 10, 1864.

51. Catton, *Grant Takes Command*, 369; James Buchanan to Brigadier General Henry B. Carrington, September 23, 1864, Provost Marshal General's Bureau, Letters Received, Indiana District 11, 1864–65, RG 110, entry no. 5314, box 7, NARA.

52. James Guthrie, *The Harrison's Bar Letter of Gen. McClellan* (N.p: 1864), 2; M. L. Deal to Henry R. Strong, September 27, 1864, Henry R. Strong Papers, folder 1, IHS; Captain D. S. Brown to Colonel James A. Wilcox, September 30, 1864, Records of United States Army Continental Commands, 1821–1920, Northern Department, Letters Received, 1864–65, RG 393, entry no. 3349, box 1.

53. Sears, *George B. McClellan: The Young Napoleon*, 374; *Harper's Weekly*, "M'Clellan's Letter," September 24, 1864.

54. Sears, *The Civil War Papers of George B. McClellan*, 590–92, 595–96; Sears, *George B. McClellan: The Young Napoleon*, 375.

55. Sears, *The Civil War Papers of George B. McClellan*, 595–96.

56. *Harper's Weekly*, "M'Clellan's Letter," September 24, 1864; John Allen Trimble to George Pendleton, September 10, 1864, Trimble Papers, box 2. While there is no evidence linking the changes in his drafts to events in Georgia, it is clear from a congratulatory letter he wrote to Sherman that he had been following events closely. "I confess that at the beginning I trembled for your long line of communications, and I have watched with the most intense interest the admirable manner in which you overcame the difficulty. Your campaign will go down to history as one of the memorable ones of the world." It is impossible to imagine that the language of his acceptance letter could not be influenced by the current events, yet most historians have overlooked the connection. See, for instance, Stephen W. Sears, "McClellan and the Peace Plank of 1864: A Reappraisal," *Civil War History* 36 (1990).

57. Nevins, *The War for the Union: The Organized War to Victory*, 104–7. Nevins argued that Blair's firing and Frémont's withdrawal from the race were not connected, although that remains a subject of some debate.

58. *O.R.*, ser. 1, vol. 43, pt. 1, 29–31.

59. Hugh McCulloch to Susan McCulloch, September 25, 1864, McCulloch MSS. To see the kinds of letters Democratic leaders were receiving, see the Marble Papers, vols. 8 and 9, which cover September 1864.

60. Younger, *Inside the Confederate Government*, 174; Sarah Woolfolk Wiggins, ed., *The Journals of Josiah Gorgas, 1857–1878* (Tuscaloosa: University of Alabama Press, 1995), 132; Jones, *A Rebel War Clerk's Diary*, 421; Ambrose Remley to Parents, Brother, and Sister, September 18, 1864, Remley MSS, LLIU.

61. This was not the first time in American history that elections had been conducted in the middle of a war, however. The War of 1812 was five months old when the 1812 election was held. My thanks to John M. Murrin for pointing this out.

CHAPTER 7

1. Sears, *The Civil War Papers of George B. McClellan*, 135.

2. James M. Greiner, Janet L. Coryell, and James R. Smither, eds., *A Surgeon's Civil War: The Letters and Diary of Daniel M. Holt, M.D.* (Kent, Ohio: Kent State University Press, 1994), 257; Charles F. Larimer, ed., *Love and Valor: Intimate Civil War Letters between Captain Jacob and Emeline Ritner* (Western Springs, Ill.: Sigourney Press, 2000), 361.

3. From 1789 until the war broke out in 1861, Southerners dominated government institutions: Two-thirds of the Speakers of the House and presidents pro tem of the Senate were from the South, and twenty of the thirty-five Supreme Court justices (where Southerners had always held a controlling majority). Southern-born men occupied the presidency for forty-nine of the nation's seventy-two years. McPherson, *Ordeal by Fire*, 144–45.

4. Vorenberg, *Final Freedom*, 165; Julie A. Doyle, John David Smith, and Richard M. McMurry, eds., *This Wilderness of War: The Civil War Letters of George W. Squier, Hoosier Volunteer*, Voices of the Civil War (Knoxville: University of Tennessee Press, 1998), 87.

5. *Miscegenation: Endorsed by the Republican Party* (N.p.: 1864), 3; Jeremiah S. Black, *Speech of Hon. Jeremiah S. Black, at the Hall of the Keystone Club, in Philadelphia* (Philadelphia: *The Age*, 1864), 3; William D. Potts, *Campaign Songs for Christian Patriots and True Democrats* (New York: William D. Potts, 1864), 13.

6. Doyle et al., *This Wilderness of War*, 89.

7. Frank Freidel, "The Loyal Publication Society: A Pro-Union Propaganda Agency," *Mississippi Valley Historical Review* 26 (1939): 362–64, 373.

8. Even abolitionist Wendell Phillips, who once vowed to cut off both hands before saying anything complimentary about Lincoln, whom he considered far too conservative on the issue of black rights, kept quiet. Why? He despised McClellan, whom he referred to as a dwarf. But he promised that

after Lincoln's reelection he would "agitate" again "till I bayonet him and his party into justice." John C. Waugh, *Reelecting Lincoln: The Battle for the 1864 Presidency* (New York: Crown, 1998), 321.

9. Ibid., 316, 334; Strong, *Diary of the Civil War*, 497; Larimer, *Love and Valor*, 373.

10. Sears, *George B. McClellan: The Young Napoleon*, 378–80; Waugh, *Reelecting Lincoln*, 315.

11. Sears, *George B. McClellan: The Young Napoleon*, 377; *World*, October 6, 1864.

12. *The Lincoln Catechism: Wherein the Eccentricities & Beauties of Despotism Are Fully Set Forth* (New York: J. F. Feeks, 1864), 21; *Address of Democratic Members of Congress to the Democracy of the United States* (Washington, D.C.: L. Towers, 1864), 3, 6–7; Potts, *Campaign Songs for Christian Patriots and True Democrats*, 9–10.

13. Curiously, the Democrats' rather divergent claims both appear in the same pamphlet. *Harrison's Bar Letter of Gen. McClellan* (N.p.: 1864), 2–3; Rowland, *Jefferson Davis, Constitutionalist*, vol. 6, 359.

14. Sears, *George B. McClellan: The Young Napoleon*, 379; James M. McPherson and Patricia R. McPherson, eds., *Lamson of the Gettysburg: The Civil War Letters of Lieutenant Roswell H. Lamson, U.S. Navy* (New York: Oxford University Press, 1997), 209.

15. *New York Herald*, November 7, 1864.

16. Jones, *A Rebel War Clerk's Diary*, 430, 437; Rowland, *Jefferson Davis, Constitutionalist*, vol. 6, 356.

17. Edwin Eckley Gray to Lucy Gray, October 10, 1864, William and Eckley Gray Papers, CL.

18. Larry E. Nelson, "Black Leaders and the Presidential Election of 1864," *Journal of Negro History* 63 (1978): 53–54.

19. J. I. Green to Augustus Belmont, October 3, 1864, Marble Papers, vol. 9; Waugh, *Reelecting Lincoln*, 333; G.W.A. [George W. Adams?] to Manton Marble, n.d., 1864, Marble Papers, vol. 9.

20. John G. Nicolay and John Hay, *Abraham Lincoln: A History*, abridged and ed. Paul M. Angle, Classic American Historians (Chicago: The University of Chicago Press, 1966), 279; Samuel S. Cox to Manton Marble, October 12, 1864, Marble Papers, vol. 9.

21. J. A. Bayard to Thomas F. Bayard, October 12, 1864, Bayard Papers, vol. 10; William P. Davis to John G. Davis, October 24, 1864, John G. Davis Papers, box 4, folder 14.

22. Tyler Dennett, ed., *Lincoln and the Civil War in the Diaries and Letters of John Hay* (New York: Da Capo Press, 1988), 229–30.

23. Doyle et al., *This Wilderness of War*, 92; Blair, *A Politician Goes to War*, 211.

24. Basler, *Collected Works*, vol. 8, 52.

25. *New York Times*, October 20, 1864.

26. Sears, *George B. McClellan*, 384; Nicolay and Hay, *Abraham Lincoln: A History*, 280.

27. Kinchen, *Confederate Operations in Canada and the North*, chaps. 5 and 6.

28. Daly, *Diary of a Union Lady*, 307; Charles Mason, Diary, October 14, 1864, Mason Collection; G.W.A. [George W. Adams?] to Manton Marble, October 26, 1864, Marble Papers, vol. 9; Sears, *George B. McClellan: The Young Napoleon*, 384–85.

29. *Dayton Daily Empire*, November 2, 1864; *World*, November 2, 1864; *Old Guard*, November 1864, 246–49.

30. *Campaign Post*, October 28, 1864; *Dayton Daily Empire*, October 31, 1864.

31. Strong, *Diary of the Civil War*, 504; Sarah A. Dooley to Rufus Dooley, October 15, 1864, Rufus Dooley Papers, box 1, folder 14, IHS.

32. Samuel M. Johnston to Major General Hoovery, October 4, 1864, Records of United States Army Continental Commands, 1821–1920, District of Indiana, 1864, RG 393, entry no. 222, box 2, NARA; Benjamin F. Covy to Colonel James A. Wilcox, October 7, 1864, Records of United States Army Continental Commands, 1821–1920, Northern Department, Letters Received, 1864–65, RG 393, entry no. 3349, box 3.

33. Anonymous to Brigadier General James B. Fry, November 1, 1864, vol. 3, Provost Marshal General's Bureau, Letters Sent, Pennsylvania Western District, 1863–66, RG 110, entry no. 3126, NARA; Anonymous to Major F.A.H. Garbel, December 6, 1864, NARA; Dodge to Brigadier General James B. Fry, ibid.

34. Baker, *The Works of William H. Seward*, vol. 5, 505–10.

35. These letters had a wider circulation than the person to whom they were addressed. Reading letters aloud to family or passing them around was fairly typical. Indeed, soldiers sometimes wrote that they did not want the contents disseminated.

36. Henry A. Peck to Tracy Peck, October 30, 1864, Henry A. Peck Papers, CL; Greiner et al., *A Surgeon's Civil War*, 245–46.

37. Margaret Brobst Roth, ed., *Well Mary: Civil War Letters of a Wisconsin Volunteer* (Madison: University of Wisconsin Press, 1960), 93; William B. Bement to Isaac Bush, November 7, 1864, Bement MSS, LLIU; John Reed Beatty to Laura, October 30, 1864, Beatty Papers.

38. Albert Castel, *Tom Taylor's Civil War*, Modern War Studies (Lawrence: University Press of Kansas, 2000), 218; Lebbie Trowbridge to George Martin Trowbridge, October 14, 1864, Trowbridge Papers. Taylor's decision had consequences close to home. When his brother-in-law, Democratic representative Chilton White, ran for reelection, Taylor declined to distribute campaign material in his unit, thereby contributing to White's defeat. Castel, *Tom Taylor's Civil War*, 218.

39. F. S. Wildman to Sam Wildman, October 1, 1864, Wildman Family Papers, box 1, OHS; Lebbie Trowbridge to George Martin Trowbridge, October 14, 1864, Trowbridge Papers.

40. Some also had gone home for the October elections. In fact, Lincoln had asked Sherman to allow as many Indiana soldiers as possible to go home and vote in the state contest as long as it did not jeopardize the army's safety. Lincoln was careful to note, though, that "this is, in no sense, an order." Basler, *Collected Works*, vol. 8, 11. For a detailed account of how soldiers got the

absentee vote, see Josiah Henry Benton, *Voting in the Field: A Forgotten Chapter of the Civil War* (Boston: Private printer, 1915).

41. Rosenblatt and Rosenblatt, *Hard Marching Every Day*, 273–76.

42. Basler, *Collected Works*, vol. 8, 100–101.

43. Strong, *Diary of the Civil War*, 508; Nicolay and Hay, *Abraham Lincoln: A History*, 281. For a complete account of the rebels' Election Day schemes, see Kinchen, *Confederate Operations in Canada and the North*, chap. 7.

44. Sears, *The Civil War Papers of George B. McClellan*, 85.

45. *New York Herald*, December 1, 1864; Nevins, *The War for the Union: The Organized War to Victory*, 138. The soldier vote probably tipped the balance in New York and Connecticut to Lincoln's favor and may also have made the difference in Indiana and Maryland, James M. McPherson argues. The soldiers also delivered several congressional seats to the Republican column. McPherson, *Ordeal by Fire*, 493.

46. McPherson, *Ordeal by Fire*, 493. One soldier even wrote McClellan to claim that the military had used its "despotic" powers to coerce the troops into voting for Lincoln, saying that the men who cast ballots for the president were offered promotions while McClellan supporters were promised demotion—a highly questionable claim given the numbers of men who voted. Anonymous to George B. McClellan, November 10, 1864, Ellen Marcy McClellan Letters to Mary Shipman, folder G, CHS.

47. Otto F. Bond, ed., *Under the Flag of the Nation: Diaries and Letters of Owen Johnston Hopkins, a Yankee Volunteer in the Civil War* (Columbus: Ohio State University Press, 1998), 202; Blair, *A Politician Goes to War*, 217; William Kepner to Isaac Barker, November 27, 1864, Isaac Barker Civil War Letters, folder 2, IHS; Strong, *Diary of the Civil War*, 514.

48. Younger, *Inside the Confederate Government*, 177; Wiggins, *The Journals of Josiah Gorgas*, 139. A year after the election, McClellan told Barlow from Europe that he had no idea "what the secesh expected to be the result of my election— but if they expected to gain their independence from me they would have been woefully mistaken." Sears, *George B. McClellan: The Young Napoleon*, 385.

49. Rowland, *Jefferson Davis, Constitutionalist*, vol. 6, 386–87; Jones, *A Rebel War Clerk's Diary*, 445, 448.

50. Basler, *Collected Works*, vol. 8, 100–101.

51. Sears, *George B. McClellan: The Young Napoleon*, 386; Shankman, "William B. Reed and the Civil War," 467, including n. 54; *Sullivan Democrat*, November 10, 1864.

52. Manton Marble to George B. McClellan, November 13, 1864, Marble Papers, vol. 10; *World*, November 9, 1864; Sears, *The Civil War Papers of George B. McClellan*, 619, n. 1.

53. *Niles Republican*, December 17, 1864; Clara Gaskill to James R.M. Gaskill, November 26, 1864, Gaskill Papers, folder 1, Lincoln Library; Strong, *Diary of the Civil War*, 511; William Kepner to Isaac Barker, November 27, 1864, Barker Letters, folder 2.

54. Basler, *Collected Works*, vol. 8, 149–50.

55. Dennett, *Lincoln and the Civil War in the Diaries and Letters of John Hay,* 237–38.

56. Andrew Johnson, who became president after Lincoln was assassinated, was a Southern Democrat before the war but ran with Lincoln under the Union Party banner.

CHAPTER 8

1. Charles E. Vetter, "A Sociological Perspective of William T. Sherman's March Through Georgia," in *The Campaign for Atlanta and Sherman's March to the Sea: Essays on the American Civil War in Georgia, 1864,* ed. Theodore P. Savas and David A. Woodbury (Campbell, Calif.: Savas Woodbury, 1994), 401.

2. Some of the troops from the Army of Tennessee were transferred to North Carolina, where they fought Sherman at Bentonville in March 1865.

3. Wiggins, *The Journals of Josiah Gorgas,* 144.

4. For a thorough discussion of the emergence of hard war, see Grimsley, *The Hard Hand of War.*

5. Strong, *Diary of the Civil War,* 522; Kinchen, *Confederate Operations in Canada and the North,* chap. 8.

6. Blair, *A Politician Goes to War,* 217; Vicki Betts, " 'Dear Husband': The Civil War Letters of Sophronia Joiner Chipman: Kankakee County, Illinois, 1863–1865," *Military History of the West* 29 (1999): 171; William R. Bennet to Colonel R. W. Thompson, October 1, 1864, Provost Marshal General's Bureau, Letters Received, Indiana District 7, 1863–64, RG 110, entry no. 5236, box 6.

7. *World,* December 25, 1864; *O.R.,* ser. 1, vol. 44, 783.

8. Wiggins, *The Journals of Josiah Gorgas,* 149; Betts, " 'Dear Husband,' " 177. This housewife, Sophronia Joiner Chipman, was mistaken about Vicksburg. Grant's victory there had not included an unconditional surrender.

9. Sherman's orders in Georgia were for official parties, appointed by brigade commanders, to "forage liberally on the country" but not to enter private homes. Livestock and wagons were open for raiding, but Sherman instructed his men to differentiate between the rich, "who are usually hostile," and the poor, who were "usually neutral or friendly." Sherman wanted his troops to destroy public buildings, railroad property, factories, and machine shops while sparing homes, libraries, and asylums. Only corps commanders could authorize the destruction of houses, cotton gins, and mills. Discipline broke down in regard to soldiers' foraging and to setting fire to cotton gins and presses. But the best study to date on the march concludes that the men torched few houses. Special Field Order 190, *World,* November 25, 1864; Lee Kennett, *Marching Through Georgia: The Story of Soldiers and Civilians During Sherman's Campaign* (New York: HarperCollins, 1995), 265–75.

10. *O.R.,* ser. 1, vol. 44, 798–800. For a comprehensive account of the burning of Columbia, see Marion Brunson Lucas, *Sherman and the Burning of Columbia* (College Station: Texas A&M University Press, 1976).

11. Basler, *Collected Works*, vol. 8, 275–76

12. Nevins, *The War for the Union: The Organized War to Victory*, 268–69; Rowland, *Jefferson Davis, Constitutionalist*, vol. 6, 465–67.

13. Strong, *Diary of the Civil War*, 552; Charles Mason, Diary, February 20 and 21, 1865, Mason Collection.

14. Alexander St. Clair Boys to W. W. Long, February 19, 1865, Boys Papers, box 1, folder 5; Alexander Long to Alexander St. Clair Boys, February 12, 1865, ibid.

15. Judith N. McArthur and Orville Vernon Burton, eds., *"A Gentleman and an Officer": A Military and Social History of James B. Griffin's Civil War* (New York: Oxford University Press, 1996), 286.

16. Basler, *Collected Works*, vol. 8, 149; Samuel S. Cox to Manton Marble, January 13, 1865, Marble Papers, vol. 10.

17. Nevins, *The War for the Union: The Organized War to Victory*, 213–14; Vorenberg, *Final Freedom*, 5; *Cong. Globe*, 38th Cong., 2nd Sess., pt. 1, 38–39, 524–31; Nicolay and Hay, *Abraham Lincoln: A History*, 348. By early May every Northern state but New Jersey and every border state but Kentucky and Delaware had ratified the amendment. The Unionist legislatures of Louisiana and Tennessee also had approved it, and the remaining Confederate states ratified it in the fall as a condition of reconstruction. The Thirteenth Amendment became part of the Constitution in December 1865.

18. Basler, *Collected Works*, vol. 8, 254–55; *Christian Recorder*, February 18, 1865.

19. "Letters of Richard Cobden to Charles Sumner, 1862–1865," 318.

20. Wiggins, *The Journals of Josiah Gorgas*, 153; Robert Hunt Rhodes, ed., *All for the Union: The Civil War Diary and Letters of Elisha Hunt Rhodes* (New York: Orion Books, 1985), 223.

21. George Frush to John Dunbar, March 26, 1865, George Frush Letter, box BL 153, folder 14, SHSI—Iowa City; Blair, *A Politician Goes to War*, 234.

22. Lee rejected the advice of some of his subordinates to cut his troops loose and allow them to prey on the Yankees as a guerrilla force. Other Confederate commanders heartily endorsed this idea, however. General Wade Hampton wrote Davis on April 19 saying that rejoining the Union would be the worst thing that could happen to the South and that *"no* sacrifice would be too great to escape this trains of horrors." He suggested disbanding the infantry, taking volunteers and mounting them as cavalry, and going to Texas to organize a resistance movement. As soon as this unit was pulled together, he would send them into the North, "and they will soon show that we are not conquered." Hudson Strode, ed., *Jefferson Davis: Private Letters, 1823–1889* (New York: Da Capo Press, 1995), 154–55.

23. Annette Tapert, ed., *The Brothers' War: Civil War Letters to Their Loved Ones from the Blue and Gray* (New York: Times Books, 1988), 234; Marcia Reid-Green, ed., *Letters Home: Henry Matrau of the Iron Brigade* (Lincoln: University of Nebraska Press, 1993), 114; Charles Mason, Diary, April 11, 1865, Mason Collection.

24. Rosenblatt and Rosenblatt, *Hard Marching Every Day*, 322–23. For a full study on Lincoln's relationship with the soldiers, see William C. Davis, *Lincoln's*

Men: How President Lincoln Became Father to an Army and a Nation (New York: Free Press, 1999).

25. David Herbert Donald, *Lincoln* (London: Jonathan Cape, 1995), 598–99.

26. Rhodes, *All for the Union*, 232.

27. Doyle et al., *This Wilderness of War*, 103; Browning, *The Diary of Orville Hickman Browning*, vol. 2, 19.

28. Strong, *Diary of the Civil War*, 587; "Death of the President," *Old Guard*, May 1, 1865.

29. There was good reason to think that Confederates may have had a role in the assassination. In the fall of 1864, there was much talk in the South about the possibility of kidnapping Lincoln, then exchanging him for two hundred thousand rebel soldiers being held in the North. A Confederate spy even made an effort to capture the president, but the heavy guard around Lincoln dissuaded the would–be kidnappers, and Lincoln was probably unaware of the attempt. Jefferson Davis encouraged the discussion of such schemes, but when someone came to him with an actual plan, he refused to endorse it, fearing the man would wind up killing Lincoln and not just kidnapping him. Donald, *Lincoln*, 549–50, 677–78n.

Bibliography

PRIMARY SOURCES

Address of Democratic Members of Congress to the Democracy of the United States. Washington, D.C.: L. Towers, 1864.

Adjutant General. Miscellaneous Civil War Correspondence. Indiana State Archives, Indianapolis.

Aplin Family Papers. Clements Library, University of Michigan, Ann Arbor.

Bailhache-Braymen Family Papers. Abraham Lincoln Presidential Library, Springfield, Illinois.

Baker, George E., ed. *The Works of William H. Seward.* Vol. 5. Boston: Houghton, Mifflin, 1884.

Barber, Henry. Papers. Abraham Lincoln Presidential Library, Springfield, Illinois.

Barker, Catharine. Papers. State Historical Society of Iowa, Des Moines.

Barker, Isaac. Civil War Letters. Indiana Historical Society, Indianapolis.

Basler, Roy P., ed. *The Collected Works of Abraham Lincoln.* Vols. 4–8. New Brunswick: Rutgers University Press, 1953.

Bayard, James A. *Two Speeches of James A. Bayard of Delaware.* Baltimore: W. M. Innes, 1863.

Bayard, Thomas F. Papers. Library of Congress, Washington, D.C.

Beatty, John R. Papers. Minnesota Historical Society, St. Paul.

Bement Manuscripts. Lilly Library, Indiana University, Bloomington.

Betts, Vicki. " 'Dear Husband': The Civil War Letters of Sophronia Joiner Chipman: Kankakee County, Illinois, 1863–1865." *Military History of the West* 29 (1999): 146–98.

Black, Jeremiah S. *Speech of Hon. Jeremiah S. Black, at the Hall of the Keystone Club, in Philadelphia.* Philadelphia: The Age, 1864.

Blair, William Alan, ed. *A Politician Goes to War: The Civil War Letters of John White Geary.* University Park: Pennsylvania State University Press, 1995.

Blight, David W., ed., *When This Cruel War Is Over: The Civil War Letters of Charles Harvey Brewster*. Amherst: University of Massachusetts Press, 1992.

Bond, Otto F., ed. *Under the Flag of the Nation: Diaries and Letters of Owen Johnston Hopkins, a Yankee Volunteer in the Civil War*. Columbus: Ohio State University Press, 1998.

Bowlus, Ezra. Civil War Letters. Indiana Historical Society, Indianapolis.

Boys, Alexander S. Papers. Ohio Historical Society, Columbus.

Brooks, Noah. *Washington in Lincoln's Time*. New York: The Century Co., 1895.

Brooks, William Gray. Papers. Massachusetts Historical Society, Boston.

Brown, Bergun H. Papers. Indiana Historical Society, Indianapolis.

Browning, Orville Hickman. *The Diary of Orville Hickman Browning*. Vols. 1 and 2. Edited by Theodore Calvin Pease and James G. Randall. Springfield: Illinois State Historical Library, 1925.

Buckingham, Governor William A. Incoming Correspondence. Connecticut State Library, Hartford.

————. Papers. Connecticut State Library, Hartford.

Burlingame, Michael, ed. *With Lincoln in the White House: Letters, Memoranda, and Other Writings of John G. Nicolay, 1860–1865*. Carbondale: Southern Illinois University Press, 2000.

Butler, Benjamin F. *Private and Official Correspondence of Gen. Benjamin F. Butler During the Period of the Civil War*. Vol. 5. Springfield, Mass.: Plimpton Press, 1917.

Campbell, James. *Speech of Hon. James Campbell, of Philadelphia, Delivered at Scranton, Pennsylvania*. Philadelphia: *The Age*, 1863.

Campbell, John. *Unionists Versus Traitors: The Political Parties of Philadelphia; or the Nominees That Ought to Be Elected in 1861*. Philadelphia: N.p., 1861.

Castel, Albert. *Tom Taylor's Civil War*. Modern War Studies, edited by Theodore A. Wilson. Lawrence: University Press of Kansas, 2000.

Cavins, Elijah H. C. Collection. Indiana Historical Society, Indianapolis.

Chamberlain, Joseph and Orville. Papers. Indiana Historical Society, Indianapolis.

The Chicago Copperhead Convention. Washington, D.C.: Congressional Union Committee, 1864.

Chittenden Papers. Indiana State Library, Indianapolis.

Church, Sanford E. *Speech by Hon. Sanford E. Church at Batavia, October 13, 1863*. N.p.: 1863.

Cincinnati Convention, October 18, 1864, for the Organization of a Peace Party. N.p., n.d.

Civil War Miscellany: Adjutant General. Indiana State Archives, Indianapolis.

"The Constitution." New York: Society for the Diffusion of Political Knowledge, 1863.

Cook, Thomas M., and Thomas W. Knox, eds. *Public Record Including Speeches, Messages, Proclamation, Official Correspondence, and Other Public Utterances of Horatio Seymour.* New York: I. W. England, 1868.

Copperhead Platform! N.p.: 1862.

Correspondence in Relation to the Public Meeting at Albany, N.Y. N.p., n.d.

Cravens Manuscripts. Lilly Library, Indiana University, Bloomington.

Crist Manuscripts. Lilly Library, Indiana University, Bloomington.

Crowe, Isaac. Papers. Minnesota Historical Society, St. Paul.

Daly, Maria Lydig. *Diary of a Union Lady: 1861–1865.* Edited by Harold Earl Hammond, with an introduction by Jean V. Berlin. Lincoln: University of Nebraska Press, 2000.

Davis, Jefferson. *The Papers of Jefferson Davis.* Edited by Lynda Lasswell Crist. Vol. 10. Baton Rouge: Louisiana State University Press, 1999.

Davis, John G. Papers. Indiana Historical Society, Indianapolis.

Davis, William C. *Jefferson Davis: The Man and His Hour, a Biography.* New York: HarperCollins, 1991.

Dean, Gilbert. *The Emancipation Proclamation and Arbitrary Arrests!!* Albany: Atlas & Argus, 1863.

Democratic National Convention. *Official Proceedings of the Democratic National Convention, Held in 1864 at Chicago.* Chicago: Times Steam Book and Job Printing House, 1864.

Dennett, Tyler, ed. *Lincoln and the Civil War in the Diaries and Letters of John Hay.* New York: Da Capo Press, 1988.

Dillon, William D., ed. "The Civil War Letters of Enos Barret Lewis, 101st Ohio Volunteer Infantry." *Northwest Ohio Quarterly* 57 (1985): 51–63, 83–100, 132–43.

Dooley, Rufus. Papers. Indiana Historical Society, Indianapolis.

Dowdey, Clifford, and Louis H. Manarin, eds. *The Wartime Papers of R. E. Lee.* New York: Bramhall House and the Virginia Civil War Commission, 1961.

Dowling, John. Papers. Indiana Historical Society, Indianapolis.

Doyle, Julie A., John David Smith, and Richard M. McMurry, eds. *This Wilderness of War: The Civil War Letters of George W. Squier, Hoosier Volunteer.* Voices of the Civil War, edited by Frank L. Byrne, Knoxville: University of Tennessee Press, 1998.

Embree, Lucius C. Papers. Indiana State Library, Indianapolis.

English, William H. Papers. Indiana Historical Society, Indianapolis.

Evans Family Papers. Ohio Historical Society, Columbus.

Facts for the People Relating to the Present Crisis. N.p.: [Indiana] Democratic State Central Committee, 1862.

Fish Family Papers. Clements Library, University of Michigan, Ann Arbor.

For Peace, and Peaceable Separation: Citizen's Democratic Address to the People of the State of Ohio, and the People of the Several States of the West and North. Cincinnati: N.p., 1863.

Frush, George. Letter. State Historical Society of Iowa, Iowa City.

Fry, Colonel James B. *Final Report Made to the Secretary of War, by the Provost Marshal General, of the Operations of the Bureau of the Provost Marshal General of the United States.* Vols. 1 and 2. N.p.: 1866.

Gardiner, William H., II. Letters, 1852–63. Massachusetts Historical Society, Boston.

Gaskill Papers. Abraham Lincoln Presidential Library, Springfield, Illinois.

Gibbons, John. Letters. Wisconsin Historical Society.

Gilbert, Henry C. Papers. Clements Library, University of Michigan, Ann Arbor.

Gillis, John A. Diaries. Minnesota Historical Society, St. Paul.

Glenn, John F. Papers. Abraham Lincoln Presidential Library, Springfield, Illinois.

Grant, Ulysses S. *Personal Memoirs of U. S. Grant.* Edited by E. B. Long. New York: Da Capo Press, 1982.

Gray, William and Eckley. Papers. Clements Library, University of Michigan, Ann Arbor.

Greenleaf, Margery, ed. *Letters to Eliza from a Union Soldier, 1862–1865.* Chicago: Follett, 1970.

Greiner, James M., Janet L. Coryell, and James R. Smither, eds. *A Surgeon's Civil War: The Letters and Diary of Daniel M. Holt, M.D.* Kent, Ohio: Kent State University Press, 1994.

Guthrie, James. *The Harrison's Bar Letter of Gen. McClellan.* N.p.: 1864.

Handley Manuscripts. Lilly Library, Indiana University, Bloomington.

Herr Papers. Duke University, Raleigh, North Carolina.

Hill Manuscripts. Lilly Library, Indiana University, Bloomington.

Hoadley Letter. Connecticut State Library, Hartford.

Howe, Daniel Wait. Collection. Indiana Historical Society, Indianapolis.

Indiana Legion Adjutant General. Papers. Indiana State Archives, Indianapolis.

Jackson, Joseph Orville, ed. *"Some of the Boys . . .": The Civil War Letters of Isaac Jackson, 1862–1865.* With a foreword by Bell Irvin Wiley. Carbondale: Southern Illinois University Press, 1960.

Jarvis, William. Letters. Connecticut Historical Society, Hartford.

John Williams & Company. Papers. Abraham Lincoln Presidential Library, Springfield, Illinois.

Johnson, George S. Papers. Indiana Historical Society, Indianapolis.

Jones, John B. *A Rebel War Clerk's Diary.* Condensed, edited, and annotated by Earl Schenck Miers. Baton Rouge: Louisiana State University Press, 1993.

King, Rufus H. Letter to Isaac H. Vrooman, August 7, 1864 [mss. 12354]. New York State Library Manuscripts and Special Collections, Albany.

Kirkwood, Governor Samuel J. Papers. State Historical Society of Iowa, Des Moines.

Lane, Joseph. Manuscripts. Lilly Library, Indiana University, Bloomington.

Larimer, Charles F., ed. *Love and Valor: Intimate Civil War Letters between Captain Jacob and Emeline Ritner.* Western Springs, Ill.: Sigourney Press, 2000.

"Letters of Richard Cobden to Charles Sumner, 1862–1865." *American Historical Review* 2 (1897): 306–19.

The Lincoln Catechism. New York: J. F. Feeks, 1864.

Little, Sidney O. Letters. Clements Library, University of Michigan, Ann Arbor.

Long, Alexander. *The Present Condition and Future Prospects of the Country: Speech of Hon. Alexander Long, of Ohio.* N.p: 1864.

Mahoney, D. A. *The Prisoner of State.* New York: Carleton, 1863.

Marble, Manton. Papers. Library of Congress, Washington, D.C.

Marshall, Jeffrey D., ed. *A War of the People: Vermont Civil War Letters.* Hanover, N.H.: University Press of New England, 1999.

Mason, Charles. Collection. State Historical Society of Iowa, Des Moines.

Mass Convention of the Democracy and Conservative Citizens of Indiana. N.p.: 1862.

McClellan, Ellen Marcy. Letters to Mary Shipman. Connecticut Historical Society, Hartford.

McClellan, George B. *The Harrison's Bar Letter of Gen. McClellan.* N.p.: 1864.

———. Papers. Library of Congress, Washington, D.C. Microfilm.

McCulloch Manuscripts. Lilly Library, Indiana University, Bloomington.

McKeon, John. *The Administration Reviewed.* New York: Van Evrie, Horton, 1862.

McPherson, James M., and Patricia R. McPherson, eds. *Lamson of the Gettysburg: The Civil War Letters of Lieutenant Roswell H. Lamson, U.S. Navy.* New York: Oxford University Press, 1997.

Meigs, Montgomery. "General M. C. Meigs on the Conduct of the Civil War." *American Historical Review* 26 (1921): 285–303.

Miscegenation: Endorsed by the Republican Party. N.p., 1864.

Morgan, Edwin Denison. Papers, 1836–83 [SC11818]. New York State Library Manuscripts and Special Collections, Albany.

Morton, Oliver P. Letterbook, September 1863–December 1866. Vol. 3. Indiana State Archives, Indianapolis.

———. Papers. Indiana State Archives, Indianapolis. Microfilm.

Parker Papers. Clements Library, University of Michigan, Ann Arbor.

Parker, Joel. *Speech of Governor Parker at Freehold, N.J.* N.p.: 1864.

Peck, Henry A. Papers. Clements Library, University of Michigan, Ann Arbor.

Pendleton, George H. *Speech of Hon. George H. Pendleton, of Ohio, in the House of Representatives, December 10, 1861.* N.p.: 1861

———. *Speech of Hon. George H. Pendleton, of Ohio, on the Enlistment of Negro Soldiers, Delivered During the Debate in the House of Representatives, January 21, 1863* Washington, D.C.: N.p.: 1862 [1863].

Perry, R. Matthew. Papers. Wisconsin Historical Society, Madison.

Pierce, Edward L., ed. *Memoir and Letters of Charles Sumner.* Vol. 4. Boston: Roberts Brothers, 1893.

Plessinger, James B. Papers. Indiana State Library, Indianapolis.

Porter, Horace. *Campaigning with Grant.* New York: Da Capo Press, 1986.

Potts, William D. *Campaign Songs for Christian Patriots and True Democrats*. New York: William D. Potts, 1864.

Prickett, Thomas. Papers. Indiana Historical Society, Indianapolis.

Provost Marshal General's Bureau. Acting Assistant Provost Marshal General, Letters Received, Iowa, 1863–65. Record Group 110, Entry Number 6356. National Archives and Records Administration (NARA), Washington, D.C.

————. Letters Received, Indiana District 7, 1863–64. Record Group 110, Entry Numbers 5232, 5236. NARA.

————. Letters Received, Indiana District 11, 1864–65. Record Group 110, Entry Number 5314. NARA.

————. Letters Sent by Chief Mustering Officer, New York Southern District, 1863–65. Record Group 110, Entry Number 1360. NARA.

————. Letters Sent, Illinois District 4, 1863–65. RG 110, Entry Number 5631. NARA.

————. Letters Sent, 1863–65, Wisconsin. Record Group 110, Entry Number 6104, Vol. 1. NARA.

————. Letters Sent, New Jersey, 1863–66. Record Group 110, Entry Number 2539, Vol. 1. NARA.

————. Letters Sent, Pennsylvania Western District, 1863–66. Record Group 110, Entry Number 3126, Vol. 3. NARA.

————. Letters Sent, Pennsylvania Western District, 1863–66. Record Group 110, Entry Number 3127, Vol. 2. NARA.

————. Letters to the Adjutant General, Pennsylvania Western District, 1864. Record Group 110, Entry Number 3127, Vol. 1. NARA.

Records of the Adjutant General's Office, 1780s–1917. Turner-Baker Papers. Letter Books. Unmicrofilmed. Record Group 94, Entry Number 179, Vol. 1. NARA.

————. Turner-Baker Papers. Letter Books. Unmicrofilmed. Record Group 94, Entry Numbers 124, 411, 475, 536, 540, 541, and 697. NARA.

————. Turner-Baker Papers. Record Group M797, Entry Number 2536, Roll 67. NARA. Microfilm.

Records of United States Army Continental Commands, 1821–1920. District of Indiana, 1864. Record Group 393, Entry Number 222, NARA.

————. District of Indiana, Letters Sent, 1864–66. Record Group 393, Entry Number 218. NARA.

————. General Burnside's Telegrams. Record Group 393, Entry Number 3511. NARA.

————. Miscellaneous Records—Post of Cincinnati, Ohio, 1862–65. Record Group 393, Entry Number 217. NARA.

————. Miscellaneous Records—Post of Philadelphia, Letters Sent, 1862–65. Record Group 393, Entry Number 1360. NARA.

————. Northern Department, Letters Received, 1864–65. Record Group 393, Entry Number 3349. NARA.

Reed, William B. *A Northern Plea for Peace: Address of the Hon. William B. Reed, of Pennsylvania.* London: Henry F. Mackintosh, 1863.

Reid-Green, Marcia, ed. *Letters Home: Henry Matrau of the Iron Brigade.* Lincoln: University of Nebraska Press, 1993.

Remley Manuscripts. Lilly Library, Indiana University, Bloomington.

Republican Party Platform, 1864.

Rhodes, Robert Hunt, ed. *All for the Union: The Civil War Diary and Letters of Elisha Hunt Rhodes.* New York: Orion Books, 1985.

Rosenblatt, Emil, and Ruth Rosenblatt, eds. *Hard Marching Every Day: The Civil War Letters of Private Wilbur Fisk, 1861–1865.* Modern War Studies, edited by Theodore A. Wilson. Lawrence: University Press of Kansas, 1992.

Roth, Margaret Brobst, ed. *Well Mary: Civil War Letters of a Wisconsin Volunteer.* Madison: University of Wisconsin Press, 1960.

Rowland, Dunbar, ed. *Jefferson Davis, Constitutionalist: His Letters, Papers, and Speeches.* Vol. 6. Jackson: Mississippi Department of Archives and History, 1923.

Scott, Robert Garth, ed. *Fallen Leaves: The Civil War Letters of Major Henry Livermore Abbott.* Kent, Ohio: Kent State University Press, 1991.

Sears, Stephen W., ed. *The Civil War Papers of George B. McClellan: Selected Correspondence, 1860–1865.* New York: Ticknor & Fields, 1989.

Seymour, Horatio. Papers [SC7008]. New York State Library Manuscripts and Special Collections, Albany.

Seymour, Thomas H. Papers. Connecticut Historical Society, Hartford.

Silber, Nina, and Mary Beth Sievens, eds. *Yankee Correspondence: Civil War Letters Between New England Soldiers and the Home Front.* A Nation Divided: New Studies in Civil War History. Charlottesville: University Press of Virginia, 1996.

Spooner, Benjamin J. Collection. Indiana State Library, Indianapolis.

Starks, Kate. Papers. Indiana State Library, Indianapolis.

Stearns Family Papers. Political Correspondence. Connecticut Historical Society, Hartford.

Steele, Robert Papers. Wisconsin Historical Society, Madison.

Strode, Hudson, ed. *Jefferson Davis: Private Letters, 1823–1889.* New York: Da Capo Press, 1995.

Strong, George Templeton. *Diary of the Civil War.* Edited by Allan Nevins. New York: Macmillan, 1952.

Strong, Henry R. Papers. Indiana Historical Society, Indianapolis.

Swift Family Correspondence. Connecticut State Library, Hartford.

Tapert, Annette, ed. *The Brothers' War: Civil War Letters to Their Loved Ones from the Blue and Gray.* New York: Times Books, 1988.

Taylor, Thomas T. Papers. Ohio Historical Society, Columbus.

Thompson, M.L.P. Letter. Ohio Historical Society, Columbus.

Throne, Mildred, ed. "An Iowa Doctor in Blue: The Letters of Seneca B. Thrall, 1862–1864." *Iowa Journal of History* 58 (1960): 97–188.

Trimble, John Allen. Papers. Ohio Historical Society, Columbus.

"The Troubles in Coles County." *Chicago Times*, March 31, 1864.

Trowbridge, George Martin. Papers. Clements Library, University of Michigan, Ann Arbor.

United States Bureau of the Census. *Historical Statistics of the United States: Colonial Times to 1957*. Washington, D.C.: Government Printing Office, 1961.

―――. *Population of the United States in 1860*. Washington, D.C.: Government Printing Office, 1864.

―――. *The United States on the Eve of the Civil War: As Described in the 1860 Census*. Washington, D.C.: U.S. Civil War Centennial Commission, 1963.

United States Census Office. *Statistics of the United States, 8th Census*. Washington, D.C.: Government Printing Office, 1866.

United States War Department. *The War of the Rebellion: A Compilation of the Official Records of the Union and Confederate Armies*. Washington, D.C.: Government Printing Office, 1880. [Cited as *O.R.*]

Vallandigham, Clement L. *The Record of Hon. C. L. Vallandigham on Abolition, the Union, and the Civil War*. 9th ed. Columbus: J. Walter, 1863.

―――. *Speech of Hon. C. L. Vallandigham, of Ohio, on Executive Usurpation*. Washington, D.C.: H. Polkinhorn, 1861.

―――. *Speeches, Arguments, Addresses, and Letters of Clement L. Vallandigham*. New York: J. Walter, 1864.

Vannest, Joseph P. Papers. Indiana Historical Society, Indianapolis.

Voorhees, Daniel W. *Speech of D. W. Voorhees, of Indiana, Delivered in the House of Representatives, March 9, 1864*. Washington, D.C.: Constitutional Union Office, 1864.

Weaver, Amos C. Papers. Indiana Historical Society, Indianapolis.

Welles, Gideon. *Diary of Gideon Welles*. Vol. 2. New York: W. W. Norton, 1960.

Wetherill, Charles Mayer. Papers. Indiana State Library, Indianapolis.

Wiggins, Sarah Woolfolk, ed. *The Journals of Josiah Gorgas, 1857–1878*. Edited by and with a foreword by Frank E. Vandiver. Tuscaloosa: University of Alabama Press, 1995.

Wilder, J. T. Papers. Indiana State Library, Indianapolis.

Wildman Family Papers. Ohio Historical Society, Columbus.

Williams, R. Manuscripts. Lilly Library, Indiana University, Bloomington.

Woodward, C. Vann, ed. *Mary Chesnut's Civil War*. New Haven: Yale University Press, 1981.

Worden Papers. Indiana Historical Society, Indianapolis.

Yates Family Papers. Abraham Lincoln Presidential Library, Springfield, Illinois.

Younger, Edward, ed. *Inside the Confederate Government: The Diary of Robert Garlick Hill Kean*. Baton Rouge: Louisiana State University Press, 1993.

PERIODICALS

Campaign Post (Boston)
Chicago Times
Christian Recorder (Philadelphia)
Crisis (Columbus, Ohio)
Congressional Globe
Dayton Daily Empire
Detroit Free Press
Dubuque Herald
Frank Leslie's Illustrated Newspaper
Harper's Weekly
La Crosse (Wisconsin) *Democrat*
New York Herald
New York Times
Niles (Michigan) *Republican*
Pilot (Boston)
Old Guard
Vanity Fair
World (New York)
Yankee Notions

SECONDARY SOURCES

Abrams, Ray H. "*The Jeffersonian,* Copperhead Newspaper." *Pennsylvania Magazine of History and Biography* 57 (1933): 260–83.

Adams, Michael C. C. *Fighting for Defeat: Union Military Failure in the East, 1861–1865.* Lincoln: University of Nebraska Press, 1992.

Baker, Jean H. *Affairs of Party: The Political Culture of Northern Democrats in the Mid-Nineteenth Century.* Ithaca: Cornell University Press, 1983.

Benton, Josiah Henry. *Voting in the Field: A Forgotten Chapter of the Civil War.* Boston: Private printer, 1915.

Bernath, Stuart L. *Squall Across the Atlantic: American Civil War Prize Cases and Diplomacy.* Berkeley: University of California Press, 1970.

Bernstein, Iver. *The New York City Draft Riots: Their Significance for American Society and Politics in the Age of the Civil War.* New York: Oxford University Press, 1990.

Bethauser, Margaret. "Henry A. Reeves: The Career of a Conservative Democratic Editor." *Journal of Long Island History* 9 (1973): 34–42.

Blake, Kellee L. "Ten Firkins of Butter and Other 'Traitorous' Aid." *Prologue* 30 (1998): 289–93.

Brown, Francis. *Raymond of the Times.* New York: W. W. Norton, 1951.

Buck, Stephen J. " 'A Contest in Which Blood Must Flow Like Water': Du Page County and the Civil War." *Illinois Historical Journal* 87 (1994): 2–20.

Carley, Kenneth. *Minnesota in the Civil War*. Minneapolis: Ross & Haines, 1961.

Catton, Bruce. *Grant Takes Command*. Boston: Little, Brown, 1968.

———. *A Stillness at Appomattox*. Garden City, N.Y.: Doubleday & Company, 1957.

Churchill, Robert. "The Sons of Liberty Conspiracy, 1863–1864." *Prologue* 30 (1998): 295–303.

Coleman, Charles H. "The Use of the Term 'Copperhead' During the Civil War." *Mississippi Valley Historical Review* 25 (1938): 263–64.

Cooney, Charles F. "Treason or Tyranny? The Great Senate Purge of '62." *Civil War Times Illustrated* 18 (1979): 30–31.

Cowden, Joanna D. *"Heaven Will Frown on Such a Cause as This": Six Democrats Who Opposed Lincoln's War*. Lanham, Md.: University Press of America, 2001.

———. "Sovereignty and Secession: Peace Democrats and Antislavery Republicans in Connecticut During the Civil War Years." *Connecticut History* 30 (1989): 41–54.

Crenshaw, Ollinger. "The Knights of the Golden Circle: The Career of George Bickley." *American Historical Review* 47 (October 1941): 23–50.

Current, Richard. *Lincoln and the First Shot*. Philadelphia: Lippincott, 1963.

Davis, William C. *Lincoln's Men: How President Lincoln Became Father to an Army and a Nation*. New York: Free Press, 1999.

Dearing, Mary R. *Veterans in Politics: The Story of the G.A.R*. Baton Rouge: Louisiana State University Press, 1952.

De Bohigas, Nuria Sales. "Some Opinions on Exemption from Military Service in Nineteenth-Century Europe." *Comparative Studies in Society and History* 10 (1968): 261–89.

DeCanio, Stephen J., and Joel Mokyr. "Inflation and Wage Lag During the American Civil War." *Explorations in Economic History* 14 (1977): 311–36.

Donald, David Herbert. *Lincoln*. London: Jonathan Cape, 1995.

Dudley, Harold M. "The Election of 1864." *Mississippi Valley Historical Review* 14 (1932): 500–518.

Dupree, A. Hunter, and Leslie H. Fishel Jr. "An Eyewitness Account of the New York Draft Riots, July, 1863." *Mississippi Valley Historical Review* 47 (1960): 472–79.

Earnhart, Hugh G. "The Administrative Organization of the Provost Marshal General's Bureau in Ohio, 1863–65." *Northwest Ohio Quarterly* 37 (1965): 87–99.

Ellis, Richard E. "The Market Revolution and the Transformation of American Politics, 1801–1837." In *The Market Revolution in America: Social, Political, and Religious Expressions, 1800–1880*, edited by Melvyn Stokes and Stephen Conway, 149–76. Charlottesville: University Press of Virginia, 1996.

Ericson, Christina, and Barbara Austen. "On the 'Front Lines' of the Civil War Home Front." *Connecticut History* 39 (2000): 150–65.

Fisher, Donald. "1863: The First Year of National Conscription." *Rochester History* 53 (1991): 3–30.

Fite, Emerson. "The Agricultural Development of the West During the Civil War." In *The Economic Impact of the American Civil War*, edited by Ralph L. Andreano, 48–63. Cambridge, Mass.: Schenkman, 1962.

Foulke, William Dudley. *Life of Oliver P. Morton*. Vol. 1. Indianapolis: Bowen-Merrill, 1899.

Freidel, Frank. "The Loyal Publication Society: A Pro-Union Propaganda Agency." *Mississippi Valley Historical Review* 26 (1939): 359–76.

Geary, James W. *We Need Men: The Union Draft and the Civil War*. DeKalb: Northern Illinois University Press, 1991.

Gienapp, William E. " 'Politics Seems to Enter into Everything': Political Culture in the North, 1840–1860." In *Essays on American Antebellum Politics*, edited by Stephen E. Maizlish and John Kushma, 14–69. College Station: Published for the University of Texas at Arlington by Texas A&M University Press, 1982.

Gray, Wood. *The Hidden Civil War: The Story of the Copperheads*. New York: Viking Press, 1942.

Greenberg, Irwin F. "Charles Ingersoll: The Aristocrat as Copperhead." *Pennsylvania Magazine of History and Biography* 93 (1969): 190–217.

Grimsley, Mark. *The Hard Hand of War: Union Military Policy Toward Southern Civilians, 1861–1865*. New York: Cambridge University Press, 1995.

Grimsted, David. *American Mobbing, 1828–1861: Toward Civil War*. New York: Oxford University Press, 1998.

Hallock, Judith Lee. "The Role of the Community in Civil War Desertion." *Civil War History* 29 (1983): 123–34.

Hammond, Bray. "The North's Empty Purse, 1861–1862." *American Historical Review* 67 (1961): 1–18.

Hanna, William F. "The Boston Draft Riot." *Civil War History* 36 (1990): 262–73.

Harsh, Joseph L. *Taken at the Flood: Robert E. Lee and Confederate Strategy in the Maryland Campaign of 1862*. Kent, Ohio: Kent State University Press, 1999.

Harstad, Peter T. "Draft Dodgers and Bounty Jumpers." *Civil War Times Illustrated* 6 (1967): 28–36.

Hess, Earl J. *Liberty, Virtue, and Progress: Northerners and Their War for the Union*, American Social Experience Series no. 10. New York: New York University Press, 1988.

Holt, Michael F. "Abraham Lincoln and the Politics of Union." In *Abraham Lincoln and the American Political Tradition*, edited by John L. Thomas, 111–41. Amherst: University of Massachusetts Press, 1986.

Hutter, J. H., and Ray H. Abrams. "Copperhead Newspapers and the Negro." *Journal of Negro History* 20 (1935): 131–52.

Jackson, William J. *New Jerseyans in the Civil War: For Union and Liberty*. New Brunswick: Rutgers University Press, 2000.

Kaplan, Sidney. "The Miscegenation Issue in the Election of 1864." *Journal of Negro History* 34 (1949): 274–343.

Kennett, Lee. *Marching Through Georgia: The Story of Soldiers and Civilians During Sherman's Campaign.* New York: HarperCollins, 1995.

Kessel, Reuben A., and Armen A. Alchian. "Real Wages in the North During the Civil War: Mitchell's Data Reinterpreted." In *The Economic Impact of the American Civil War*, edited by Ralph Andreano, 11–30. Cambridge, Mass.: Schenkman, 1967.

Kinchen, Oscar A. *Confederate Operations in Canada and the North.* North Quincy, Mass.: Christopher, 1970.

Kirkland, Edward Chase. *The Peacemakers of 1864.* New York: Macmillan, 1927.

Klaus, Samuel, ed. *The Milligan Case, Civil Liberties in American History.* New York: Da Capo Press, 1970.

Klement, Frank L. " 'Brick' Pomeroy: Copperhead and Curmudgeon." *Wisconsin Magazine of History* 35 (1951): 106–13.

———. "Clement L. Vallandigham's Exile in the Confederacy, May 25–June 17, 1863." *Journal of Southern History* 31 (1965): 149–63.

———. *The Copperheads in the Middle West.* Chicago: University of Chicago Press, 1960.

———. *Dark Lanterns: Secret Political Societies, Conspiracies, and Treason Trials in the Civil War.* Baton Rouge: Louisiana State University Press, 1984.

———. *The Limits of Dissent: Clement L. Vallandigham and the Civil War.* New York: Fordham University Press, 1998.

———. *Lincoln's Critics: The Copperheads of the North.* Shippensburg, Pa.: White Mane Books, 1999.

———. "Middle Western Copperheadism and the Genesis of the Granger Movement." *Mississippi Valley Historical Review* 38 (1952): 679–94.

———. "Midwestern Opposition to Lincoln's Emancipation Policy." *Journal of Negro History* 49 (1964): 169–83.

———. "Sound and Fury: Civil War Dissent in the Cincinnati Area." *Cincinnati Historical Society Bulletin* 35 (1977): 99–114.

———. "Vallandigham as an Exile in Canada." *Ohio History* 74 (1965): 151–68.

Levine, Peter. "Draft Evasion in the North During the Civil War, 1863–1865." *Journal of American History* 67 (1981): 816–34.

Levstik, Frank R. "The Toledo Riot of 1862: A Study of Midwest Negrophobia." *Northwest Ohio Quarterly* 44 (1972): 100–106.

Long, E. B., and Barbara Long. *The Civil War Day by Day.* New York: Da Capo Press, 1971.

Long, Roger. "Copperhead Clement Vallandigham." *Civil War Times Illustrated* 20, no. 8 (1981): 22–29.

Lucas, Marion Brunson. *Sherman and the Burning of Columbia.* College Station: Texas A&M University Press, 1976.

Mabee, Carleton. *The American Leonardo: A Life of Samuel F. B. Morse.* Rev. ed. Fleischmanns, N.Y.: Purple Mountain Press, 2000.

Maizlish, Stephen E. "The Meaning of Nativism and the Crisis of the Union: The Know-Nothing Movement in the Antebellum North." In *Essays on American Antebellum Politics*, edited by Stephen E. Maizlish and John Kushma, 166–98. College Station: Published for the University of Texas at Arlington by Texas A&M University Press, 1982.

Man, Albon P., Jr. "Labor Competition and the New York Draft Riots of 1863." *Journal of Negro History* 36 (1951): 375–405.

McArthur, Judith N., and Orville Vernon Burton, eds. *"A Gentleman and an Officer": A Military and Social History of James B. Griffin's Civil War*. New York: Oxford University Press, 1996.

McCoy, Drew R. *The Elusive Republic: Political Economy in Jeffersonian America*. Chapel Hill: University of North Carolina Press, 1980.

McKay, Ernest A. *The Civil War and New York City*. Syracuse, N.Y.: Syracuse University Press, 1990.

McKitrick, Eric L. "Party Politics and the Union and Confederate War Efforts." In *The American Party Systems: Stages of Political Development*, edited by William Nisbet Chambers and Walter Dean Burnham, 117–51. New York: Oxford University Press, 1967.

McPherson, Edward. *The Political History of the United States of America During the Great Rebellion*. Washington, D.C.: Philip & Solomons, 1864.

McPherson, James M. *Crossroads of Freedom: Antietam*. Pivotal Moments in American History, edited by David Hackett Fischer and James M. McPherson. New York: Oxford University Press, 2002.

———. *For Cause and Comrades: Why Men Fought in the Civil War*. New York: Oxford University Press, 1997.

———. "No Peace Without Victory, 1861–1865." *American Historical Review* 109 (February 2004): 1–18.

———. *Ordeal by Fire: The Civil War and Reconstruction*. 3rd ed. Boston: McGraw-Hill, 2001.

Merrill, R. G. "The Court-Martial of Private Spencer." *Civil War Times Illustrated* 27 (1989): 34–40.

Milano, Anthony J. "The Copperhead Regiment: The 20th Massachusetts Infantry." *Civil War Regiments* 3 (1993): 31–63.

Milton, George Fort. *Abraham Lincoln and the Fifth Column*. New York: Vanguard Press, 1942.

Mitchell, Reid. "The Northern Soldier and His Community." In *Toward a Social History of the American Civil War*, edited by Maris A. Vinovskis, 78–92. New York: Cambridge University Press, 1990.

———. *The Vacant Chair: The Northern Soldier Leaves Home*. New York: Oxford University Press, 1993.

Mott, Frank Luther. *American Journalism: A History of Newspapers in the United States through 250 Years, 1690 to 1940*. New York: Macmillan, 1941.

Murdock, Eugene C. "Horatio Seymour and the 1863 Draft." *Civil War History* 11 (1965): 117–41.

Murrin, John M. "The Great Inversion, or Court Versus Country: A Comparison of the Revolution Settlements in England (1688–1721) and America (1776–1816)." In *Three British Revolutions: 1641, 1688, 1776,* edited by J.G.A. Pocock, 368–453. Princeton: Princeton University Press, 1980.

Neely, Mark E., Jr. *The Fate of Liberty: Abraham Lincoln and Civil Liberties.* New York: Oxford University Press, 1991.

————. *The Union Divided: Party Conflict in the Civil War North.* Cambridge: Harvard University Press, 2002.

Nelson, Larry E. "Black Leaders and the Presidential Election of 1864." *Journal of Negro History* 63 (1978): 42–58.

Nevins, Allan. *The War for the Union: The Improvised War, 1861–1862.* New York: Charles Scribner's Sons, 1959.

————. *The War for the Union: The Organized War, 1863–1864.* New York: Charles Scribner's Sons, 1971.

————. *The War for the Union: The Organized War to Victory, 1864–1865.* New York: Charles Scribner's Sons, 1971.

————. *The War for the Union: War Becomes Revolution, 1862–1863.* New York: Charles Scribner's Sons, 1960.

Nicolay, John G., and John Hay. *Abraham Lincoln: A History.* Abridged and edited by Paul M. Angle. Classic American Historians. Chicago: University of Chicago Press, 1966.

Niven, John. *Connecticut for the Union: The Role of the State in the Civil War.* New Haven: Yale University Press, 1965.

Noe, Kenneth W. " 'The Conservative': A Civil War Soldier's Musical Condemnation of Illinois Copperheads." *Illinois Historical Journal* 84 (1991): 268–72.

O'Connor, Thomas H. *Civil War Boston: Home Front and Battlefield.* Boston: Northeastern University Press, 1997.

Olson, James C. *J. Sterling Morton.* Lincoln: University of Nebraska Press, 1942.

Palladino, Grace. *Another Civil War: Labor, Capital, and the State in the Anthracite Regions of Pennsylvania, 1840–68.* Urbana: University of Illinois Press, 1990.

Paludan, Phillip Shaw. "The American Civil War Considered as a Crisis in Law and Order." *American Historical Review* 77 (1972): 1013–34.

————. *"A People's Contest": The Union and Civil War.* 2nd ed. Modern War Studies, edited by Theodore A. Wilson. Lawrence: University of Kansas, 1996.

Pocock, J.G.A. *The Machiavellian Moment: Florentine Political Thought and the Atlantic Republican Tradition.* Princeton: Princeton University Press, 1975.

Potter, David M. *Lincoln and His Party in the Secession Crisis.* New Haven: Yale University Press, 1962.

———. *The South and the Sectional Conflict.* Baton Rouge: Louisiana State University Press, 1968.

Ramsdell, Charles W. "Lincoln and Fort Sumter." *Journal of Southern History* 3 (1937): 259–88.

Randall, J. G. *Constitutional Problems under Lincoln.* Rev. ed. Urbana: University of Illinois, 1964.

Rehnquist, William H. *All the Laws but One: Civil Liberties in Wartime.* New York: Knopf, 1998.

Remini, Robert V. *The Revolutionary Age of Andrew Jackson.* New York: Harper Torchbooks, 1987.

Richardson, Heather Cox. *The Greatest Nation of the Earth: Republican Economic Policies During the Civil War.* Cambridge: Harvard University Press, 1997.

Risjord, Norman K. *The Old Republicans: Southern Conservatism in the Age of Jefferson.* New York: Columbia University Press, 1965.

Roseboom, Eugene Holloway, and Francis Phelps Weisenburger. *A History of Ohio.* Edited by Carl Wittke, Prentice-Hall History Series. New York: Prentice-Hall, 1934.

Sampson, Robert D. " 'Pretty Damned Warm Times': The 1864 Charleston Riot and 'the Inalienable Right of Revolution.' " *Illinois Historical Journal* 89 (1996): 99–116.

Sears, Stephen W. *George B. McClellan: The Young Napoleon.* New York: Ticknor & Fields, 1988.

———. "McClellan and the Peace Plank of 1864: A Reappraisal." *Civil War History* 36 (1990): 57–64.

Seyfried, Vincent F. "The Civil War in Queens County." *Long Island Historical Journal* 5 (1993): 146–56.

Shankman, Arnold. " 'Soldier Votes' and Clement L. Vallandigham in the 1863 Ohio Gubernatorial Election." *Ohio History* 82 (1973): 88–104.

———. "William B. Reed and the Civil War." *Pennsylvania History* 39 (1972): 455–69.

Siegel, Alan A. *Beneath the Starry Flag: New Jersey's Civil War Experience.* New Brunswick: Rutgers University Press, 2001.

Silbey, Joel H. *A Respectable Minority: The Democratic Party in the Civil War Era, 1860–1868.* Norton Essays in American History. New York: Norton, 1977.

———. "The Surge of Republican Power: Partisan Antipathy, American Social Conflict, and the Coming of the Civil War." In *Essays on American Antebellum Politics,* edited by Stephen E. Maizlish and John Kushma, 199–229. College Station: Published for the University of Texas at Arlington by Texas A&M University Press, 1982.

Smith, George Winston. "Broadsides for Freedom: Civil War Propaganda in New England." *New England Quarterly* 21 (1948): 291–312.

Smith, Reed W. *Samuel Medary and the Crisis.* Columbus: Ohio State University Press, 1995.

Sprague, Dean. *Freedom Under Lincoln*. Boston: Houghton Mifflin, 1965.

Stampp, Kenneth M. *The Imperiled Union: Essays on the Background of the Civil War*. New York: Oxford University Press, 1980.

———. *Indiana Politics During the Civil War*. Edited by Dorothy Riker and Gayle Thornbrough. Vol. 31, Indiana Historical Collections. Indianapolis: Indiana Historical Bureau, 1949.

———. "The Milligan Case and the Election of 1864 in Indiana." *Mississippi Valley Historical Review* 31 (1944): 41–58.

Starr, Stephen Z. "Was There a Northwest Conspiracy?" *Filson Club Historical Quarterly* 38 (1964): 323–41.

Sterling, Robert E. "Civil War Draft Resistance in the Middle West." Ph.D. diss., Northern Illinois University, 1974.

Thomas, Emory M. *The Confederacy as a Revolutionary Experience*. Englewood Cliffs, N.J.: Prentice-Hall, 1971.

Thornbrough, Emma Lou. *Indiana in the Civil War Era, 1850–1880*. Indianapolis: Indiana Historical Bureau and Indiana Historical Society, 1965.

Tredway, G. R. *Democratic Opposition to the Lincoln Administration in Indiana*. N.p.: Indiana Historical Bureau, 1973.

Vetter, Charles E. "A Sociological Perspective of William T. Sherman's March through Georgia." In *The Campaign for Atlanta & Sherman's March to the Sea: Essays on the American Civil War in Georgia, 1864*, edited by Theodore P. Savas and David A. Woodbury, 375–410. Campbell, California: Savas Woodbury, 1994.

Volwiler, A. T. "Letters from a Civil War Officer." *Mississippi Valley Historical Review* 14 (1928): 508–29.

Von Clausewitz, Carl. *On War*. Translated and edited by Michael Howard and Peter Paret. Princeton: Princeton University Press, 1976.

Vorenberg, Michael. *Final Freedom: The Civil War, the Abolition of Slavery, and the Thirteenth Amendment*. New York: Cambridge University Press, 2004.

Waugh, John C. *Reelecting Lincoln: The Battle for the 1864 Presidency*. New York: Crown, 1998.

Weber, Jennifer L. "All the President's Men: The Politicization of Union Soldiers and How They Saved Abraham Lincoln." Publication forthcoming.

Wedgwood, Wm. B. *The Reconstruction of the Government*. New York: John H. Tingley, 1861.

Welles, Gideon. "The History of Emancipation." *Galaxy*, December 1872, 538–51.

Wheeler, Kenneth H. "Local Autonomy and Civil War Draft Resistance: Holmes County, Ohio." *Civil War History* 45 (1999): 147–59.

White, Ronald C., Jr. *The Eloquent President: A Portrait of Lincoln Through His Words*. New York: Random House, 2005.

Wiley, Bell Irvin. *The Life of Billy Yank: The Common Soldier of the Union*. Baton Rouge: Louisiana State University Press, 1993.

Williams, Frank J. *Judging Lincoln*. Carbondale: Southern Illinois University Press, 2002.

Williams, T. Harry. "Frémont and the Politicians." *Journal of the American Military History Foundation* 2 (1938): 178–91.

———. *Lincoln and His Generals*. New York: Vintage Books, 1952.

Wilson, Charles R. "New Light on the Lincoln-Blair-Frémont 'Bargain' Of [1864?]." *American Historical Review* 42 (1936): 71–78.

———. "The Original Chase Organization Meeting and the Next Presidential Election." *Mississippi Valley Historical Review* 23 (1936): 61–79.

Wood, Forrest G. *Black Scare: The Racist Response to Emancipation and Reconstruction*. Berkeley: University of California Press, 1970.

Woodworth, Steven E. *Cultures in Conflict: The American Civil War*. Greenwood Press Cultures in Conflict Series. Westport, Conn.: Greenwood Press, 2000.

Wubben, Hubert H. *Civil War Iowa and the Copperhead Movement*. Ames: Iowa State University Press, 1980.

Index